AF262920

GOTHIC BY DESIGN

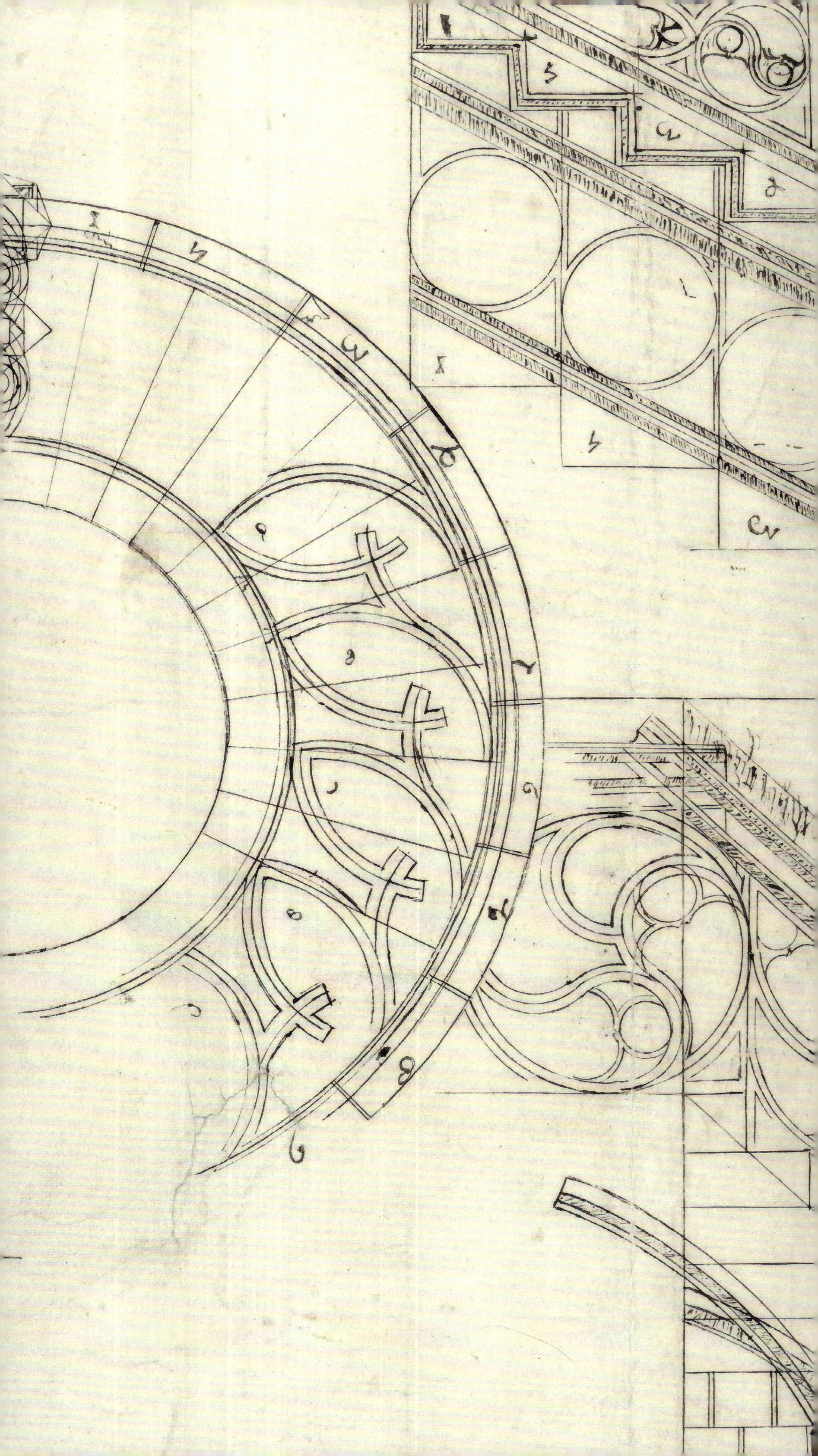

GOTHIC BY DESIGN

THE DAWN OF
ARCHITECTURAL DRAFTSMANSHIP

Femke Speelberg
with an essay by Melanie Holcomb

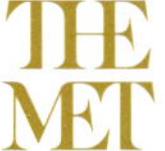

The Metropolitan Museum of Art, New York
Distributed by Yale University Press, New Haven and London

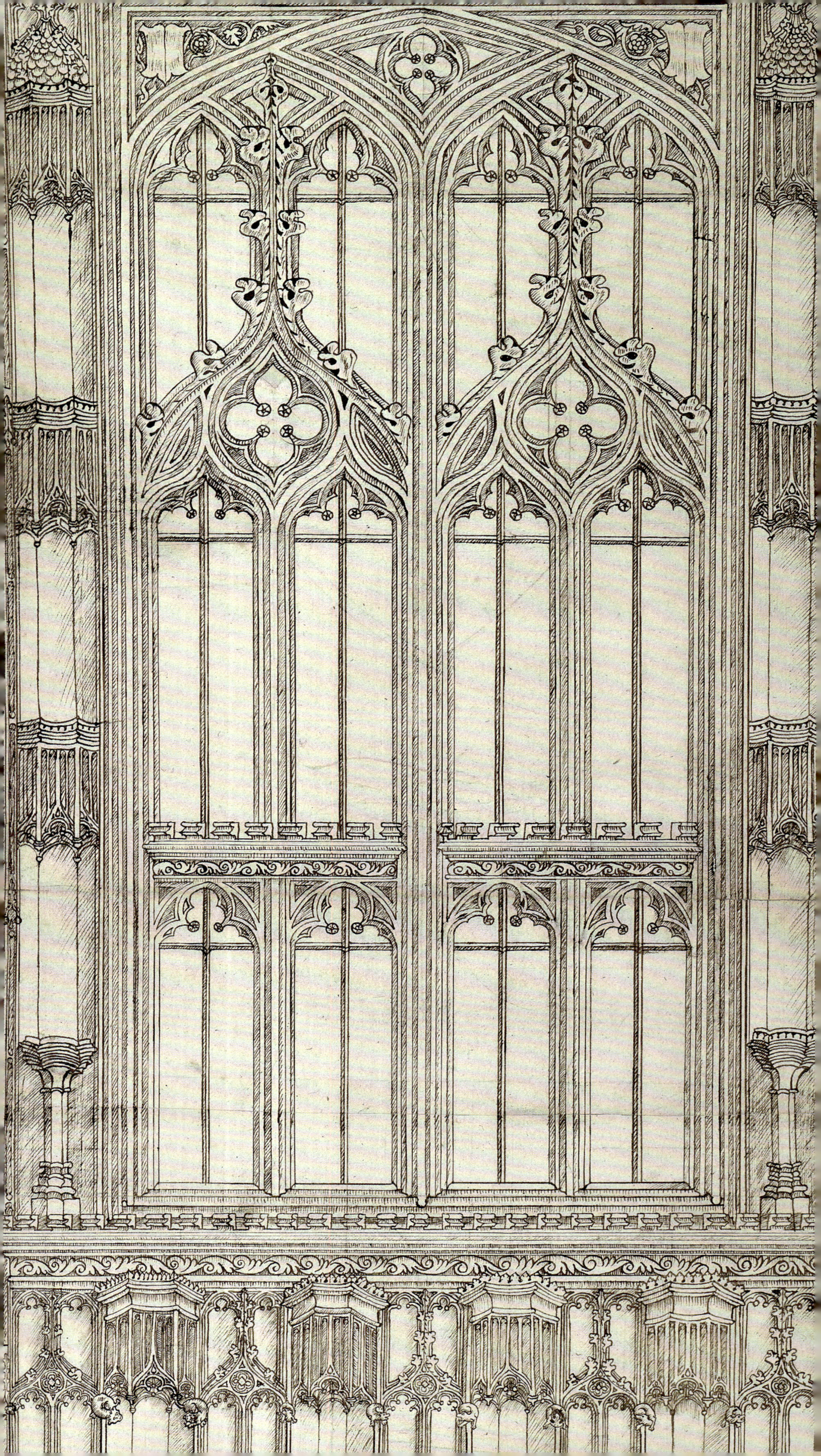

CONTENTS

The opening of the exhibition *Gothic by Design: The Dawn of Architectural Draftsmanship* coincides almost to the day with the seventh anniversary of the fire that severely damaged the iconic Cathedral of Notre Dame in Paris. This devastating incident, and the heroic efforts to restore the monument to its former glory, placed a marked emphasis on our enduring reverence for the architectural wonders of the Gothic era. The towering presence of these structures—built centuries ago to function as the beating heart of religious and civic life—remains an indelible fixture of the urban skyline of numerous cities across the European continent.

Ironically, many such structures started their lives as the result of similar incidents. Cathedrals like those of Strasbourg and Canterbury, discussed in this publication, are prominent examples of architectural sites where fire and other forms of damage provided the unforeseen incentive to begin afresh with ambitious plans that surpassed their predecessors in splendor and size. During the Gothic period, the development of those plans came into focus through the making and preservation of elaborate architectural drawings that informed, and gradually transformed, the building process.

More than six hundred Gothic drawings for architecture and adjacent disciplines survive from the period between the thirteenth and sixteenth centuries. The great majority of these remarkable works on parchment and paper reside in European collections, often not far from the original construction sites for which they were conceived. Principally known among locals and small groups of experts, their existence can arguably be counted among the better-kept secrets of art history. The exhibition *Gothic by Design* marks the first time that a representative group of these extraordinary designs will travel to the United States.

The impetus for this seminal exhibition was The Met's acquisition in 2022 of the monumental design for a sacrament house by the German architect Lorenz Lechler. A collaborative effort between the Department of Medieval Art and The Cloisters and the Department of Drawings and Prints, this purchase underscored the Museum's commitment to the representation of medieval architecture as an art form. The exhibition and its accompanying catalogue represent a continuation of those collaborative efforts. Spearheaded by Femke Speelberg, curator in the Department of Drawings and Prints, but with the steadfast support of the team of expert curators in the Department of Medieval Art and The Cloisters, *Gothic by Design* offers a once-in-a-lifetime opportunity for our audiences to immerse themselves in the earliest history of architectural draftsmanship, and to discover the roots of modern architecture.

First and foremost, I want to express my gratitude to all the institutions who have graciously agreed to lend works to the exhibition, a decision that was anything but matter of fact given the age, size, and fragility of these precious drawings on parchment and paper. Bringing them together in an illuminating display in our Drawings, Prints, and Photographs Galleries would not have been possible without the generous financial support of the Placido Arango

Fund, the Gail and Parker Gilbert Fund, The Schiff Foundation, Gilbert and Ildiko Butler, The Michael and Patricia O'Neill Charitable Fund, and Susan Schulman and Lawrence Eyink. I also wish to thank the Diane W. and James E. Burke Fund, Hubert and Mireille Goldschmidt, and Ann M. Spruill and Daniel H. Cantwell for their critical donations toward the production of this exhibition catalogue.

Max Hollein
Marina Kellen French Director and CEO
The Metropolitan Museum of Art, New York

The seed for *Gothic by Design: The Dawn of Architectural Draftsmanship* was sown during the early stages of the COVID-19 lockdown, when an innocent research question about a fifteenth-century architectural print inadvertently steered me into the realm of Gothic architectural drawings. Having visited the stupendous facade elevation known as Drawing F at Cologne Cathedral during a college excursion many years prior, I knew such plans existed, but—like many of my peers—I had no idea of the sheer number that survive, nor of the wealth of knowledge they contain. The Met's acquisition of Lorenz Lechler's design for a sacrament house, in 2022, created a welcome opportunity to tell the little-known history of Gothic architectural drawings to a wide audience.

First and foremost, I would like to thank The Met's Nadine M. Orenstein, Drue Heinz Curator in Charge of the Department of Drawings and Prints, and C. Griffith Mann, Michel David-Weill Curator in Charge of the Department of Medieval Art and The Cloisters, for their staunch support during the initial development of this project. I am also deeply indebted to Max Hollein, Marina Kellen French Director and CEO, for greenlighting the exhibition in its present form, and for his continued encouragement of a scholarship-driven exhibition program. Quincy Houghton and her team in the Exhibitions Office are the driving force that keep that program afloat, and *Gothic by Design* would not have been possible without their guidance. I would like to thank in particular Christine McDermott, as well as Marci King, for their close attention to every detail of the organization and loan process.

Early on, the research for this exhibition benefited from several trips to Europe. The American Austrian Foundation's Curatorial Exchange Program allowed for an extended stay in Vienna, where Katharine Eltz-Aulitzky made me feel extremely welcome and encouraged me to take advantage of the opportunities afforded by the program. The Met's Professional Travel Grant program enabled an extensive tour of sites across France, Germany, and Switzerland. I would like to thank the Grants Committee for recognizing the importance of on-site visits and collection research, and Elizabeth Perkins for spearheading this program. I would also like to extend my gratitude to Andrea Bayer and Inka Drögemüller for championing these invaluable Met staff travel opportunities.

My research was greatly helped by the curators, conservators, collection managers, archivists, and other staff at the institutions I visited, most of whom became lenders to the show. I thank the extremely obliging colleagues at the core collections for Gothic architectural drawings in Vienna, Strasbourg, and Ulm, whose enthusiasm during my initial visits convinced me of the feasibility of this exhibition: In Vienna, René Schober and Andreas Hartl, Academy of Fine Arts Vienna, and Andreas Nierhaus and Andreas Gruber, Wien Museum, provided me with access to their collections while most of the world was still in lockdown. In Strasbourg and Ulm, where the collections are jointly shepherded by still-active building lodges and the affiliated institutions that house the drawings, I was welcomed wholeheartedly by Sabine Bengel, Fondation de l'Oeuvre Notre-Dame, Strasbourg (celebrating eight hundred years in 2026), and Cécile Dupeux and Jean-David Touchais, Musée de l'Oeuvre Notre-

Dame, Strasbourg, as well as Heidi Vormann and Andreas Böhm, Münsterbauhütte in Ulm, and Gudrun Litz, then at the Haus der Stadtgeschichte—Stadtarchiv Ulm.

For help during additional research visits and with loan approvals, I would also like to thank the staff of the following institutions: in Amsterdam, the Rijksprentenkabinet, Rijksmuseum; in Basel, the Kupferstichkabinett, Kunstmuseum Basel; in Berlin, the Kupferstichkabinett and Kunstgewerbemuseum, Staatliche Museen zu Berlin; in Cologne, the Dombauarchiv; in Erlangen, the Graphische Sammlung, Universitätsbibliothek der Friedrich-Alexander-Universität (FAU) Erlangen-Nürnberg; in Frankfurt am Main, the Graphische Sammlung, Historisches Museum Frankfurt; in Freiburg im Breisgau, the Augustinermuseum; in Houston, the Department of Prints and Drawings, Museum of Fine Arts, Houston; in London, the Department of Prints and Drawings, The British Museum, the Word and Image Department, V&A South Kensington, and the Royal Institute of British Architects (RIBA); in Mechelen, the Museum Hof van Busleyden; in Munich, the Präsenzbibliothek, Bayerisches Nationalmuseum; in Nuremberg, the Graphische Sammlung, Germanisches Nationalmuseum; in Reims, the Archives de la Marne, Centre de Reims; in Strasbourg, the Fondation de l'Oeuvre Notre-Dame and the Musée de l'Oeuvre Notre-Dame; in Stuttgart, the Kunst- und Kulturgeschichtliche Sammlung and the Landesmuseum Württemberg; in Ulm, the Evangelische Gesamtkirchengemeinde and the Haus der Stadtgeschichte—Stadtarchiv Ulm; in Vienna, the Academy of Fine Arts Vienna, the Graphische Sammlung, Albertina, the Library and Works on Paper Collection, MAK—Museum of Applied Arts, and the Architektursammlung, Wien Museum; and, last but not least, in Zurich, the Block Research Group, Institute of Technology in Architecture (ITA), Federal Institute of Technology (ETH) Zurich, and Vaulted AG.

I would like to express special thanks to Merlijn Hurx, KU Leuven; Mauro Mussolin, Università degli Studi Roma Tre; Olivia Horsfall Turner, RIBA, London; Ariane Mensger, Kunstmuseum Basel; Christof Metzger and Eva Michel, Albertina, Vienna; Christian Rümelin, Germanisches Museum, Nuremberg; and Dena M. Woodall, Museum of Fine Arts, Houston, for the stimulating conversations and words of encouragement regarding this project. Martijn van Beek, Utrecht University, Donato Esposito, independent scholar, and Peter Völkle, Münsterbauhütte Bern, have also helped tremendously by providing much-needed research resources. I am also grateful to Sam Fogg and Jana Gajdošová for their generosity in sharing images and information. I would be remiss if I did not also thank Arthur K. Watson Chief Librarian Ken Soehner and his incredible staff in The Met's Thomas J. Watson Library, and Robyn Fleming in particular, for their resourcefulness and grace in processing the constant stream of requests and interlibrary loans.

Additional gratitude is owed to Peter Fuhring for his unwavering support, curiosity, and expertise. Repeated consultations with Robert Bork, University of Iowa, and Nancy Wu have proven invaluable, as have conversations with The Met's unparalleled academic staff. In the Department of Medieval Art and The Cloisters, Melanie Holcomb generously agreed to share her insights in the book's introductory essay, while Shirin Fozi, Paul and Jill Ruddock Associate Curator, and Julia Perratore discussed objects from the Museum's holdings with me. Abraham Thomas, Daniel Brodsky Curator of Modern Architecture, Design, and Decorative Arts, Department of Modern and Contemporary Art, and Wolfram Koeppe, Marina Kellen French Senior Curator, Department of European Sculpture and Decorative Arts, were also among the early supporters of this project. Finally, all my curatorial colleagues in the Department of Drawings and Prints offered much-needed encouragement and proved extremely helpful as sounding boards at various stages of this project. Liz Zanis, Casey Davignon, Ricky Luna, and David del Gaizo deserve special mention for their help in sorting out the (digital) logistics of the exhibition and book.

The physical work of making an exhibition at a place like The Met is as intricate and complex as running a small city. I am indebted to all involved, named or unnamed. The principal person to thank is Yana van Dyke in the Department of Paper Conservation, whose enthusiasm for the project and expertise with works on parchment was invaluable. Mecka Baumeister in the Department of Objects Conservation kindly stepped in as interpreter and translator on international calls. I am also extremely grateful to Rachel Mustalish, Sherman Fairchild Conservator in Charge of the Department of Paper Conservation, and her predecessor Marjorie Shelley for their support of this project, and to Martin Bansbach for his craftsmanship. For their care of and advice on objects in The Met collection, I would also like to express gratitude to Lucretia Kargère and Jennifer Schnitker, Department of Objects Conservation; Sophie Scully, Department of Paintings Conservation; and Christine E. Brennan, Jeff Elliott, and Andrew Winslow, Department of Medieval Art and The Cloisters.

Lucian Simmons, Head of Provenance Research in the Director's Office, as well as Emily Balter and Susie Garcia, Office of the Secretary and General Counsel, were a tremendous help in filing legal paperwork for international loans. Becca Young, Registrar's Office, deserves praise for expertly and calmly navigating the roster of lenders and all the complexities that come with it. In the Design Department, Ezra Wu, Kamomi Solidum, Aichi Lee, and Jourdan Ferguson were responsible for making the installation of the exhibition a success. For their involvement in the design and installation, I would also like to thank Alicia Cheng, Chelsea Garunay, and Mortimer Lebigre in Design, Frederick J. Sager and his team in the Department of Objects Conservation, and Matthew Lytle, Lal Bahcecioglu, and the rest of the incredible staff in the Buildings Department. The Digital Department proved fundamental in creating and finessing the presentation of several interpretative media throughout the show, and I would like to thank Melissa Bell, Kate Farrell, Lela Jenkins, Christopher Alessandrini, Isabella Garces, Paul Caro, Peter Berson, and Kaelen Burkett for their incredible work. Special thanks are also due to Zoltán Bereczki, University of Debrecen, Hungary, who collaborated with Robert Bork to create custom digital content for the show. I am further indebted to Margaret-Anne Logan in The Met's Communication Department, and Gretchen Scott, Marketing and Digital Content Department, for generating interest in the exhibition, and to Heidi Holder, Frederick P. and Sandra P. Rose Chair of Education, and her dynamic staff for their tremendous work in interpreting and enriching the exhibition experience for visitors of all ages and backgrounds.

For the all-important task of perpetuating the narrative of the exhibition in book form, special thanks go to The Met's Publications and Editorial

Department. I want to express my great appreciation to Mark Polizzotti, Michael Sittenfeld, and Peter Antony for their enthusiasm and interest in the subject. Above anyone, Elizabeth Benjamin, editor of both the catalogue and the exhibition labels, deserves praise for her ability to juggle both the big-picture narrative and a close attention to detail. I'm also grateful to our bibliographic editor, Julia Oswald, for keeping us honest, as well as to Richard Koss and Elizabeth Tucker for proofreading, and Theresa Duran for indexing. The Met's Lauren Knighton, as well as Michael Dyer, Remake, expertly shepherded the book into its present form, while The Met's Shannon Cannizzaro did tremendous work sourcing the illustrations. In the Imaging Department, I would like to thank Katherine Dahab, Anna-Marie Kellen, Paul Lachenauer, Mark Morosse, Bruce Schwarz, and Juan Trujillo for taking new photographs of all objects in The Met collection.

Finally, I want to emphasize that this project would not have been possible without the generous financial contributions that were made toward the exhibition and book. In Institutional Advancement, I want to thank Kate Lester Thompson and her colleagues in Corporate Programs and Government and Foundation Giving for the thoughtful connections and relationships they have forged. I am exceedingly grateful to the Placido Arango Fund and the Gail and Parker Gilbert Fund for their support of this exhibition. I also share my thanks with The Schiff Foundation, Gilbert and Ildiko Butler—members of the Visiting Committee for the Department of Drawings and Prints and early enthusiasts of the show—and The Michael and Patricia O'Neil Charitable Fund, as well as Susan Schulman and Lawrence Eyink for a critical gift toward the conservation of one of the loan objects. For their contributions to the catalogue, I sincerely thank the Diane W. and James E. Burke Fund, and Visiting Committee members Hubert and Mireille Goldschmidt, and Ann M. Spruill and Daniel H. Cantwell.

Femke Speelberg
Curator, Department of Drawings and Prints

Academy of Fine Arts Vienna

Albertina, Vienna

Archives de la Marne, Centre de Reims

Bayerisches Nationalmuseum, Munich

Block Research Group, Institute of Technology in Architecture (ITA), Federal Institute of Technology (ETH) Zurich / Vaulted AG

The British Museum, London

Evangelische Gesamtkirchengemeinde Ulm

Fondation de l'Oeuvre Notre-Dame / Musée de l'Oeuvre Notre-Dame, Strasbourg

Germanisches Nationalmuseum, Nuremberg

Haus der Stadtgeschichte—Stadtarchiv Ulm

Historisches Museum Frankfurt

Kunstmuseum Basel

Landesmuseum Württemberg, Stuttgart

MAK—Museum of Applied Arts, Vienna

The Metropolitan Museum of Art, New York

Museum Hof van Busleyden, Mechelen

The Museum of Fine Arts, Houston

Royal Institute of British Architects (RIBA), London

Staatliche Museen zu Berlin
 Kunstgewerbemuseum
 Kupferstichkabinett

Wien Museum

CONTRIBUTORS

Philippe Block (PB)
Full Professor of Architecture and Structures, Co-Director, Block Research Group, ITA, ETH Zurich, and Co-Founder and Chairman, Vaulted AG

Alessandro Dell'Endice (ADE)
Senior Researcher, Block Research Group, ITA, ETH Zurich, and COO, Vaulted AG

Melanie Holcomb
Curator and Manager of Collection Strategy, Department of Medieval Art and The Cloisters, The Metropolitan Museum of Art, New York

Francesco Ranaudo (FR)
Co-Founder and CEO, Vaulted AG

Femke Speelberg (FS)
Curator, Department of Drawings and Prints, The Metropolitan Museum of Art, New York

Tom Van Mele (TVM)
Senior Scientist, Co-Director, Block Research Group, ITA, ETH Zurich, and Co-Founder and CTO, Vaulted AG

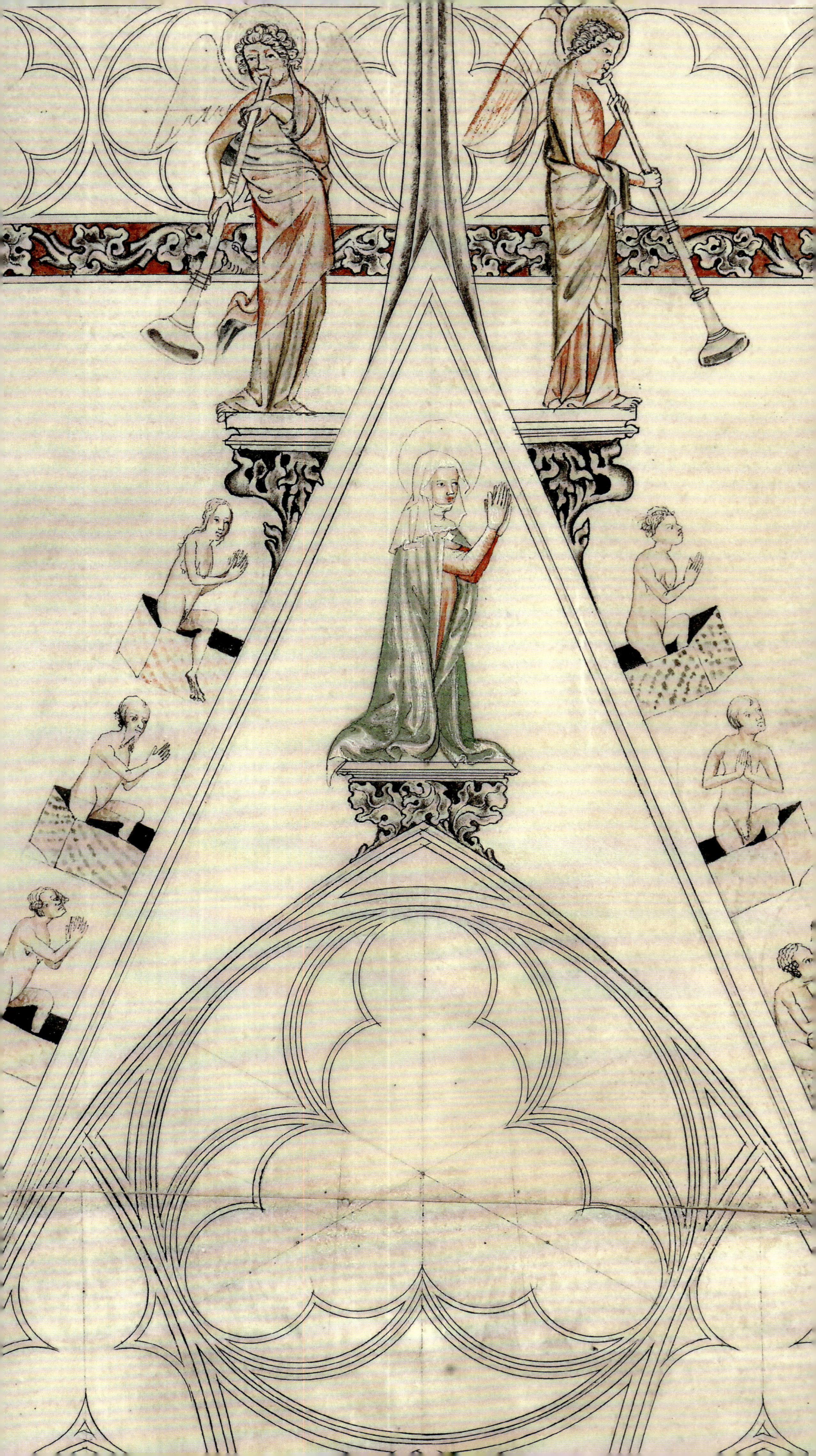

ROUGH SKETCHES
A PREHISTORY OF ARCHITECTURAL DRAWING IN THE MIDDLE AGES

Melanie Holcomb

Drawing makes me happy.
—Frank Gehry[1]

The conceptual drawings of the architect Frank Gehry cannot fail but delight (FIG. 1). Formed from a nearly continuous line, his exquisite scribbles almost pass as a flamboyant signature. Gehry describes his drawings as an instinctive response to a prospective site, the expression of a germ of an idea that will take increasingly concrete form. "I simply look at what is before my eyes. Afterwards, I simply react." From there, "you go to the model, then comes the computer and finally, the studio."[2] Part of the pleasure in looking at these early ideations derives from the way they conjure a building without resembling a building at all. Using frenetic strokes of the pen to communicate a visual and proprioceptive experience of a structure, they sidestep the fundaments of whether and how an edifice can stand up. Were it not for a long tradition of understanding drawings as direct traces of the mind at work—indeed the very marks of genius—Gehry's sketches might fail to convince. But the conventions of automatic drawing and calligraphic abstraction to which Gehry is so clearly indebted provide a foundation of trust between architect and patrons, draftsman and viewers. Even without structural or spatial cues, his scrawled evocations coax us into making an imaginative leap from two dimensions to three, from the flat plane of the paper to a structure that sits in and defines space.[3]

Gehry's sketches may seem an unlikely starting point for a consideration of medieval architectural drawings before 1250, that is, before master masons began amassing the professional plans, elevations, and other designs that *Gothic by Design: The Dawn of Architectural Draftsmanship* rightly celebrates. Scholars have long been perplexed by the discrepancy between the architectural daring of the 1100s, epitomized by Early Gothic cathedrals, and the utter lack of surviving drawings that we presume were needed to achieve those physical, conceptual, and aesthetic heights.[4] This void in the history of graphic design has even led some to declare that drawings played no role in the design and construction process.[5] Yet Gehry's penned meanderings remind us that architectural drawings can take surprising forms and need not solve technical problems at all. More than that, they invite us to pay attention to the cultural assumptions, cognitive habits, and social conditions that allow two-dimensional renderings of buildings to communicate effectively. In this arena, medieval draftsmen offer tantalizing clues. The conventions they use and their own explanations of how their sketches function provide oblique testimony to a long-standing culture of thinking about architecture through drawing. From there, it is surely a short step to the mason's yard.

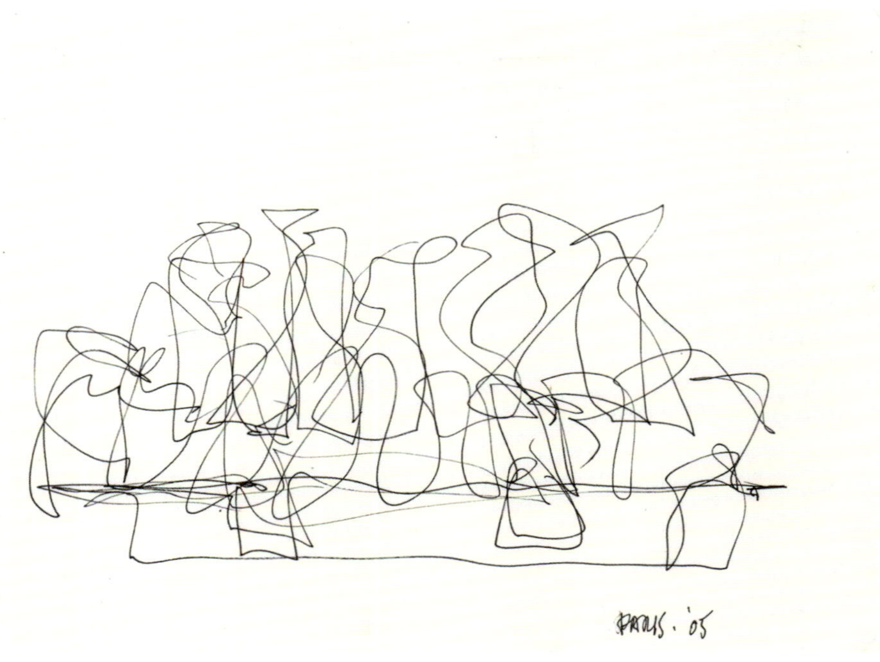

FIG. 1 Frank Gehry (American, born Canada, 1929–2025). Conceptual sketch for the Fondation Louis Vuitton, 2005. Ink on paper, 9 1/16 × 12 in. (23 × 30.5 cm). Fondation Louis Vuitton, Paris

One of the earliest architectural plans to be preserved appears in ninth-century copies of the treatise *De locis sanctis* (Concerning sacred places), originally composed in the seventh century by Adomnán, abbot of the Monastery of Iona.[6] His text describes pilgrimage sites in the Holy Land, Alexandria, and Constantinople, and includes schematic floor plans of four church complexes.[7] Adomnán's floor plans conform in several respects to the conventions of most surviving medieval drawings. That is, they are all finished, not spontaneous, works. Though they vary in quality and elaboration from manuscript to manuscript, all are laid out with a straightedge and compass to signal the care with which they have been copied and their trustworthiness as sources of information. And like most medieval drawings, they are manifestly intertwined with text. Adomnán's sketches (or, more accurately, later copies of his sketches) are not only embedded in his descriptions of buildings, but also use text as a significant design element. Created with the same tools, inks, and colors as the script, these images were used to extend the meaning and experience of reading about a distant structure, one that Adomnán assumes few of his readers have seen.

The illustration devoted to the Church of the Holy Sepulchre in Jerusalem is his most elaborate, and presents the monument within a network of three adjacent churches articulated as simple circles, squares, and rectangles (FIG. 2). Cartographic historians have commented upon the plan's seeming indebtedness to Roman surveyors' maps, with walls expressed by outlines, doorways shown as breaks in those lines, and an arrangement of spaces that conveys their relative proportion and placement to one another.[8] The drawings also show furnishings and key relics—the sepulchral slab, altars, crosses, lamps, and a chalice—that work alongside discursive passages to identify the buildings and call attention to their most noteworthy features.

No drawing can entirely capture a building in all its complexity, and Adomnán's description acknowledges that shortcoming. One virtue of a floor plan, though, as he notes, is its capacity to suggest a comprehensive view of a building through its presentation of geometric relationships and spatial arrangements. As cursory as Adomnán's plans may seem, they should not blind us to the considerable interpretive skills required to read them. As the art historian Michael Baxandall noted about similar drawings from a much later period, one has to understand the conventions of a floor plan: the way it supposes a vantage point from on high and expects the viewer to imagine an elevation from its footprint.[9] In his description of the Church of the Holy Sepulchre, Adomnán evokes the conceptual projection that the floor plan solicits. "Well, this extremely large church . . . shaped to wondrous roundness on every side, *rises up from its foundations* in three walls."[10] Both design and description make plain a degree of architectural literacy. Adomnán assumes his readers come to his text with enough experience of other buildings and enough familiarity with the patterns of a floor plan to allow them to make appropriate, if general, inferences as to what the structures he describes look like.

Adomnán was by no means the architect of these buildings, and he makes clear that he never laid eyes on them. Rather, he presents as his interlocuter one Arculf, a cleric staying at Iona, who did.[11] The images that accompany Adomnán's text, we are told, mimic sketches that Arculf showed him, etched into wax tablets:

> *We have drawn these plans of the four churches after the model which . . . the holy Arculf sketched for me on a wax surface. Not that it is possible to exhibit their likeness in a drawing, but in order that the* monumentum *[tomb] of the Lord might be shown, placed as it is in the middle of the round church, albeit in a rough sketch, or that it might be made clear which church is situated near or far away from it.*[12]

Again and again, Adomnán reminds us of his images' reliability, because Arculf frequented the site, saw it with his own eyes, and measured it with his own hands. The leading scholar on Adomnán, Thomas O'Loughlin, argues that Arculf is a literary device, a means of giving credibility to Adomnán's account by supplying him with a firsthand witness.[13] But even if Arculf were a fiction, the activities attributed to him had to be believable to be rhetorically effective. His invocation, whether the man himself be real or invented, attests to a general practice of architectural sketching—both communicating a building's features through a few quick strokes on a wax tablet and translating a building's form into a cogent, if simple, plan. The juxtaposition of Arculf's wax tablets with Adomnán's text is equally telling, in that it conveys medieval attitudes toward the disposability and preservation of such works. The drawings on Arculf's wax tablets are mere aide-mémoire, erased once they have served their purpose. The drawings in Adomnán's text, by contrast, affirm the intentions and circumstances required to preserve them. Floor plans were worth saving because they provided an architectural affirmation of Christian truths meant to be shared across monastic communities.

Insofar as Adomnán's sketches supplement religious commentary, they provide an early instance of the most frequent context for architectural repre-

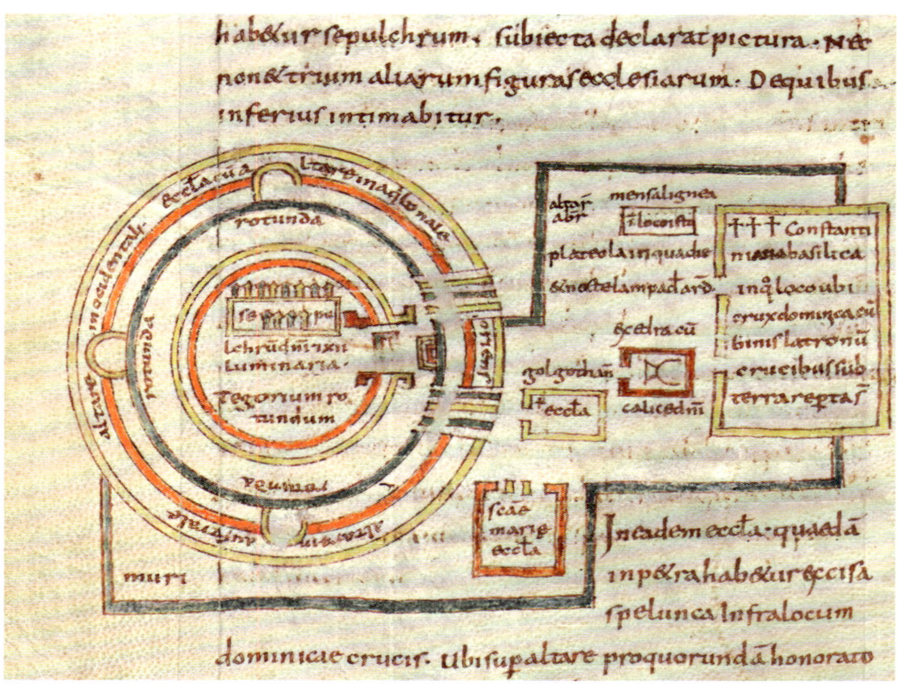

Plan of the Church of the Holy Sepulchre, detail of fol. 4v from *De locis sanctis* (Concerning sacred places) by Adomnán (ca. 629–704). Austria, 9th century. Opaque watercolor and ink on parchment, 11 × 7⁵⁄₁₆ in. (28 × 18.5 cm). Österreichische Nationalbibliothek, Vienna (Cod. 458, fol. 4v)

sentations before 1250. Architecture, in an abstract sense, was intimately linked to cognition, and provided a framework for mnemonic activities.[14] It also reinforced the fundamental idea that the world could be understood through the divine gift of geometry and, in turn, that that elegant geometry could demonstrate the pervasive guiding hand of an orderly God.[15] Elaborate arcades were thus frequently used to frame the organization of complex information, whether in the form of canon tables in Gospel books or diagrams for computing the movable feasts of the Christian calendar (FIG. 3).

At the same time, biblical scholars, both Christian and Jewish, studied and attempted to draw the architecture described in the Bible to deepen their understanding of the sacred text. The Book of Ezekiel, which presents visionary descriptions of the destroyed Temple in Jerusalem, particularly lent itself to such study. The eleventh-century Rabbi Solomon ben Issac of Troyes, known as Rashi, and the twelfth-century canon Richard of St. Victor were two scholars who used drawing to help resolve that text's contradictory and confusing passages (FIG. 4).[16] As the art and architectural historian Karl Kinsella has remarked, these impressive efforts to reconstruct the Temple through both plan and section must have "functioned within a preexisting visual language of architecture."[17]

The many sketches of the Temple found in the *Commentary on the Mishnah* by the Jewish physician and philosopher Maimonides (Rabbi Moshe ben Maimon), now in the Bodleian Libraries in Oxford, are linked to this tradition.[18] The Bodleian's *Commentary* is an extraordinary survivor. Scholars debate whether its Judeo-Arabic text is written in its author's own hand, or was copied by a scribe and emended with Maimonides's handwritten notes and corrections.[19] In either case, it is clear that the book was his personal working

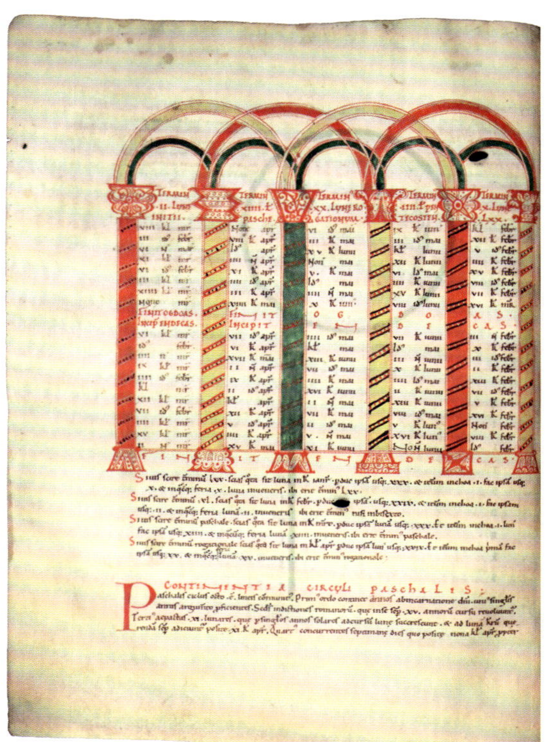

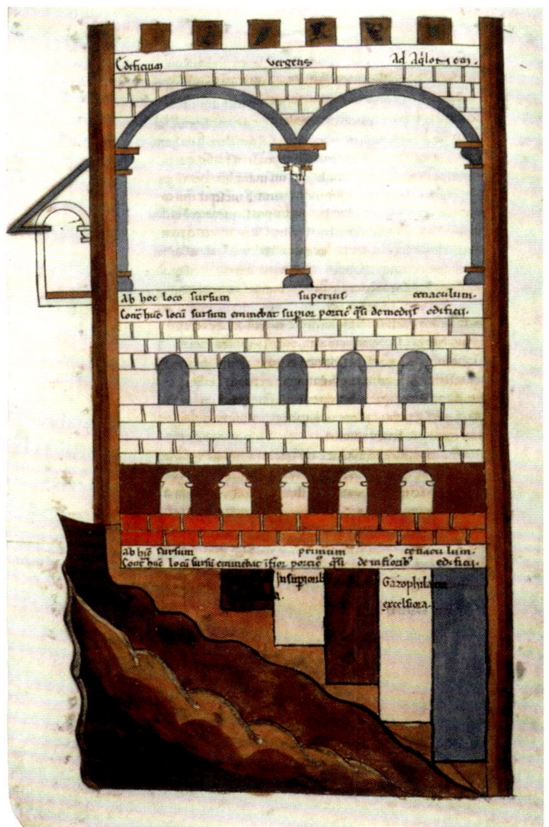

FIG. 3 Table of lunar termini for major movable feasts, fol. 28v from the Thorney Computus. Thorney Abbey, Cambridgeshire, England, 1110. Opaque watercolor and ink on parchment, 13 ⅜ × 9 ¹³⁄₁₆ in. (34 × 25 cm). St John's College, University of Oxford (MS 17, fol. 28v)

FIG. 4 Temple gatehouse, lateral elevation, fol. 162v from *In visionem Ezechielis* (Commentary on Ezekiel's Temple vision) by Richard of St. Victor (died 1173). England, 12th century. Opaque watercolor and ink on parchment, 9 ¹³⁄₁₆ × 6 ⅝ in. (25 × 16.8 cm). Bodleian Libraries, University of Oxford (MS Bodl. 494, fol. 162v)

copy. In turning its pages, we do not need to worry about the vagaries of copyists, as is almost always the case with medieval manuscripts. When the text directs the reader to look at the figures the author has drawn, it means the very ones we see.

The *Commentary* was a multiyear project that made accessible to the general reader the compendium of Jewish law known as the Mishnah. Maimonides's text clarifies the teachings of the Mishnah, often relying on the earlier Talmudic commentary on the Mishnaic text.[20] There are a handful of drawings sprinkled throughout the *Commentary*, but the greatest concentration comes in the discussion of the tractate Middoth (Measurements), in which Maimonides trains his attention on the Mishnah's articulation of the architectural features of the lost Temple.[21] In this short section—a mere ten folios out of some three hundred—nineteen sketches appear as if in a frenzied rush.[22] Some are discreetly tucked into the written text, so cursory as to be difficult to spot. Other more complex works take up a quarter or half of the page, with the concluding drawing—a detailed floor plan of the Temple with its furnishings and courts—accorded an entire page to itself (FIG. 5). None exhibit artistic finesse. Even those inscribed by means of a straightedge display a degree of carelessness, characterized by stop-and-start lines of varying thickness that often overshoot their corners. Explication, not ornamentation, would seem the aim.

Where they fall short in quality, the sketches excel in variety, subject, and type. In addition to several floor plans and site plans that clarify the interior layout of the Temple and some of its outbuildings, as well as their placement within the larger precinct, Maimonides includes simple geometric forms that approximate the distinctive shapes of certain features, such as the semicircular steps of the Nicanor Gate, which separated the Court of the Women from the Court of the Jews, the triangular ramp that led up to the altar, and the trapezoidal footprint of the sanctuary. The draftsman's pen also captures the complex construction of the Temple walls with side chambers, the graduated beams above the principal doorway, and the configuration of the inner folding doors. A stately bar graph demonstrates the hundred-cubit height of the facade (FIG. 6), while an evocative line of identifying text descending in delicate zigzags traces the approach from the Shushan (or Eastern) Gate to the Temple entrance via various courtyards and staircases (FIG. 7). In the text, local building terms and practices are regularly used as helpful comparatives.

In many ways this section of the *Commentary* is an homage to drawing's capacity to suggest a building, clarify its features, and solve technical problems. It represents a sustained and highly inventive effort that both partakes of and departs from established diagrammatic conventions. Maimonides uses every schematic at his disposal to tackle the building's measurements, geometries, spatial arrangements, and sightlines. He considers its relationship to its site, its visual impact, its approach, and the decorative details that make it unique. Any and all of these issues would be addressed in an architect's portfolio today. Throughout, Maimonides makes evident his assumption that the Temple and its features are more efficiently understood and explained through drawings than through text: "Look at the figure . . . and it will become clear to you what is written here." "Although everything is explained to the reader, I am still drawing it so that it can be understood quickly." "This requires a lot of explanation, so let your heart picture what I am telling you."[23] The drawings thus fulfill the

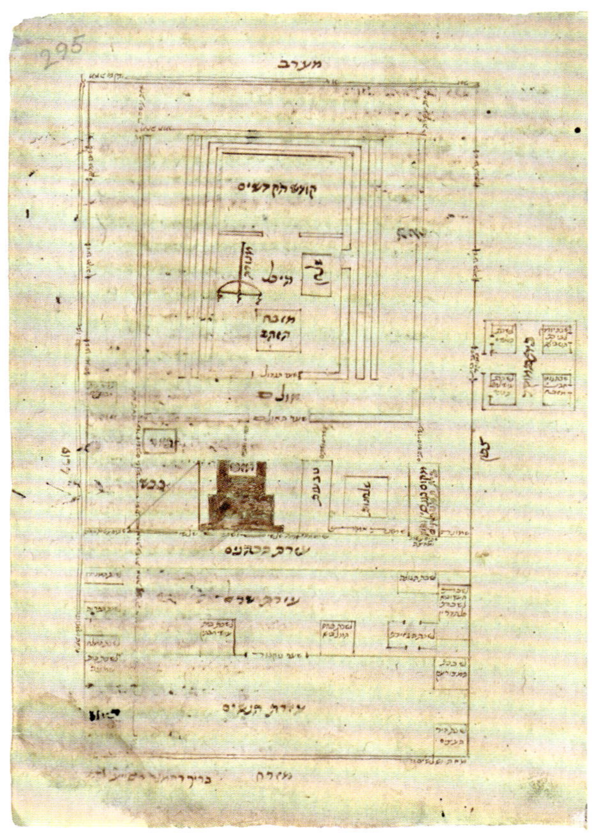

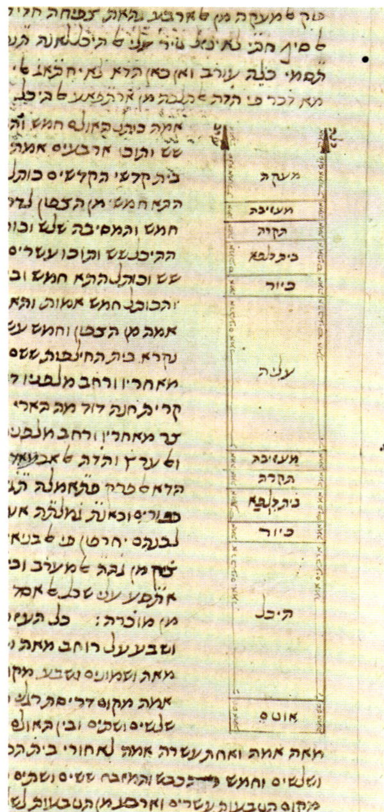

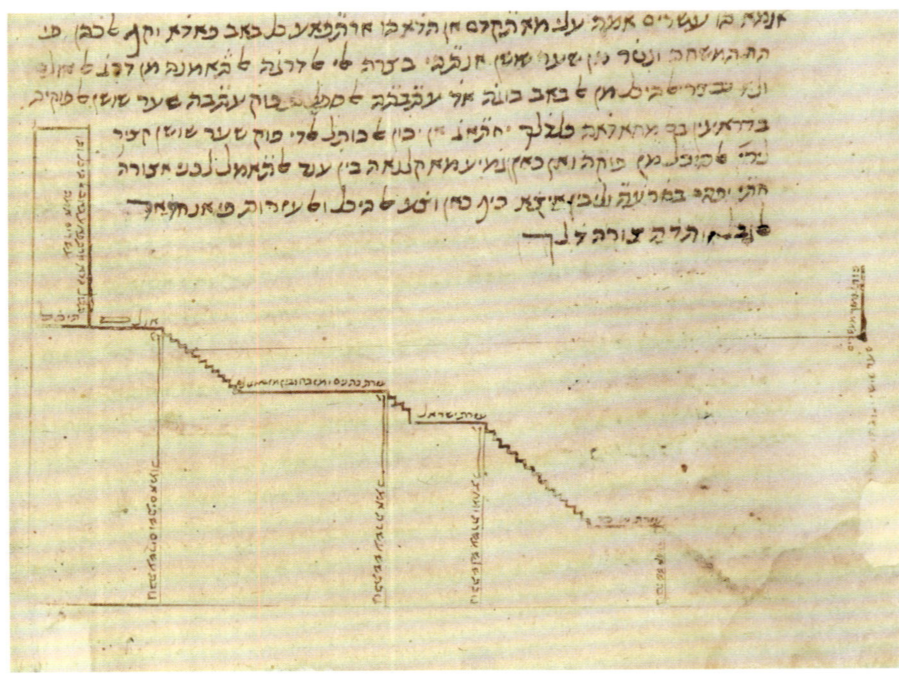

Approach to the Temple from the Shushan Gate, detail of fol. 288v from *Commentary on the Mishnah* (see fig. 5)

aims of the *Commentary* project, providing a clarification of the Mishnah and consolidating legal discussion of its content. They also serve as a helpful guide for the beginner and easy reference for the expert, so that "whatever he had read will become perfectly and permanently clear in his mind."[24] If the Mishnah and Maimonides's commentary on it are exercises in ekphrasis, the accompanying drawings constitute an attempt to reverse engineer the Temple, to give concrete form to it in the mind's eye. While recuperative, the text and drawings also look to the future, presenting a set of precise requirements, a metaphorical blueprint, for a temple to be rebuilt in the Messianic Age.

If the abstract concerns of a Jewish legal scholar seem a long way from the practical needs of the Gothic cathedral construction site, the thirteenth-century portfolio of the French artist Villard de Honnecourt helps to bridge the conceptual gap (FIG. 8). The portfolio—an idiosyncratic assemblage of drawings stitched into a pigskin envelope—has long been held up by scholars as providing the earliest-surviving architectural drawings from the Middle Ages.[25] While few scholars these days claim that Villard was himself an architect, his drawings emphatically convey his own engagement with the graphic possibilities that architecture and its study invited.[26] The portfolio is a compendium of haphazardly arranged graphic types: floor plans, elevations, cutaway views, diagrams, narrative scenes, figural and physiognomic studies, and investigations of foliate forms, patterns, and geometric structures. They reflect a curious mind, a draftsman as interested in geometry and masonry techniques as he is in nifty technologies and the patterns of drapery folds. Even amid the variety, a particular acuity for things architectural emerges, whether in the form of designs for roof construction, window or floor pavements, vaulting schemes, or sculptural details. Deep immersion in the cathedrals at Cambrai, Reims, and Laon, conveyed through multiple detailed sketches, counters the restlessness that characterizes the rest of the portfolio.

Most of the monuments he draws are not his own inventions but structures he has seen firsthand, as he regularly reminds his readers: "I once saw a Saracen tomb that looked like this." "I have been in many lands. . . . In no place did I ever see such a tower as that at Laon." "I was once in Hungary. . . . There I saw the pavement of a church made in such manner."[27] Villard's direct knowledge from his travels, like that of Adomnán's eyewitness informant, Arculf, lends special authority to his drawings. Interestingly, Villard also resembles Arculf in his dependence on an ephemeral support for recording his observations. The substandard and irregular bits of parchment he carried with him on his travels were the castaways of proper book production. Only later, it would seem, did he impose order on the loose sheets he had compiled and turn them into a bound volume (of sorts), adding inscriptions that included a bid for remembrance and the long-term utility of his efforts:

> *Villard de Honnecourt salutes you and prays to all who will work with the devices that one will find in this book that they will pray for his soul and remember him. For in this book you are able to find sound advice on the great techniques of masonry and on the devices of carpentry. Likewise, you are able to find the technique of representation as the discipline of geometry requires and instructs [it to be done].*[28]

Like Maimonides, Villard used an array of graphic conventions to make sense of buildings. Both were clearly invested in the idea that drawing helps one "see" a structure's complex forms. Villard, though, is a true draftsman—a visual thinker and explicator. Just as Maimonides returned repeatedly to his text to correct and clarify, Villard reworked his sketches, moving from leadpoint to ink back to leadpoint, to refine their contours and, presumably, his own thoughts.

Scholars have long seized on Villard's perceived shortcomings as a draftsman. Some critique his architectural drawings for their errors and imprecision and his figural drawings for their awkwardness and ambiguous relationship to his claims of firsthand observation.[29] Yet among the draftsmen whose work survives from the Middle Ages, Villard stands out for his insistent and consistent use of drawing as a mode of inquiry. In his sketchbook, we see him mulling over problems by repeating designs and juxtaposing similar forms, as an opening halfway through his notebook amply demonstrates (SEE FIG. 8). There, ready for comparison, are floor plans for three different chevets, the symbolically and liturgically charged space at the eastern end of a church that became the focus of much innovation and experimentation during the Gothic period. Two of the drawings can be linked to specific French churches, one at Cambrai and the other at Meaux, while the plan at top right is a theoretical design that Villard tells us was devised by himself and someone named Pierre de Corbie.[30] All three plans are highly schematized. Piers have been reduced to simple circles, while the ribs of the side chapels have been quickly inscribed with little concern for perfect proportions. Accuracy in form or measure is clearly less important than the overall impact. The Meaux plan in particular sets the stage for the hypothetical plan directly above it, which plays with the idea of radiating chapels that alternate in shape, size, and vaulting pattern.

Other sketches wrestle with the inherent incapacity of a single drawing to capture a building in its totality. The pages devoted to the tower of the

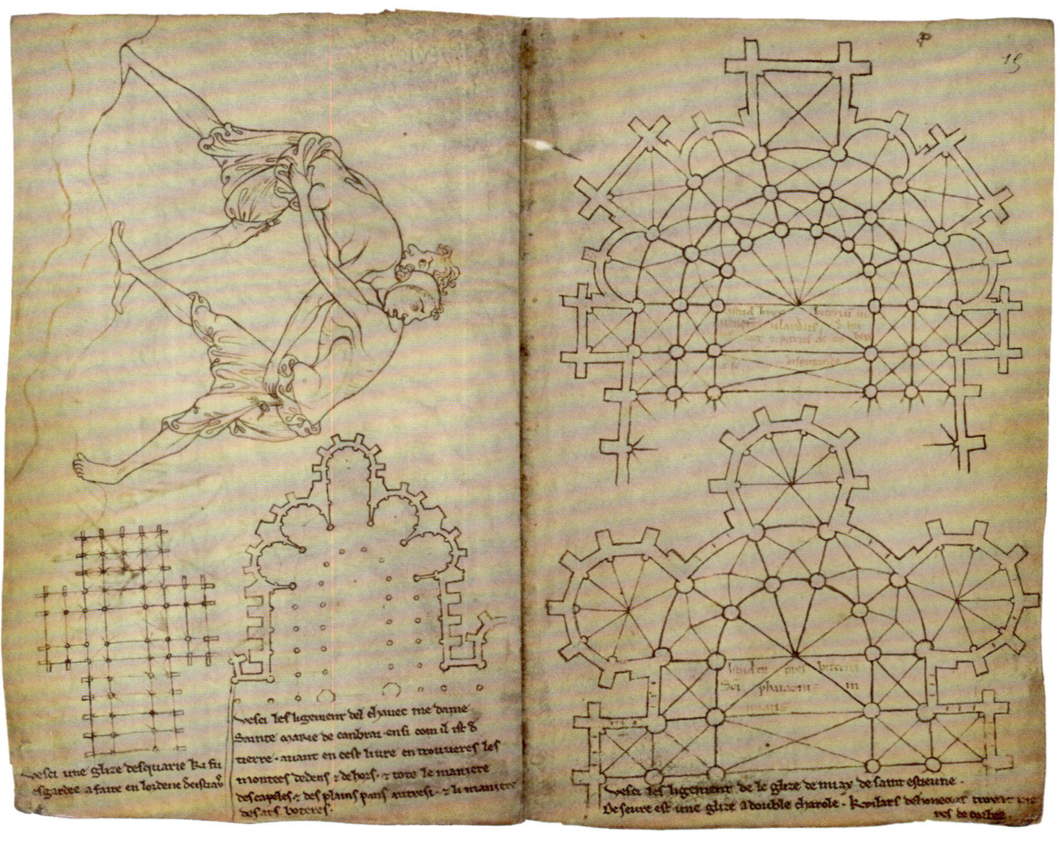

FIG. 8 Villard de Honnecourt (French, active ca. 1220–40). Two wrestlers and plans of a Cistercian church and the chevet of the Cathedral of Notre Dame, Cambrai (fol. 14v, left); plans of a double-ambulatory chevet and the chevet of the Cathedral of Saint-Étienne, Meaux (fol. 15r, right), from the *Portfolio of Villard de Honnecourt*. France, ca. 1230. Pen and ink on parchment, fol. 14v: 9⁷⁄₁₆ × 6 in. (24 × 15.3 cm), fol. 15r: 9⁷⁄₁₆ × 6⅛ in. (24 × 15.6 cm). Bibliothèque Nationale de France, Paris (MS Fr. 19093, fols. 14v–15r)

Cathedral of Laon show the structure in plan, elevation, and detail (see fig. 12). Villard's exterior rendering employs compound perspective to convey the many facets of the tower's structure and decoration. How do things look from different sides? What can a spectator see and not see from where they stand? What is the relationship between what one knows about a building and what one observes? Such questions run as an undercurrent throughout the portfolio. The enlarged aedicula, or niche for a statue, of the upper story of the Laon tower and the outsize sculpted oxen it shelters do not reflect the actual proportions of the monument as much as Villard's wonder before it.

The image of interlocked wrestlers among the chevet drawings in figure 8 explores these preoccupations outside the architectural sphere. The subject, a contest between opposing sides, allows the two figures to mirror one another, a strategy Villard deploys elsewhere in the portfolio.[31] Through a single sketch he adeptly considers the relationship between the frontal and dorsal sides of the naked torso, as the concavity of the one man's chest, traced with the most delicate of lines, finds its partner in the convexity of his opponent's back, its roundness accentuated by the subtle placement of a hand.

It is difficult to understand the relationship between Villard's drawings and actual building practice, particularly as we are not even sure of his profession. Some still assert he was an architect.[32] Others argue he was a carpenter, a goldsmith, or a lay representative of the chapter of Cambrai Cathedral.[33] His drawings successfully suggest the buildings he claims to depict, but they often convey misunderstandings of elementary principles of Gothic cathedral design. The anthropologist Edward Robbins reminds us that architectural drawings are fundamentally social endeavors, created in part to put a building into the center of a conversation.[34] What Villard's portfolio most certainly reveals is the perceived utility of drawing as a way to think and talk about architecture. Villard makes this claim himself in his preface, quoted above, in which he argues for his book's instructional value, promising to illuminate the basics of masonry and carpentry. Even more audaciously, he promises to teach techniques of representation based on geometry. Not only will his sketches show interested readers how to construct buildings, but they will also show how to *draw* buildings. Whether Villard's drawings in fact accomplish these tasks is beside the point. His assertion that they will assumes the expectation that they can.

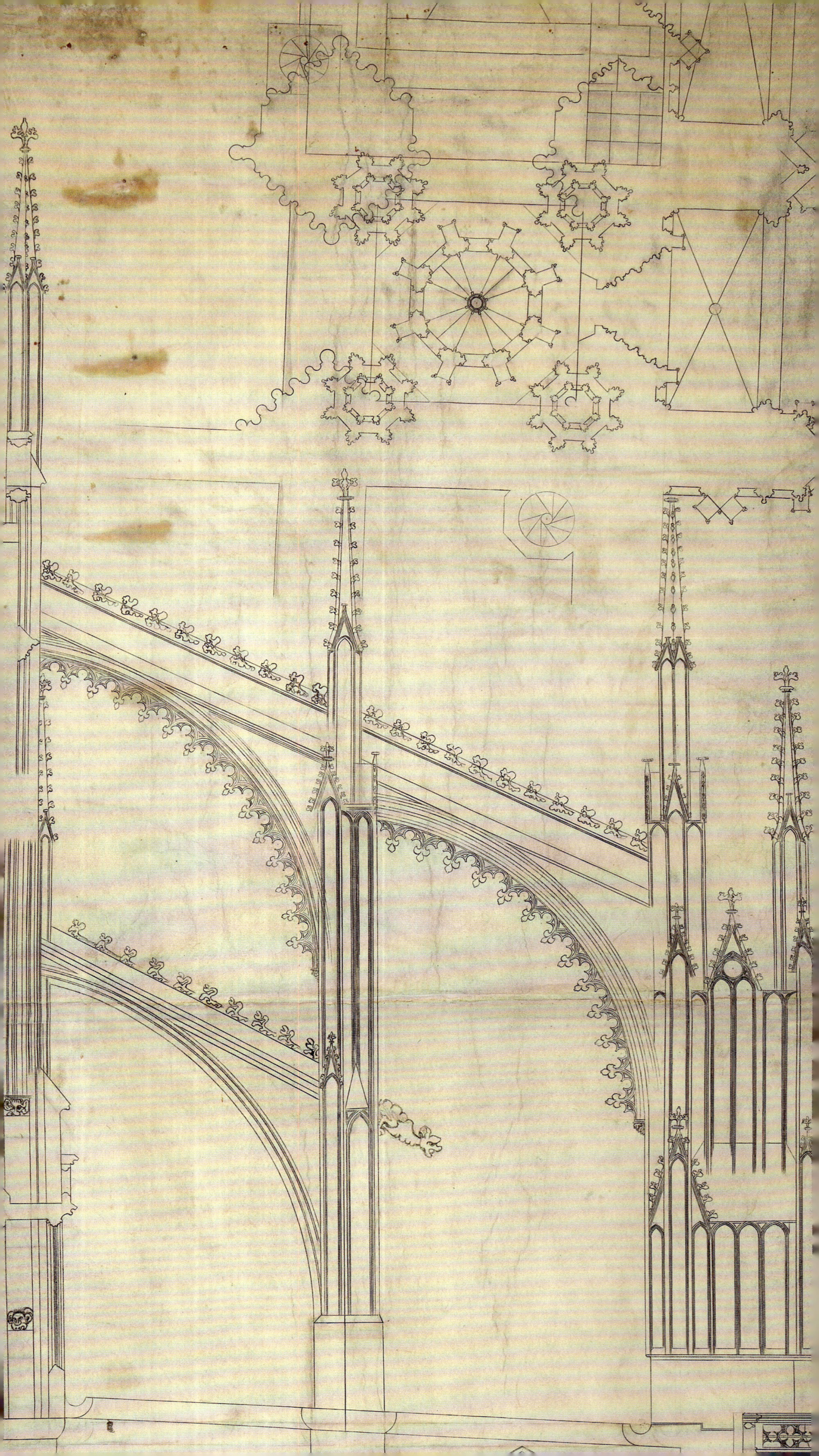

VISION MADE VISIBLE
THE GOTHIC BUILDING TRADITION AND ARCHITECTURAL DRAFTSMANSHIP

Femke Speelberg

The Gothic [tradition] thus invented a new medium—the architectural drawing.
—Roland Recht[1]

In 1770, the German poet Johann Wolfgang von Goethe visited the Cathedral of Notre Dame in Strasbourg (FIG. 9). Having come of age in the time of neoclassicism—a movement inspired by ancient Greek and Roman art, in which architecture was governed by strictly codified rules—he was predisposed to dislike the Gothic structure. Nothing, however, could have been further from the truth, and the visit fundamentally changed Goethe's views on architecture. He was so impressed with the building's grandeur and "thousand harmonizing details" that he concluded it must be the work of a single ingenious architect, whom he identified as Erwin von Steinbach on the basis of inscriptions preserved in the cathedral itself.[2] Goethe was correct in one sense—Erwin had indeed been employed as its architect—but in truth he was neither the first nor the only master of works to make his mark on its construction.

As with many monumental medieval churches, it took more than one generation of builders to complete Strasbourg's imposing cathedral. In fact, the site was under construction virtually nonstop from 1176, after the previous eleventh-century edifice was destroyed by fire, until well into the sixteenth century.[3] During this period, plans were adjusted and expanded numerous times, but the successive architects responsible for the structure's completion were nevertheless able to create a building that, to Goethe's eyes, formed a unified whole. In addition to their expertise and professional judgment, the medieval builders were aided by their access to a vital resource: their predecessors' carefully drawn elevations and plans. This invaluable archive allowed them to understand the thought processes and design choices that had shaped the building up to its current state, enabling a relatively seamless continuation of the work.

The use of drawings in the field of architecture may seem self-evident from our modern-day perspective, but the graphic archive accumulated by the Strasbourg building lodge (the official body in charge of the construction site) is the earliest of its kind. It also contains what may be the oldest true architectural drawing to have been preserved, now referred to, fittingly, as Drawing A (FIG. 10). Created between about 1250 and 1275, it shows a partial elevation of the west facade of Strasbourg Cathedral up to the level of its rose window with a rudimentary design for the entrance portals. It is not a quick sketch, but a carefully thought-out design. Methodically placed pen-and-ink lines follow a preparatory network of blind ruling (shallow, inkless incisions in the parchment) made with the help of a stylus, compass, and straightedge to ensure the exact alignment and curvature of the different building elements (FIG. 11). The time and care it took to create this single partial elevation present compelling

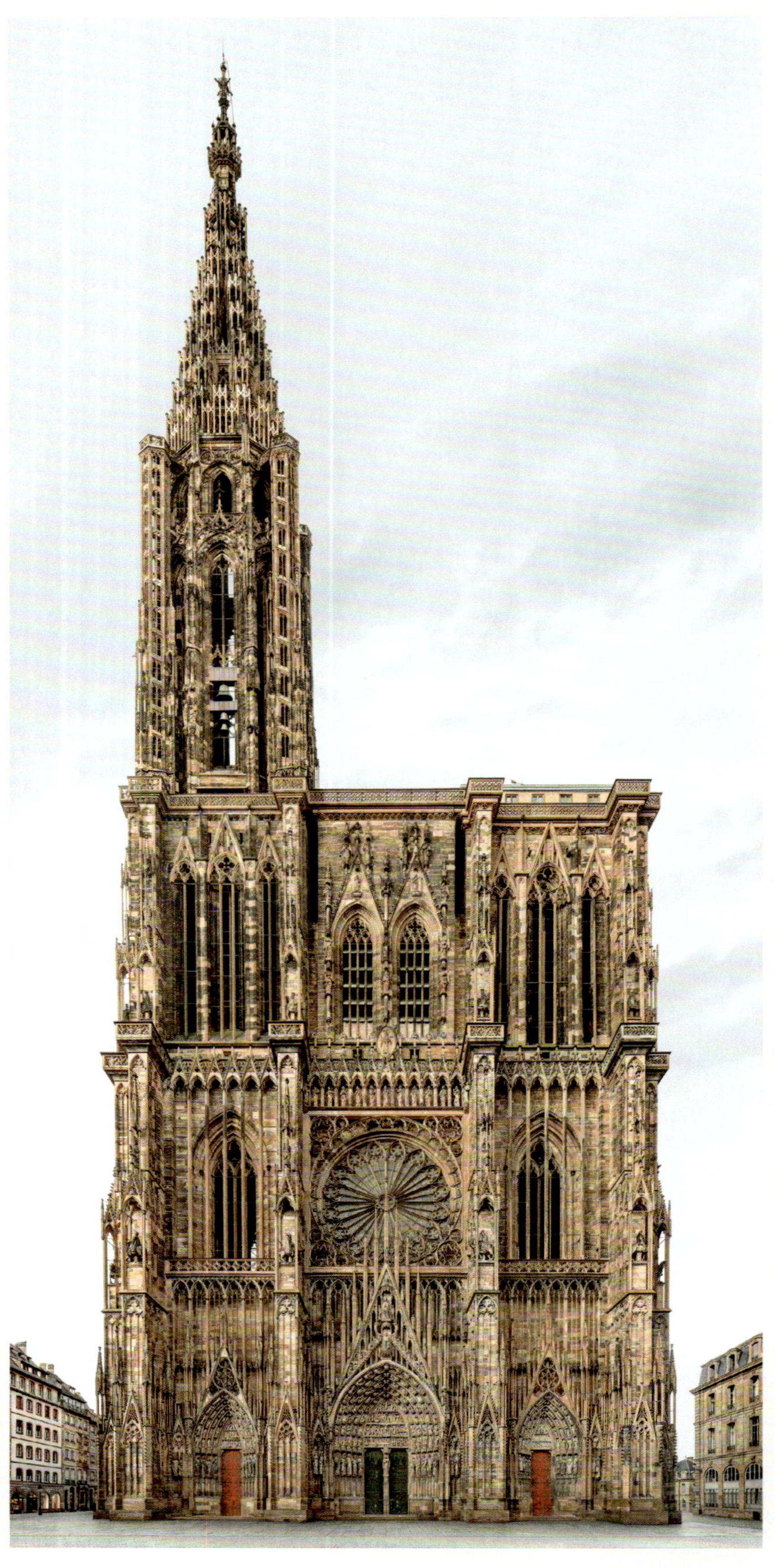

FIG. 9 Markus Brunetti (German, born 1965). *Strasbourg, Cathédrale Notre-Dame*, 2009–14. Archival pigment print

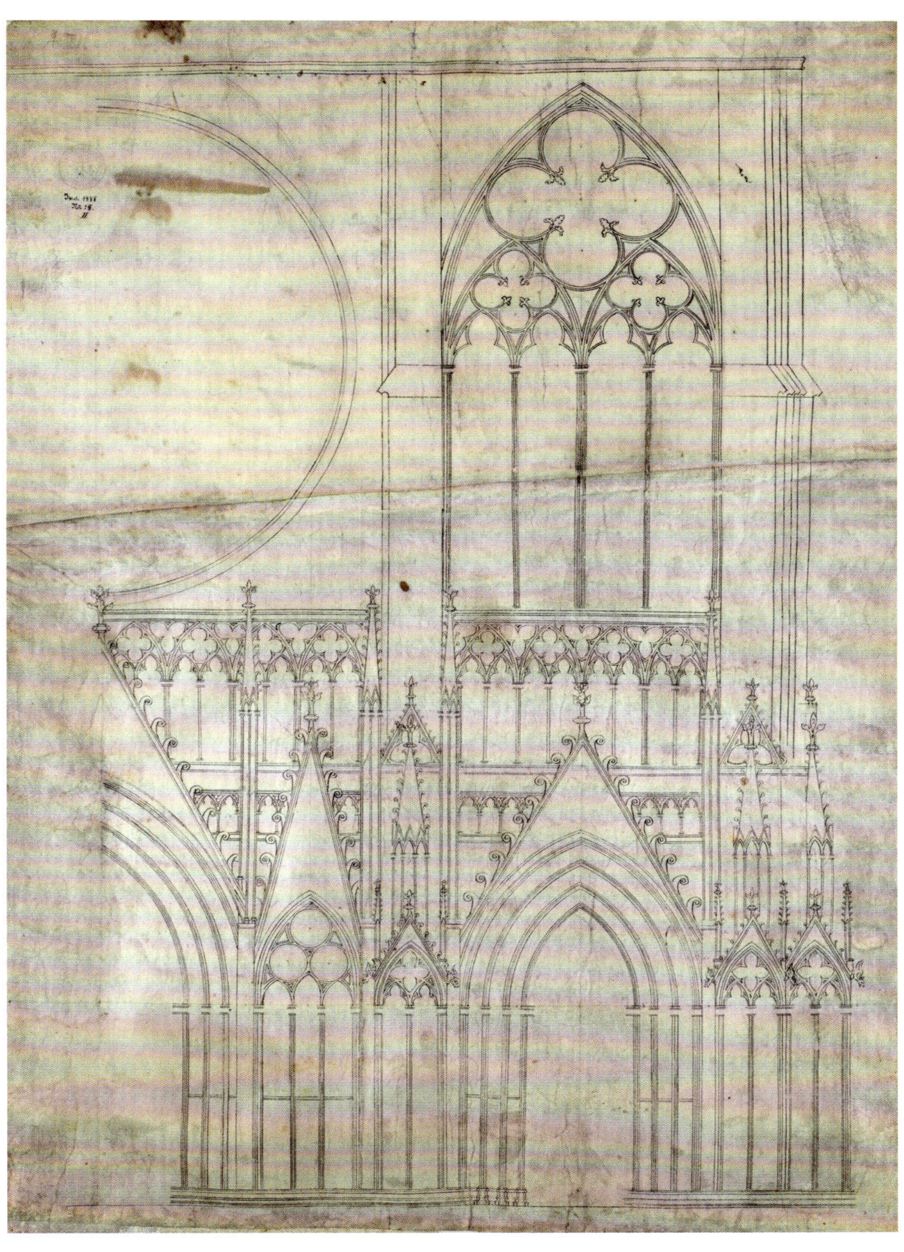

FIG. 10 Attributed to Master Rudolph the Elder (German, died 1276). Partial elevation of Strasbourg Cathedral (Drawing A), ca. 1250–75. Pen and ink over blind ruling on parchment, 33 ⅞ × 24 ⁷⁄₁₆ in. (86 × 62 cm). Fondation de l'Oeuvre Notre-Dame, in custody of Musée de l'Oeuvre Notre-Dame, Strasbourg (D.22.995.0.10 [OND 1])

evidence of the fundamental place drawing had already come to hold in the Gothic building process.

Nowadays, this parchment sheet is one of more than six hundred surviving architectural drawings created across Western and Central Europe from the thirteenth to the sixteenth century. While this number is impressive, it represents only a fraction of the thousands of drawings produced over the nearly four-hundred-year period now associated with Gothic art. The transformative effect of their integration into the process of architectural planning undoubtedly contributed to the Gothic tradition's establishment as one of the most expressive and diverse architectural styles to have been developed in the Western world. To date, the knowledge and study of these drawings have been the focus of a relatively small group of scholars, predominantly of architectural history. These experts have made great strides in analyzing the drawings' content with respect to the activities of specific architects and building sites. Without this research, the present exhibition and book, *Gothic by Design: The Dawn of Architectural Draftsmanship*, would not have been possible.[4] While a few studies have taken a broader, transnational approach to examining the impact of drawing on Gothic architecture, there remains much to be explored.[5] Similarly, to date, art historical surveys of early drawings rarely include examples with architectural subjects. Along with its accompanying catalogue, Melanie Holcomb's 2009 exhibition at The Met, *Pen and Parchment: Drawing in the Middle Ages*, constitutes an important exception. Asking the defiant question, "What did it mean to draw before the Renaissance?," the project surveys the evolution of line drawing from about 800 to 1200 across a variety of disciplines.[6] While the material does not yield easily to a comprehensive historical narrative, owing to the fragmented survival of objects, Holcomb's study nevertheless makes clear that the medium of drawing provided an increasingly potent means of representation and communication during this period.

Picking up chronologically where Holcomb left off and focusing on the genre of architectural drawing, *Gothic by Design* investigates the status and function of drawing in the process of creation and beyond. The present chapter offers an introduction to the subject, from its uncertain beginnings in the twelfth or thirteenth century to the early sixteenth century. This period is marked by a significant shift in the status of drawing, which evolved from an essentially ephemeral practice to a potent means of recording and preserving design solutions. Examples from cathedral archives in Strasbourg, Ulm, Vienna, and elsewhere highlight the diverse functions drawings served in the building process and make clear that the use of drawing was by no means an incidental phenomenon during the Gothic period. The following chapter steps back from the building site to consider the design principles that fueled the work of Gothic architects. From the curriculum of the master mason to the instructional publications of a late-career master of works, the graphic media of drawing and, later, print encouraged innovation, invited collaboration among artists within and outside the architectural profession, and offered an autonomous means of professional representation. Above all, this book argues that while the Gothic period is not widely known for its individual designers, the Gothic style as we have come to know it is the product of a focused attention to design that went hand in hand with a thriving practice of draftsmanship.

Despite Goethe's early embrace of Erwin von Steinbach as the visionary architect of Strasbourg Cathedral, and despite the survival of hundreds of drawings by Erwin and his peers, the history of Gothic architecture is rarely told through the achievement of ingenious individuals, as is standard for Western architecture from the Renaissance onward. This is in part because, compared to their successors, relatively little is known about the people who designed Gothic buildings. Notwithstanding numerous efforts to reconsider the history of cathedrals "through the eyes of their builders," a paradigm shift has so far been impeded by a lack of detailed records.[7] For example, as the architectural historian Peter Kurmann emphasized in the 1989 exhibition catalogue *Les bâtisseurs des cathédrales gothiques* (The builders of the Gothic cathedrals), more architects were named in archival documents of the thirteenth century than ever before. Yet, few of these individuals can be linked to a significant body of work or even securely associated with the specific parts of a building to which they contributed—an archival gap that greatly diminishes the significance of the survival of their names.[8] Likewise, although many medieval architects were revered in their own day, few remaining primary source documents, such as letters and treatises or secondary biographical materials, offer a deep understanding of their career paths, ideas, practices, or artistic networks. As Holcomb noted in her 2009 exhibition catalogue, there is simply no medieval equivalent to the Italian artist and biographer Giorgio Vasari's *Lives of the Most Excellent Painters, Sculptors, and Architects* (1550; expanded 1568) to lift these artists and their works from obscurity.[9] As a result, the few documents that *do* survive have played a significant role in shaping our perception of the history of Gothic architecture, even if they outline only a partial picture.

For one, the twelfth-century chronicles of the Benedictine Abbot Suger, which detail the renovation and expansion of the Royal Abbey of Saint-Denis, just north of Paris, provide Gothic architecture with a potent origin story and an illustrious protagonist. Suger documented the transformation of the decaying Romanesque abbey, which began in about 1135 to 1137, into what has often been interpreted as the first comprehensive demonstration of the new Gothic style.[10] In his dual role as supervisor and chronicler, he left behind a narrative built around the manifestation of his personal vision: "And bright is the noble edifice which is pervaded by the new light; / Which stands enlarged in our time, / I, who was Suger, being the leader while it was being accomplished."[11] Accordingly, Suger is often heralded as the father of Gothic architecture. However, even when celebrated as a "great builder," his role should principally be understood as patron and overseer and not as the building's architect.[12]

Indications to this effect can be found in Suger's own writing. For example, the fact that he pays very little attention to the practical details of the building process, especially as compared to his lengthy descriptions of spatial aggrandizement and material splendor, has been taken to mean that his knowledge in this area was limited.[13] Furthermore, in his account of the church's consecration, written in about 1144–47, he remarks, "Thus, when ... that which we proposed to carry out had been designed with perspicuous order, we brought together an assembly of illustrious men ... and ... laid the first stones."[14] The passive

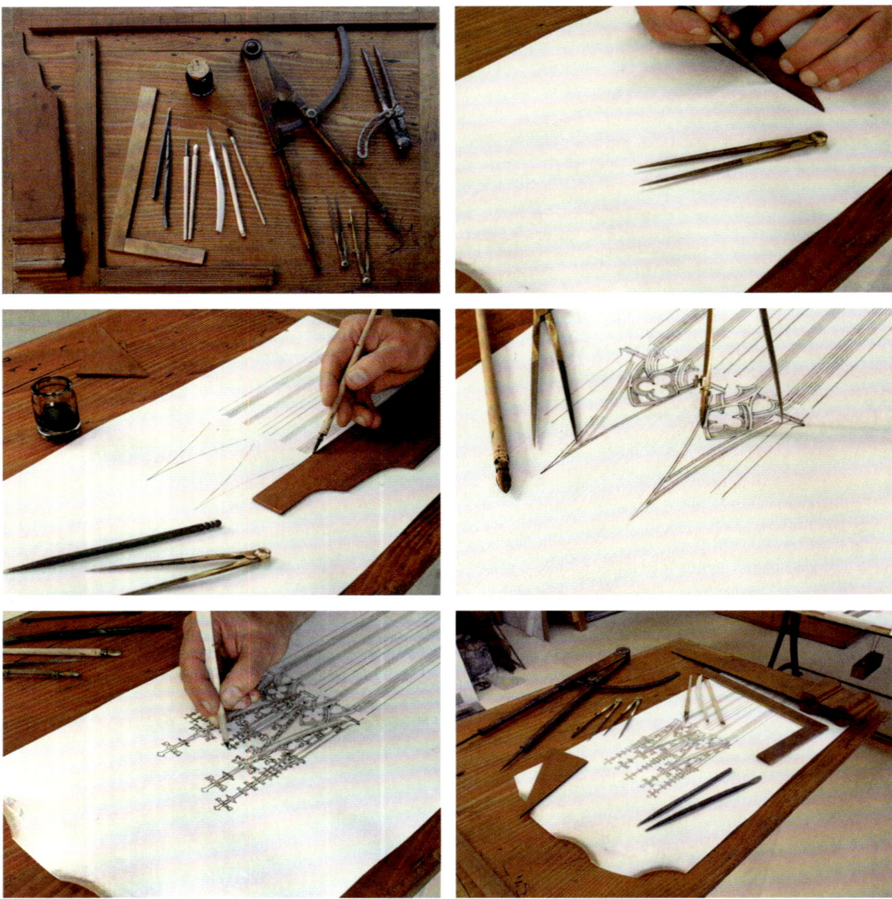

phrasing and specific choice of the words *designatum est* (had been designed) emphasize that while he had a clear vision for the outcome of the renovation—a monumental building that could accommodate and beguile large crowds of pilgrims—Suger relied on his unnamed architect (or architects) to execute the design plans that would ensure the physical manifestation of his ideas.[15]

The bound collection of thirty-three parchment leaves with drawings by Suger's countryman Villard de Honnecourt from about a century later was long thought to offer a glimpse at such early architectural plans (FIG. 12). Among the approximately two hundred and fifty drawings that fill both sides of the parchment sheets are numerous floor plans and elevations of identifiable churches, as well as geometric studies and designs for stone moldings, wood scaffolds, and other building devices, which convinced the nineteenth-century historian Jules Quicherat that they were the work of an important thirteenth-century architect.[16] The bound volume was later more specifically deemed a lodge book (*Bauhüttenbuch*), an album with professional annotations and drawings collected by an architect.[17] More recently, however, the status of the drawings has been called into question.[18] The discovery that the drawings began their lives as loose sheets with little or no organization and only later were bound into a booklet with interpretative inscriptions unmoors the collection's designation as a lodge book.[19] Analysis of the drawings has also identified more than one hand, such that several architectural subjects and annotations are no longer attributable to Villard.[20]

The most prominent argument for a reconsideration of the drawings, however, is the level of accuracy of the renderings in Villard's hand. While he used a ruler and compass in most of his underdrawings, suggesting a careful process of preparation, the finished pen-and-ink drawings that overlay them give the appearance of having been done freehand. As a result, his drawings have been interpreted as informal sketches rather than scaled architectural designs of the type seen in figure 10.[21] More importantly, Villard's renderings of known buildings sometimes contain unrealistic ideas and proportions, and often deviate considerably from the completed structures, as can be seen by comparing his elevation of a tower of Laon Cathedral with the facade's appearance today (FIGS. 12, 13).[22] While these anomalies have been interpreted in numerous ways, there is universal agreement that Villard was not the architect responsible for the design of any of the churches he depicted; neither are his drawings believed to be working designs for any building site. Consequently, it is thought highly unlikely that Villard was an architect at all. His employment in related professions such as masonry, goldsmith's work, and carpentry has been proposed.[23] Alternatively, the art historian Carl F. Barnes Jr. has put forward the possibility that Villard functioned as a lay representative for the chapter of Cambrai Cathedral and visited other building sites on the organization's behalf while Cambrai was under construction.[24] Neither these alternate careers nor the inaccuracies in Villard's drawings are reasons to divorce them from contemporaneous architectural practice altogether, however. Whether professionally or otherwise, Villard was intimately familiar with many aspects of the building process and was conversant enough in its visual and structural vocabulary that he confidently designed his own floor plans.[25] More importantly, his drawings undeniably reflect modes of rendering that have become conventions of architectural representation. As such, they form irrefutable evidence of a tradition of architectural draftsmanship that was firmly established by his lifetime, even if other direct physical evidence is lacking.[26]

In addition to Villard's drawings, there are other indications that the tradition of architectural drafting is much older than surviving examples suggest. For one, the level of sophistication and maturity demonstrated in extant thirteenth-century drawings for architectural projects implies a process of development over multiple generations (SEE FIG. 10, PLS. 4–6, 8, 9).[27] Furthermore, it would be difficult to explain the influence of numerous Early Gothic cathedrals—such as Saint-Denis, Notre Dame de Paris, and Reims—on the designs of other churches, often at great distances, without the use of carefully rendered architectural drawings as visual aids. Later accounts attest to the fact that such drawings were made on request or were brought along by architects and masons who migrated from building site to building site for their employment.[28]

On a more fundamental level, however, architectural historians have long argued that the medium was integral to the transition from the Romanesque to the Gothic style. While this shift is generally defined by seemingly simple changes in form—privileging pointed over rounded arches and a vertical rather than horizontal orientation—these developments went hand in hand with a much greater structural complexity.[29] For good reason, the historian Jacques Le Goff characterized the construction sites of Gothic cathedrals as "the prin-

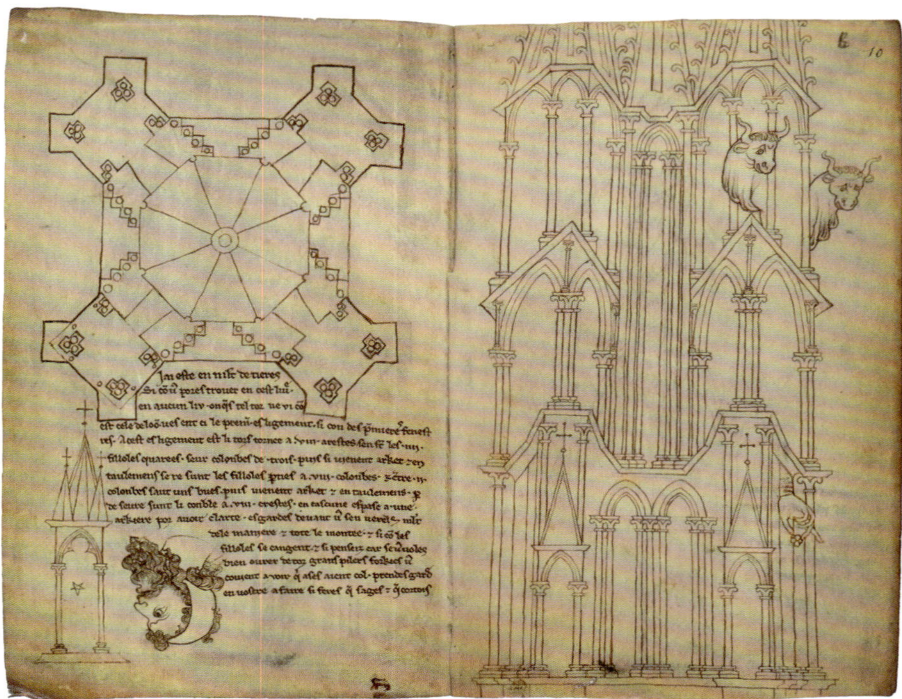

FIG. 12 Villard de Honnecourt (French, active ca. 1220–40). Floor plan (fol. 9v, left) and elevation (fol. 10r, right) of one of the west towers of Laon Cathedral, ca. 1230–35. Pen and ink on parchment, fol. 9v: 9⅜ × 6¹/₁₆ in. (23.8 × 15.4 cm), fol. 10r: 9³/₁₆ × 6¼ in. (23.3 × 15.9 cm). Bibliothèque Nationale de France, Paris (MS Fr. 19093, fols. 9v–10r)

cipal laboratories of technological innovation."[30] Accordingly, the building process required increasingly more advanced planning that benefited greatly from visual methods of communication.[31] The pointed, or ogival, arch, for example, depended on geometry both for its form and strength, which were determined through the manipulation and interplay of circles (PL. 1).[32] While an arch was relatively easy to draw with the help of a compass, the specifications of its design were notoriously difficult to communicate otherwise.[33] Its execution, moreover, required precise coordination among the architects, stone masons, and carpenters to ensure the correct placement and measurements of its individual elements. This process was facilitated by the use of accurate renderings as well.[34] Consequently, by the middle of the thirteenth century, drawing had become so integral to building that a contemporary dictionary equated the one with the other, translating the Latin verb *architectari* (to construct) into French as *pourtrere* (*pourtraire*, to delineate).[35]

Other near-contemporary sources confirm that the descriptive and instructional potential of drawings had become widely recognized during the first century of Gothic architecture.[36] The French writer Bishop William of Auvergne, for instance, characterized the function of drawing as a "material description" of a "mental image," an aide-mémoire for craftsmen, similar to how Villard de Honnecourt's drawings have been perceived.[37] This function would have only gained in importance in the context of building projects that could take decades if not centuries to complete. The English Benedictine monk and illuminator Matthew of Paris further emphasized the fact that drawings could

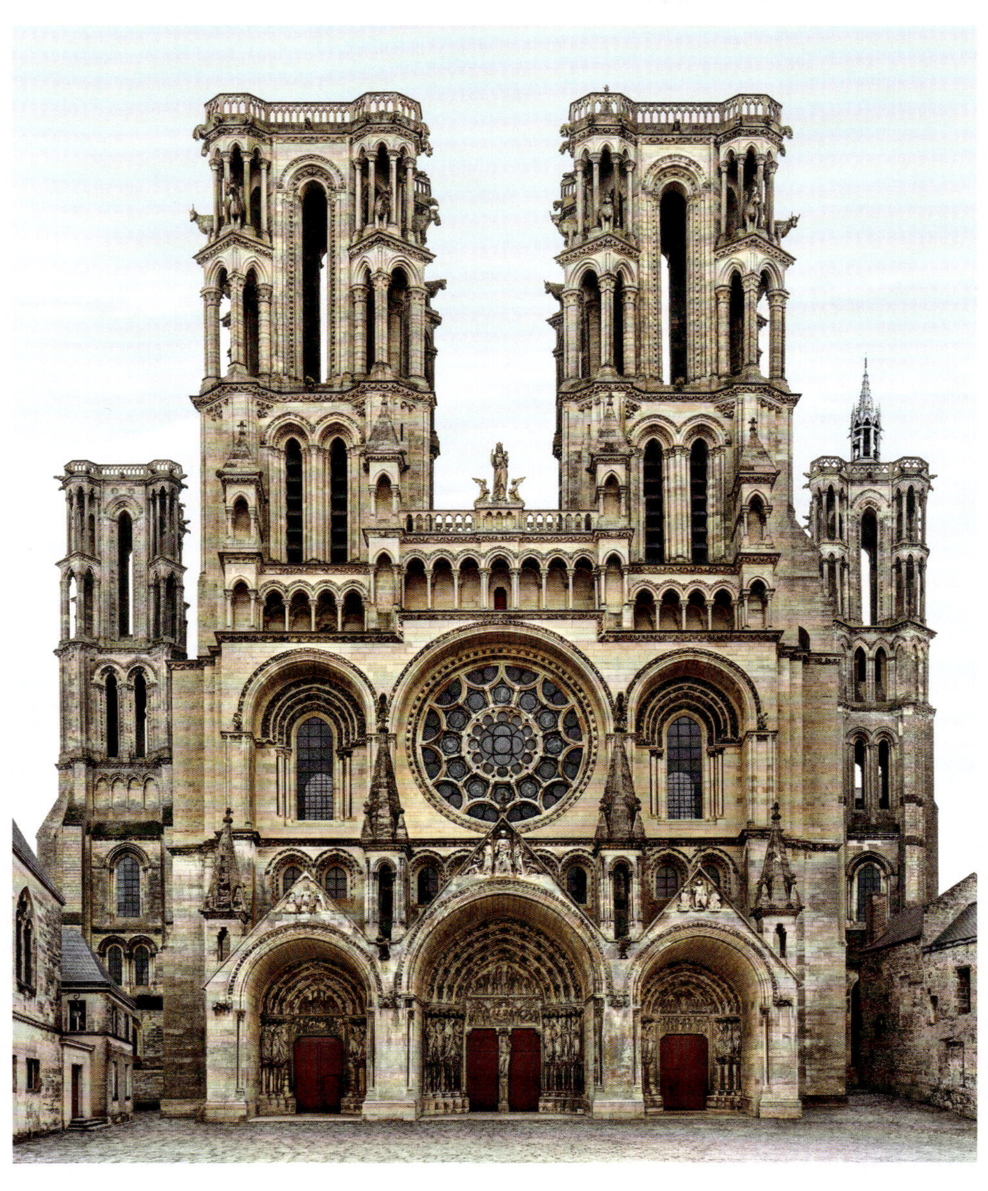

FIG. 13 Markus Brunetti. *Laon, Cathédrale Notre-Dame,* 2013–15. Archival pigment print

capture "what cannot be described in words."[38] He made this observation when recording a fleeting solar phenomenon in 1233, by which point many other subjects, such as anatomy, genealogy, geography, and even theological concepts, were already being communicated through diagrammatic illustrations.[39]

Closest to the subject of architecture are diagrammatic plans of buildings, such as the early ninth-century ideal plan for the Monastery of Saint Gall, Switzerland, and another from the late twelfth century detailing the waterworks that serviced Canterbury's Romanesque cathedral and outbuildings.[40] Although less architectural in appearance, the waterworks plan offers compelling evidence of the practice of drawing on parchment around the same time as the rebuilding of Canterbury Cathedral. As at Strasbourg, Canterbury's Romanesque edifice was largely destroyed by fire, in 1174. Following the example of Abbot Suger's account of the expansion of Saint-Denis, the English monk Gervase of Canterbury recorded the subsequent rebuilding campaign.[41] Compared to Suger, Gervase extended noticeably more agency to the architect(s) entrusted with the renovation. He described, for example, how Guillaume of Sens, "a man of great abilities, and a most curious workman in wood and stone," was chosen from a group of architects gathered from across England and France to lead the project.[42] For five years, Guillaume managed and controlled the building site by ordering materials, making devices for unloading ships and hauling materials, assembling masons and other workers, and delivering templates for cutting stones. Even when he was gravely injured after a fall from the scaffolding, Guillaume communicated what needed to be done from his sickbed to "a certain ingenious monk," possibly Gervase himself, who was chosen as overseer in his stead.[43]

Linking Gervase's mention of templates, or "models for cutting the stones," to Guillaume's ability to supervise the building work remotely, the art and architectural historian Alain Erlande-Brandenburg proposed that portable architectural drawings were, by this time, already integrated into the Gothic building process, although he remained unsure about their precise form.[44] At this early moment, a consistent vocabulary had not yet been developed to refer to specific kinds of drawings, and Guillaume and his contemporaries might have employed several different media.[45] One common method was treating a support, often a wood board, with a layer of plaster (or another chalk-based material) to create a drawing surface. The relatively soft chalk layer could be easily incised with a sharp drawing tool. For legibility, the incised lines were sometimes traced with colored chalk or charcoal. Once a design had served its purpose, the support would be replastered and used again. While no examples survive from the twelfth century, a version of this technique was already described in the context of making stained-glass windows in the early twelfth-century treatise *De diversis artibus* (On diverse arts) by Theophilus Presbyter, possibly a pseudonym for the German goldsmith and metalworker Roger of Helmarshausen.[46] A pair of fourteenth-century wood planks in Girona, Spain, further attests to the pervasive use of this technique over a large geographic area and a long period of time.[47] Notably, at the end of the twelfth century, the English scholar Abbot Alexander Neckam referenced the same technique being employed in a goldsmith's workshop, where apprentices might be given "a waxed tablet, or one anointed with whiting or rubbed over with clay," on which to "draw little flowers . . . in various manners."[48] The latter description is of particular interest since it points not only to a professional practice of making working drawings, but also to one of sketching. All cases suggest a predominantly ephemeral practice wherein any drawing existed for a relatively brief time.

The method of incising a plaster-covered board is closely related to other on-site practices, including drawing on walls and floors, either directly or by first covering them with a layer of plaster. Among the oldest-known examples is a fragment of a rose window drawn around 1190 to 1200 on a floor slab in Byland, North Yorkshire.[49] By the early thirteenth century, the custom was employed in churches across England, France, Germany, and Spain (FIG. 14).[50] So-called drafting floors—located either in the church proper or in a building erected for the purpose—were often used to produce to-scale designs that could subsequently serve as prototypes for various building elements and be transferred to stone or wood by way of templates (SEE PL. 88). Floor-slab drawings at cathedrals in Wells and York, in England, and at Clermont-Ferrand, in France, are still extant.[51] Scaled-down drawings, more often found scratched into walls, are thought to have been used in the moment to think through specific problems or design solutions. For example, in Soissons, France, two thirteenth-century wall drawings depict existing rose windows from the cathedrals of Chartres and Laon. They likely functioned as reference material while the Soissons builders worked on their own rose window.[52] The occurrence of numerous rose window designs among the surviving ephemeral drawings underscores the role of the medium as a necessary aid in figuring out designs of a more complex geometrical makeup. However, walls and plastered supports did not allow for the same level of detailed reflection and planning that a scaled drawing in pen and ink on parchment or paper could provide. It is therefore assumed that the need for works on parchment or paper increased as building designs became even more complex. At the same time, it is also quite possible that the complexity of designs increased as a direct result of introducing a preliminary drawing phase into the initial stages of planning a building.[53]

If any architectural plans for Early Gothic structures such as Saint-Denis and Canterbury Cathedral *were* drawn on parchment, the Reims Palimpsest might explain why they have not survived.[54] Dating to the second half of the thirteenth century, the French manuscript was compiled entirely from recycled sheets of parchment of various origins. Before their reuse for a necrology, they were washed and cut down into uniform pages. Not all of the previous content was effaced during this process, however. While the ink was successfully re-moved, folios 85–96, 99–106, and 111–12 retained fragments of the blind-ruled underdrawings of at least six architectural designs, which were first recon-structed by the art and architectural historian Robert Branner (PL. 4). The designs were all made by a single person or workshop, active in or around Reims between about 1230 and 1260.[55] The palimpsest therefore provides incontestable evidence that a sophisticated design practice had already been established by the early thirteenth century.[56]

The subject matter of the underdrawings ranges from church facades and details of pinnacles to clerestory windows and choir stalls. None repre-sent a finished design for a specific project. Rather, they appear to be itera-tive sketches, exercises, and record drawings used to work toward other more well-defined ideas.[57] Their ephemeral function is underlined by Sheet E, which

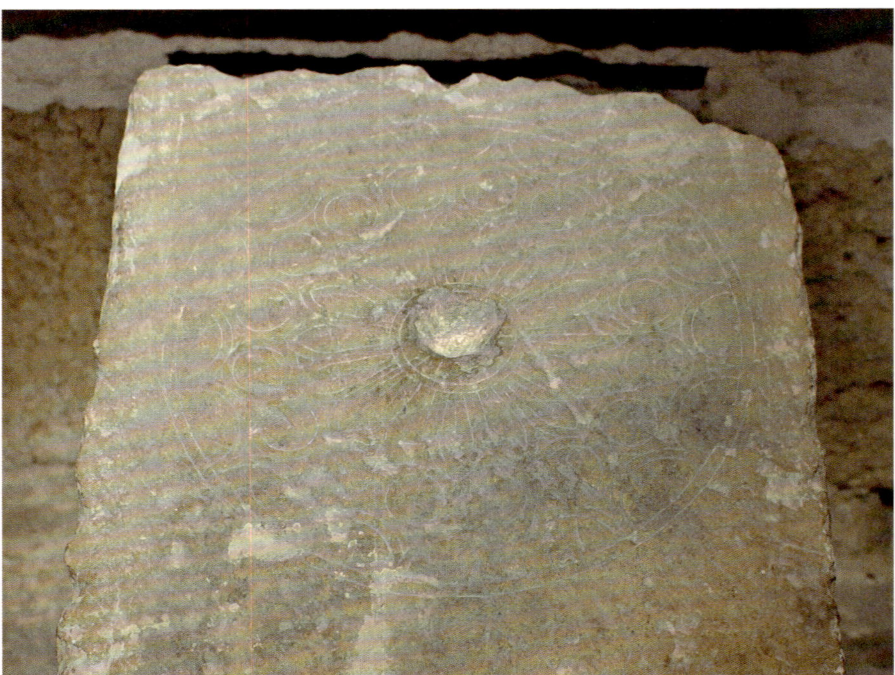

is now scattered across manuscript folios 99r, 100v, 105r, and 106v. It contains not one but two superimposed drawings—one depicting clerestory windows and another showing an undefined architectural element with colonnettes in plan view—which provide clear evidence for the active reuse of parchment even within the confines of the architectural workshop.[58] Similar traces of reuse are also found in the near-contemporary drawings of Villard de Honnecourt, discussed above.[59]

The reuse of parchment underscores both the material value and relative flexibility of the medium as a support for drawing. It also provides vital early evidence for the prolific use of drawing as a method of ideation. In this respect, the Reims Palimpsest drawings are the exact type one would expect to find in architectural workshops, but few such others survive from before the fifteenth century.[60] This does not mean they never existed. Instead, the palimpsestic drawings in the Reims manuscript indicate that their absence can be explained by the contemporary prioritization of material over archival preservation.[61] Once a drawing had served its purpose—or an architect passed away, or a workshop ceased to exist—the functional value of the parchment outweighed its content. The unexpected rediscovery of Gothic architectural drawings in the bindings of various manuscripts further illustrates this point. They include fragments of designs for Cologne Cathedral found in the lining of a manuscript bound at the end of the fifteenth century in the scriptorium at Altenberg, a design for an unidentified wall elevation used as the cover of a sixteenth-century math book at Eberbach Abbey, and a rare late medieval English elevation for a timber-framed secular building hidden in the binding of a manuscript belonging to the Diocese of Worcester.[62] Such examples underscore the architectural historian Nancy Wu's observation that the recycling of parchment has deprived us of many early architectural drawings and therefore of a clear understanding of the medium's beginnings.[63] Only those lucky few drawings that found safety bound in manuscript form and preserved on library shelves—think of Villard de Honnecourt's collection, or the plans of Saint Gall and the Canterbury waterworks—escaped this fate. Not long after the production of the Reims Palimpsest, however, a shift in attitude toward the preservation of this type of content led to the formation of the first permanent collections of architectural designs in several cities across Europe.

Preserving Design History:
The Strasbourg Drawing Archive

In his treatise on poetry from around 1200, the grammarian Geoffrey of Vinsauf muses on the planning phase that precedes construction: "If a man has a house to build, his impetuous hand does not rush into action. The measuring line of his mind first lays out the work . . . in a definite order. The mind's hand shapes the entire house, before the body's hand builds it."[64] In contrast to the flurry of activity often depicted in medieval illustrations of building sites, the preliminary process Vinsauf describes is calm, premeditated, and intentional.[65] While he does not reference the making of drawings explicitly, his formulation, coupled with William of Auvergne's definition, mentioned above, of drawing as the "material description" of a "mental image," suggests why the medium came to fulfill an essential role in maintaining control of the building process. Every phase constituted a new moment to reflect and, when necessary, to redraw plans to correct, improve, or elaborate on an existing design. For this reason, architectural drawings were created, consulted, and refined with a certain frequency from early on. The two oldest surviving designs for Strasbourg Cathedral present compelling evidence for this practice.

Shortly after the partial design for the facade of Strasbourg Cathedral, Drawing A, was created (SEE FIG. 10), a close variant known as Drawing A′ was made (PL. 5).[66] The draftsman of this second version of the facade elaborates on the first by filling previously blank areas with sculptural details such as column capitals, leaf ornaments, and tracery configurations. Drawing A is generally attributed to Master Rudolph the Elder, who served as the master of works (*magister operis*) for an undetermined amount of time prior to the appointment of Erwin von Steinbach.[67] The second drawing, A′, is credited to Erwin on the basis of similarities with other renderings made during his tenure in Strasbourg. At the time he made Drawing A′, however, Erwin was almost certainly still subordinate to Master Rudolph in the building lodge hierarchy. There is no documentary evidence to clarify his exact position, but the fact that he was allowed to make drawings suggests that he was either in the final stages of his apprenticeship to become a master mason, or had completed his training and held the role of foreman (*parlier*). Owing to the star status Erwin adopted later in life, his Drawing A′ has been interpreted as an effort to enliven and modernize Master Rudolph's seemingly more conservative design.[68] However, this falsely assumes that each work represents a complete concept—a misperception that extends too much agency to any one drawing. In actuality, Rudolph's design did not address ornamentation because that was not the intended function of the drawing. Just as he reserved a large circular field for a rose window whose design would have been worked out at a later moment, he undoubtedly also intended for the blank wimpergs (gables over the portals) and the empty spandrels (triangular areas above the curves of an arch) to be filled with tracery or other forms of sculptural decoration. Erwin's Drawing A′ does just that. Rather than compete with one another, the two designs reflect consecutive phases of the building process: Master Rudolph's version determines overall proportions and material allocations, while Erwin's drawing addresses the subsequent sculptural work on the facade. This division and sequence of work is confirmed by a slightly later color-coded rendering in the Strasbourg archive, known as Drawing C, in which the colors blue and red correspond to Drawings A and A′, respectively.[69]

In the time between the execution of Drawings A and A′, the structural makeup of the facade did not undergo any changes. The new sculptural additions could therefore easily have been drawn directly on the existing sheet. Rather than altering Drawing A, however, Erwin obtained the architectural outline of Drawing A′ by using the existing work as a template before filling the blank areas with decorations.[70] This more laborious process seems to indicate reverence for the integrity of the original design and, by extension, different design states. Indeed, both sheets were kept even after the design of the facade changed considerably in 1277, after which point they no longer served a direct purpose in the building process (PL. 6).[71] This new inclination to preserve design drawings signifies a clear departure from the earlier practice of recycling parchment. For the Strasbourg building lodge, in particular, the establishment of a design archive aligned with a significant course adjustment within the building campaign. While the initial rebuild, begun in 1176, adhered to the Alsatian Romanesque tradition, a growing awareness of the new Gothic style inspired a stylistic rethinking in Strasbourg. This change first manifested in the nave, which was built over a twenty-five-year period starting around 1250. The original facade design proposed in Drawings A and A′ would have marked the natural completion of this project, but work had scarcely begun by 1275.[72] The death of Master Rudolph in 1276 almost certainly paused proceedings, and the subsequent leadership transition was the impetus for the first of many revisions, both large and small, to Strasbourg's facade project.

The decision to preserve drawings related to the ongoing work on the Strasbourg facade means that it is now the best visually documented building project of the Middle Ages. Not counting the plans for its two octagonal towers (only one of which was built), no fewer than sixteen distinct drawings for the facade have been preserved.[73] Moreover, there is enough evidence to conclude that the current body of fifty-eight design drawings that can be connected to the Strasbourg building lodge represents only a fraction of the number that were once held in the archive.[74] According to Louis Schneegans, historian and archivist in Strasbourg in the nineteenth century, as many as 366 remained there in the second half of the seventeenth century. There is some doubt about the accuracy of this figure, but the fact that 428 drawings are still found in the archive of Vienna's Stephansdom (Saint Stephen's Cathedral) confirms that Strasbourg's holdings could easily have numbered nearly as many.[75]

Not all building sites would have relied on drawings to the same extent as Strasbourg or Vienna, but it is abundantly clear that many more drawings were made—and retained for a considerable amount of time—than can be accounted for today. For example, the archive of the minster lodge in the Upper Rhine city of Freiburg im Breisgau, active alongside Strasbourg's archive in the thirteenth and fourteenth centuries, is no longer preserved in situ. While various drawings related to its celebrated west tower survive, none remain in Freiburg itself.[76] The inadvertent dispersal of this archive seems to have happened intermittently over time. The architect Gregor Hauser, for instance, took several drawings with him when he left Freiburg to take up a new post in Vienna around 1514. Other drawings ended up in Stuttgart.[77] In the fifteenth century, the building lodge in Ulm took measures against this phenomenon by stipulating in the contract of a new master of works (*Dombaumeister*) that all designs made for the minster were considered property of the lodge and could not be taken elsewhere or used in other commissions.[78] The lodge's longevity as well as this preemptive method of safeguarding intellectual property undoubtedly contributed to the preservation of a sizable archive in Ulm, today one of the three most important collections of its kind alongside those in Strasbourg and Vienna.[79] Such measures could not prevent loss due to unforeseen calamities, however. The once-considerable cathedral archive in Cologne, for example, became a casualty of the city's invasion and subsequent pillaging by French Revolutionary troops, while the great majority of English drawings—few of which survive despite ample attestation in written sources—likely fell victim to the categorical repossession and destruction of Church property following King Henry VIII's break with Rome in 1534 (PLS. 8, 18).[80]

A comparatively benign but nevertheless regrettable form of loss is related to the relatively fragile nature of both parchment and paper. Of the two, parchment is the more robust material and was often the medium of choice for large and/or important drawings, even after paper became available in greater quantities over the course of the fourteenth century. However, as a hygroscopic material that reacts to fluctuations in moisture level, parchment is particularly vulnerable to environmental stressors. Two early designs for the facade of the Duomo of Orvieto, dating to about 1290 to 1320, demonstrate the effects of prolonged exposure to the Mediterranean's hot, dry summers and cool, wet winters: The sheets are warped due to a process of constant shrinking and expanding. They have further suffered from insect damage (FIG. 15). Together with a fifteenth-century fragment showing the sculptural surround of the rose window, they are the only survivors of a group of drawings that, in 1825, still counted at least thirteen distinct sheets.[81] Aside from climate, other storage conditions caused challenges. In 1847, for example, the architect Gustave Klotz expressed his concern about the state of the Strasbourg archive, where rolled-up drawings had been casually piled on the shelves of a cabinet.[82]

The dispersal of architectural drawings is a contributing factor in the loss of knowledge about their authorship, dating, and subject matter. This is the case, for example, for the so-called Nuremberg Drawing (*Nürnberger Riss*) (PL. 9).[83] The somewhat misleading name of this drawing derives not from its place of origin or subject matter, discussed below, but from its current location at the Germanisches Nationalmuseum in Nuremberg, where it once belonged to the museum's founder, the nineteenth-century Franconian Baron Hans von und zu Aufseß.[84] The recent determination that the drawing's likely place of conception was, in fact, Strasbourg, underlines the fact that even this

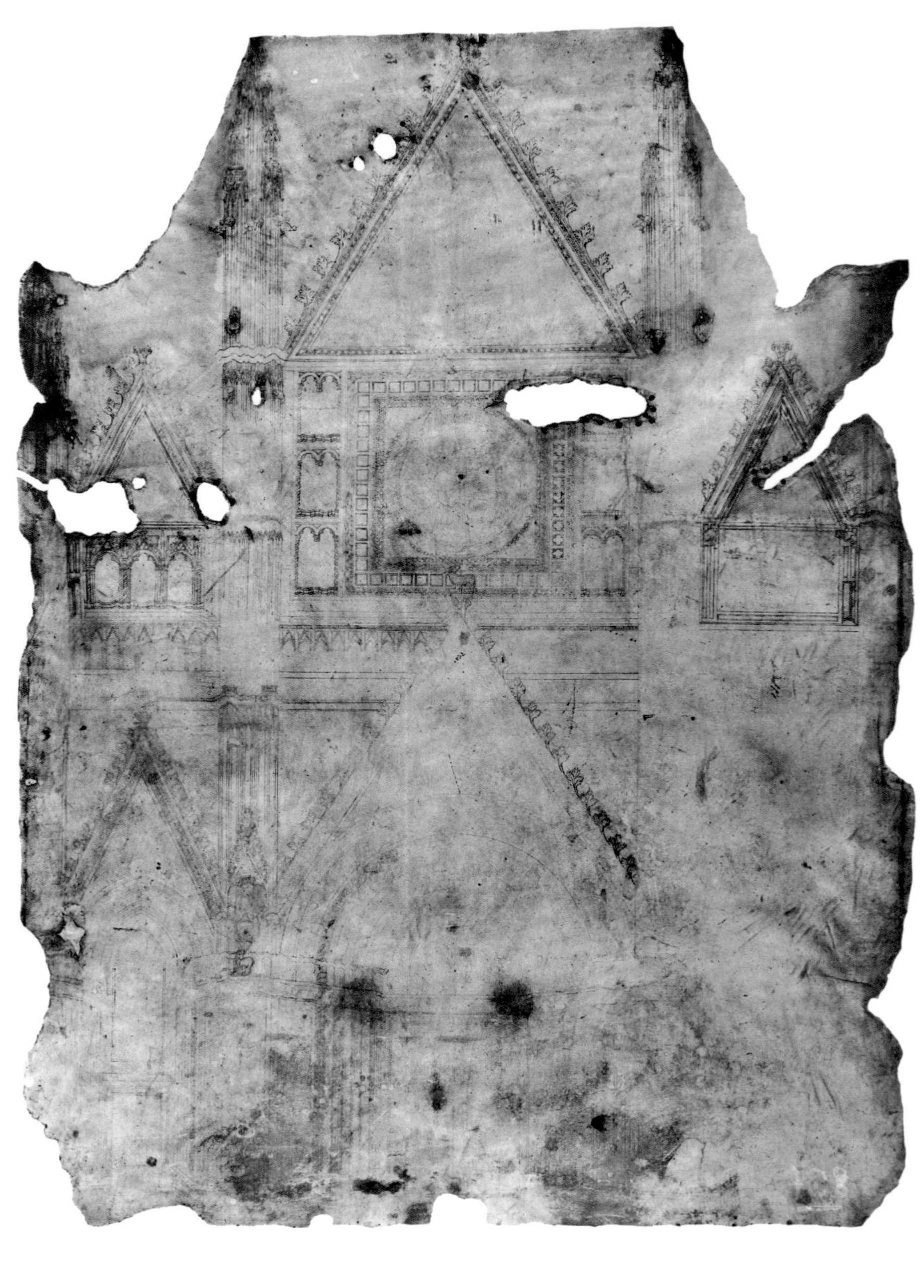

FIG. 15 Attributed to Lorenzo Maitani (Italian, ca. 1275–1330). Design for the facade of the Duomo
of Orvieto, ca. 1310. Pen and brown ink with red pigment over blind ruling, 48 1/16 × 35 1/16 in.
(122 × 89 cm). Museo dell'Opera del Duomo di Orvieto (Q3)

relatively well-preserved archive suffered from the gradual displacement of some of its contents.

That Strasbourg was the Nuremberg Drawing's place of origin is not immediately evident, because none of the visible designs on either side of the sheet relate to the cathedral. Instead, the elevation and floor plan that fill the length of the recto represent the western entrance portal and tower of Freiburg Minster.[85] The sheet's extreme height (just shy of ninety-two inches), achieved through the collation of three fairly even pieces of parchment, correlates closely with the overall proportions of the tower, which indicates that this was the first subject to be drawn. The verso of the sheet was subsequently used for elevations and floor plans of other projects, two of which are identified as preliminary designs for churches in Thann and Breisach, towns that are located, like Freiburg, in the Upper Rhine region, south of Strasbourg.[86] In his annals of Thann of 1724, Malachias Tschamser alluded to the involvement of Erwin von Steinbach in the design of all three buildings, but this notion was rejected in the early twentieth century.[87] More recently, the attribution has been resuscitated based on a stylistic comparison with Erwin's work in Strasbourg.[88] Careful examination of the parchment by the architectural historian Johann Josef Böker reveals, moreover, that at least one of the sheets was recycled to make the Nuremberg Drawing and still contains traces of an erased drawing related to Strasbourg's rose window.

The Nuremberg Drawing is now interpreted as a collection sheet (*Sammelblatt*)—an archive of separate designs from Erwin's tenure in Strasbourg, copied onto the double-sided sheet for the purposes of preservation. The original drawings were likely sent to Freiburg, Breisach, and Thann to be used on-site for the execution of their respective buildings.[89] The Freiburg elevation itself may even have been pieced together from several separate drawings, as not all parts of the building are equal in scale.[90] That the copyist (or copyists) responsible for making the Nuremberg Drawing took some liberties with the scale is otherwise apparent from the extremely oversize leaf-shaped crockets and finial adorning Freiburg's openwork tower. These expressive, heavily shaded ornaments suggest that architectural accuracy and archival objectivity were temporarily abandoned to showcase the precocious draftsman's ability to render such sculptural details in the round. Nevertheless, in its function as a storehouse of multiple designs, the Nuremberg Drawing provides indisputable evidence that the archive in Strasbourg was, from the beginning, the result of a concerted effort on the part of the building lodge to retain the designs that had been made under its auspices.

Seeing the Big Picture:
A Closer Look at Monumental Facade Elevations

While the Nuremberg Drawing, at nearly ninety-two inches in height, can be called monumental by any standard, its size is by no means exceptional among architectural drawings of the Gothic period. The extreme height of Gothic structures necessitated the production of oversize drawings, most of which were much taller than they were wide. To ensure that the intricate details of facade and tower designs were legible, the scale of an elevation could only be reduced by so much. While Gothic drawings typically lack measurements or scale bars—for various reasons, proportions were favored over exact dimensions—barring some exceptions, the ratio of drawing size to building height tends to fall between 1:10 and 1:20. An impressive number of such monumental drawings have survived, likely because their sheer size prevented them from being carried around or consulted with ease. By comparison, Barbara Schock-Werner, the architect who served as the master builder of Cologne Cathedral from 1999 until 2012, has suggested that a majority of the smaller, more practical drawings that were used on-site have probably been lost due to such use. She surmised that those designs that remain were either not used at all, or contain initial ideas and overall impressions that would have been developed further elsewhere.[91]

As the Nuremberg Drawing has already illustrated, however, monumental architectural drawings functioned as more than exact blueprints. This was likely the case for the fourteenth-century elevation of the central bay of the Strasbourg facade, commonly known as Drawing 5 (FIG. 16).[92] The parchment surface consists of five collated sheets that, in total, measure more than thirteen feet high. In addition to its impressive size, Drawing 5 stands out owing to the application of color to indicate polychromy in the sculptural program. Notably, the color is only applied to the top half of the structure. This is consistent with the fact that, apart from the mischievous lions scaling the wimperg above the central portal, most of the facade's figurative sculpture is missing from the lower half of the drawing (SEE FIG. 18).

These incongruities are among several that indicate that the enormous drawing, like the facade itself, was not conceived in a single campaign. The differences between the lower section of the drawing (comprising the entrance portal, rose window, and sculpture gallery) and the uppermost sheet (containing the belfry) most likely correlate with their authorship. The lower section of the building was designed and executed by three generations of Steinbach architects: Erwin von Steinbach, his son Johannes, and grandson Master Gerlach. Gerlach is generally thought to have "summarized" all three architects' designs for the lower section of Drawing 5. The work may originally have also included a proposal for the building's resolution at the top, which was later replaced with the current uppermost sheet with the colorful belfry. It is unclear when and by whom the later addition was made.[93] The belfry itself was ultimately executed under Claus von Lohre, the master of works from 1390 to 1399, but not according to the design proposed in Drawing 5. Documentary evidence indicates that plans to connect the north and south towers with a belfry were in place as early as the time of Gerlach's successor, Master Conrad.[94] Conrad's tenure from 1372 to 1382 coincided with a double celebration: the bicentennial of the entire rebuilding campaign (1376), and the centennial of the facade project (1377). Although the idea is difficult to corroborate without documentary evidence, it is tempting to think that the vividly colored uppermost sheet of Drawing 5 was created to celebrate either or both events. The fact that a separate artist, likely a painter of Bohemian origin, was commissioned to draw the sculptural program of the belfry substantiates the idea of a special occasion.

The drawing's extremely large size and general lack of architectural complexity further suggest that it was produced primarily to impress. In this sense, it might be compared to a near-contemporary presentation drawing attributed to Lando di Pietro, which has been tentatively identified as a proposal for a

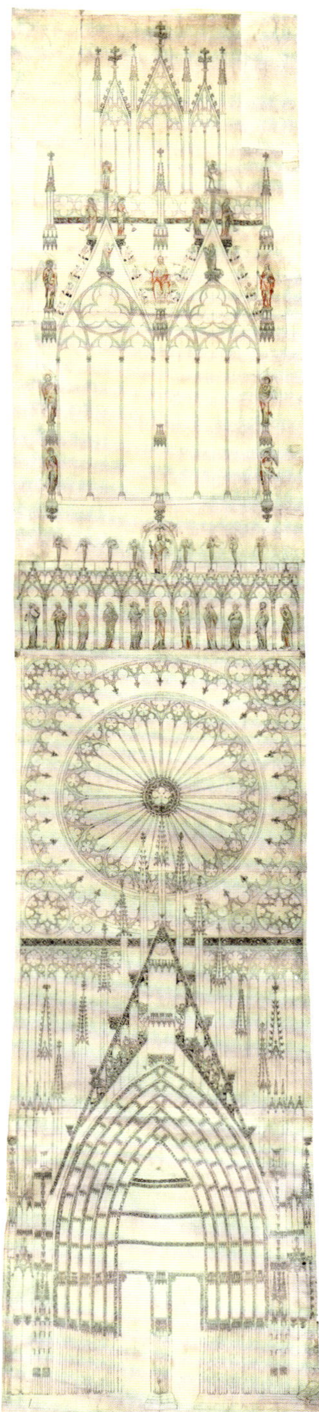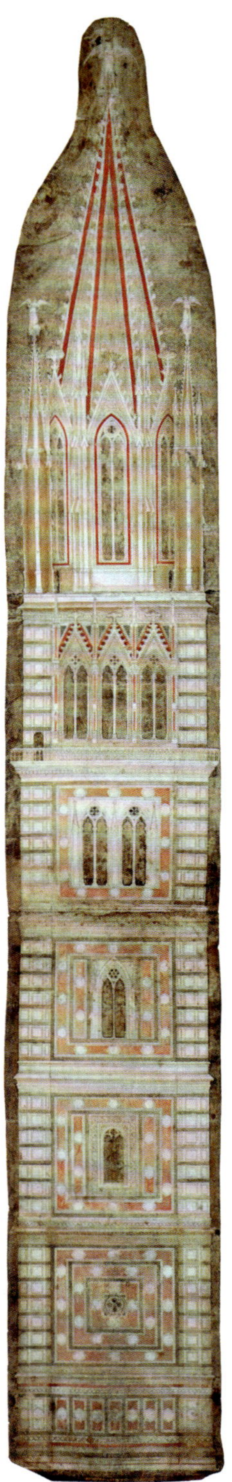

FIG. 16 Master Gerlach(?) (German, born Upper Rhine region, active 1341–70), partially after Erwin von Steinbach (German, born Upper Rhine region, died 1318) and Johannes von Steinbach (German, born Upper Rhine region, active 1318–39), with additions by unidentified German artist (14th century) and unidentified Bohemian artist (14th century). Elevation of the central bay of the west facade of Strasbourg Cathedral (Drawing 5), ca. 1360–70. Pen and ink over blind ruling, with wash and watercolor, on parchment, 16 ft. 4 7/8 in. × 3 ft. 10 1/16 in. (500 × 117 cm). Fondation de l'Oeuvre Notre-Dame, in custody of Musée de l'Oeuvre Notre-Dame, Strasbourg (D.22.995.0.14 [OND 5])

FIG. 17 Attributed to Lando di Pietro (Italian, ca. 1280–1340). Design for the campanile of Siena, after 1334. Brown ink and colored pigments on parchment, 87 3/8 × 12 5/8 in. (222 × 32 cm). Museo dell'Opera Metropolitana del Duomo di Siena (154)

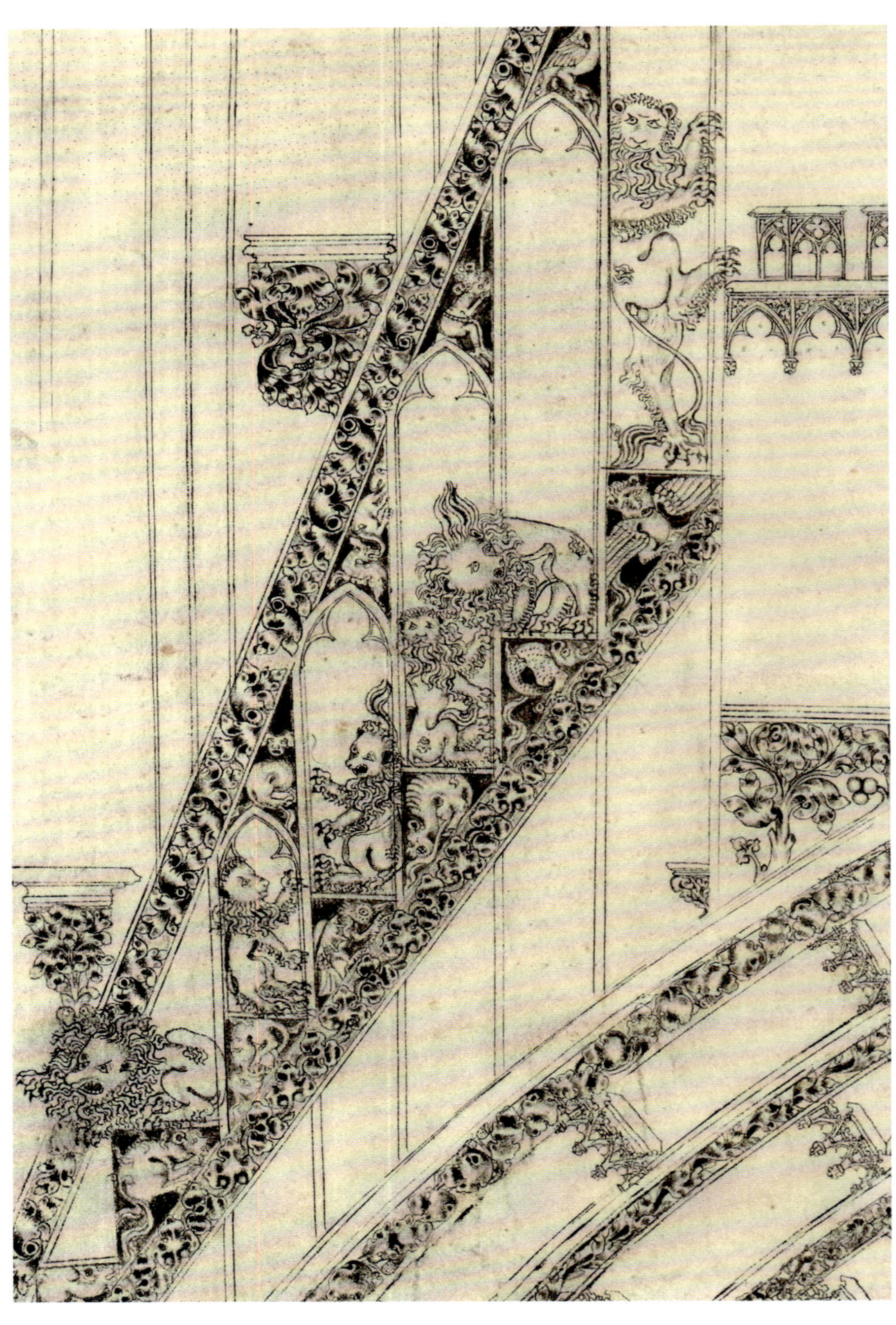

FIG. 18 Detail of the lion statuary on the main gable in Strasbourg Drawing 5 (see fig. 16)

new (unbuilt) campanile for the Duomo of Siena (see fig. 17).⁹⁵ Executed in brown ink with cream, green, and red coloring that reflects the stonework characteristic of Italian trecento architecture, Di Pietro's drawing offers a vivid picture of what the tower would look like when built. Strasbourg's Drawing 5 is similarly evocative, but since the execution of the facade was already well underway when it was made, the design is not, strictly speaking, a presentation drawing (typically rendered at the outset of the project to elicit support). Instead, it seems to celebrate the distinct phases that led to the facade's completion, and may have been created in honor of the civic donations that enabled the realization of the campaign.

An almost contemporary and even more monumental example from Cologne Cathedral served a very different purpose: that of a master plan. One of the archive's few survivors, Drawing F provides a comprehensive view of the cathedral's facade and two towers (fig. 19).⁹⁶ While not quite as tall as the Strasbourg elevation, it is nearly twice as wide and far more detailed in its execution. The drawing surface consists of twenty pieces of parchment that range dramatically in size and shape. Eleven large sheets relate roughly to the different building registers of the north and south sides of the facade, while nine smaller sheets were used to piece them all together. This parchment patchwork suggests that the elevation in its present form was not planned from the start but came about in stages, likely beginning with the sheet representing the lowest tier of the south tower. This area corresponds to the portion of the facade that was executed first, and the one for which the most preparatory drawings have survived (see pl. 8).⁹⁷ Unlike Strasbourg Drawing 5, Cologne Drawing F displays coherent draftsmanship throughout, indicating that once the plan to collate the full elevation had been decided, the drawing was executed over a relatively short time.

Its date—and with it, its attribution—has fluctuated immensely, from as early as about 1280 to 1290 to various periods in the early to mid-fourteenth century.⁹⁸ The execution of the facade did not commence until the second half of the fourteenth century, but nevertheless followed the design proposed in Drawing F. By and large, it would remain the guiding scheme for the execution of Cologne's west facade and towers over the following centuries. The steadfast adherence to the initial design was undoubtedly encouraged by the comprehensive nature of the structural and decorative programs, and possibly helped further by the extremely long tenure of Michael von Savoyen, who was master of works of Cologne Cathedral and spearheaded the facade project from 1353 until about 1390. While work remained incomplete after building activity stagnated in the sixteenth century, it was picked up again in the nineteenth century. The miraculous 1840 restitution of Drawing F, which had been looted during the French invasion nearly fifty years earlier, inspired a new building campaign from 1869 to 1880 that finally gave the Cologne facade its two iconic openwork towers (fig. 20).⁹⁹ Barring a handful of exceptions—including the facade of the Duomo of Orvieto, which over its two-hundred-fifty-year building campaign largely stayed true to a design of about 1310 (see fig. 15)¹⁰⁰—few other long-term medieval construction projects remained as faithful to an original design over such an extended period of activity.¹⁰¹

Most other multigenerational building projects were subject to constant revision as needs, fashions, and leadership changed. The completion of

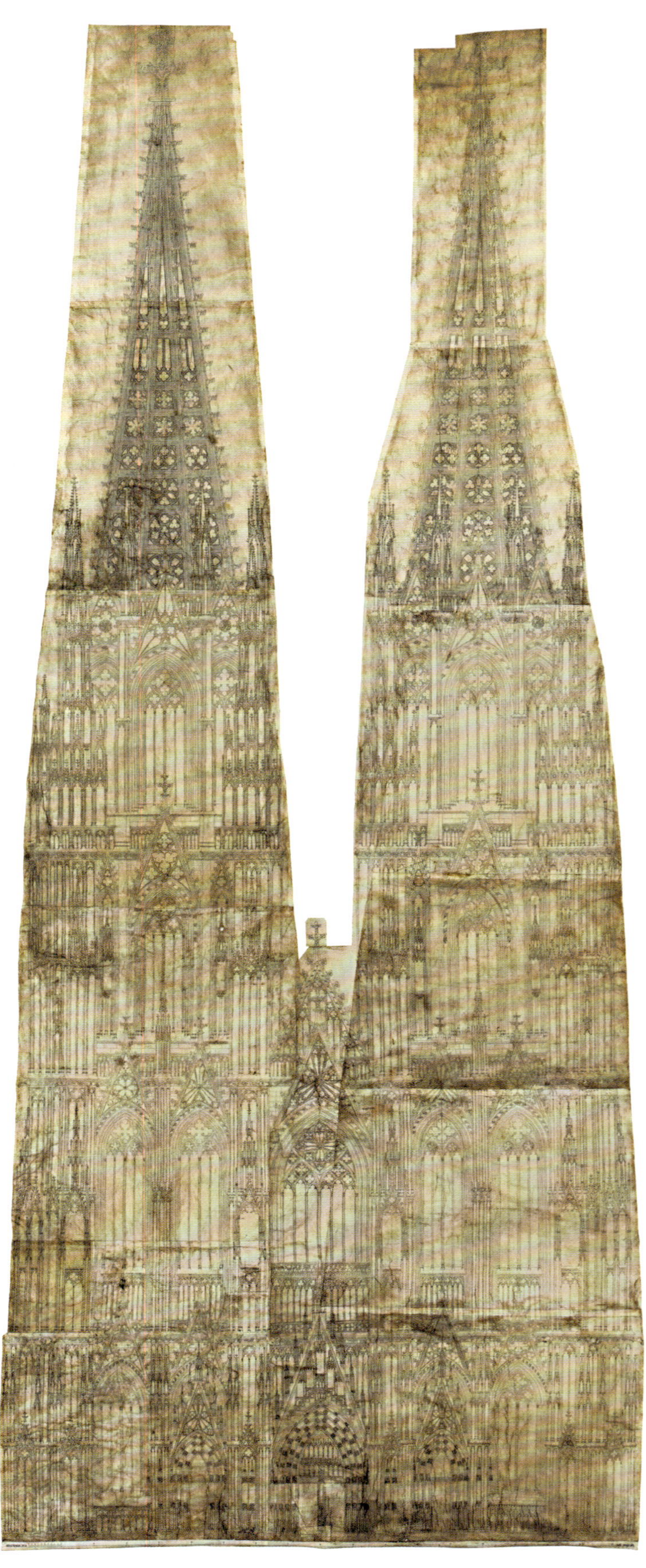

FIG. 19 Unidentified German artist (late 13th or early 14th century). Elevation of the facade of Cologne Cathedral (Drawing F), 1280 or after. Pen and ink over blind ruling on parchment, 13 ft. 3¹³⁄₁₆ in. × 5 ft. 5⁹⁄₁₆ in. (406 × 166.5 cm). Dombauarchiv, Cologne (R 0001)

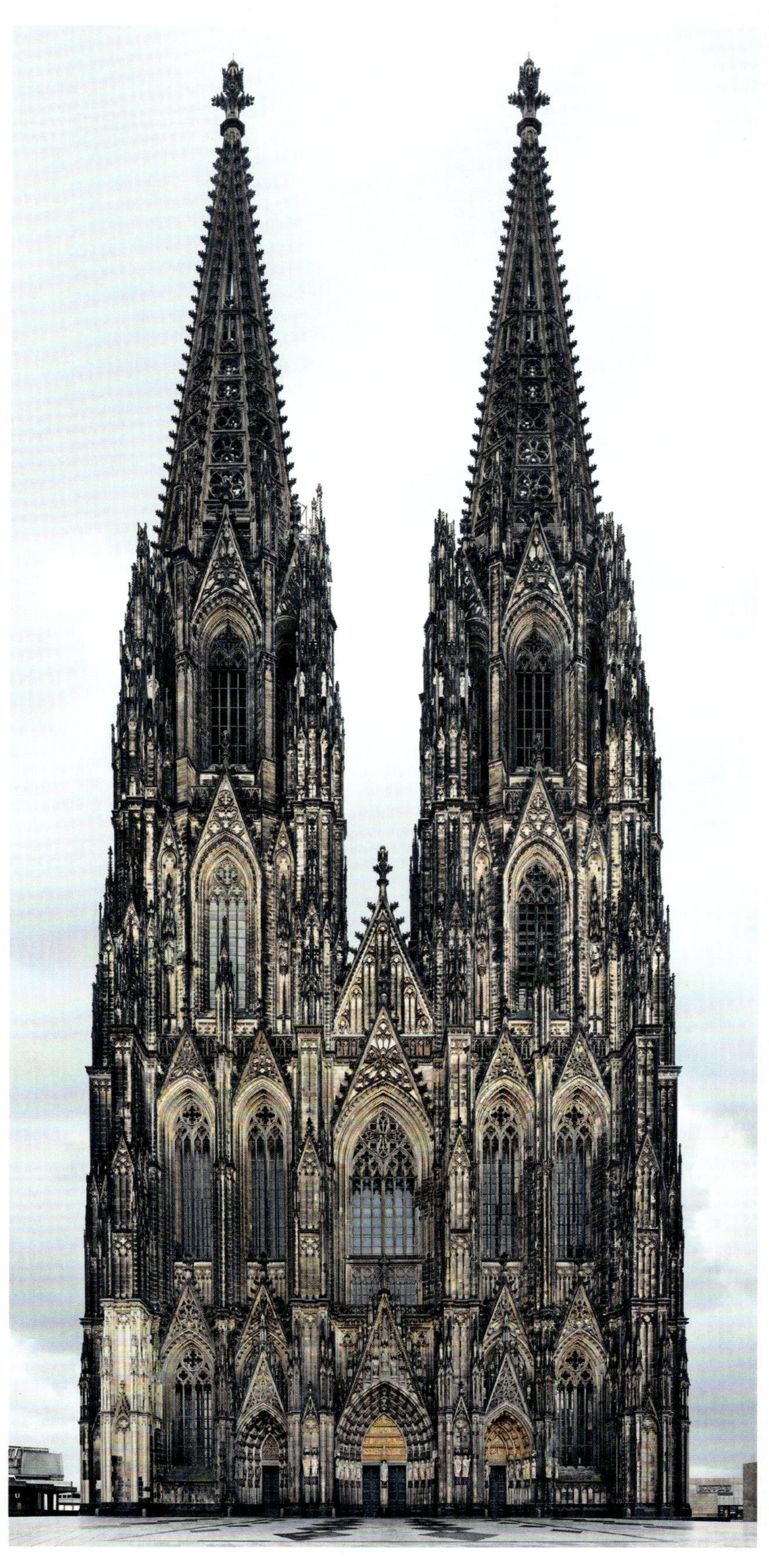

FIG. 20 Markus Brunetti. *Köln, Hohe Domkirche St. Petrus*, 2008–14. Archival pigment print

the west-end tower of the Dom (imperial cathedral) in Frankfurt am Main is a case in point. Beginning with the 1414 acquisition of the old town hall that was demolished to make space for it, the tower was under construction for nearly a century.[102] Over that time, three or possibly four distinct designs guided the process.[103] A drawing attributed to Ulrich von Ensingen that was recently identified as an initial proposal for the Frankfurt tower indicates an ambitious beginning.[104] Ensingen had extensive experience in the design and construction of church towers from his work on building sites in Esslingen, Ulm, Basel, and Strasbourg. As a recognized tower expert, he was most likely approached to supply a design for Frankfurt that was to be executed under the supervision of the local master of works, Madern Gerthener.[105] As observed above in the context of the buildings depicted in the Nuremberg Drawing, by the turn of the fourteenth century, Erwin von Steinbach had already engaged in arrangements of this kind by rendering structures for projects outside of Strasbourg. The practice became much more common over the course of the fourteenth and fifteenth centuries and gave rise to a class of sought-after star architects. It also created a new distinction between those who design and those who make, disrupting the established working methods of the building lodges.[106] It is no wonder, therefore, that this type of custom-designed but remotely executed work was one of the prominent topics discussed during a (now legendary) meeting of architects and masons from the most important building sites across the Rhine and Danube river basins, held in Regensburg in 1459 to establish rules and regulations that were codified in the Regensburg Ordinance.[107]

The same statute touched on the contractual role of drawings, stipulating that a master of works was to adhere strictly to the design drawing that had been agreed upon by all parties involved. If revisions were to be made, a comprehensive new design had to be drawn, presented, and approved before any changes could be implemented.[108] This appears to have been the case in Frankfurt several times over. Ulrich von Ensingen's initial proposal for a tower adorned by an openwork spire was abandoned even before the building process commenced, likely due to financial constraints. A new design attributed to Madern Gerthener appears to have informed the early building stages instead. While only a partial floor plan survives for the unexecuted top half of this design, it is assumed that the first two stories of the tower follow Gerthener's original idea.[109] Two elevations by Gerthener's successors, Lienhardt von Schopfheim and Michael Kurtze, who held the position of master of works consecutively in the 1430s, demonstrate that the design of the tower had once again been revised. With slight variations, the two drawings document an octagonal upper tower crowned by a cupola with a lantern (SEE PL. 16).[110] This design guided construction throughout much of the fifteenth century, until further financial concerns forced another change of plans. A drawing by Nicolaus Quecke, dating from his appointment as master of works in the 1490s, proposed eliminating the spire and closing off the octagonal tower with a tracery balustrade (SEE PL. 17). This simple, cost-effective solution did not meet with the council's approval, however.[111] In 1504, it was decided to revert back to the cupola design, because "the old design is the best" (*der alt ryss sy der best*).[112] In this respect, the retention of outmoded design drawings by the Frankfurt building lodge paid off in a very immediate way. This proved true again in the nineteenth century, when fire damage prompted the completion of the tower. After consulting the surviving drawings, the somewhat controversial decision was made to cherry-pick "the best" elements from the different iterations of the tower design.[113]

The Sum of Its Parts:
Drawing Buildings from the Ground Up

In their sweeping monumentality, large-scale facade and tower elevations like Cologne's Drawing F or Strasbourg's Drawing 5 might speak most eloquently to our modern imagination, but the day-to-day reality of the medieval building process required breaking up such comprehensive views into countless detailed, granular studies. The most practical type of working drawing was the profile template, which masons used to transfer design outlines directly onto blocks of stone (SEE PL. 88). Few other drawings boasted such an unmediated relationship with on-site production. Rather, as the architectural historian John White suggests, most other drawings represented studies that could still be altered in the course of execution, not unlike the preparatory sketches other artists make for paintings and sculpture.[114]

Two designs found today in the archive originating from the Stephansdom building lodge in Vienna are examples of such working drawings: a porch elevation for Regensburg Cathedral (PL. 11) and a study for the buttressing system of the Cathedral of Saint Vitus (Veitsdom) in Prague, discussed below. Neither work originated in Vienna, but both appear to have entered the archive relatively early, likely as objects of study. The porch design may have been brought to Vienna following the abovementioned meeting in Regensburg in 1459, at which, in addition to approving ordinances, participating architects and masons exchanged, copied, and discussed numerous drawings.[115] The Regensburg entrance portal would have sparked particular interest due to its unique triangular design.[116] Developed around 1400, the idea for the portal was first recorded in a monumental elevation that proposed radically changing the west facade by replacing its more traditional two-tower scheme in the style of Strasbourg and Cologne with a single central tower.[117] Although this course correction was ultimately not implemented, the idea for the triangular porch found favor and was developed further in the Vienna drawing.[118] While the Vienna design appears highly finished, subtle details nevertheless reveal that it, too, is a preliminary study. Among other variations, it contains minor differences between the porch's left and right sides, as well as suggestions for decorations that were unrealized, notably in the intimation of a superstructure above the portal. Interpreted either as a decorative echo of the triangular portal, or as a functional, loggia-like balcony for the display of relics, no such superstructure was ever built, and the portal was instead finished with a tracery balustrade.[119]

The second example of a working drawing from the Vienna archive is the comparatively more technical study for the Cathedral of Saint Vitus by Peter Parler, a preeminent member of the Parler dynasty of medieval architects.[120] His pedigree seems to have contributed to his appointment as master of works in Prague at the remarkably young age of twenty-three. Peter inherited the

Saint Vitus building project from a French predecessor, Matthias of Arras, who had already built part of the choir.[121] Peter's drawing focuses on this section of the building and shows part of the choir with the external buttressing system (PL. 10).[122] Several details indicate that he used the drawing as a study sheet to think through the construction, a process surely complicated by the fact that he had to reconcile his own additions with the existing architecture of the choir.[123] The many visible alterations made as part of this graphic thinking process refute the long-held assumption that the drawing is a copy after a lost original: in actuality, Peter's drawing was brought from Prague to Vienna by his son Wenzel, who became head of the Stephansdom lodge around 1400.[124]

That Peter's drawing can be assigned the status of a study sheet is also evident from a floor plan that was casually jotted above the buttressing system in the upper right corner. The sketch bears no relation to the choir and has instead been interpreted as an initial idea for the cathedral's west facade.[125] From a layperson's perspective, it might seem odd that an initial idea would take the form of a floor plan rather than that of an elevation, but Gothic architects tended to think and design from the ground up. Within the Gothic system of architectural representation, floor plans were crucial to fully understanding any design that was to be executed in three dimensions. Because elevations were drawn in orthographic projection (straight-on, flat, frontal views), floor plans explained the actual footprint of the architectural body. Without a floor plan, for example, it might be difficult to understand that the Regensburg porch in plate 11 was meant to protrude in triangular fashion from the facade.

More so than with renderings of later traditions, a trained eye is required to make sense of Gothic floor plans. A double-sided parchment sheet in the Ulm Minster archive clearly illustrates this point (PL. 73).[126] Both sides show floor plans, but their treatments are strikingly different. The recto relates to Ulm Minster itself (FIG. 21). The floor plan shows an early design for the minster's west facade, entrance hall, and octagonal tower attributed to Matthäus Ensinger (Ulrich von Ensingen's son), who became master of works in Ulm in 1446.[127] As is customary in Gothic floor plans, the drawing details both the tower's horizontal layout *and* the vertical relationship of its floors by superimposing them. Specific aspects of the construction are also called out in different areas of the rendering. The northwest wall of the tower, for example, includes a unique view of the internal metal armature (FIG. 22). As the architectural historian and current master builder of Freiburg Minster Anne-Christine Brehm has noted, this confirms that the master of works was also responsible for planning the most structurally intricate parts of the construction, although the execution would have been left to specialists.[128] At Ulm Minster, this work may have happened in or after 1461, when payment records testify to the acquisition of the necessary metal parts.[129]

While the term "floor plan" suggests a view seen from above, Gothic examples often offer the opposite vantage point. Because the flooring held little or no interest during the initial construction process, the blank space within the footprint was frequently used to include information about the vaulted ceiling (SEE PLS. 8, 72, 73, 92). A combination of such views was implemented within the floor plan of the octagonal tower of Strasbourg Cathedral, which appears on the verso of plate 73. Of the tower's four external spiral staircases,

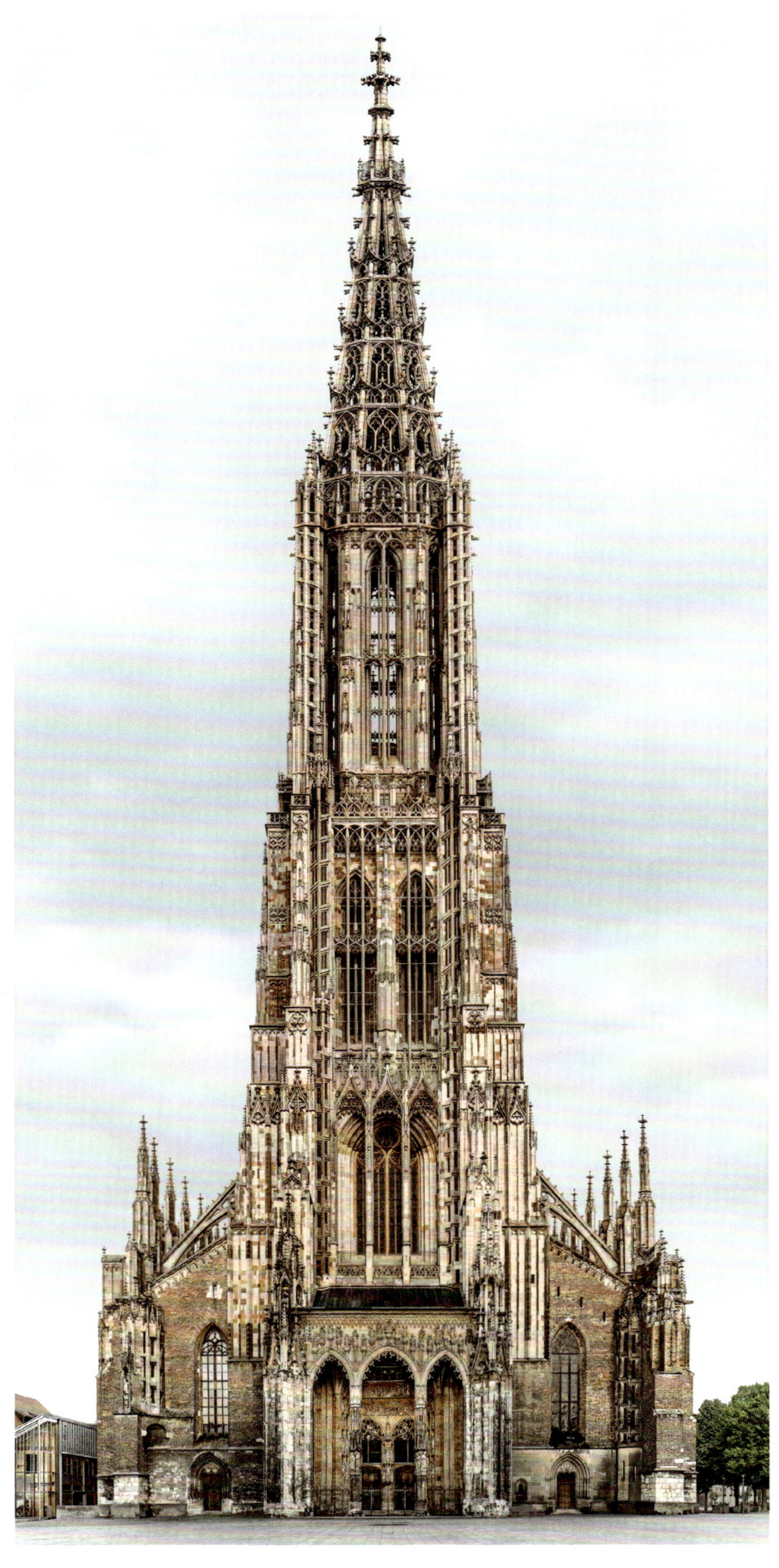

FIG. 21 Markus Brunetti. *Ulm, Münster,* 2007–14. Archival pigment print

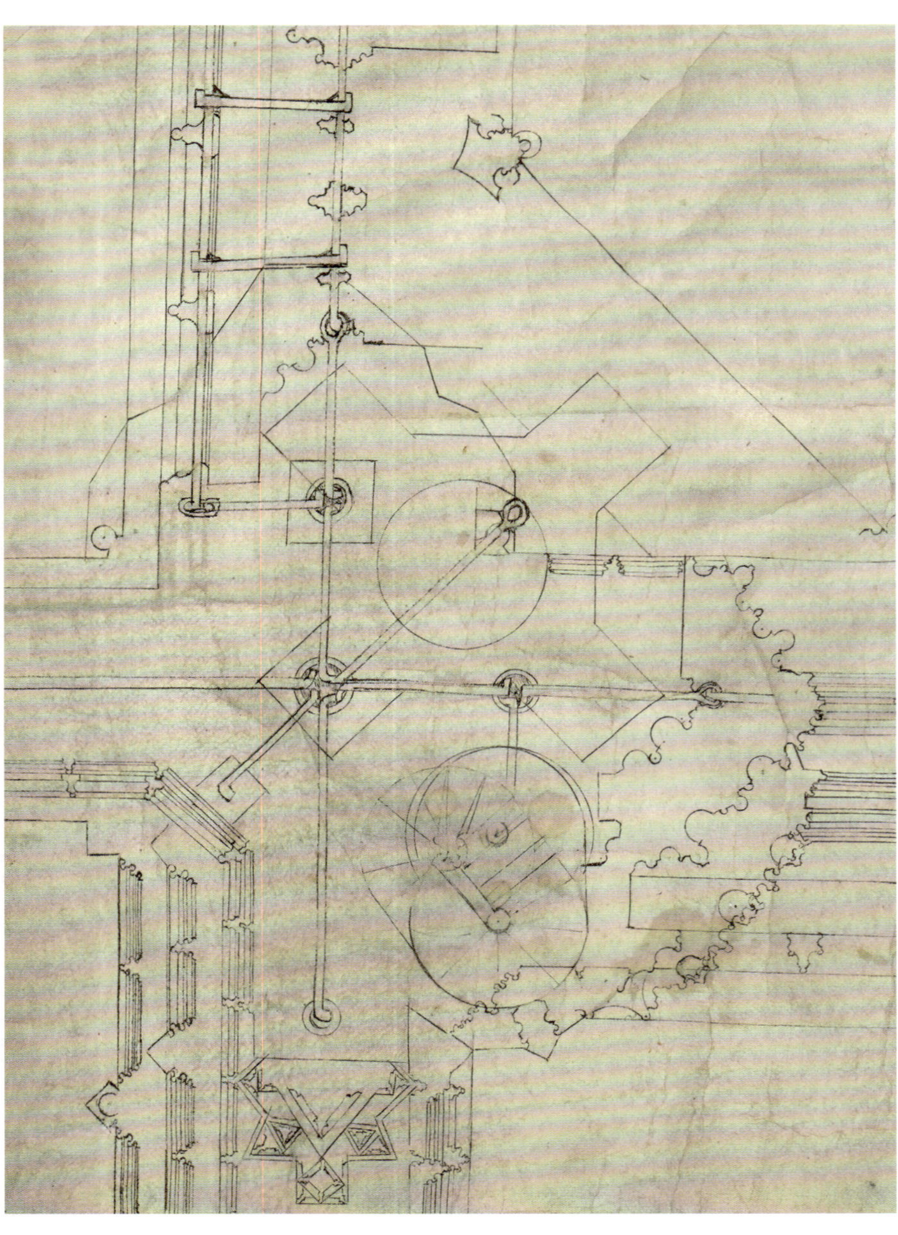

FIG. 22 Detail of the floor plan of the tower of Ulm Minster showing the metal armature inside the walls, from the recto of Ulm Drawing IIIC (see pl. 73)

three are shown as if looking down the stairs, while one focuses on the vault above the stairwell. In addition, in lieu of showing the floor in the main body of the tower, the draftsman has collapsed the spire crowning the tower to reveal the structural makeup of the octagonal pyramid (COMPARE WITH FIG. 9). To visualize the spire in elevation, imagine attaching a string at center and pulling the structure upward. Gothic architects in German-speaking regions referred to the ability to understand this representational device—and to extrapolate three-dimensional information from a two-dimensional plan—as *Auszug* (pulling out), which was considered a trade secret.[130]

The combination of elevation and floor plan thus provided the experienced Gothic architect with the information necessary to execute a design. In this respect, the pairing was far more functional than a perspectival depiction of the same structure. This might be surprising, since the adoption of point perspective is often perceived as a sign of progress through its association with the classicizing ideals of the Italian Renaissance.[131] Its advent in the fifteenth century did little to revolutionize Gothic architects' well-established representational techniques, however. By contrast, Renaissance architectural draftsmanship underwent its most important revolution when it adopted the systematic integration of plans, elevations, and sections into one fully comprehensive design, as had been customary in Gothic architecture for the better part of three centuries.[132]

Surviving late fifteenth- and sixteenth-century drawings nevertheless demonstrate that a number of Gothic architects added perspectival depictions to their arsenal. An impressively detailed design for the upper part of a crossing tower and its spire for the Cathedral of Notre Dame in Rouen forms a striking example (FIG. 23).[133] The structure is presented at a forty-five-degree angle, as if in the round, breaking the perceived visual barrier between the flat picture plane and the viewer's three-dimensional, lived-in environment. This compelling spatial effect was likely introduced to persuade the prospective patron of the efficacy of the design, since the commission for Rouen's crossing tower, to replace a wood structure that had burned down in 1514, proved hard-won.[134] Vying over commissions was much more common outside German-speaking regions, where building projects were less often organized by an established lodge run by a master builder. In such cases, architects increasingly had to contend with artists from other disciplines as well as with their peers. Such outside influences could not but impact their working methods, including representational devices.

The sense of competition is felt most prominently in a letter written by a Dutch master carpenter named Michiel Heynrich to King Christian II of Denmark in 1521. Defending his drawings of a wood spire for the royal castle in Copenhagen, Heynrich acknowledges that his rendering might not be "as beautiful" as a painter might produce but notes that he has included a floor plan to convey the building's "real measurements"—intimating that, to his mind, point perspective has little to do with architectural accuracy.[135] In its designer's effort to produce a beautiful drawing of the kind disparaged by Heynrich, the Rouen crossing tower sheet lays bare the limitations of conveying spatial information in quasi-perspective. The tower's angled presentation both skews and complicates objective analysis of the design. The intended proportions, connections between parts of the building, and even the exact shapes of the windows and

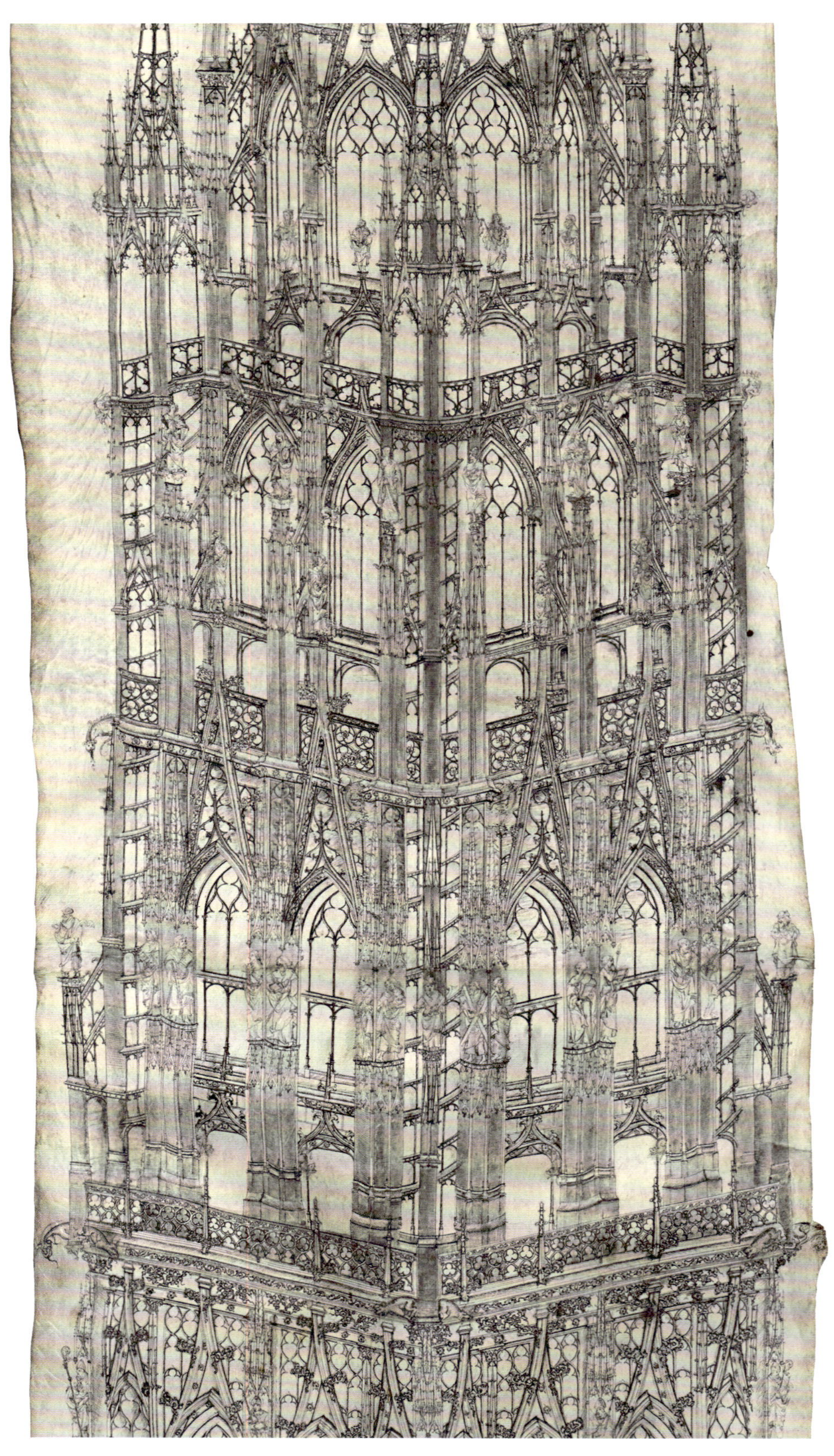

FIG. 23 Detail of the Rouen crossing tower (see pl. 19)

tracery are not easily defined. While it is not impossible to reconstruct a floor plan from the Rouen elevation, as the architectural historian Robert Bork has done, doing so necessitates making certain informed assumptions.[136]

This process of extrapolating spatial information from perspectival depictions is far more effective for buildings designed in the classical tradition, composed as they are from cubes, spheres, and other elementary volumes, than for the more geometrically complex edifices of the Gothic period.[137] The architectural historian Mario Carpo aptly summarized this dichotomy by comparing a Doric capital to a Gothic pinnacle:

> *Anyone who has seen a Doric capital should be in a position to produce another one that is, as far as appearances go, identical to its model. . . . The external appearance of a Gothic pinnacle, on the contrary, does not betray the internal design of its structural proportions. These proportions are physically present in the building's masonry, if the builders observed them carefully. But they are hidden.*[138]

The legibility and reproducibility of classicizing architecture was aided further by the increasing availability of published treatises that offered unprecedented access to its design principles. The lack of equivalent publications from the Gothic tradition long had an adverse effect on the aesthetic and historic reception of its architecture. The next chapter demonstrates how many of the fundamental design strategies of Gothic architecture can, nevertheless, be gleaned from surviving drawings as well as from excursions into the new medium of print.

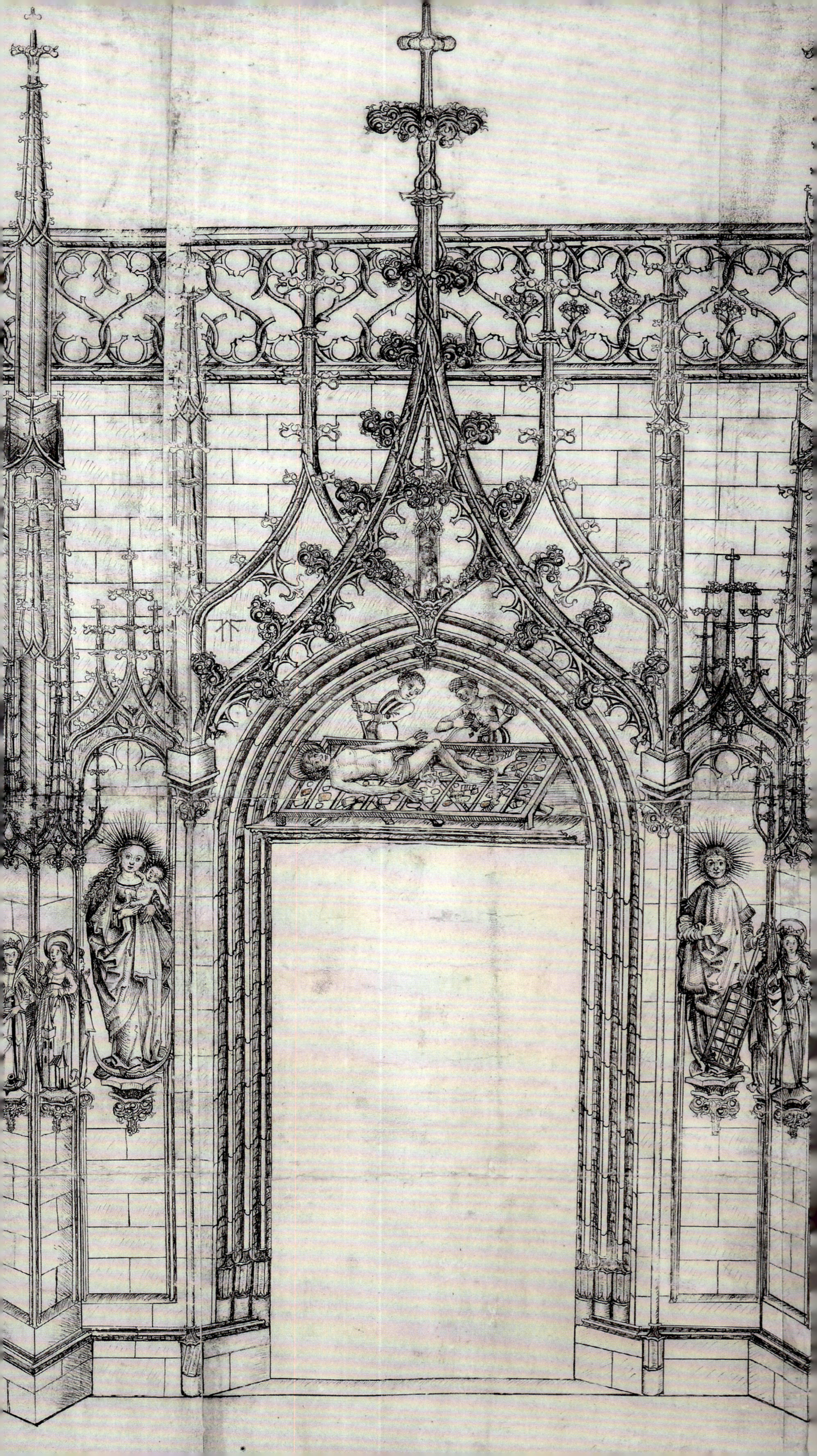

"ENDOWING MASSIVE WALLS WITH VARIETY"
STRUCTURE, ORNAMENT, AND ARTISTIC EXPRESSION IN GOTHIC DESIGN

Femke Speelberg

We . . . who must always protect ourselves against the weather, and everywhere surround ourselves with walls, have to revere the genius who discovered the means of endowing massive walls with variety, of apparently breaking them through, and of thus occupying the eye in a worthy and pleasing manner.
—Johann Wolfgang von Goethe[1]

In 1494, the architect Jakob von Landshut designed a portal for the north side of Strasbourg Cathedral that would function as an alternative to the main (west) entrance and provide direct access to the new Chapel of Saint Lawrence (PL. 15).[2] Made in anticipation or at the onset of construction, Landshut's drawing presents diverging approaches for the sculptural decoration. On the left side of the portal, he shows an elaborate scheme in which the arched window is incorporated into a blind tracery arcade and crowned by a wimperg (ornamental gable) that matches the portal in height. On the right side, he proposes a more sober option that leaves the stone wall largely uninterrupted and employs a less complicated pattern for the window tracery. The fact that two directions were up for consideration emphasizes that the sculptural details were by no means an afterthought. Instead, they played a role of fundamental importance in determining the tenor of the overall design. In this case, ornament won out. Not only was Landshut's more elaborate design selected, but the final scheme was even richer in execution than the version in the drawing (FIG. 24).[3]

Landshut's design for the Saint Lawrence portal is indicative of a heightened attention to the expressive potential of architectural elements in Gothic architecture, which increased in intensity from the thirteenth century onward. In addition to the soaring height and ethereal light associated with Gothic design, the articulation of almost every surface—from heavily sculpted facades and intricate rib-vaulted ceilings to delicately carved capitals and geometric window tracery—became a central preoccupation. This vigorous pursuit of formal innovation gave rise to national, regional, and local substyles as well as entirely unique expressions of Gothic design. Indeed, when the German writer Johann Wolfgang von Goethe visited Strasbourg Cathedral some three centuries later and marveled at "the genius who discovered the means of endowing massive walls with variety," he was celebrating the moment when the act of building became an art form capable of "occupying the eye in a worthy and pleasing manner."[4]

Despite Goethe's enthusiasm, this exuberant display of creative ingenuity was long mistaken for decadence and decline, with art and architectural historians alike interpreting the turn to ornament as a perversion of the

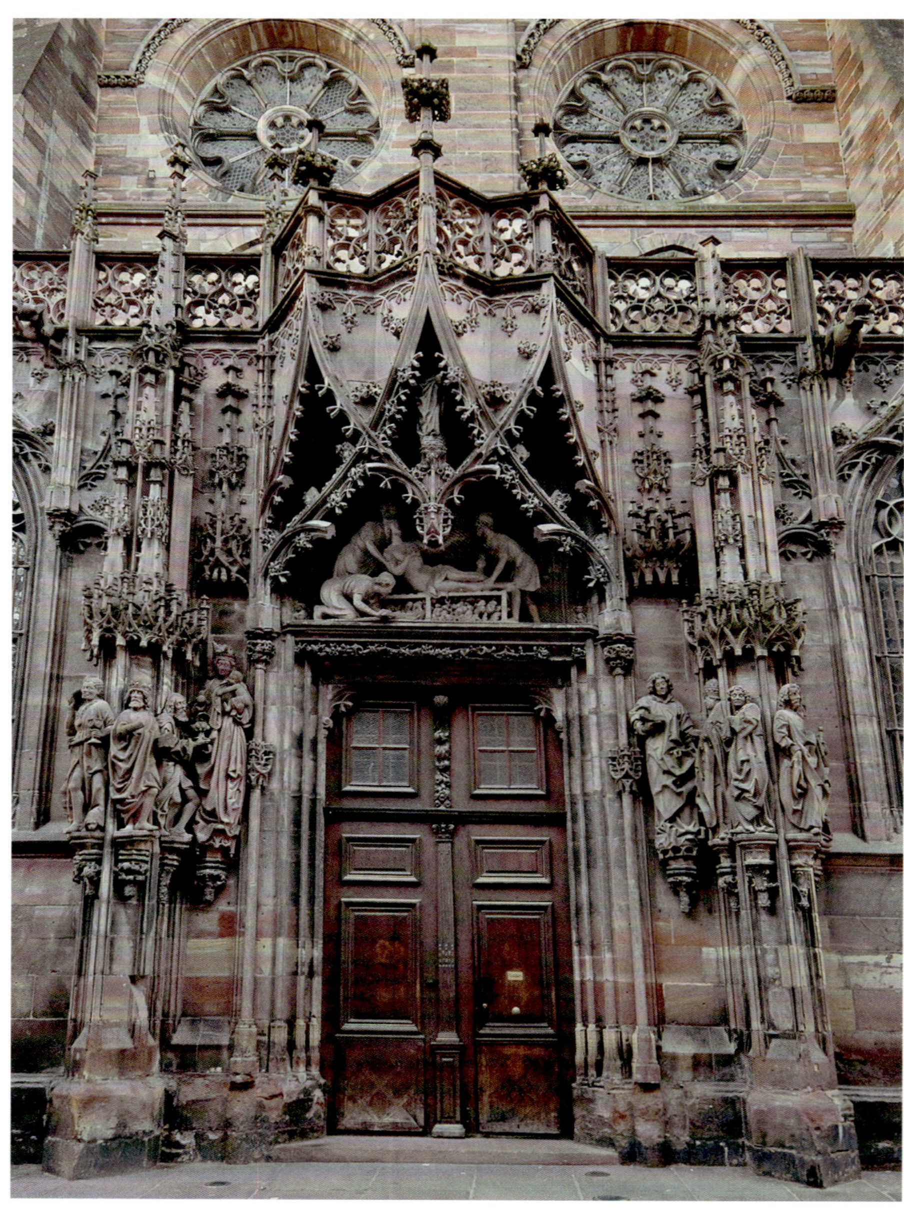

FIG. 24 Jakob von Landshut (German, ca. 1450–1509). Portal of Saint Lawrence on the north side of Strasbourg Cathedral, 1494. Photograph by Simon Woolf

structural innovations achieved during the first century of the Gothic building tradition.[5] Two misconceptions fueled this point of view. First, that structure and ornament could be understood as anything other than two sides of the same coin. More so than architects of other periods, Gothic master masons were both builders *and* sculptors who understood stone equally as a building block and as a means of decoration. This dual function was central to their advanced training, in which the principles of geometry and draftsmanship together were marshaled to transform rough-hewn quarried stone into every element a building might require, whether structural or decorative.[6]

The second misconception lay in the belief that the Gothic design process lacked a coherent foundational method. This misunderstanding took hold early on, owing in large part to the sixteenth-century writings of the Italian artist and biographer Giorgio Vasari. Accusing Gothic architects of ignoring every familiar idea of order, Vasari maintained that good design, or *disegno*, could only result from the introduction of variety within a clear system of rules.[7] One reason neither Vasari nor subsequent generations could easily discern the rules governing Gothic architecture was that its design principles were not passed down in authoritative treatises, such as *De architectura* (*Ten Books on Architecture*; 1st century BCE) by the Roman architect Vitruvius, or the manifold publications it inspired from the fifteenth century onward. This left the achievements of Gothic architects vulnerable to neglect and misinterpretation, at least until the nineteenth century, when the Gothic Revival movement and historicism, more generally, renewed interest in the period.[8] Since then, scholars have tried to unearth the underlying methods of Gothic architectural design, predominantly by analyzing and comparing the characteristics of existing buildings and, to a lesser extent, drawings.

The art and architectural historian François Bucher, more than anyone, was certain that "each step of Gothic construction was . . . based on a highly coordinated system of geometric progression."[9] Believing that the surviving body of architectural drawings would unlock "a complete theory of Gothic planning," he derived many of his ideas from drawings containing technical studies and exercises, which offer tantalizing glimpses of the design strategies taught to, and employed by, Gothic architects. Whereas the monumental facade drawings discussed in the previous chapter present views of an advanced stage in the design process, study sheets take us back to the germination of forms and ideas. Building on Bucher's efforts, the first half of this chapter focuses on two educational resources: a printed pamphlet on the proper construction of pinnacles by Mathes (or Matthäus) Roriczer, and a hand-drawn collection of leafcutter's motifs by Hans Böblinger the Elder. Both unassuming in appearance, their contents nevertheless powerfully demonstrate that the Gothic architectural design process was informed and systematic, its strategies epitomized by and in drawings.

The second half of this chapter highlights how architects and other artists employed these design strategies to showcase their talent, collaborate with their peers, and, with advances in print culture, even disseminate some of their knowledge and designs in print. Special attention is paid to designs for comparatively small-scale structures, such as sacrament houses, baldachins, and reliquaries—self-contained projects that, unlike monumental cathedrals, could be realized in a relatively short time and formed ideal vehicles for artistic expression. Similarly, print techniques introduced at the close of the Gothic period offered architects a way to share and preserve their designs in an autonomous manner. Only a handful of artists explored the medium's potential through engravings, woodcuts, and printed booklets, but together with the surviving body of drawings, these works nevertheless form a lasting testament to a strong and self-aware design tradition. By drawing on parchment and paper, Gothic architects could think through, experiment with, and predetermine both the overall structure of a building and the smallest details of its decor. While their contributions were often subsumed into the greater whole, making it difficult to celebrate specific architects for their ideas and contributions, their drawings form intimate reminders of the talented individuals who helped shape the Gothic style.

Roriczer's Pinnacle:
The Method Behind Gothic Structural Design

In the 1480s, toward the end of his career, the Regensburg master mason Mathes Roriczer published several booklets on topics related to his profession (PL. 3). Up to this point, Gothic architectural theory was predominantly conveyed from master to apprentice orally and in drawings, rather than articulated in written form. Roriczer's decision to publish, possibly prompted by his patron Wilhelm von Reichenau, bishop of Eichstätt, broke with this tradition. By committing his knowledge to print, Roriczer opened up carefully guarded, trade-specific knowledge to his contemporaries, and—unbeknownst to him—enabled future historians to discover the working methods of the Gothic master mason.

Of Roriczer's three booklets, one discusses geometric procedures that are related but not exclusive to architectural design. The other two are dedicated to the correct way to design a pinnacle (*Das Büchlein von der Fialen Gerechtigkeit*; 1486) and a wimperg (*Wimpergbüchlein*; ca. 1486–90).[10] The ostensible modesty of their subject matter—each concerns the step-by-step construction of just a single architectural element—is reflected in their humble appearance. The octavo-size booklets are printed in letterpress with simple woodcut illustrations and consist of ten and two folios, respectively (PL. 80). Nevertheless, they boast significant contributions to the history of architectural publications in the Western world. For one, as far as we know, they are the first printed architectural texts in the German language (or any vernacular); for another, they are the first to be illustrated. By way of comparison, although the first printed edition of Vitruvius's *De architectura* was published in Rome in the same year, 1486, it was written in Latin, and, notably, unillustrated (it would be another twenty-five years before an illustrated edition appeared). For a brief moment, then, some of the teachings of Gothic architecture were more accessible to a lay reader than their classical counterpart. However, in Roriczer's effort to prevent his students from making mistakes—one of the reasons he turned to publishing—he produced densely procedural instructions that proved difficult to follow, even if aided by illustrations. Consequently, the deeper implications of his texts were long misunderstood, dismissed, or entirely overlooked.[11]

Yet, within these modest publications lies the key to understanding the unifying system of structural design that Vasari, some sixty years later, would declare lacking. In actuality, Roriczer's method of designing a pinnacle (a spire-shaped crowning element) models fundamental principles that were applicable to other parts of a building as well as to entire structures.[12] In his booklet, Roriczer describes the highly coordinated system of geometric progression from floor plan to elevation, which he refers to as "drawn-out stonework" (*auszgeczogenes stainwerch*, dubbed "dynamic unfolding" in modern scholarship).[13] Using a compass and straightedge, an architect first created a floor plan by manipulating geometric shapes—principally the circle, as well as the square, triangle, pentagon, octagon, and hexagon. Then, by a process of modular extrusion (*Auszug*, or pulling out), the architect extrapolated the proportions and internal relationships of the structure's vertical elevation from the plan.[14] Roriczer's design for a pinnacle is a relatively simple example of this practice, rooted as it is in squares alone, but it can just as easily be applied to much more complicated structures, such as the canopylike baldachin of a sacrament house (used for storing consecrated bread for Communion), or the tower of a cathedral (PLS. 63, 74–76, 78).[15] Roriczer did not invent this system, nor did he claim to; he noted in his introduction that it had long been practiced by the Parler family, one of the principal architectural dynasties that dated to at least the late thirteenth century.[16]

While Roriczer ultimately codified this system in printed text, the method he painstakingly describes is practice-based rather than theoretical, and rooted in the design process itself. In this process, geometry and drawing go hand in hand. As Bucher emphasized, the architect's drawing instruments, comprising the straightedge, square, compass, and divider, provided the practical, geometric underpinnings of Gothic architectural design, to a greater extent than abstract mathematical theory.[17] Unsurprisingly, therefore, as the practice of drawing was adopted more widely, geometrically informed designs became more sophisticated. Bucher illustrated this point by asserting that a fifteenth-century builder would have done away with the perceived "inconsistencies" in the geometry of the early thirteenth-century rose window of the Cathedral of Lausanne by designing it in a regularized, predictable fashion (FIG. 25).[18]

In actuality, however, fifteenth-century Gothic architecture was rarely formulaic or predictable. Indeed, every effort was made to avoid designs that answered to either adjective. For example, there is little about the rose window of Lausanne that prepares us for the artistic license of the flamboyant fifteenth-century tracery decorations on the facade of the Abbey Church of the Holy Trinity in Vendôme, or any other Late Gothic church (FIG. 26).[19] In his celebration of Strasbourg Cathedral, Goethe rightly highlighted that variation rather than standardization lay at the heart of the Gothic design process.[20] As will be discussed below, resources related to a master mason's training, such as exercise drawings, demonstrate that the pursuit of variation was not random, but intentional and systematic. Much more so than the monumental drawings discussed in the previous chapter, these intimate, iterative exercises demonstrate the central role of drawing in the process of form finding. As the architectural historian Peter Kidson has emphasized, this preliminary stage of attention encouraged the development of "cosmetic details of unusual complexity" that adorn Gothic churches and their furnishings.[21]

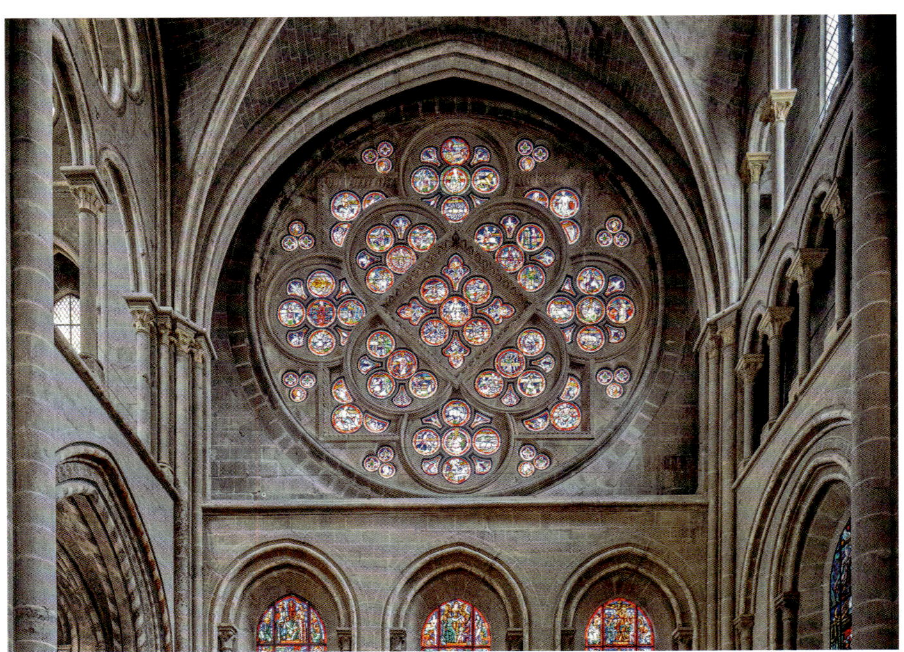

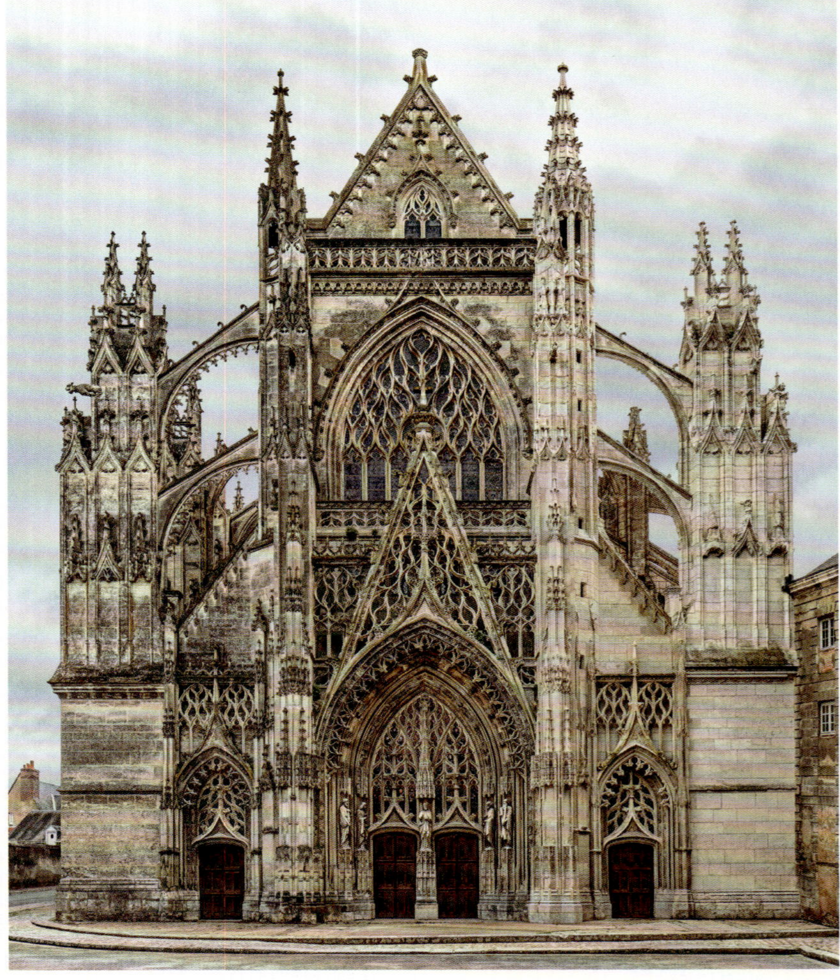

FIG. 25 Unidentified French artist (13th century). Rose window in the south transept of the Cathedral of Lausanne, early 13th century. Photograph by Dominik Gehl

FIG. 26 Markus Brunetti (German, born 1965). *Vendôme, Église de la Trinité*, 2013–18. Archival pigment print

Böblinger's Leaves:
Exercises in the Variation of Form and Ornament

Jakob von Landshut's proposal of variant designs for the Saint Lawrence portal in Strasbourg gives us a rare glimpse into the preliminary stages of the design process. Even so, before he put pen to paper to make his presentation drawing, many decisions had already been made through a more exploratory phase to which we are not privy. Some indication of what this process looked like can be reconstructed from surviving exercise drawings made by master masons as part of their education. A unique booklet preserved at the Bayerisches Nationalmuseum in Munich is a prominent example. Often identified as a leafcutter's design book (*Laubhauermüsterbuch*), it comprises twenty pages of hand-drawn leaf motifs (PL. 51).[22] The drawings' connection to architecture would not be immediately apparent were it not for the proud signature on the first page: *1435 [mason's mark] / ich hanns von / boeblingen ain stain metz* (I, Hans von Böblingen, a stone mason). Known today as Hans Böblinger the Elder, patriarch of three generations of Gothic architects, he is chiefly associated with the Frauenkirche (Church of Our Lady) in Esslingen, near Stuttgart. In 1435, however, the twenty-two-year-old Böblinger had only just completed, or was in the process of completing, his education to become a master mason.

Böblinger's basic training to become a stone mason would have commenced around age fourteen and lasted four to five years. For anyone aspiring to become a master mason, this trajectory was followed by an additional program to acquire the advanced skills needed to both design and manage building projects. No set curriculum survives for this second phase of the education, and it may have been tailored to the individual trainee's skills and aspirations, both in terms of duration and content. Among the areas of focus were the construction of structurally complex building components such as vaults and winding staircases; the carving of detailed stonework, including leaf ornaments and other figurative sculpture; and, most important in the context of this discussion, the ability to draw and create designs for these projects.[23] Based on the booklet's date and subject matter, and Böblinger's modest identification as a stone mason, it has long been conjectured that the artist created his leaf drawings during this second stage of his education.[24] More details about the precise context in which Böblinger made the drawings have only surfaced recently. We now know that he made the drawings while working as a journeyman at the minster in the Swiss town of Bern.[25] Brief stints as journeymen at various locations offered master-masons-in-training experience with distinct phases of the building process and the opportunity to observe different architects' techniques. The custom was regulated in 1459 in the Regensburg Ordinance, a list of statutes to guide the building profession, agreed upon by the leading architects of the Rhine and Danube river basins. According to the ordinance, a journeyman was to be allowed access to a building site for at least one week (equal to a payment cycle) to ensure proper remuneration for their work before they moved to another site.[26]

Böblinger appears to have stayed in Bern for about six to eight weeks, working on at least three carving projects that are signed with his mason's mark. His time there also overlapped with a campaign for carving naturalistic leafwork on the capitals that adorn the choir (FIG. 27). He seems to have taken full advantage of the opportunity to study this process closely, and it is possible that he came to Bern to do just that.[27] The technical progression of his leaf drawings suggests that the freehand motifs were entirely new to him when he began but that he quickly gained dexterity, learning to follow the curling shapes of the leaves and to adopt hatching and shading techniques suggestive of depth and movement (FIG. 28). Of the thirty-one drawings in his booklet, seven are direct copies after carved motifs found in Bern Minster, while six others are closely related. The rest are variants from which Böblinger learned to design such decorations independently, and how to adjust a design to fit a specific application or attach it to a neighboring motif.[28] The capitals in Bern, for example, are often filled with a number of different leaf motifs that were combined, mirrored, or intertwined to cover the surface. The placement of these motifs and other ornaments often followed the same rules of geometry and proportion as the architecture they adorn—as can also be seen in a technical exercise by Hans Hammer, in which the architect elaborates on Roriczer's system to determine the placement of the leaf-shaped crockets of a pinnacle (FIG. 29).[29]

While Böblinger's drawings show a lively range of different types of plants with sprigs of flowers, berries, or grapes, it appears that a number of these designs had become stock motifs that were applied across vast distances. For example, he depicted the motif of a leaf growing from a cruciferous root vegetable that can be traced to the Cathedral of Saint John in 's-Hertogenbosch in the Netherlands, where it was carved between 1380 and 1400, before it made its way to Konstanz (in present-day southern Germany) and Bern, Switzerland, by the 1420s. Drawn by Böblinger in 1435, the motif was ultimately published between about 1470 and 1490 by the South Netherlandish artist known only as Master W with the Key, who was active in or near Bruges.[30] The repetition and spread of one and the same motif across multiple building sites likely resulted from stone masons migrating from one work site to another, but also indicates some level of standardization in the education of leafcutters or figurative stone carvers more broadly.

Just as Böblinger learned to draw, copy, vary, and design leaf motifs by working from examples in Bern, the as-yet unidentified artist of a bound collection of drawings in the Universitätsbibliothek Basel learned to design window tracery patterns with help from existing designs for the Cathedral of Saint Vitus (Veitsdom) in Prague and Basel Minster (FIG. 30).[31] Like Böblinger's drawings, some patterns follow a model while others appear to be experiments by the mason-in-training. Invariably, they are drawn in the same rigorous manner, beginning with a blind-ruled geometric framework, constructed with the help of a compass and ruler, which was then traced over in pen and ink. Since even the copied patterns were treated in this manner, this two-step process of composition appears to have been the main objective of the exercise. For example, the underdrawing of one of the more complicated patterns of the group—the tracery design from Saint Vitus at upper left—clearly shows that the construction of the geometric framework proved challenging for the draftsman.[32] This underscores that the motif was not his own design, and that he was making a concerted effort to understand its process of construction. Had he been interested only in the design itself, he could

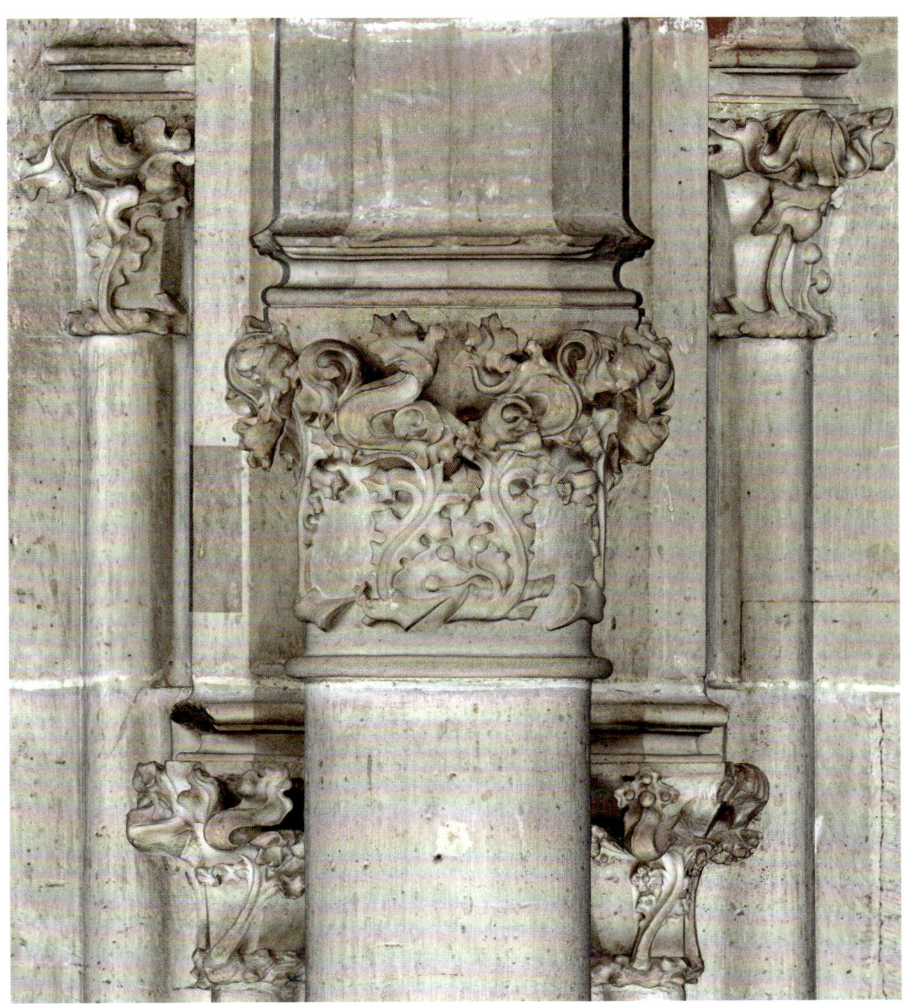

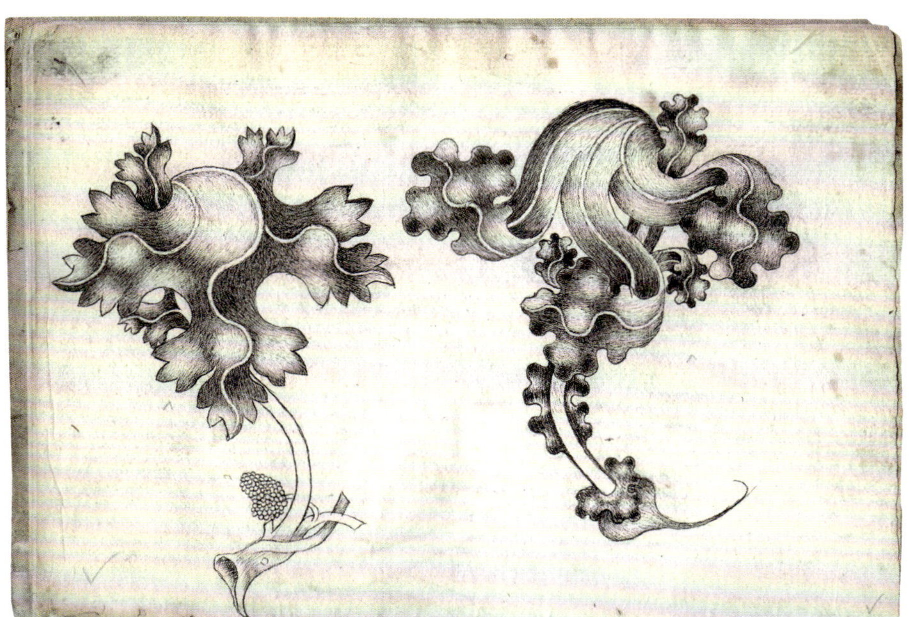

FIG. 27 Unidentified Swiss(?) artist (15th century). Capitals with carved leafwork on pier 125 south in Bern Minster, ca. 1435. Imaged in 3D photogrammetry by Jan-Ruben Fischer

FIG. 28 Detail of a page from Hans Böblinger the Elder's stone mason's book of leaf designs (*Laubhauermüsterbuch*) (see pl. 51)

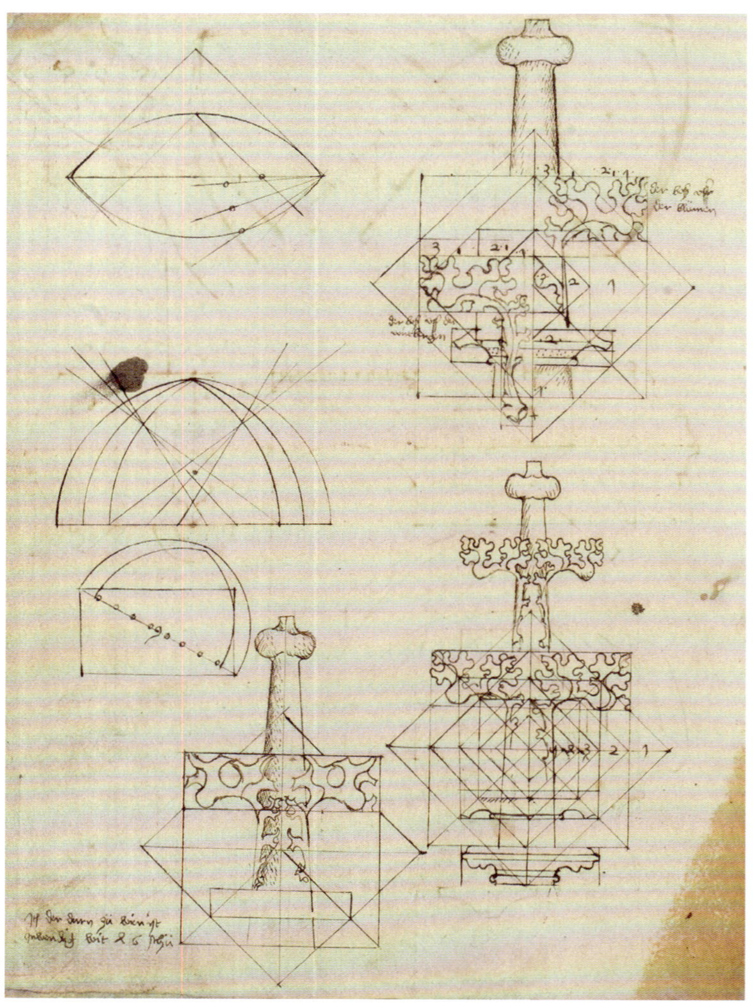

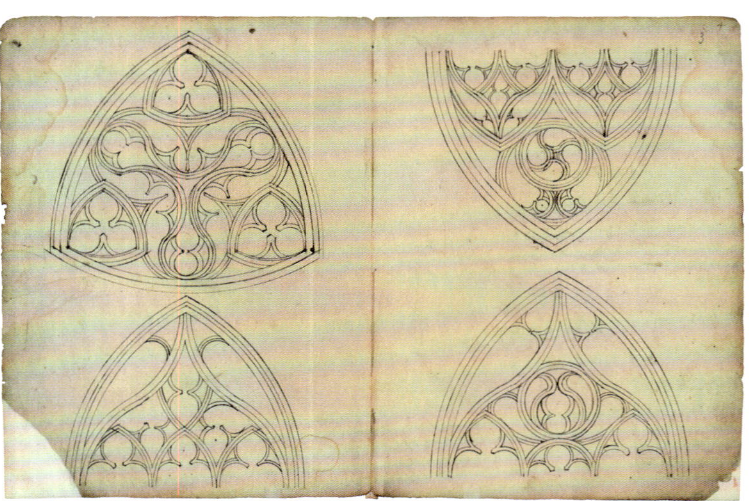

FIG. 29 Hans Hammer (German, 1440/45–1519). Album page with proportional studies for the placement of the leafwork crockets of a pinnacle (and other sketches), ca. 1460–1519. Pen and ink on paper, 11⁷⁄₁₆ × 8¼ in. (29 × 21 cm). Herzog August Bibliothek Wolfenbüttel (Cod. Guelf. 114.1 Extrav., fol. 17v)

FIG. 30 Unidentified Swiss(?) artist. Album pages with tracery motifs for arched windows, ca. 1450–75. Pen and ink over blind ruling on paper, closed: 11¹³⁄₁₆ × 8¹¹⁄₁₆ in. (30 × 22 cm). Universitätsbibliothek Basel (UBH L II 22, fols. 2v–3r)

more easily have copied it freehand. It was the geometric, compass-built, and blind-ruled armature hidden beneath the pen-and-ink drawing, however, that guided every step of the Gothic design process. Mastering it was an imperative step toward becoming a full-fledged architect. Over a dozen similar drawings in the archive of the Stephansdom (Saint Stephen's Cathedral) in Vienna indicate that these exercises were implemented more widely in the education of master masons (SEE PL. 46), while similar drawings in an album by the Italian artist Pisanello suggest that their influence also reached well beyond the German-speaking lodges.[33]

Once in full control of the necessary design and drafting skills, a master mason could effortlessly produce a sheet like the example attributed to the Frankfurt master of works Madern Gerthener (PL. 47).[34] Dated to between about 1400 and 1415, it shows ten ideas for the tracery of a pointed arch in a square frame as well as one larger round arch. The penmanship is lively and the designs are playful in nature, but Gerthener was nevertheless highly methodical in his approach—his use of a compass and ruler is evident throughout. He created variant designs systematically, by changing the scale of the geometric shapes that make up the basic compositional structure and adding or subtracting shapes accordingly; breaking open circles into C- and S-shapes and turning them inward or outward at will; and interlacing tracery elements in structured or organic patterns. The presentation of these variations in a grid helps the eye to notice their differences easily, and possibly imagine even more.[35] A very similar page in the late sixteenth-century architectural treatise of the Bruges master mason Charles De Beste, now in the Koninklijke Bibliotheek van België, indicates that this method of creating permutations was still in use nearly two hundred years later.[36] Moreover, the technique was not restricted to window tracery alone. Surviving mason's albums like that of Hans Hammer (SEE FIG. 29), as well as numerous single-sheet drawings by students and masters alike, show it was applied to the designs of balustrades, tracery screens (both blind and open), vaulting patterns, openwork spires, and floor-plan progressions (SEE PLS. 45, 46, 61–63, 90, 91).

These exercises for copying motifs and creating variations, intended to build both manual and mental dexterity in draftsmanship and design, are no different from the methods implemented in Italy during the Renaissance as the foundations of an education in drawing and design (*disegno*).[37] Since only scattered examples survive from the Gothic period, it is difficult to pinpoint when these techniques were first introduced, but two sources give a rough idea. For one, visual instructions in the early thirteenth-century drawings of Villard de Honnecourt already encouraged repetition with variation as a method for learning to render human figures of different proportions and in different poses.[38] Even earlier, at the end of the twelfth century, the English scholar Abbot Alexander Neckam referenced the practice of letting apprentices in a goldsmith's workshop sketch flowers "in various manners."[39] There can therefore be no doubt that, from early on, Gothic architects developed their figurative vocabulary through exercises like those described above, gradually transforming them from small, uniform, symmetrical, and repetitive details into a programmatic means of expression that could imbue any architectural element with visual interest.

The extent to which Gothic architects were able to employ their own design vocabulary—as opposed to following existing designs—came down, in part, to chance. The extended period of time it took to construct a church or similarly scaled building meant that an individual architect was rarely involved from start to finish. With few exceptions, most buildings can therefore not be attributed to, or celebrated as, the design of a single person. A certain amount of luck was involved in the alignment of one's career with the timing of work on a building's more visible elements. The architect Ulrich von Ensingen, for example, was able to become a tower expert because several cathedral projects happened to reach that stage of the building process in his lifetime.[40] Others were less fortunate and spent their careers either following the designs of their predecessors or fixing their mistakes.

This is undoubtedly one of the reasons why Gothic architects relished opportunities to design smaller structures, such as tabernacles, baldachins, rood screens, tombs, pulpits, and baptismal fonts. The self-contained nature and relatively short construction time of such projects enabled architects to showcase their ability and realize their artistic vision without need for compromise. As a result, some of the most interesting, personal, and at times witty expressions of Gothic architectural design belong to this group of small-scale projects. François Bucher characterized such projects as "sophisticated model experiments."[41] In his view, this was increasingly where the vanguard of architecture was to be found, as the buildings themselves "became mere shelters" for the smaller but more daring monuments.[42] Whether the distinction between a monumental church and these small-scale structures was truly so dramatic is difficult to ascertain, not least because, as the philosopher Gaston Bachelard observed, "a geometrician sees *exactly the same thing* in two similar figures, drawn to different scales."[43] Indeed, various medieval accounts confirm that the ability to play with scale—to amplify or to miniaturize in order to arrive at the appropriate proportions for the design at hand—was greatly admired in Gothic art and architecture.[44]

In modern scholarship, this group of small-scale projects tends to be classified with goldsmith's work as "microarchitecture," a somewhat misleading term given the works' artistic importance and often rather monumental proportions.[45] The German *Zierarchitektur*, which roughly translates to ornamental or decorative architecture, is similarly deceptive, since most such structures performed increasingly important, often liturgical, functions, and were designed with the same rigor as the buildings in or near which they were installed.[46] The universal acknowledgment of their importance at the time can be deduced from the fact that their successful completion—and in some cases their design alone—served as proof of competence, helping several architects to secure coveted positions as master of works.

This seems to have been the case for Matthäus Böblinger, the son of Hans Böblinger the Elder. In 1474, he designed a freestanding monument dedicated to the Mount of Olives—the site where Christ prayed before his arrest and crucifixion—for the square near Ulm Minster (PL. 14).[47] Although no commission is documented, and although Matthäus was not officially invited to oversee the project until funding was secured three years later, an inscription on the drawing explains that he promptly set about carving the stone.[48] Despite this advanced start, most, if not all, of the monument was completed only after his death, between 1516 and 1526.[49] In the interim, Böblinger's design drawing and evident enthusiasm served to recommend him to the city council in Ulm, which sought to replace Moritz Ensinger as master of works (*Dombaumeister*) after his departure in 1477.[50] The drawing for the Mount of Olives monument indicates that Böblinger had a comprehensive grasp of everything required of a lead architect. Various elements of the monument's openwork spire even prefigure his design for the minster tower, which underscores the idea that these smaller structures functioned as prototypes to showcase an architect's creative aspirations and abilities.[51]

Matthäus Böblinger remained in Ulm for almost two decades, a period during which he contributed considerably to the execution of Ulm Minster's tower, although he was replaced before his vision for its spire could be realized.[52] While the circumstances of his dismissal were unfavorable—part of the tower had collapsed during his tenure—his elevation drawing was nevertheless emended by two inscriptions on strips of paper to indicate the exact progress he had made on the tower during his time as master of works.[53] His Mount of Olives drawing carries a similar note, as does a drawing by his son, Hans Böblinger the Younger, depicting a chapel that Matthäus had erected in Esslingen.[54] These inscriptions convey that the Böblinger family recognized works on paper as a means of documenting individual artistic achievement, a preservationist trait that can undoubtedly be traced back to Hans Böblinger the Elder's signed booklet of leaf motifs, which had remained in the family. The conservation of the Mount of Olives drawing in particular proved fundamental both for the execution of the project forty years after its conception and for our understanding of the monument, which fell victim to iconoclasm soon after its completion and was fully demolished in 1807.[55] This, sadly, was the fate of many architectural projects in this category: They were relatively easy to build, but also more easily destroyed or replaced during political conflicts, interior renovations, and urban development. While many church buildings stood the test of time, most smaller structures and especially those erected in public spaces were lost, thus giving us a diminished sense of how pervasive the Gothic style once truly was.

The architect Hans Hammer had better fortune with the preservation of his design for a pulpit, one of his earliest independent projects for Strasbourg Cathedral. Registered in Strasbourg as a stone mason since 1471, Hammer had spent a decade as a journeyman, visiting and working at cathedral building sites such as the Stephansdom in Vienna and Saint Vitus in Prague. By 1481, enriched by his experience, he returned to Strasbourg, where he was soon appointed to the position of foreman (*parlier*). In this capacity, he designed a sacrament house, in 1483, and a pulpit just one year later.[56] While nothing remains of the sacrament house, both the pulpit and its presentation drawing survive (FIG. 31, PL. 26). The drawing depicts the structure in elevation. Its monumental winding staircase unfolds to showcase the elegant tracery of the balustrade, whose downward trajectory terminates in a portal crowned by a wimperg and spires.[57] A second sheet contains several technical drawings, including two floor plans and a top view of the staircase. The two sheets were

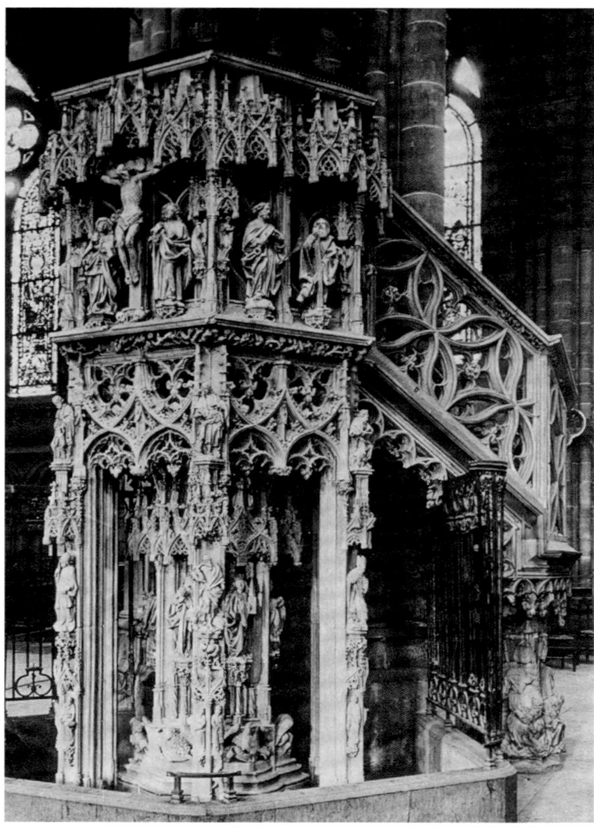

collated at a later moment, which undoubtedly ensured the survival of the technical studies. Although intended to be read together, Gothic elevations and floor plans frequently were separated over time and, more often than not, only the elevations were preserved, owing to their greater visual appeal and legibility. It is the combination of the two elements, however, that emphasizes Hammer's prowess as both a structural thinker and a sculptural designer, qualities that recommended him as the replacement for Hans Niesenberger as master of works of Strasbourg Cathedral in 1486.[58]

Hammer attested to his authorship in both the drawing and the pulpit itself with the inclusion of his mason's mark. Compared to some of his contemporaries, this manner of signature was rather modest. The architect Lorenz Lechler, for example, signed his work in a different fashion, by adding a self-portrait to a keystone in the vault of his rood screen (1486–89) for the Church of Saint Dionys in Esslingen.[59] The rood screen and a related sacrament house appear to have been among Lechler's first independent commissions as a master mason. Even at this early stage, his ambition was palpable, and not wholly without reason—his sacrament house in Esslingen is now recognized as one of the most pivotal and influential designs of its kind for the late Middle Ages.[60] Setting his sights high, he convinced the Esslingen city council to suggest to the Milanese cathedral building lodge (*fabbrica del duomo*) that he should oversee the completion of their cupola.[61] His bid for the position was not wholly implausible, since several of his compatriots, including Heinrich Parler, Ulrich von Ensingen, and Hans Niesenberger, had been employed in Milan, but Lechler's relatively limited experience at the time probably spoke against

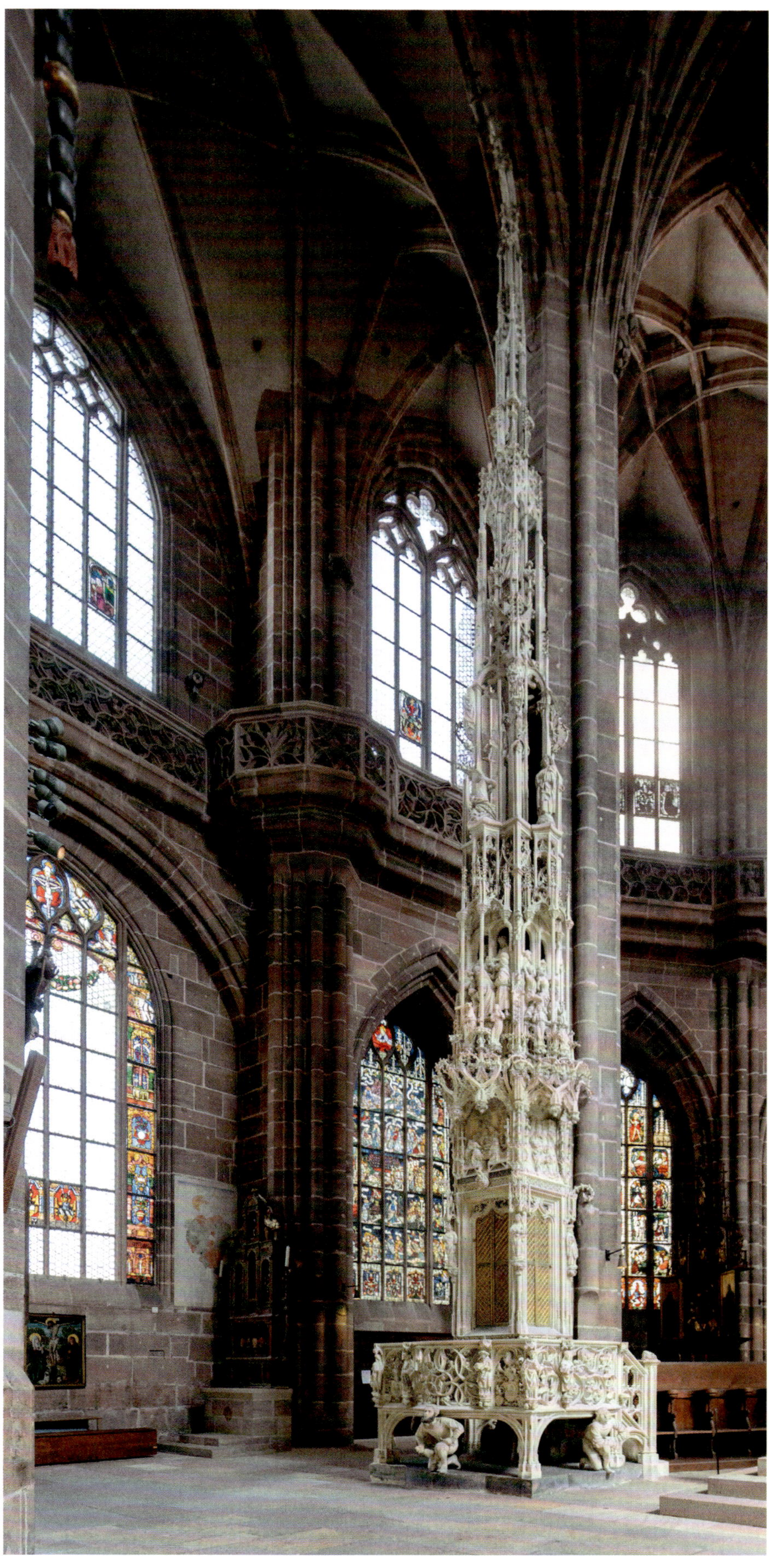

FIG. 32 Adam Kraft (German, ca. 1455–1509). Sacrament house in the Church of Saint Lorenz, Nuremberg, 1493–96. Photograph by B. O'Kane

his candidacy.[62] In 1503, just over a decade later, he finally did secure a leading position as the master gunsmith and architect (*Büchsen- und Baumeister*) of the Rhenish Palatinate in Heidelberg.[63]

It is very likely that Lechler strengthened his candidacy for this prestigious role with his highly finished design for a sacrament house of 1502, now at The Met (PL. 25). The drawing proposes a monumental structure, a projected sixty feet in height, that would rival its two most celebrated precedents at Ulm Minster and the Church of Saint Lorenz in Nuremberg (FIG. 32). The ambitious plan would have appealed to Philipp I, Elector Palatine of the Rhine, who is known to have been an enthusiastic patron of the arts.[64] Yet, while Lechler earned the appointment as Philipp's master gunsmith and architect, his sacrament house was never built, most likely because the War of the Succession of Landshut (1503–5) greatly impacted Philipp's final years and kept Lechler occupied in his role as master gunsmith. Philipp's death in 1508 almost certainly ended any plans for its completion, as his son, Ludwig V, who inherited the Palatinate and became Lechler's new employer, had no interest in ecclesiastical commissions.[65]

Unlike his colleagues Matthäus Böblinger and Hans Hammer, Lechler did not draw the figurative sculpture program for the sacrament house design himself. He was certainly capable, having created his self-portrait and some of the statuary in Esslingen.[66] However, since the structure was conceived as a speculative proposal without a confirmed location, Lechler possibly deferred making decisions about its iconographic program until his patron could approve the scheme.[67] Given the ambition of the design, it also seems likely that Lechler would have opted to work with an experienced sculptor and workshop. This type of partnership was customary even for much smaller sacrament houses, for example, the 1449 sacrament house in the Church of Saint Sulpice in Diest, Belgium, which was realized by two stone masons, a sculptor, a painter, and a smith.[68] An even larger team of carpenters, stone masons, iron- and coppersmiths, sculptors, and at least one painter was employed to realize Matthäus Böblinger's Mount of Olives monument in Ulm when it was finally built in the first decades of the sixteenth century.[69] Without the existence of drawings, such logically complex collective efforts would have proven difficult to manage.

Silver Cathedrals and Printed Tabernacles:
Architecural Design as an Interdisciplinary Practice

Not only was the execution of the small-scale architectural monuments discussed above often collaborative, but records also indicate that drawings facilitated interdisciplinary crossover during the design process itself. Just as architects sometimes opted to scale down, practitioners of architecture-adjacent fields had the ambition to scale up. For instance, the Ulm-based sculptor Jörg Syrlin the Elder, best known for the execution of the choir stalls in Ulm Minster, also submitted a design for the church's monumental sacrament house, and even created an alternate design for the completion of the minster's west tower. Both drawings have been preserved and are indistinguishable from the work of contemporary architects.[70] Similarly, toward the end of the fifteenth century, the preeminent Augsburg goldsmith Jörg Seld supplied design drawings for execution by masters in a range of disciplines, including monumental architecture.[71]

While fewer drawings survive by artists who, like Syrlin and Seld, worked outside the direct confines of the architectural profession, scattered testimonies suggest that the practice thrived, particularly among gold- and silversmiths, from the late twelfth century onward.[72] The custom of supplying designs to be executed by others is mentioned in a contract of 1272 for the silver reliquary of Saint Gertrude in the collegiate church in Nivelles, Belgium. Two goldsmiths were tasked with executing the vessel after a design by yet another goldsmith, referred to alternately as Master Jakenez or Jakemon d'Anchin, and as the monk of Anchin. It has been speculated that the drawing or drawings for this cathedral-shaped reliquary would have looked quite similar to, or may even have been inspired by, contemporary architectural designs like Drawings A and A' from Strasbourg Cathedral (SEE FIG. 10, PL. 5).[73] The oldest-surviving drawing for a piece of goldsmith's work dates to a century later, and depicts a design for a cup in the shape of a rooster standing atop an architectural base.[74] By 1476, drawing had become a deeply integrated practice in the field. That year, a statute of the Salzburg goldsmiths' guild required that all pupils demonstrate their progress by bringing "something engraved or designed" to quarterly meetings.[75] Jörg Seld was roughly a contemporary of this generation, and appears to have become a particularly gifted draftsman and designer.

Like the output of many of his contemporaries, Seld's work in precious metals has a strong architectural character, but his knowledge of and commitment to architectural design far exceeds that of his peers (PL. 41). In 1502 and 1503, he worked on a commission from the Augsburg city council to design a bell tower for the Church of Saint Peter am Perlach. Although it was never executed, the wood architectural model produced in his workshop is the oldest to survive north of the Alps.[76] Seld also provided several designs for the interior of the Church of Saint Moritz in Augsburg. His design for a stone sacrament house was executed by the workshop of the preeminent architect Burkhard Engelberg (PL. 2)—a friend and close associate—while the sculptors Adolf Daucher the Elder and Gregor Erhart worked on an altar after Seld's design. In 1514, Seld was also asked to design a sacrament house for the Dom (cathedral) in Augsburg.[77] That structure does not survive, but a drawing in the Germanisches Nationalmuseum in Nuremberg, signed with the initials *IS* and dated 1514, is here cautiously identified as Seld's original design for the commission (PL. 24). Like Hans Hammer's pulpit design, the elevation is accompanied by a separate sheet with floor plans and vaulting plans, as well as a top view of a staircase that is not pictured in the elevation. These technical drawings show Seld's great facility with Gothic architectural design methods, and hence, his ability to communicate effectively with the masons and other professionals who executed structures following his designs.

Beyond these projects, Seld also appears to have experimented with publishing his designs in print. This relatively new reproductive medium offered an autonomous platform for his ideas (no commission was needed) and had the potential to reach a much wider audience than any single drawing. Two rare woodcuts, here ascribed to Seld for the first time, depict a reliquary and an altar (FIGS. 33, 34). Their attribution is based on the close similarity

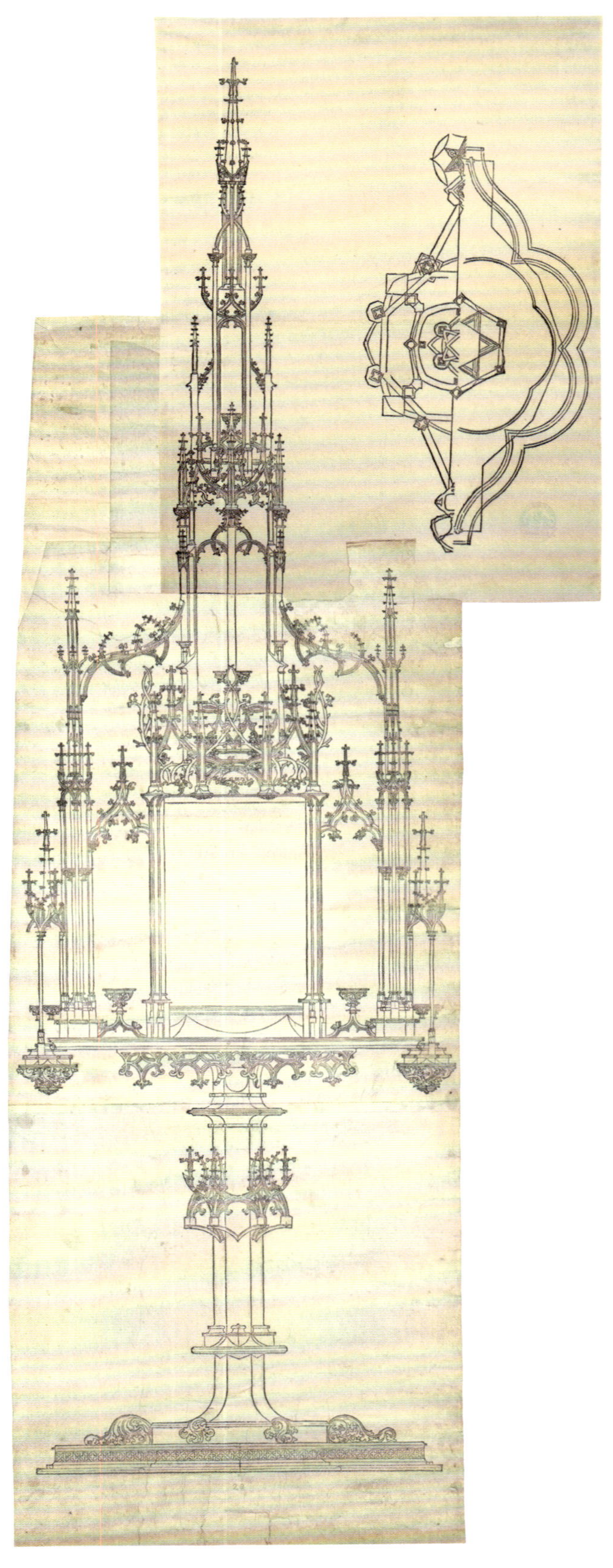

FIG. 33 Attributed to Jörg Seld (German, ca. 1454–1527). Orthographic elevation of a reliquary with its floor plan (digital reconstruction of two uncollated sheets), ca. 1500–1520. Woodcut, spire and plans (top sheet): 15 11/16 × 11 7/16 in. (39.8 × 29 cm). Friedrich-Alexander-Universität Erlangen-Nürnberg, Graphische Sammlung (H62/AH 84); corpus and foot (bottom sheet): 33 11/16 × 11 15/16 in. (85.6 × 30.4 cm). Stadtarchiv Ulm (F 1 Münsterrisse 28)

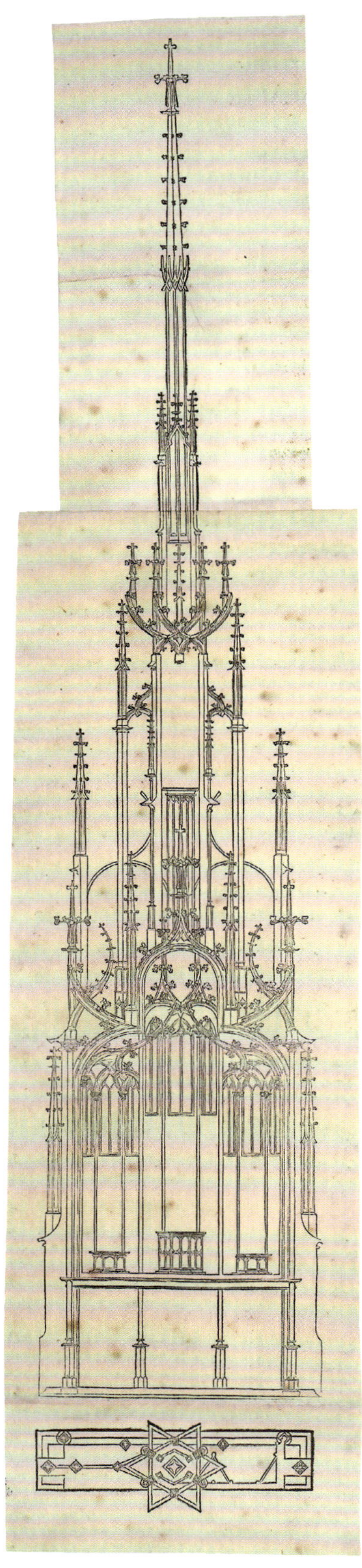

FIG. 34 Attributed to Jörg Seld (German, ca. 1454–1527). Orthographic elevation of an altar with its floor plan, ca. 1500–1520. Woodcut, spire (top sheet): 8⅞ × 4⁵⁄₁₆ in. (22.6 × 11 cm), altar and baldachin (middle sheet): 15¹³⁄₁₆ × 6¹⁄₁₆ in. (40.2 × 15.4 cm), floor plan (bottom sheet): 2⅝ × 6¹⁄₁₆ in. (6.6 × 15.4 cm). Albertina, Vienna (DG1928/407)

between the reliquary and Seld's design for a similar object, now preserved in Stuttgart (SEE PL. 41). There is no doubt, moreover, that the reliquary and altar woodcuts were produced together: They are represented as coequal, rendered in a strictly orthographic elevation, and paired with their floor plans. All nonstructural elements, including statuettes and surface decorations, have been left out to emphasize the architectural nature of both designs. While Seld's motive for publishing these designs is unknown, he was certainly aware of the power and permanence of the print medium. The execution of several monumental print commissions for the Holy Roman Emperor Maximilian I had turned his hometown into the epicenter of woodcut production.[78] Seld's biographer Norbert Lieb has tentatively suggested that his workshop was directly involved in these efforts through the production of the black-letter type (*Fraktur*) known as Kaiser-Fraktur, which was used for the so-called First Prayer Book of Maximilian (1513) and *The Tales of the Knight Theuerdank* (1517).[79] Seld was also more prominently engaged in the production of the first monumental bird's-eye view of Augsburg, known today as the Seld Plan (designed 1514–16, printed 1521), for which he provided the drawings, carved in woodblock by Hans Weiditz the Younger.[80]

Seld's woodcuts form the capstone to a modest print tradition north of the Alps that included the publication of Gothic architectural subjects. Its onset can be situated to around the time of Mathes Roriczer's pamphlets, published in the 1480s. This period was also characterized by architects' heightened interest in self-promotion—naturally aided by prints—as can be seen in the increased production of portraits, both self-made and by fellow artists (PLS. 2, 3, 83). The notion that architects ought to write something to be remembered by, first put forward in antiquity by Vitruvius, might have influenced some practitioners (or their patrons) to record their work in print as well.[81] We know Roriczer was encouraged to publish by the cultured bishop of Eichstätt, his dedicatee, but ultimately it was the architect himself who stood to gain most from the venture. Born into a dynasty of master builders, he himself remained childless, and little about his legacy would have been remembered had it not been for his publications.[82] That said, professional competition may also have been a contributing factor. In the late 1480s, the Nuremberg goldsmith Hanns Schmuttermayer issued a booklet on pinnacles (*Fialenbüchlein*) that covered much of the same ground as Roriczer's 1486 guide on the same topic. Not only did Schmuttermayer do a better job of summarizing the prescribed method, he also helpfully included instructions on how to design a wimperg.[83] Roriczer's two-folio addendum on wimpergs, published between 1486 and 1490, undoubtedly came about in response.

Around the same time, in nearby Ulm, the printmaker Wenzel von Olmütz created a series of instructional engravings for the design of Gothic baldachins that are closely related to the minster's sacrament house, and were possibly commissioned by its building lodge (SEE PLS. 74–76).[84] While Olmütz's prints are not accompanied by text, their systematic presentation underscores their educational nature. Picking up where Roriczer and Schmuttermayer left off, Olmütz addresses the design of structures that are geometrically far more complex than those covered in the earlier booklets. As such, his engravings undoubtedly spoke to contemporary architects who collected the prints and used them as inspiration for their own designs.[85]

Printmaking enabled artists to share more widely their designs for executed as well as unrealized or conceptual work. The Netherlandish master mason Alart du Hameel seems to have turned to the medium for this reason especially. Among his prints are designs for a baldachin, a statue of the apostle Peter on a leafwork console, and other leafwork designs reminiscent of the motifs in the *Laubhauermüsterbuch* of his predecessor Hans Böblinger the Elder.[86] Du Hameel also produced an engraving of a monstrance (a decorative vessel for the display of consecrated Communion bread). It is almost certainly the piece he designed for the Cathedral of Saint John in 's-Hertogenbosch, which was executed in 1484 by the Cologne-based goldsmith Hendrik de Borchgrave (PL. 40).[87] While the monstrance itself has since been lost, preventing a comparison between the two objects, the print features a distinctive crowning element in the shape of a small onion dome, an echo of the original west and lantern towers of the Cathedral of Saint John, which strongly suggests its association with the church.[88] At more than forty-three inches in height, the print is much taller than any of Du Hameel's other engravings, indicating that he replicated the object (or more likely his design drawing) to scale (COMPARE TO PLS. 41, 43). Du Hameel signed the print with his first and last name, mason's mark, and the place of production. This signature, unusually elaborate for the period—for both drawings and prints—is a unique testament to his regard for the print medium as a powerful vehicle of self-promotion and his strong awareness of the concepts of artistic and intellectual property.[89]

The floor plan below the monstrance may be perceived as its own kind of signature. Represented in shorthand, it contains only one-eighth of the structural blueprint. Those already proficient in the language of Gothic architectural plans would have recognized it as a highly efficient carrier of information, but few members of the general public would have been privy to this form of communication.[90] Here then, as with Olmütz and even Seld, is evidence of an architect speaking to other architects. Printmaking was perceived by Gothic architects as a direct extension of their long-standing, self-contained, and highly successful design and drawing traditions, rather than an entirely new avenue of communication with a mass audience. First and foremost, it offered a novel means to celebrate, share, and preserve designs among an audience of patrons and peers. In this sense, the turn to printmaking can be viewed as a somewhat more democratic sublimation of the corporate archival efforts that were set in motion by cathedral building lodges in the late thirteenth century, as described in the previous chapter. The fact that the building lodge in Ulm itself turned to printmaking speaks volumes. We owe the surviving body of Gothic architectural drawings and prints to this preservationist attitude. These works offer tangible glimpses into the painstaking, methodical, and highly creative design practices of countless generations of architects, in whose dedication to draftsmanship we have discovered the true genius of "endowing massive walls with variety" and of "occupying the eye in a worthy and pleasing manner."

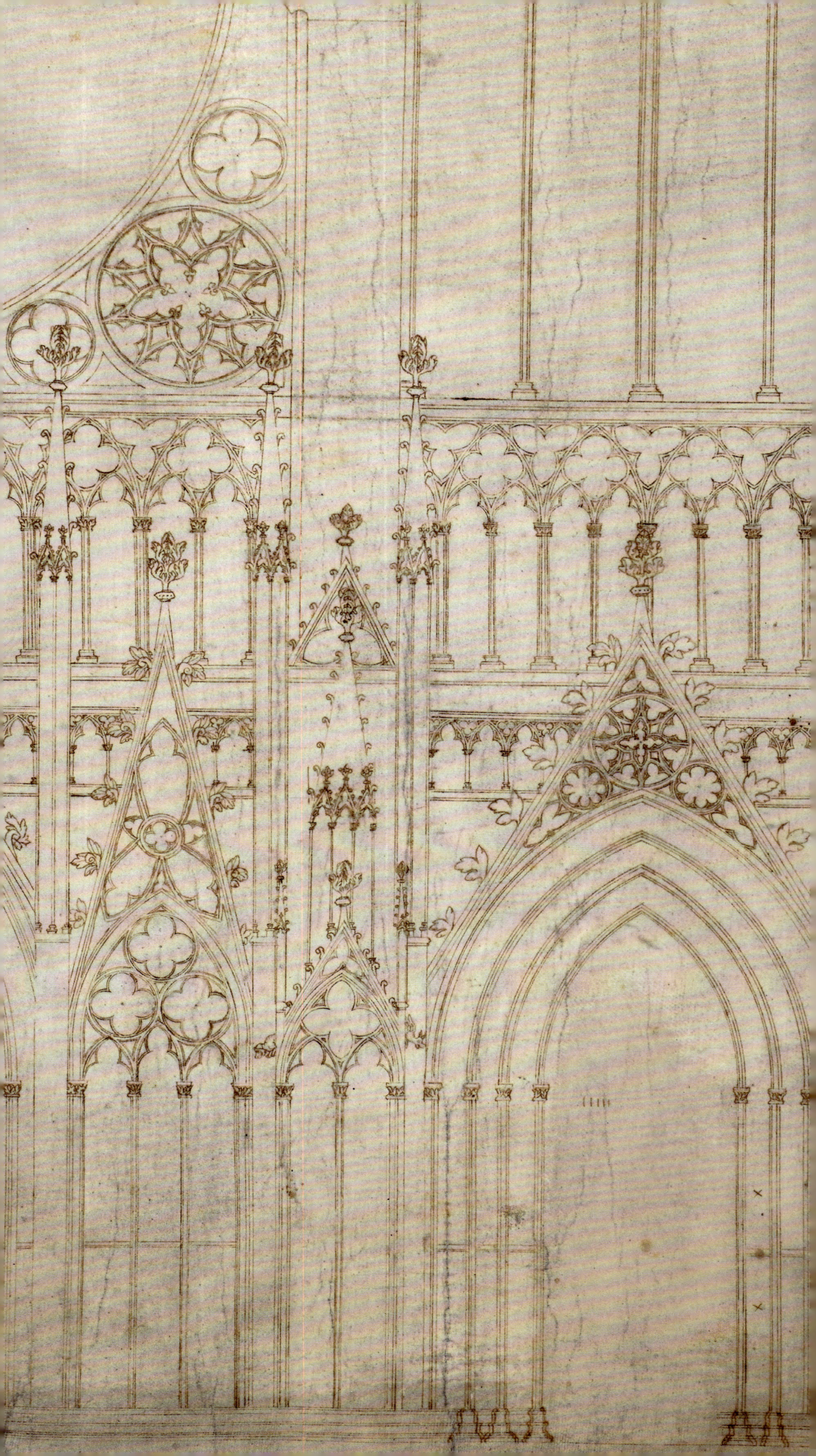

Making
Their Marks

While many Gothic cathedrals and churches stand firm as fixtures of the European cityscape, opportunities are few to come face-to-face with the people who designed and built them. Hans Holbein the Elder's silverpoint portraits of several Late Gothic architects are a rare exception (PLS. 2, 3). Individualized and lifelike, his portraits are worlds apart from those of the generic stone masons who populate most medieval depictions of building sites. More than likely, these men were drawn from life during an encounter with the artist, whose professional and social milieus would have overlapped with theirs. Some, such as Mathes (Matthäus) Roriczer (PL. 3) and Konrad Würffel, are easily identifiable as master masons because Holbein included their personal mason's marks.[1] Sporadically found on drawings or completed monuments in lieu of a full signature, such marks were most often used on the individually cut stone segments of a building.[2]

For example, a mason's mark in the shape of a cross moline can be found on a fragment of the tracery arcade from Canterbury Cathedral that is now in The Met collection (PL. 1). The cross is one of several markings incised into the stone as part of the working process. Another, in the form of a more casually carved *X*, appears twice on the piece. It is likely an assembly mark, which served a variety of practical functions, including the actual assembly of building elements. Here, the informal *X* probably references the template that would have been used to outline the molding pattern (see, for a later example, pl. 88). Placed on an uncut block of stone, templates were traced with a sharp implement or a piece of chalk to inform the carving process.[3] In this case, the same template for one half of the arcade profile was efficiently used twice, with the perpendicular line incised at center ensuring correct alignment. While many such assembly marks would ultimately disappear or become obscured in the final stages of finishing and installing building elements, mason's marks were often left visible. Those found on walls and pillars today are enduring reminders of the numerous stone masons who helped build Gothic churches.

Another of Holbein's silverpoint portraits, of the architect Burkhard Engelberg, is somewhat unusual among the group (pl. 2). Having chosen three-quarter views for Roriczer and Würffel, in this image Holbein depicts his sitter in profile and wearing a luxurious fur-lined hat, aspects that speak to Engelberg's status as a well-to-do citizen. References to the architectural profession, however, are absent. This omission could have to do with the drawing's intended function (now unknown), but might also be explained by Engelberg's widespread fame at the time, or by Holbein's personal familiarity with his subject. Considering Engelberg's career-long involvement in the rebuilding of the Basilica and Cloisters of Saints Ulrich and Afra in Augsburg, he almost certainly belonged to Holbein's circle of professional acquaintances in the city.[4] During his tenure at the basilica, Engelberg was also appointed city architect in Augsburg and, in 1493, took on an additional position as master of works (*Dombaumeister*) in Ulm.[5]

Owing to these prominent postings and to the status that came with them, Engelberg became a sought-after architect. Involved in the design and execution of a broad array of ecclesiastical and secular buildings, his reach stretched across a vast geographic area in Central Europe, from as far northeast as the Neckar Valley (Heilbronn) to Switzerland (Konstanz and Bern) and Tyrol (Bolzano) in the southwest and southeast, respectively.[6] As such, Engelberg may be counted among several so-called star architects who were able to build cross-regional or even truly international careers by supplying designs primarily through drawings rather than being tied to a single building site or masons' lodge.[7]

One of the earliest testaments to the emergence of the trans-local designer-architect as a profession is the Nuremberg Drawing, from about 1300. The double-sided sheet records designs for building projects in the Upper Rhine region, all thought to have originated from the mind of Strasbourg master of works Erwin von Steinbach (PL. 9). After archival copies were made on both sides of the parchment, the individual plans were sent to their respective building sites, where they were executed by local (master) masons.[8]

Over the course of the fourteenth and fifteenth centuries, others followed in Steinbach's footsteps and built careers as star architects.[9] The tower expert Ulrich von Ensingen and Rombout II Keldermans, heir to a dynasty of entrepreneurial South Netherlandish stone masons (PL. 21), may be counted among them.[10] The tracery arcade in The Met collection, similarly, was the product of designs by either Stephen Lote or Thomas Mapilton, the English master masons who were successively in charge of the Canterbury Cathedral project but who were both far too busy with royal commissions to be on-site for long periods of time.[11] Ironically, it is therefore unusual to find physical marks of their involvement on the buildings they so markedly helped shape.

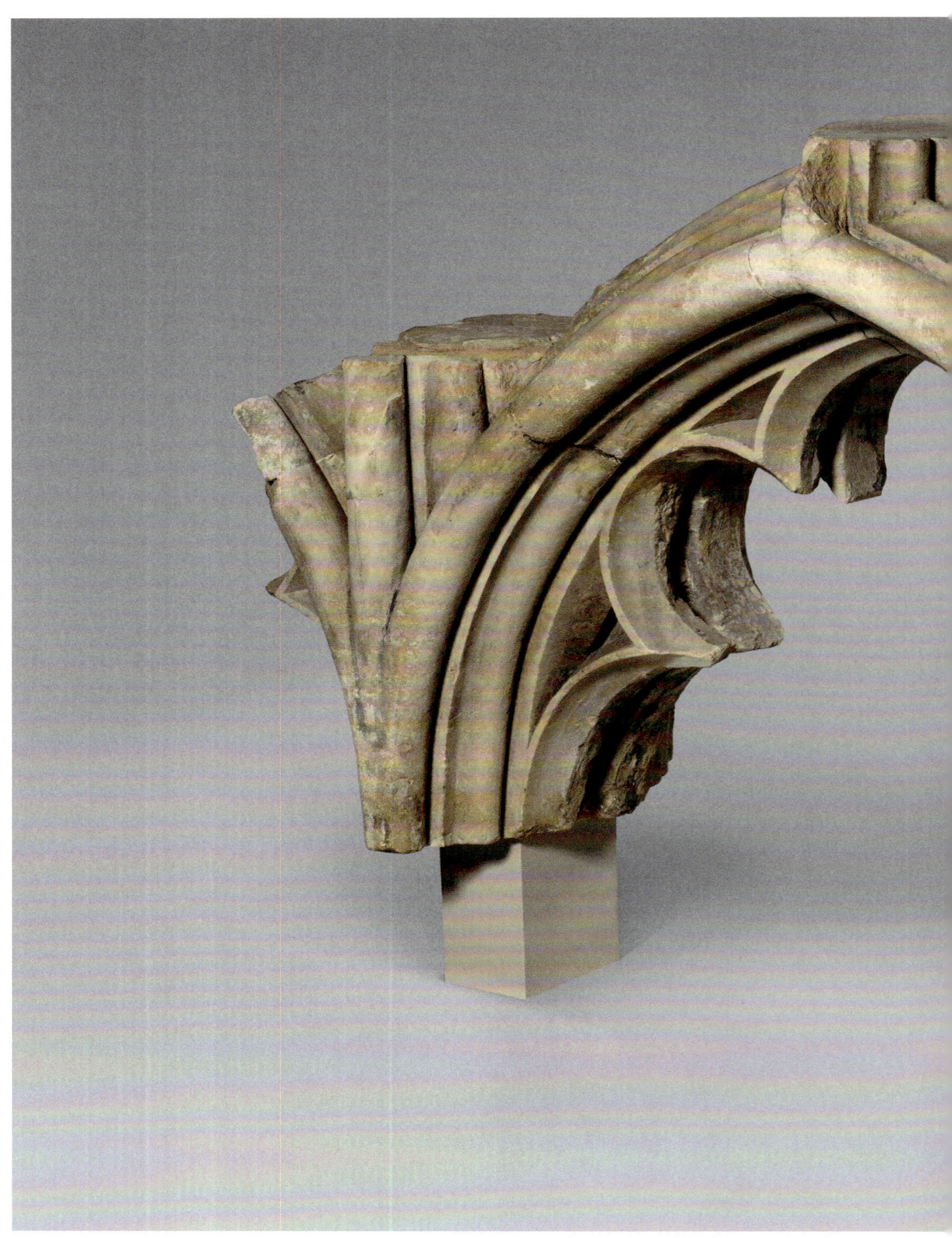

After a design by Stephen Lote or Thomas Mapilton. Tracery Arcade from the Great South
Window of Canterbury Cathedral, with a Detail of a Mason's Mark, ca. 1426–35

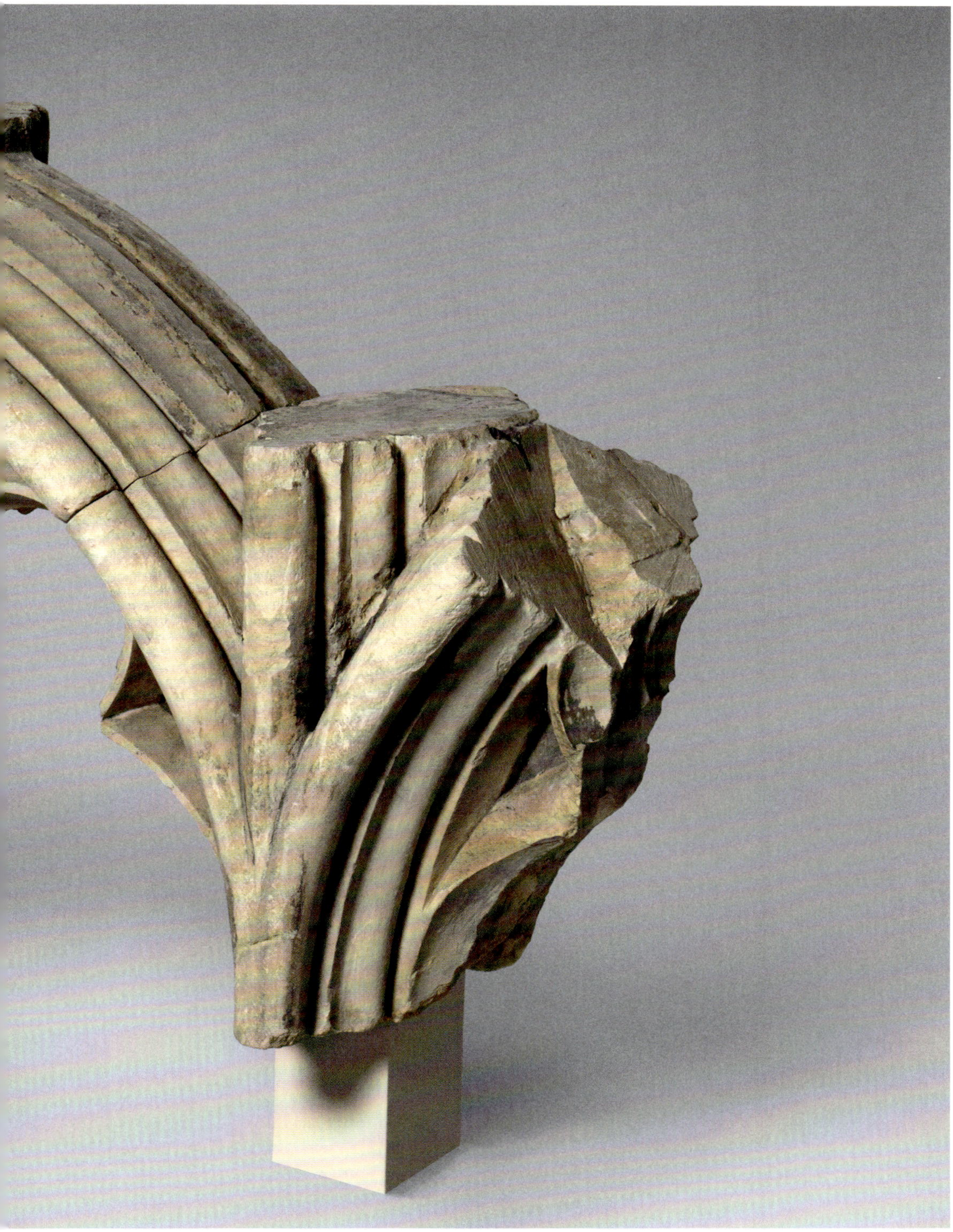

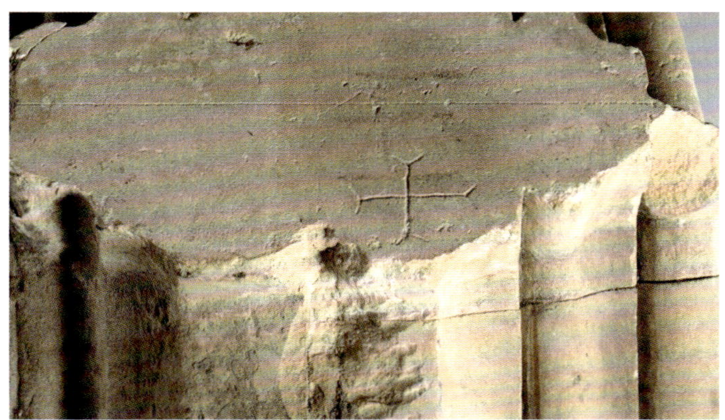

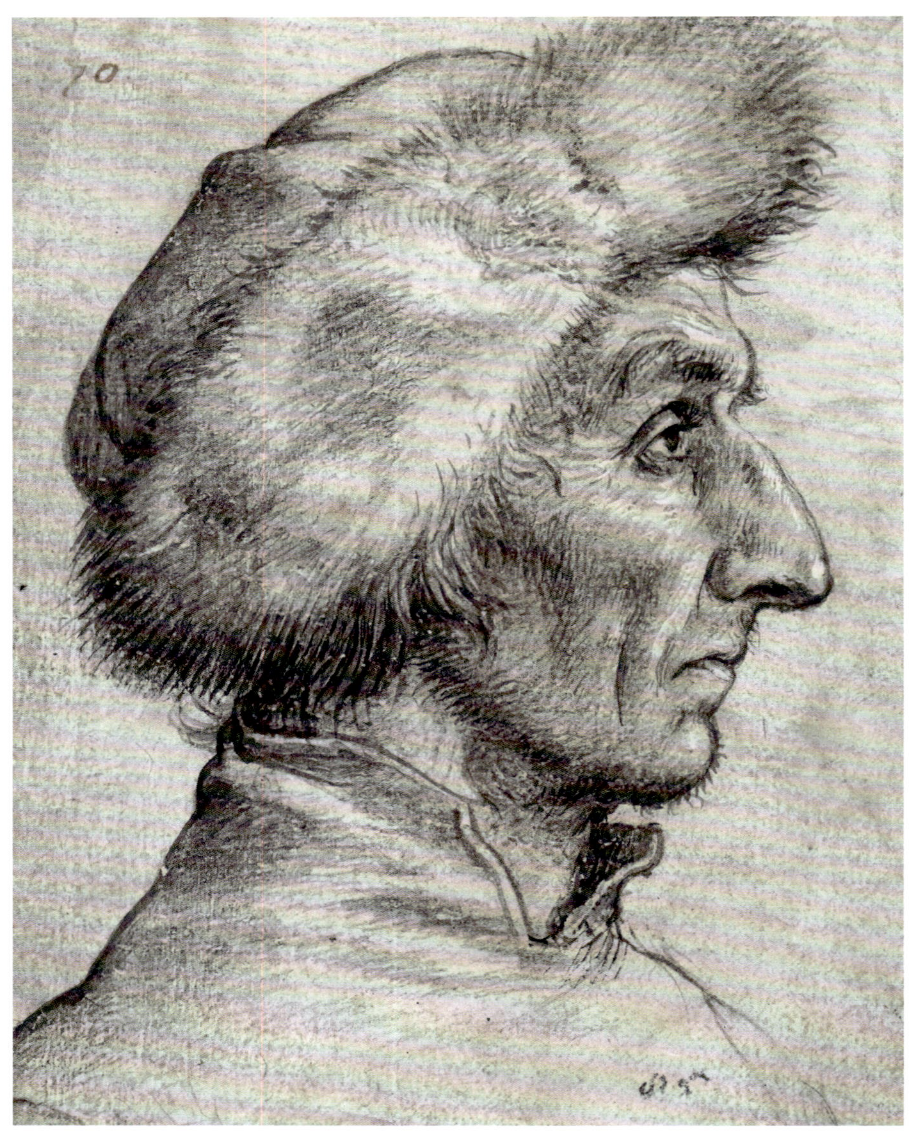

PLATE 2

Hans Holbein the Elder. Portrait of the Architect Burkhard Engelberg, ca. 1490–1510

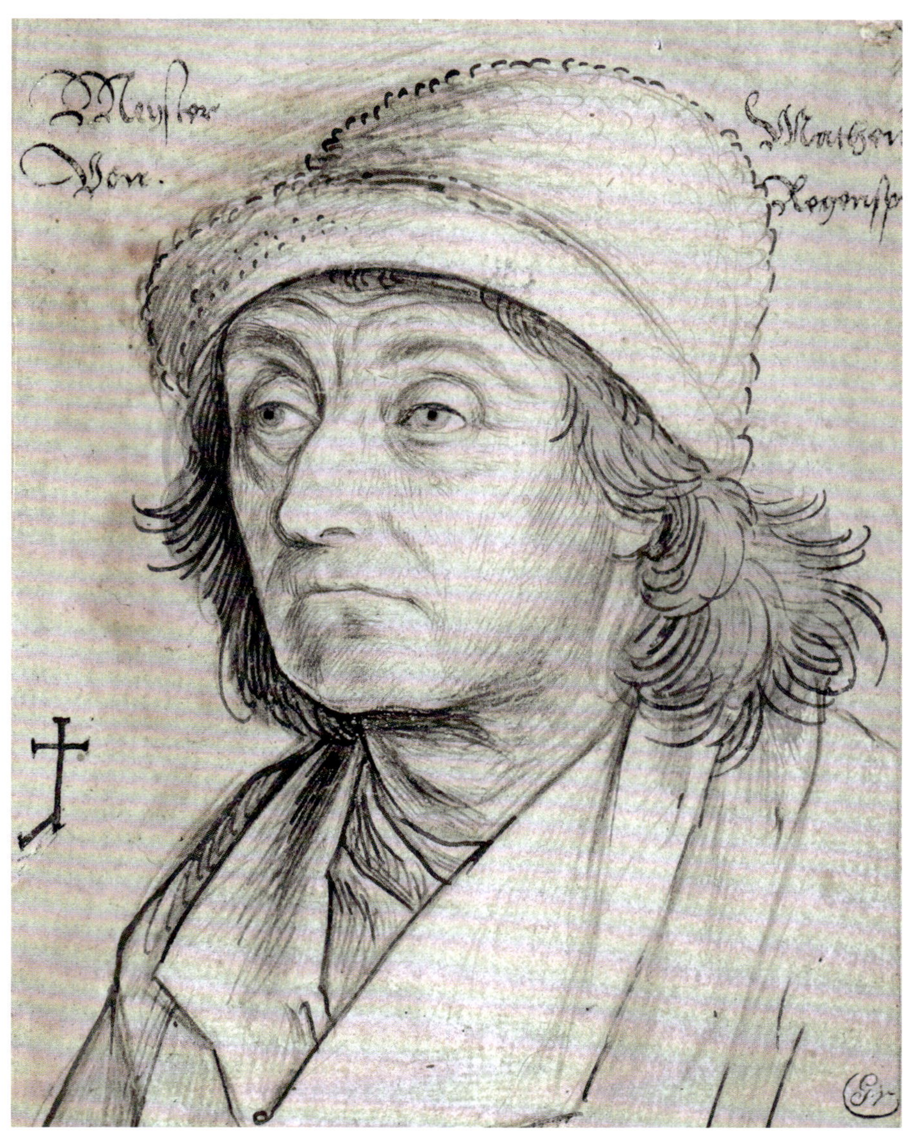

PLATE 3

Hans Holbein the Elder. Portrait of the Architect Mathes (Matthäus) Roriczer, ca. 1490–93

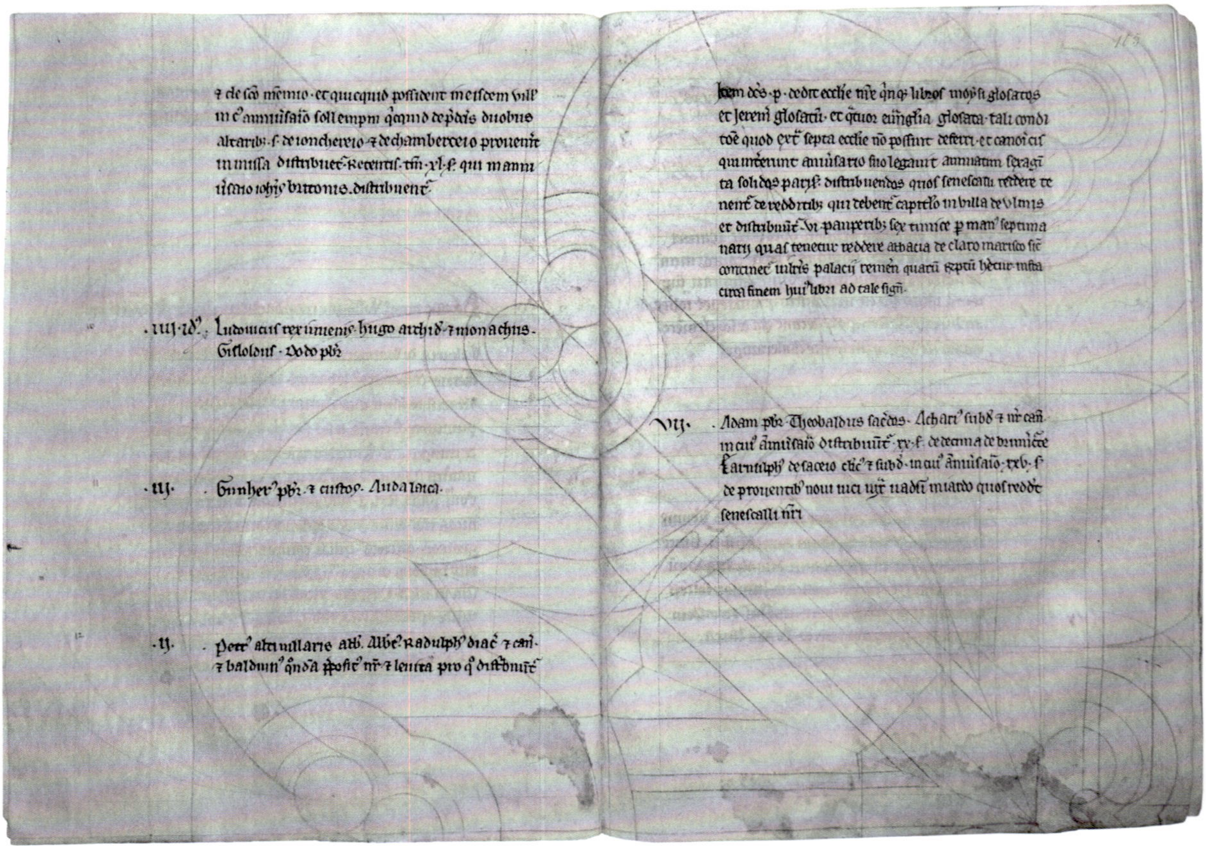

PLATE 4

Remnants of Erased Architectural Drawings from the Reims Palimpsest (*Martyrologe et Nécrologe de l'Église de Reims*; digital reconstruction of Sheet E, pages 100v and 105r), ca. 1230–60; text ca. 1263–70

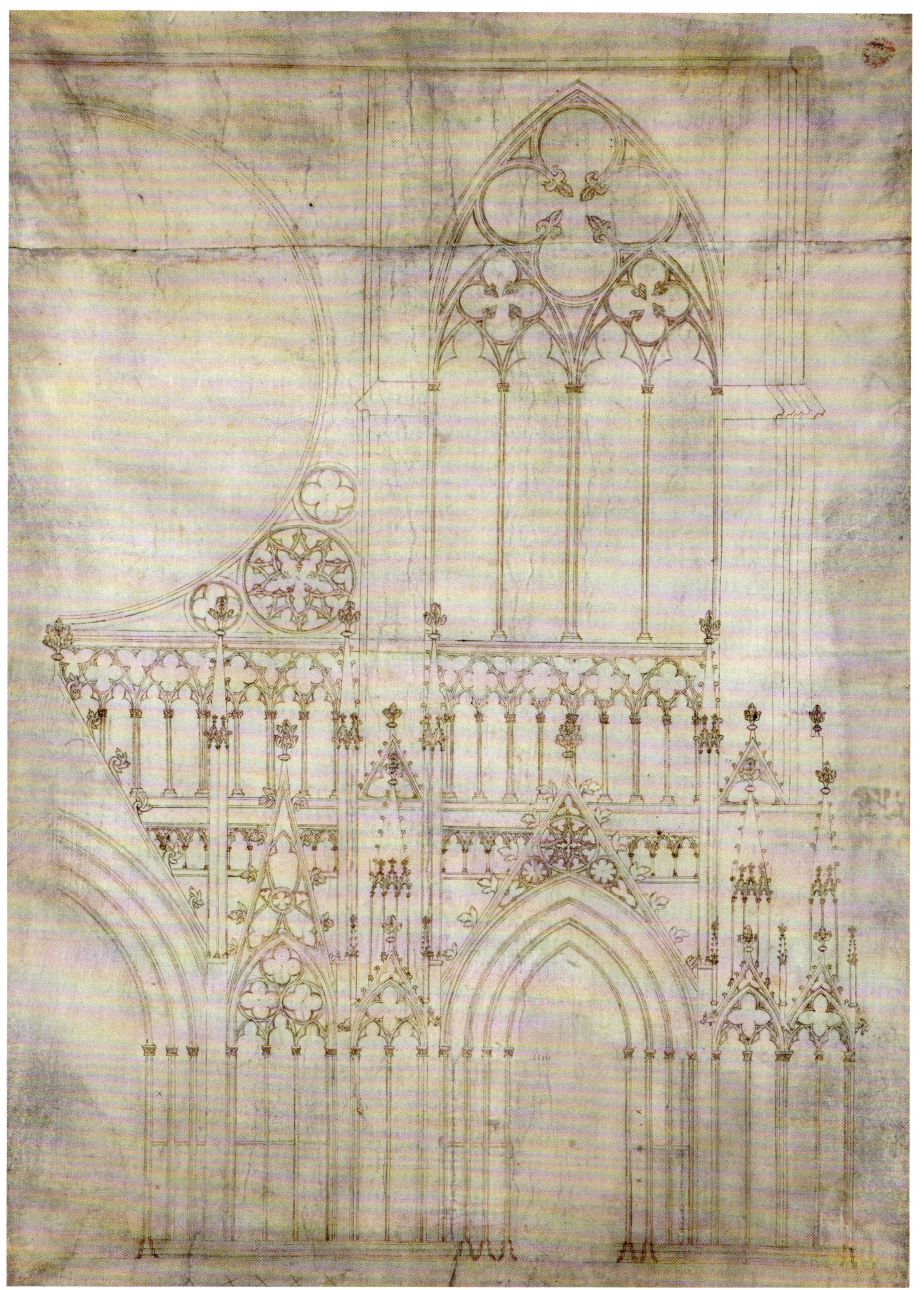

PLATE 5

Attributed to Erwin von Steinbach, partially after Master Rudolph the Elder. Partial Elevation of the Facade of Strasbourg Cathedral (Drawing A'), ca. 1260–70

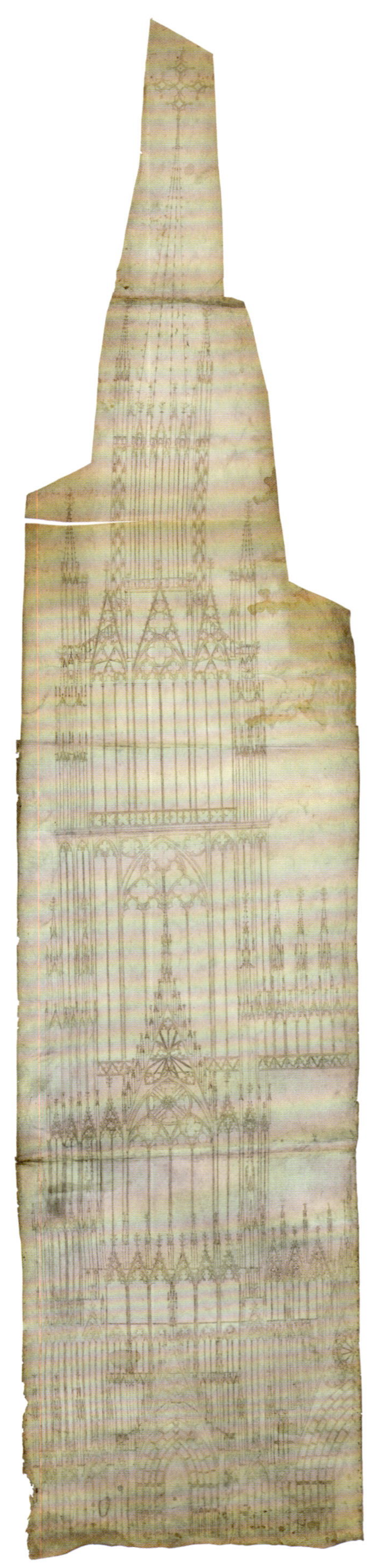

After Erwin von Steinbach. Partial Elevation of the Facade of Strasbourg Cathedral with its North Tower (Drawing B′), ca. 1278–1300

90

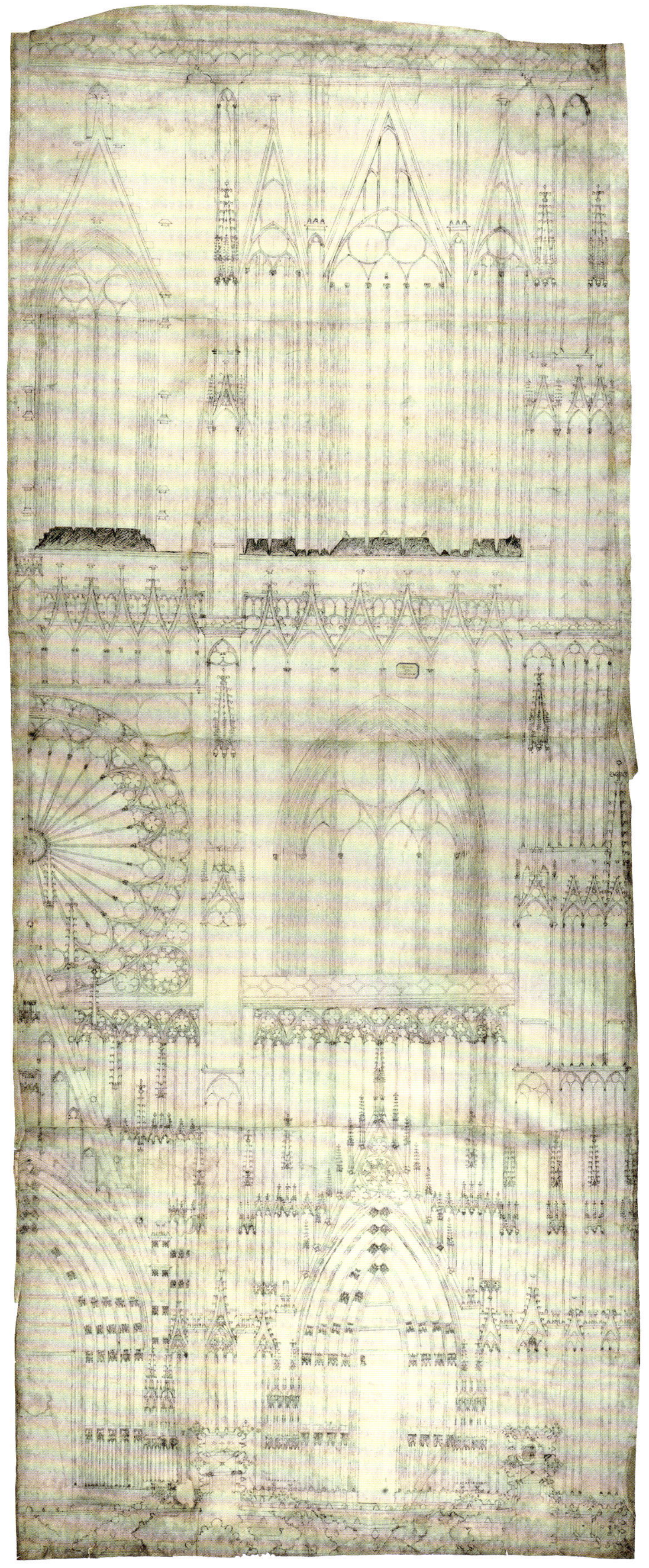

PLATE 7

Variously attributed to Michael von Freiburg or Claus von Lohre. Partial Elevation and Plan of the Facade of Strasbourg Cathedral, ca. 1380–1400

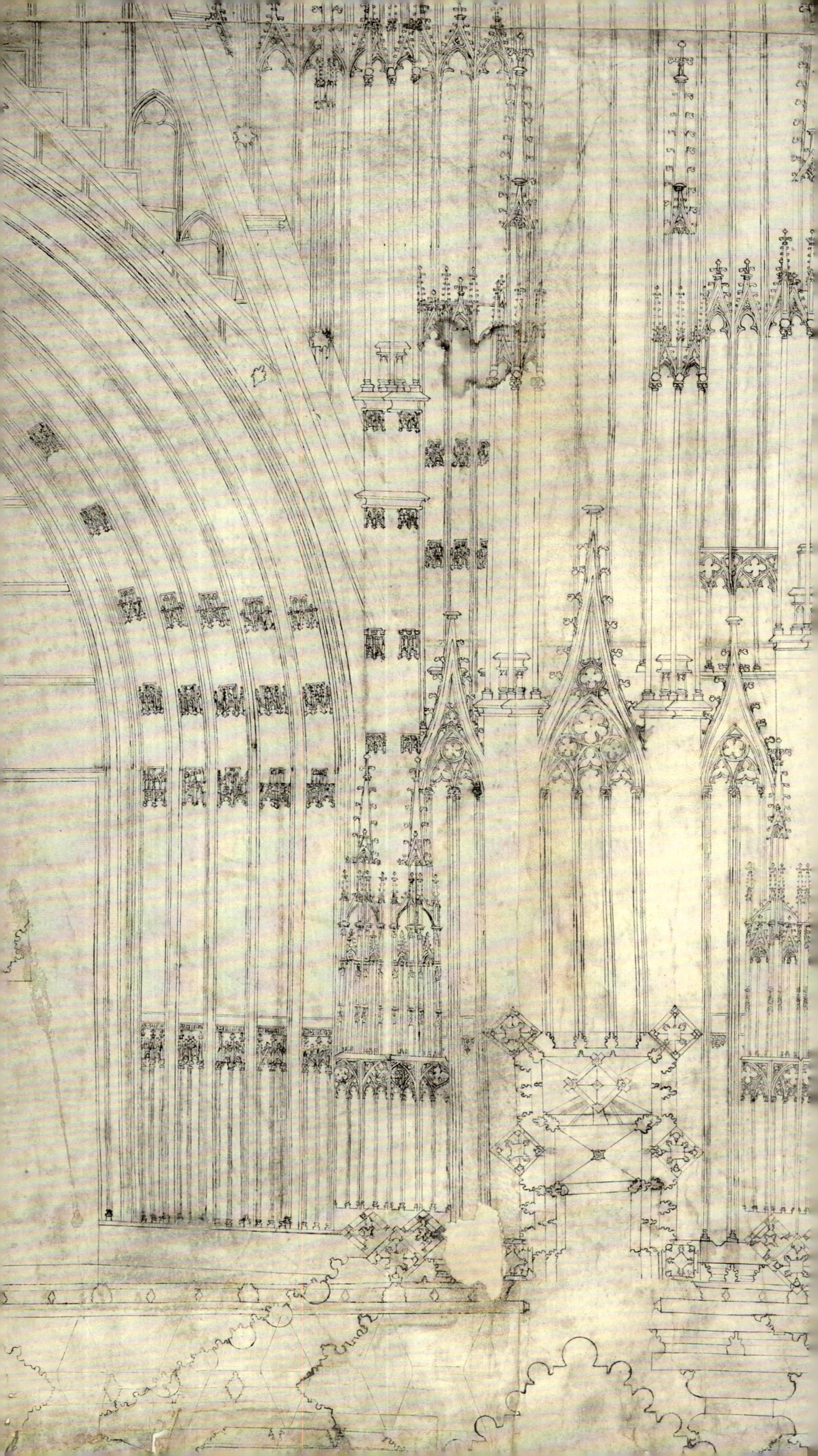

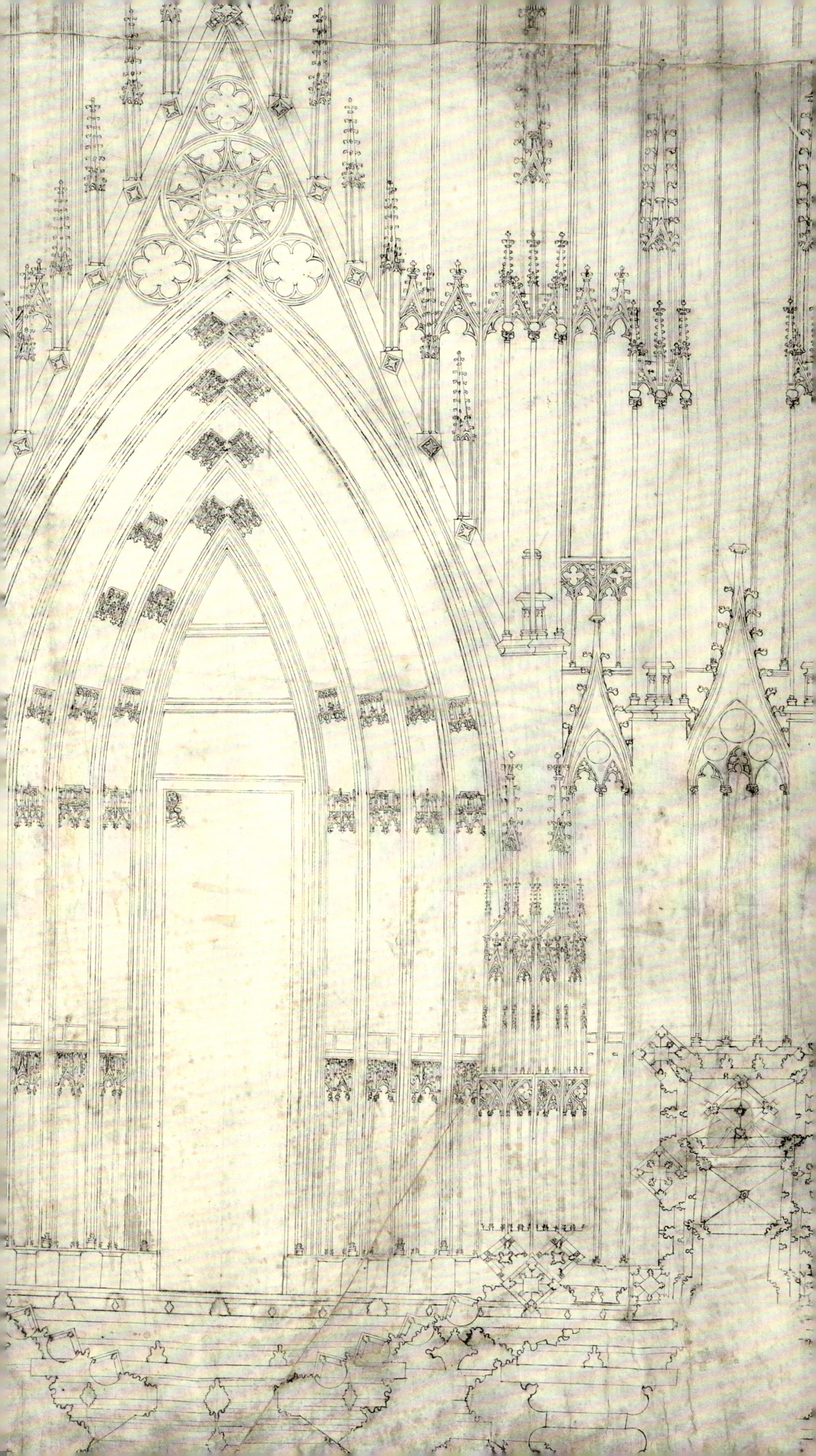

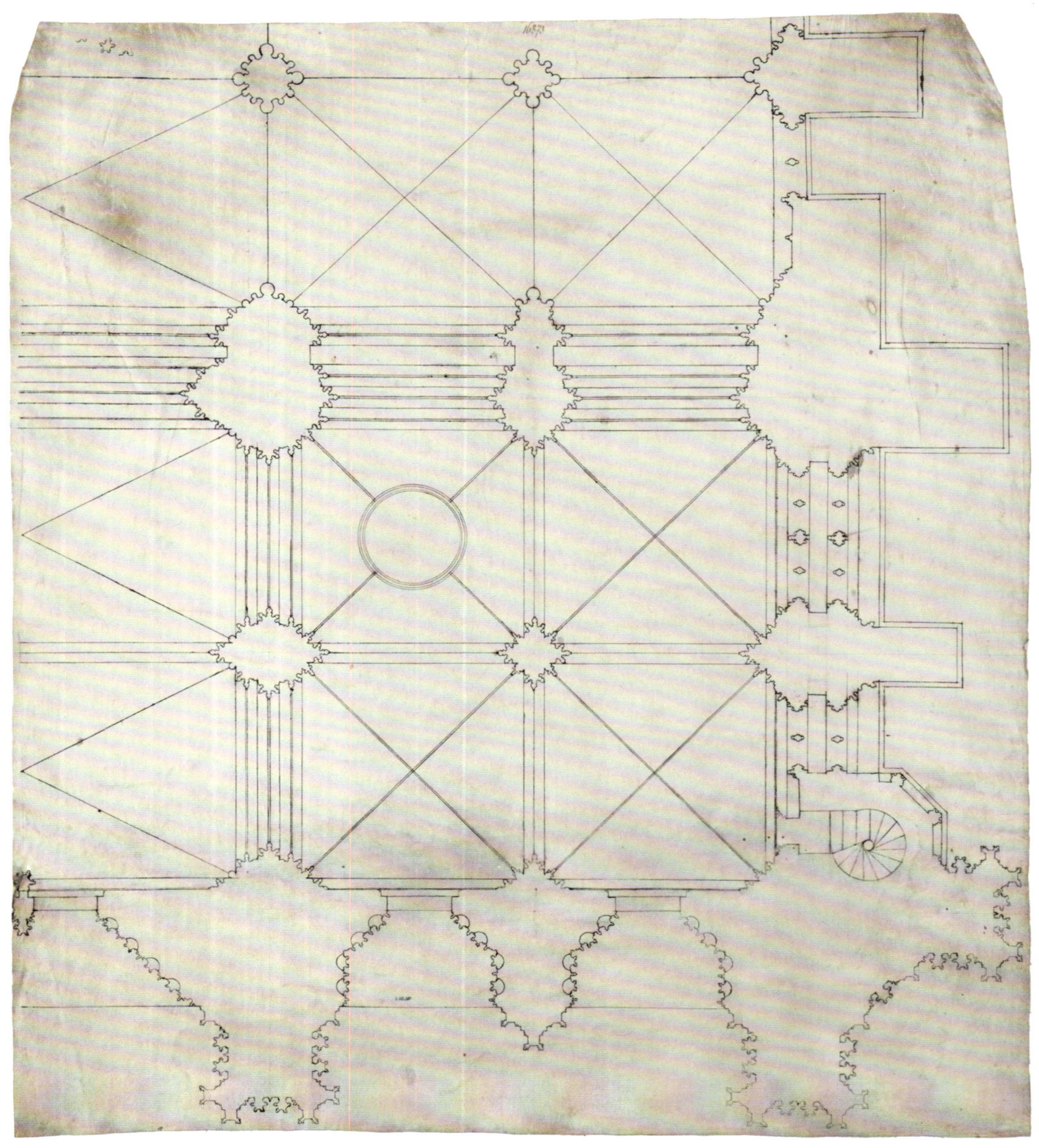

PLATE 8
Unidentified German artist. Partial Floor Plan of the Facade and South Tower of Cologne
Cathedral, ca. 1300–1350

PLATE 9
Circle of Erwin von Steinbach. Recto (left): Elevation for the Tower of Freiburg Minster;
verso (right): Various Floor Plans and Elevations (Nuremberg Drawing), ca. 1300

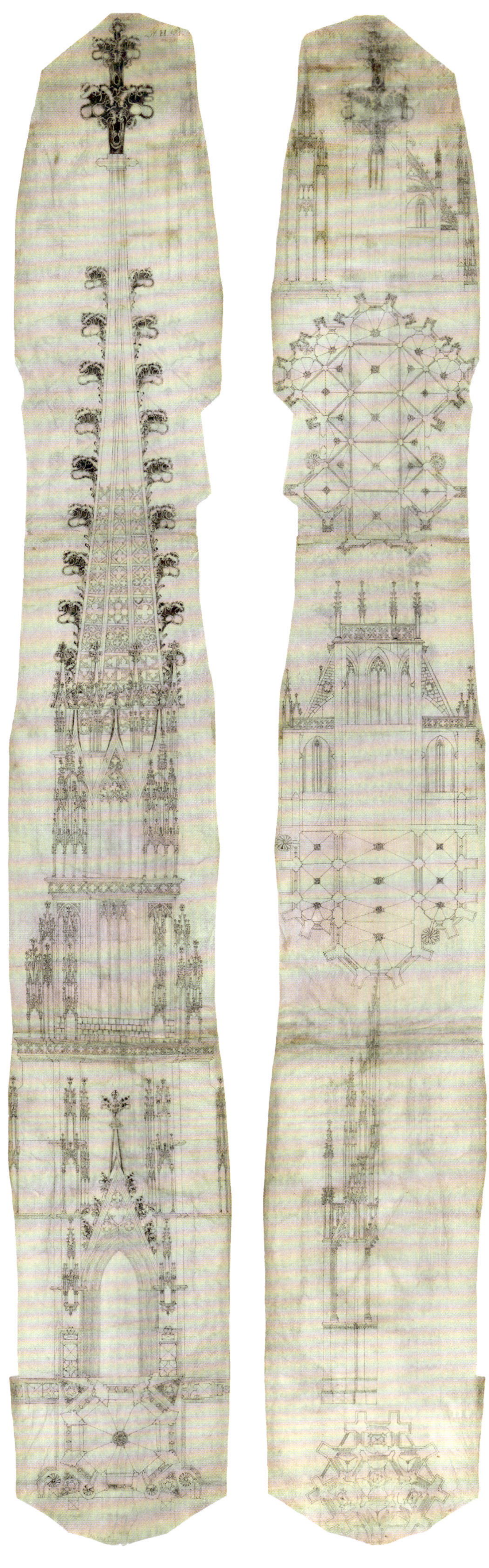

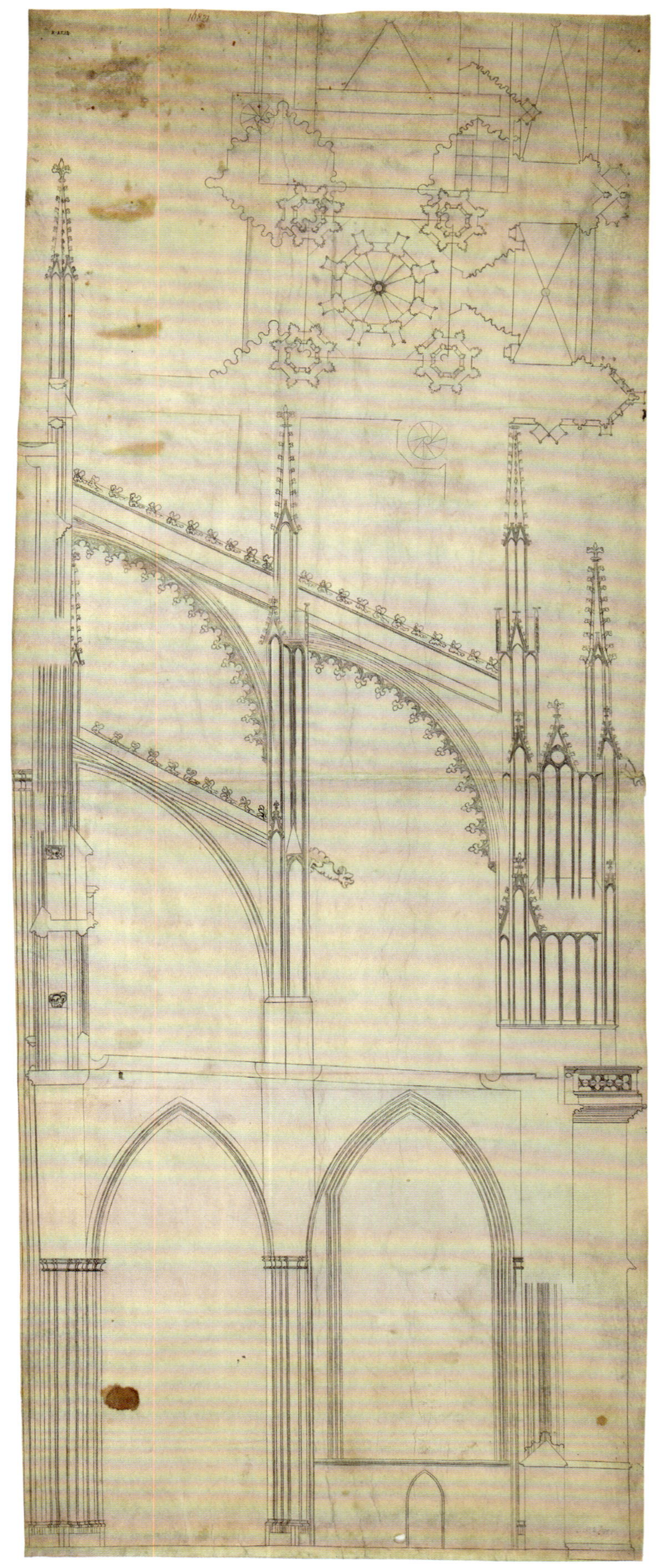

PLATE 10

Peter Parler. Cross Section of the Northern Half of the Choir and Flying Buttresses of the Cathedral of Saint Vitus (Veitsdom), Prague, ca. 1360

96

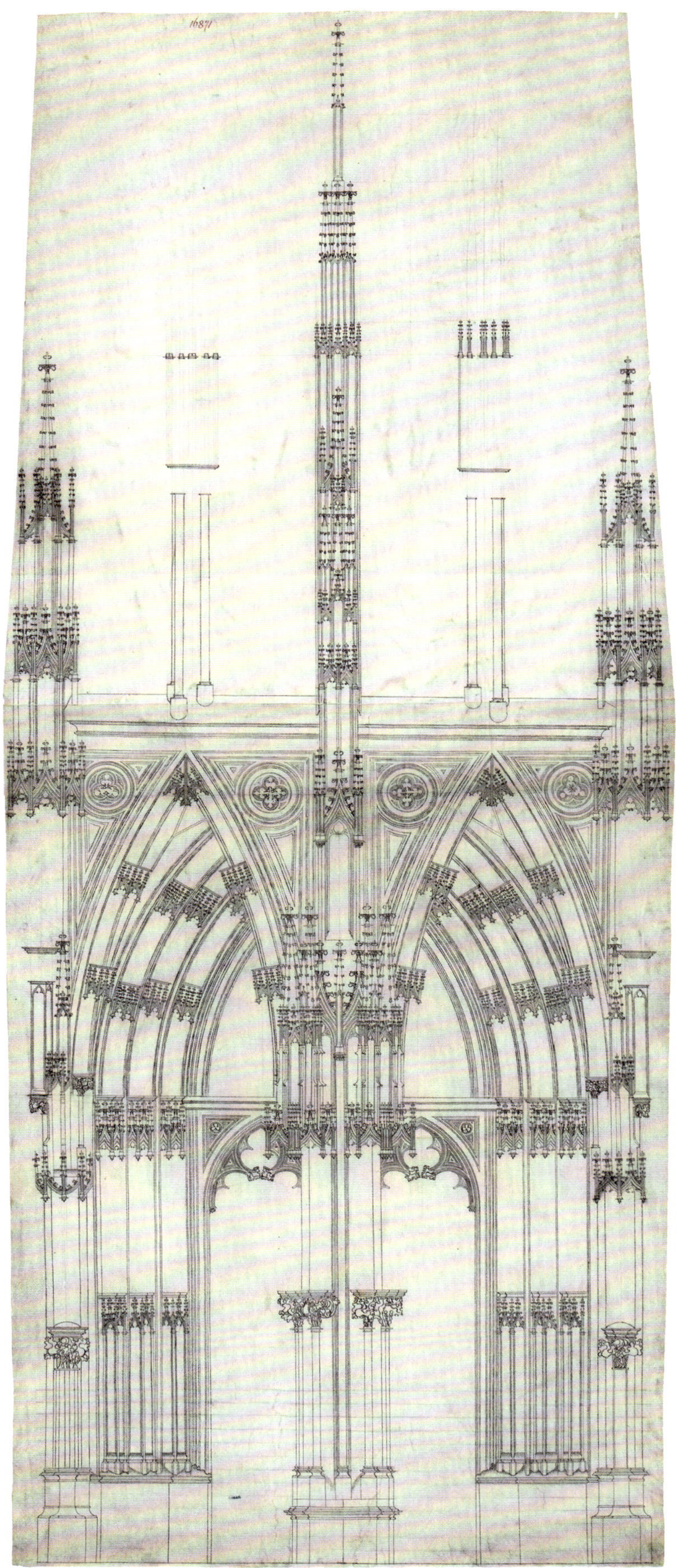

PLATE II

Possibly by Wenzel Roriczer. Design for the Entrance Portal of Regensburg Cathedral,
ca. 1390–1410

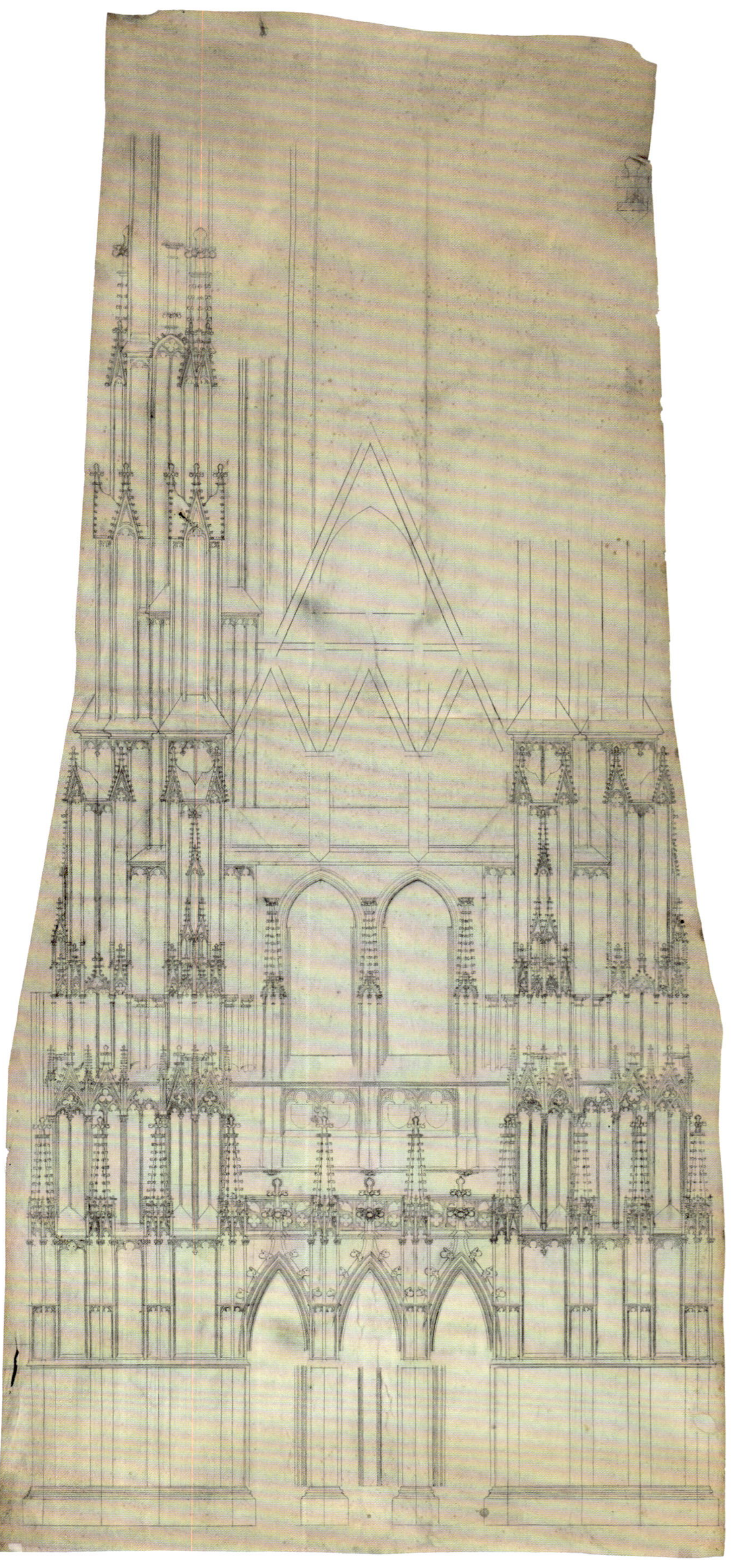

PLATE 12
Attributed to Peter von Prachatitz. Partial Elevation of the South Tower of the Stephansdom
(Saint Stephen's Cathedral), Vienna, ca. 1400–1410

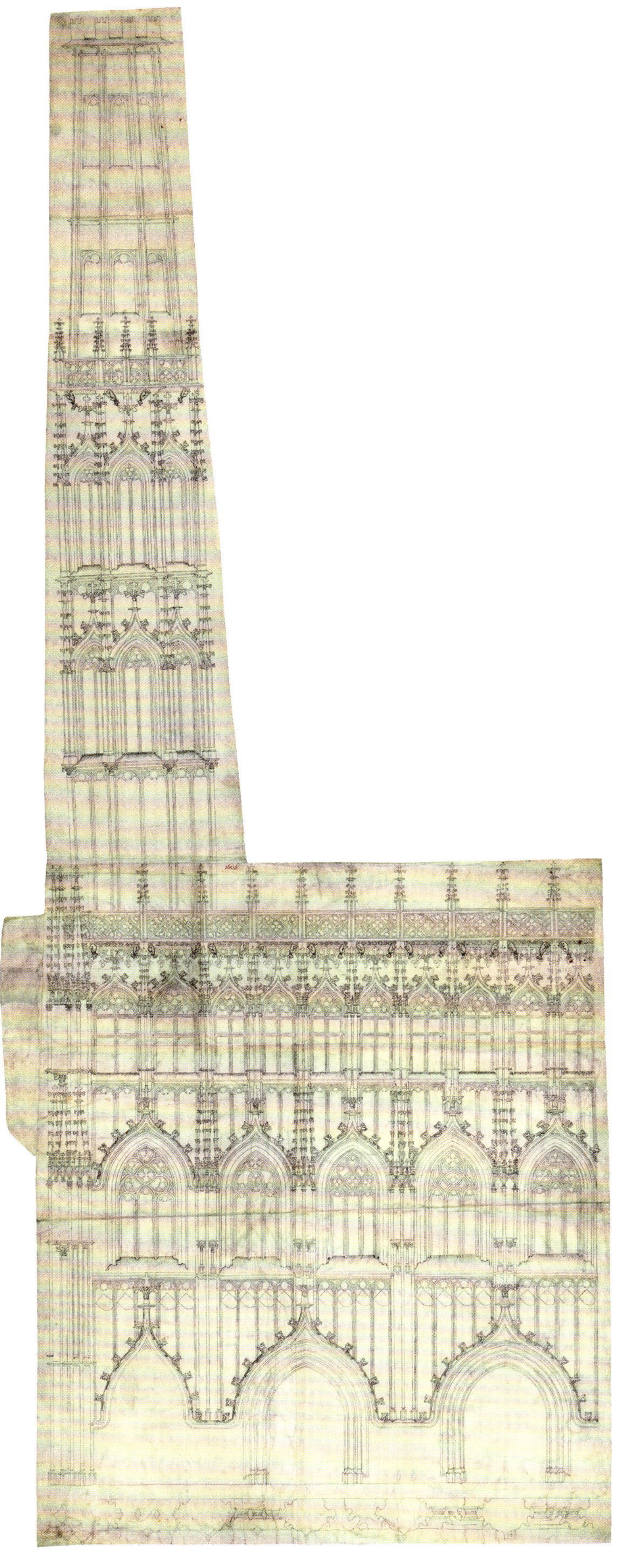

PLATE 13

Lorenz Spenning. Design with an Elevation for the Town Hall of Vienna, ca. 1455

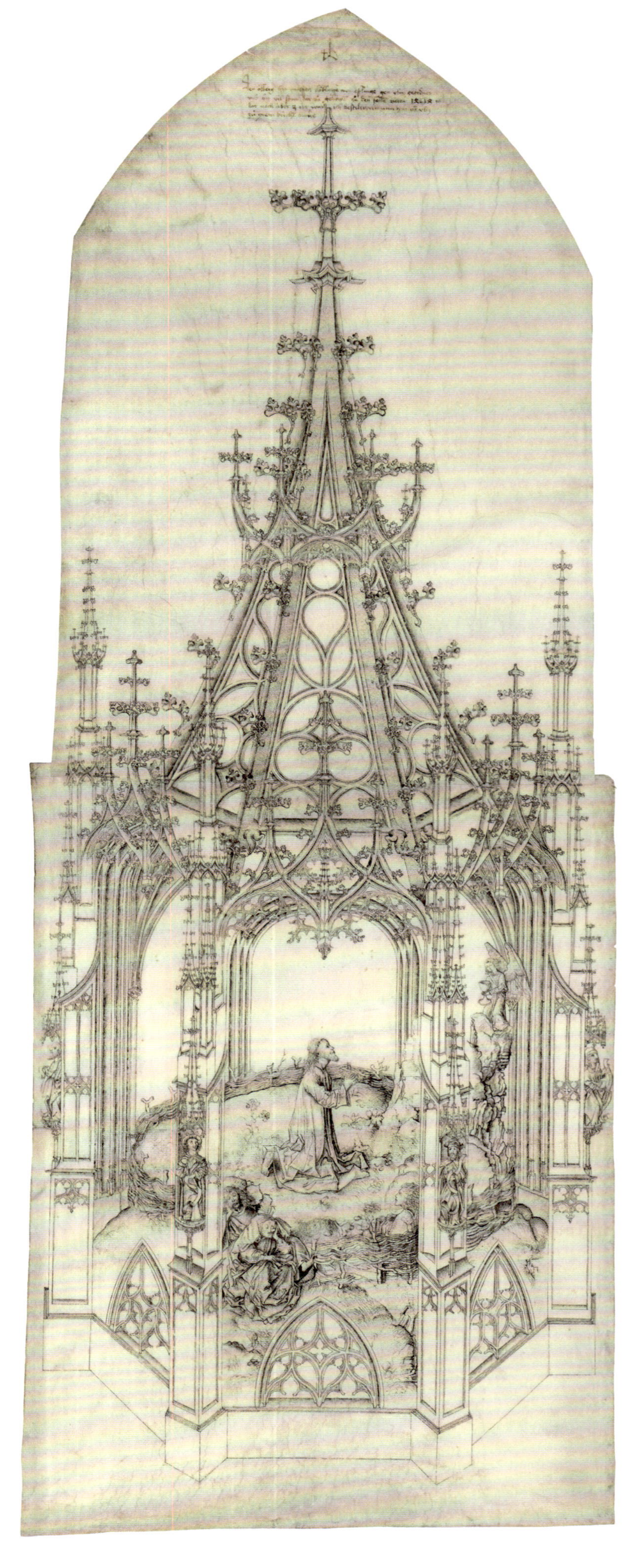

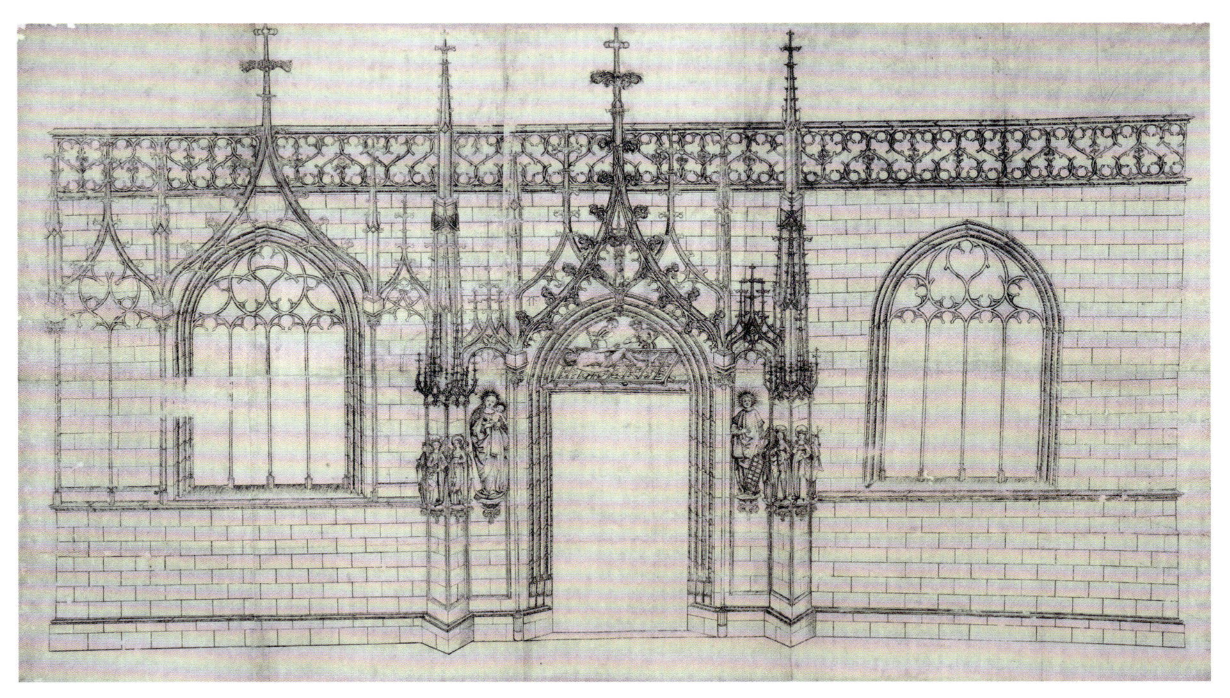

PLATE 14
Matthäus Böblinger. Design for a Mount of Olives Monument for the City of Ulm, 1474

PLATE 15
Jakob von Landshut. Design for the Saint Lawrence Portal on the North Side of Strasbourg
Cathedral, 1494

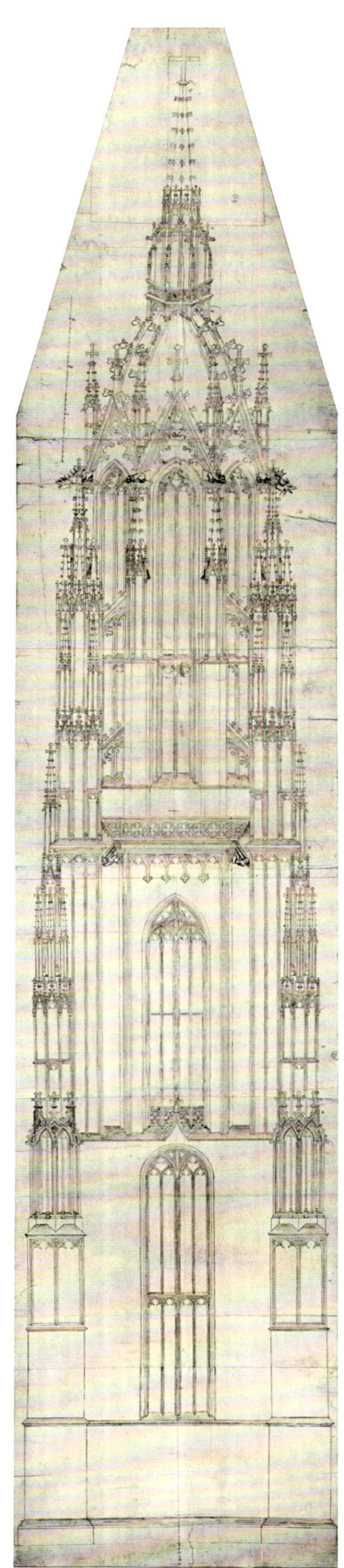

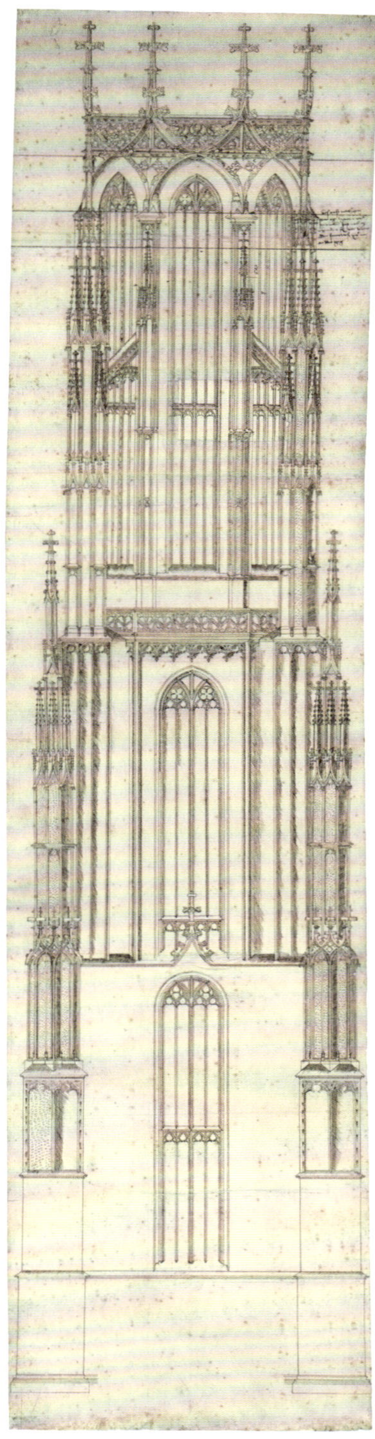

Michael Kurtze, possibly after Madern Gerthener. Elevation of the Tower of the Dom (imperial cathedral) in Frankfurt am Main (Drawing A), 1434–38

Nicolaus Quecke. Elevation of the Tower of the Dom (imperial cathedral) in Frankfurt am Main (Drawing C), ca. 1494–97

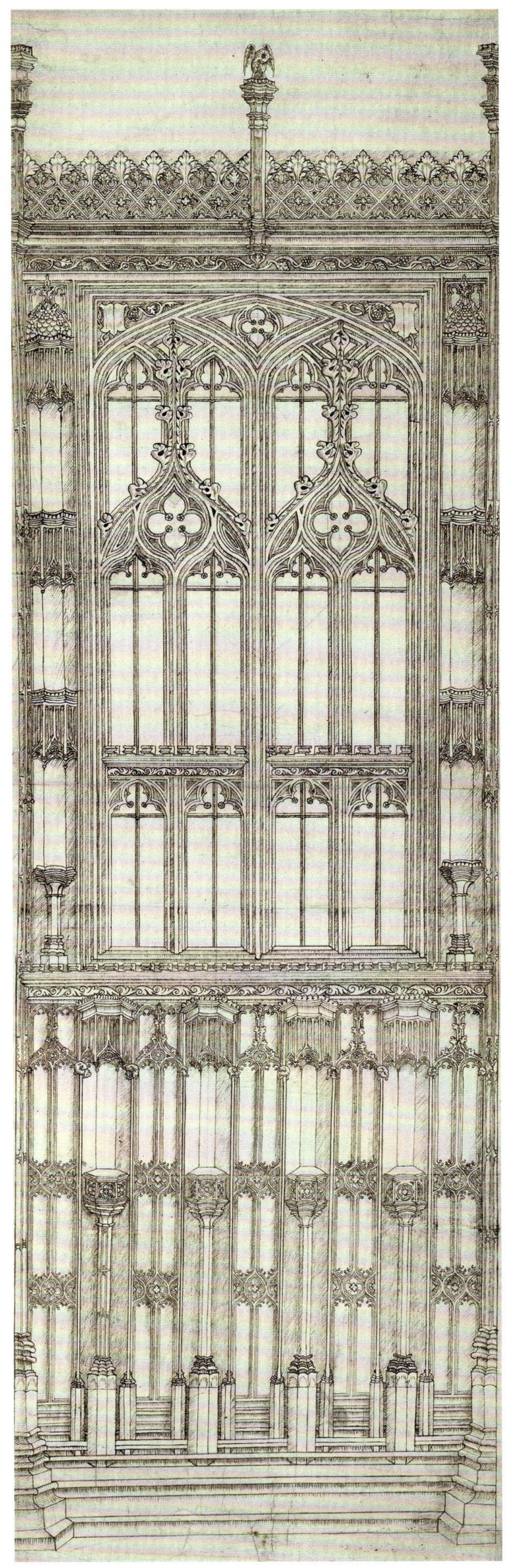

Unidentified English artist, after a design by Humphrey Coke and William Vertue. Elevation of One Bay of Bishop Fox's Chantry in Winchester Cathedral, ca. 1508

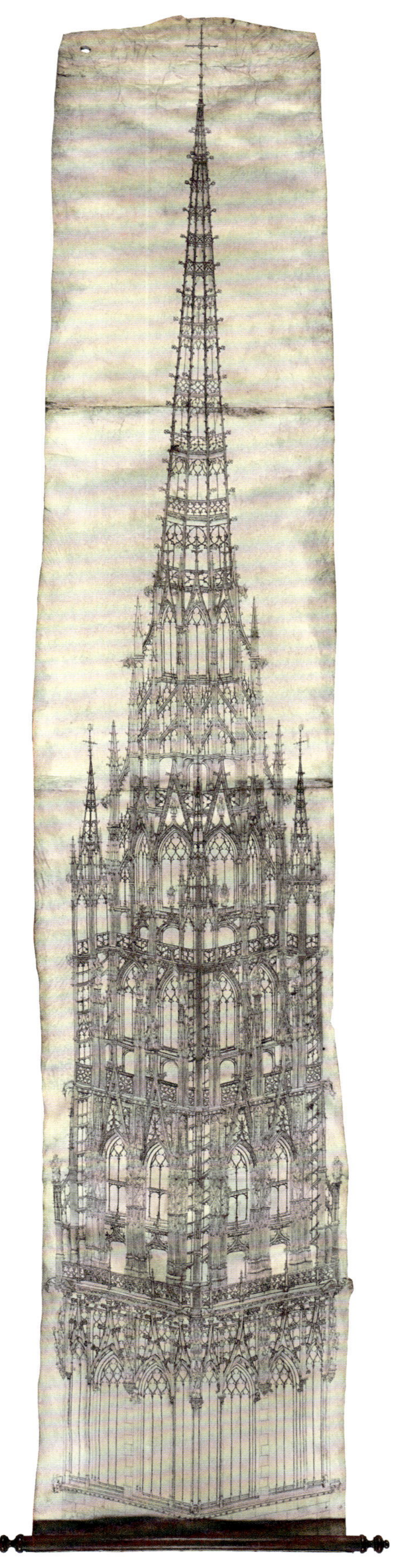

PLATE 19

Attributed to Roulland Le Roux, probably with Pierre des Aubeaux. Design for the Crossing Tower of Rouen Cathedral, 1516; later wood spool

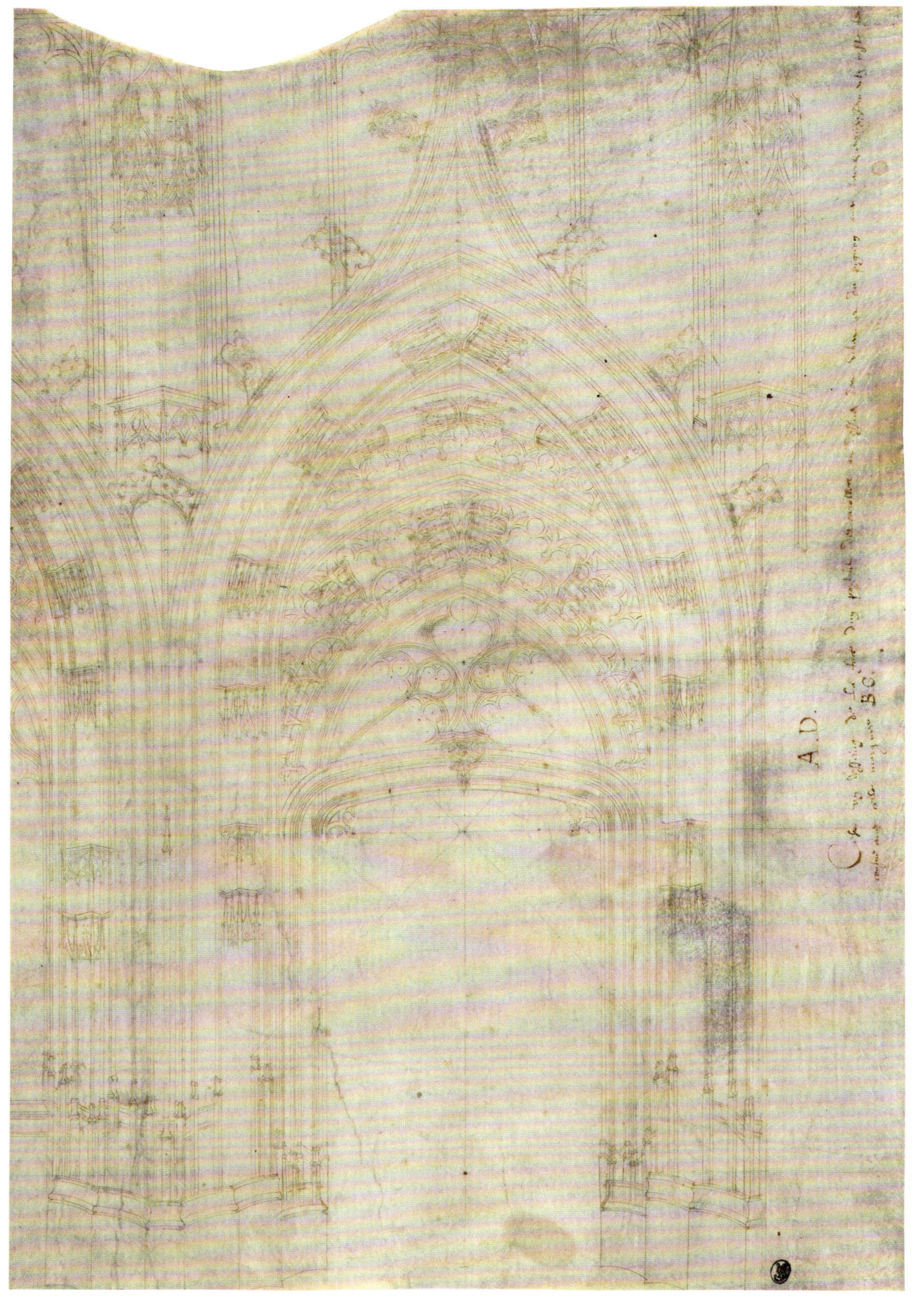

PLATE 20

Unidentified French artist. Fragment of a Facade Elevation with an Entrance Portal, ca. 1450–75

Attributed to Rombout II Keldermans. Design for the Palace of the Great Council in Mechelen,
ca. 1525

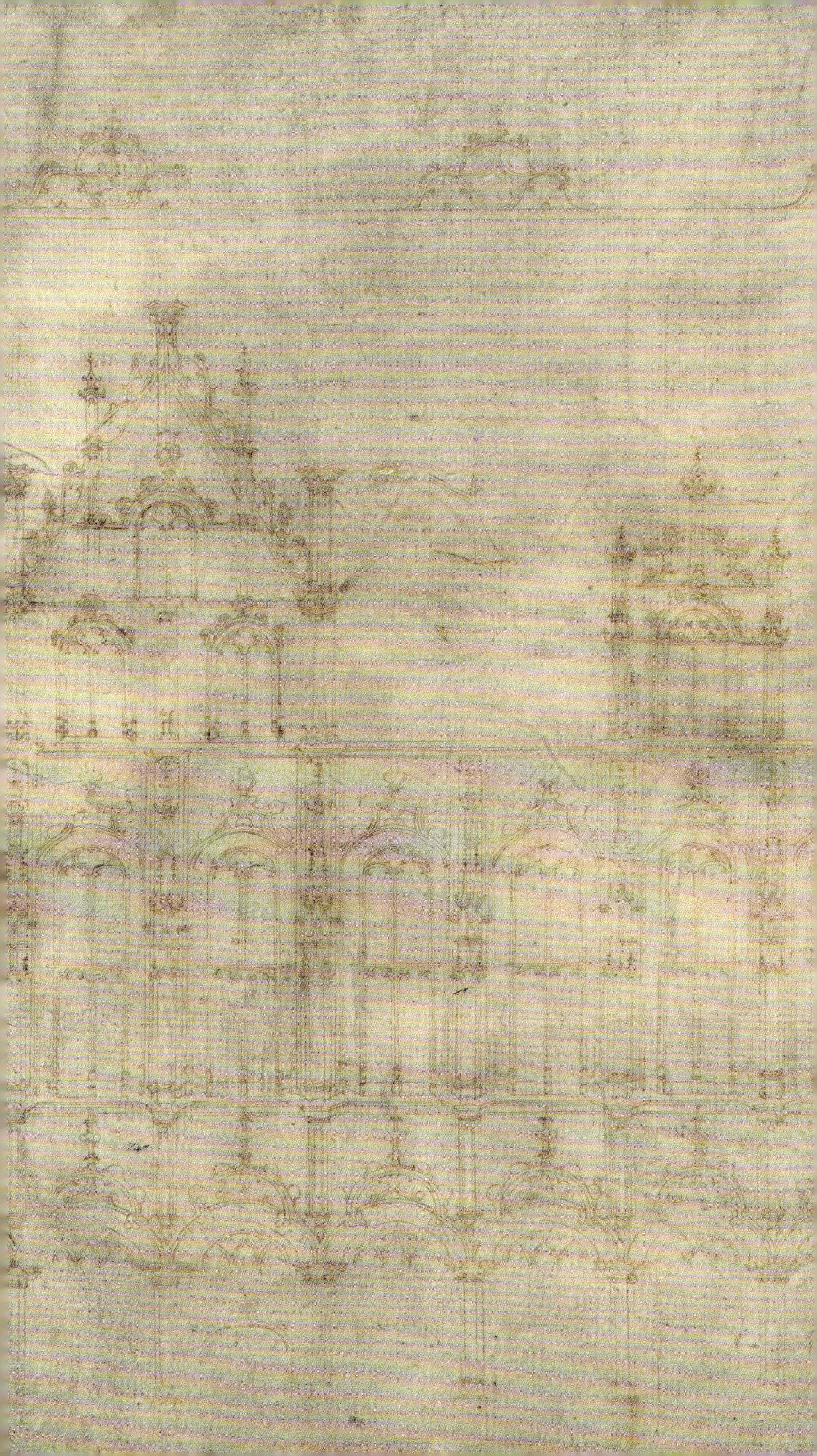

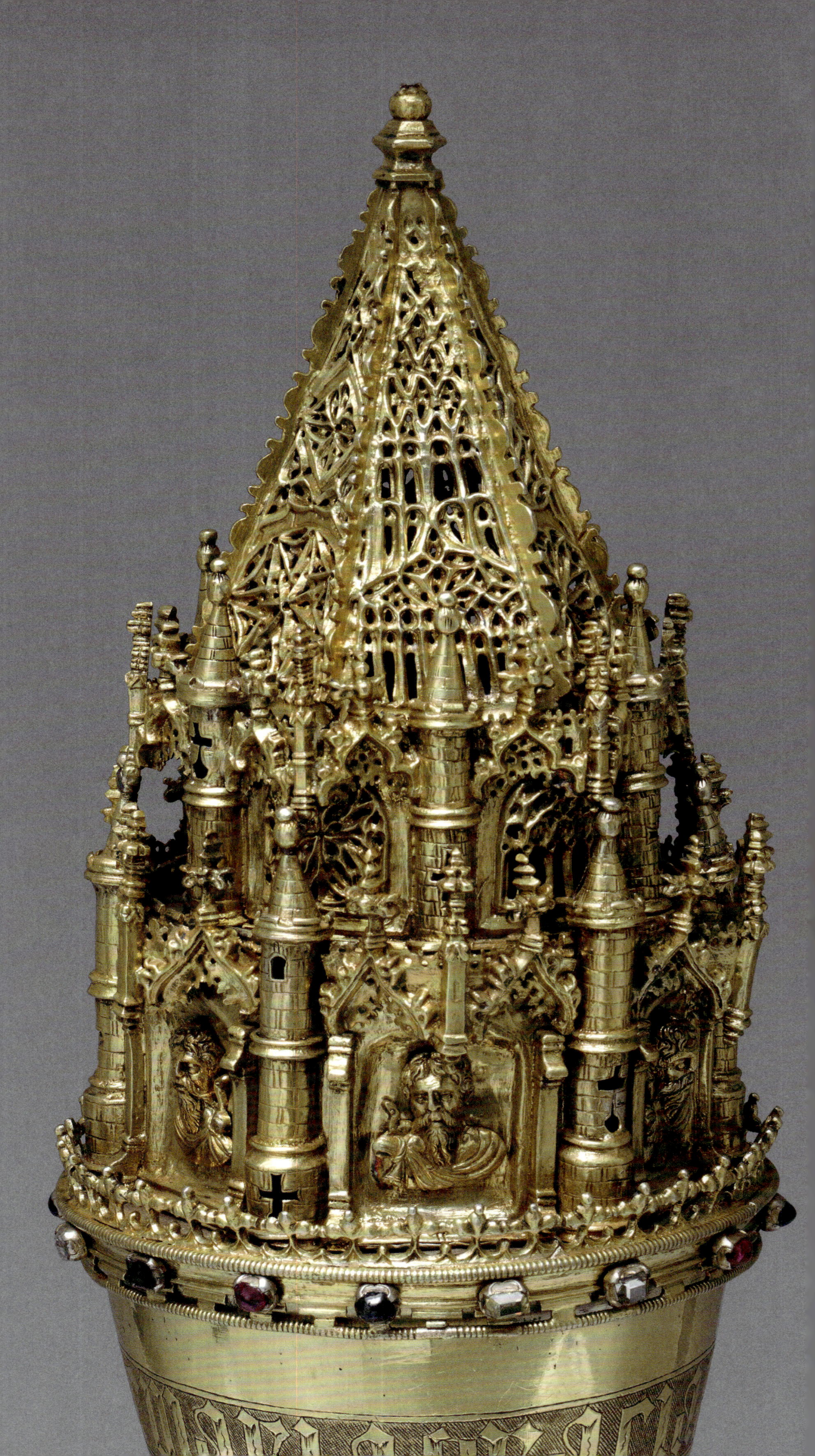

Scaled Architecture

From the thirteenth century onward, the architectural vocabulary that we associate with the imposing cathedrals of the Gothic tradition also began to influence the design of works of art of vastly different scales. The incorporation of architectural elements in freestanding monuments, secular and nonsecular furniture, statuary, stained glass, and precious objects of various kinds was not an entirely new phenomenon, but previously such designs were generally modeled after much older prototypes that did not resemble the style of the buildings in which they were housed.[1]

The art historian James Bugslag suggested a direct link between this shift toward the use of a more contemporary architectural vocabulary and the widespread adoption of scaled architectural drawings in the building process. He argued that the portability of parchment drawings allowed for new designs to be shared more readily with artists from other workshops. Moreover, he proposed that the scaled-down drawings of architectural elements facilitated their translation to objects of smaller size. Beyond these benefits, Bugslag also alluded to a more profound effect: Namely, that there was a direct correlation between the act of making drawings and the emergence of the Gothic tradition as an all-encompassing style. The preliminary phase of design, which took place away from the actual building site, introduced a pivotal moment of holistic reflection that resulted in a greater stylistic uniformity between the architectural exterior and everything one might encounter once inside.[2]

Certainly not everything in a church interior came about as part of a unified design concept (a so-called *Gesamtentwurf*). However, the idea that various artists sought to create a harmonious aesthetic experience through architectural assimilation offers a more constructive way of thinking across media than do traditional categorizations based on size, whereby monumental cathedrals and their smaller counterparts (from goldsmith's work to pulpits and sacrament houses) have been classified, respectively, as macro- and microarchitecture. This method of distinction does not always make sense. For one, the same person could create designs for works in both categories.[3] In addition, immense variation could occur within each of these sweeping categories, and even among objects of a similar function. For example, had they been built, the modest turriform monument in Johannes Weckerlin's drawing would have been dwarfed by Lorenz Lechler's sacrament house, with its projected sixty feet in height (PLS. 22, 25).[4] Moreover, deviations in scale could occur even within a single structure. The art historian Jacob Burckhardt, for example, characterized the graduating diminution of a tapering baldachin (like that of Lechler's sacrament house) as resembling "housing for ever-smaller figures" (*Gehäuse für kleine und kleinere Figuren*).[5]

The notion of size per se (whether something is big or small) does not seem to have factored into the medieval aesthetic experience of art objects. Instead, descriptions from the period emphasize the variety, complexity, and accomplishment of the object at hand. The technical difficulty of scaling certain elements up or down to a size that best suited the object also inspired admiration. For this reason, a carefully worked prayer nut or small piece of goldsmith's work could be just as captivating and awe-inspiring as a monumental cathedral.[6] Following this logic, it is almost surprising that the idea, found in a print by the South Netherlandish Master W with the Key, to outfit a censer with gargoyles and flying buttresses seems to be the only one of its kind (PL. 32). The engravings by this prolific fifteenth-century printmaker and several of his contemporaries demonstrate the effectiveness of designing

on parchment and paper as a tool to visualize scalar transforma-
tions. Baldachins and canopies are effortlessly transplanted from
designs for architectural structures, such as chapels and niches,
to small-scale objects like monstrances, censers, croziers, and
morses (vestment clasps) (SEE PLS. 31, 34, 35, 37, 40). The
prints simultaneously formed a welcome outlet for a designer's
creativity and offered inspiration for the other artists (or patrons)
who collected them. Each sheet individually contains numerous
ideas that could be implemented, substituted, simplified, or elaborated upon. A comparison of several such sheets could further
amplify this creative process by suggesting permutations of form
in a manner similar to the iterative exercise drawings that master-
masons-in-training made to learn how to introduce variation.[7]

These sources of inspiration were especially welcome in cities
with large and/or multiple centers of devotion. For example, a
Viennese booklet from 1502 (a so-called *Heiligtumsbuch*) details
that the treasury of the Stephansdom (Saint Stephen's Cathedral) alone contained 255 relics, each preserved individually in a
custom-made, richly adorned reliquary, as befit its holy contents
(PL. 38). Their splendor was meant to incite the veneration of
spectators during masses, processions, or when glimpsed through
the latticework enclosure of a sacrament house.[8] The woodcut re-
productions of these precious vessels in the *Heiligtumsbuch* are by
no means exact. Yet, in their multitude, they nevertheless perfectly
illustrate the primacy of architectural form in Gothic design. As
the art historian Johann Michael Fritz observed, amid the "concert
of different voices" that informed the design of goldsmith's work
during this period, architecture steadfastly played "first violin."[9]

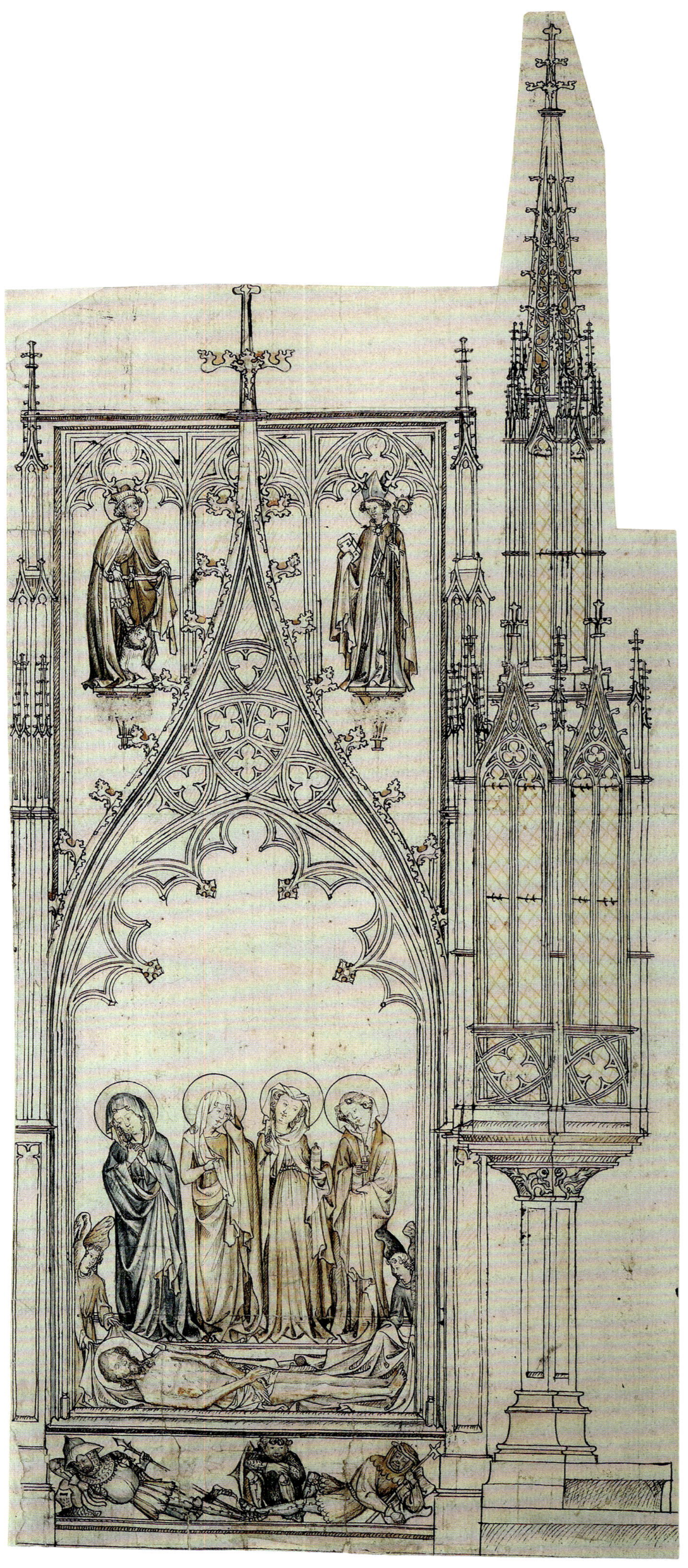

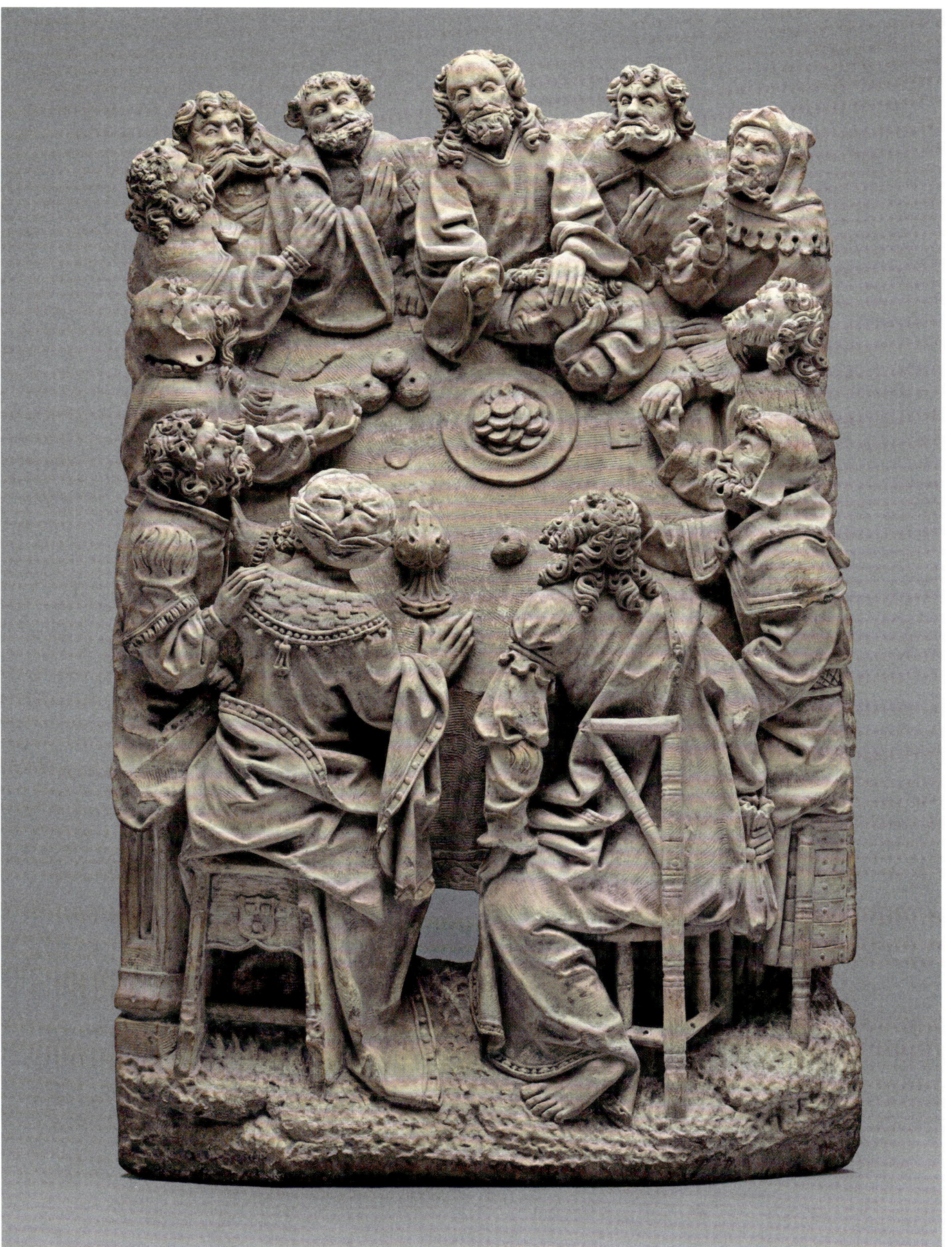

Attributed to Johannes Weckerlin. Funerary Monument and *Totenleuchter* (Memorial Lantern) or Sacrament House, ca. 1420–40

Unidentified German or South Netherlandish artist. The Last Supper, ca. 1500–1530

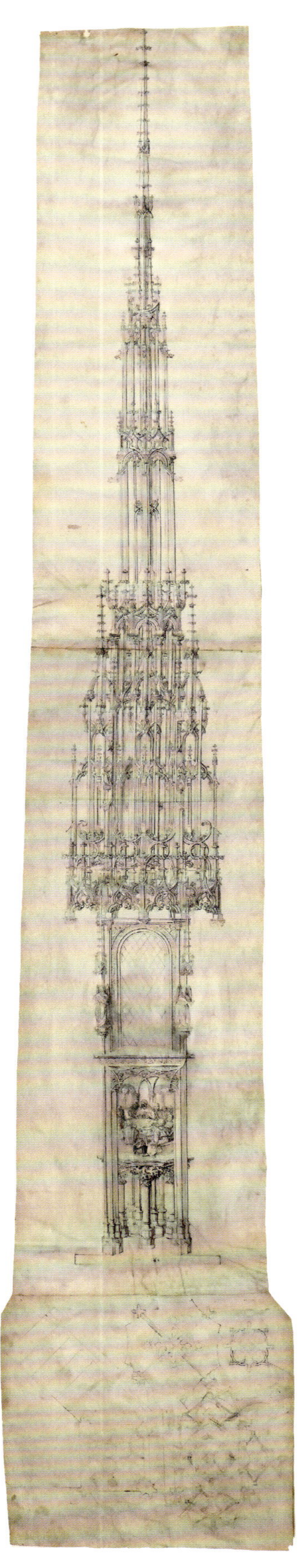

PLATE 24

Attributed to Jörg Seld. Design for a Sacrament House with the Last Supper, 1514

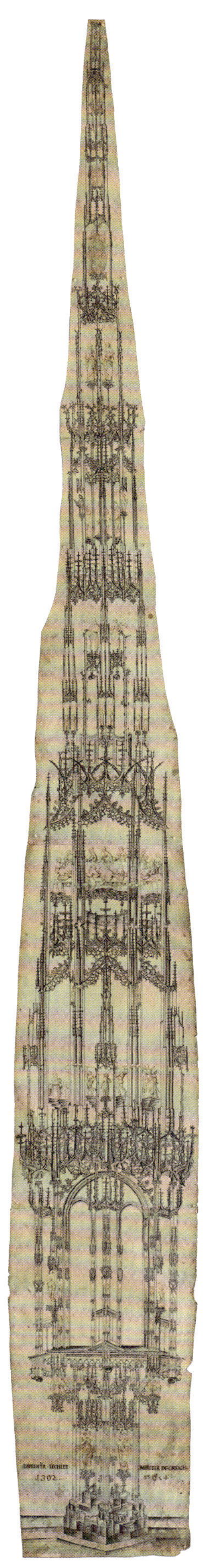

PLATE 25

Lorenz Lechler and unidentified Central European artist. Design for a Monumental Sacrament House, 1502; additional inscription 17th century

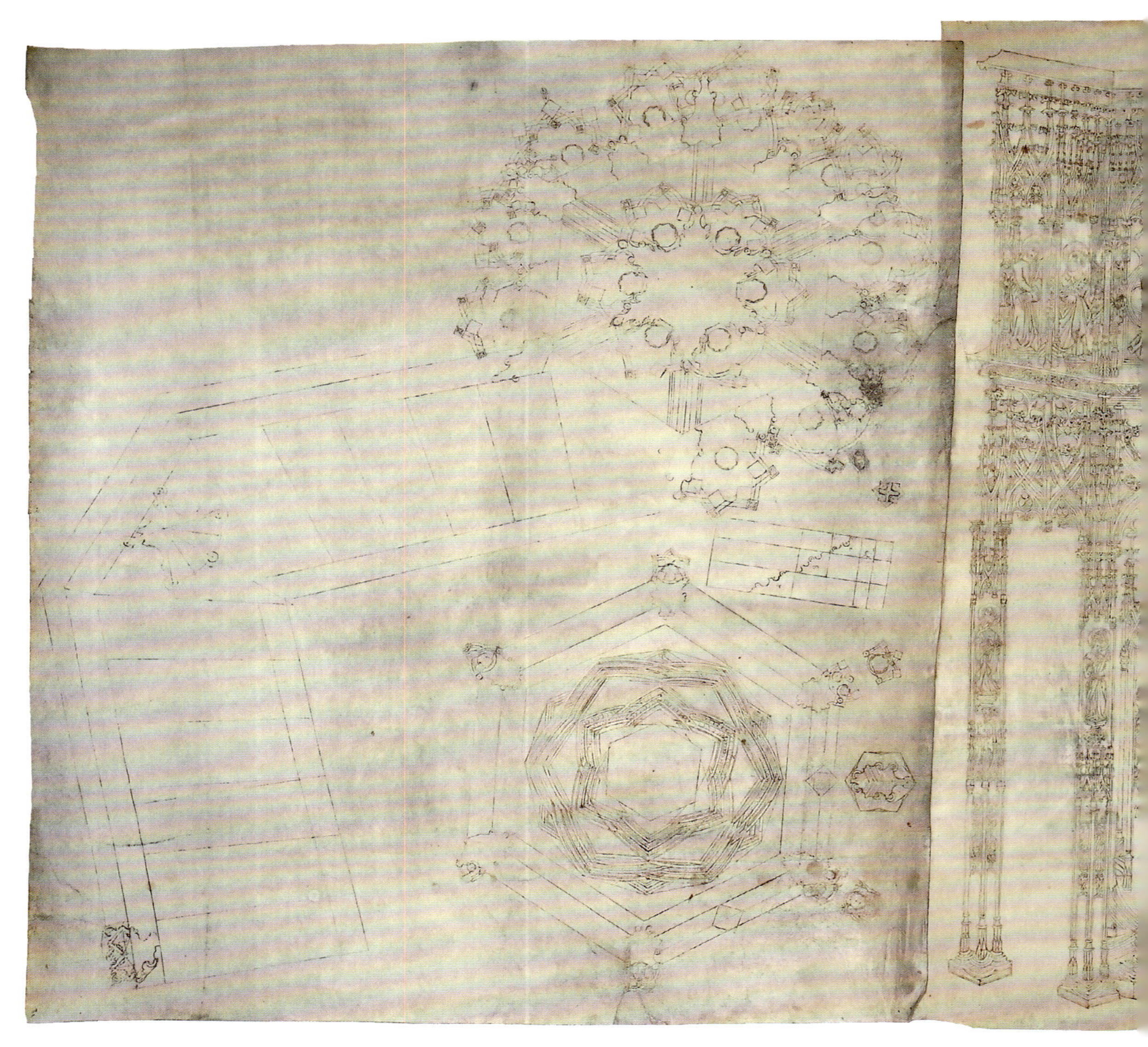

Hans Hammer. Elevation and Plans for the Pulpit of Strasbourg Cathedral, 1484

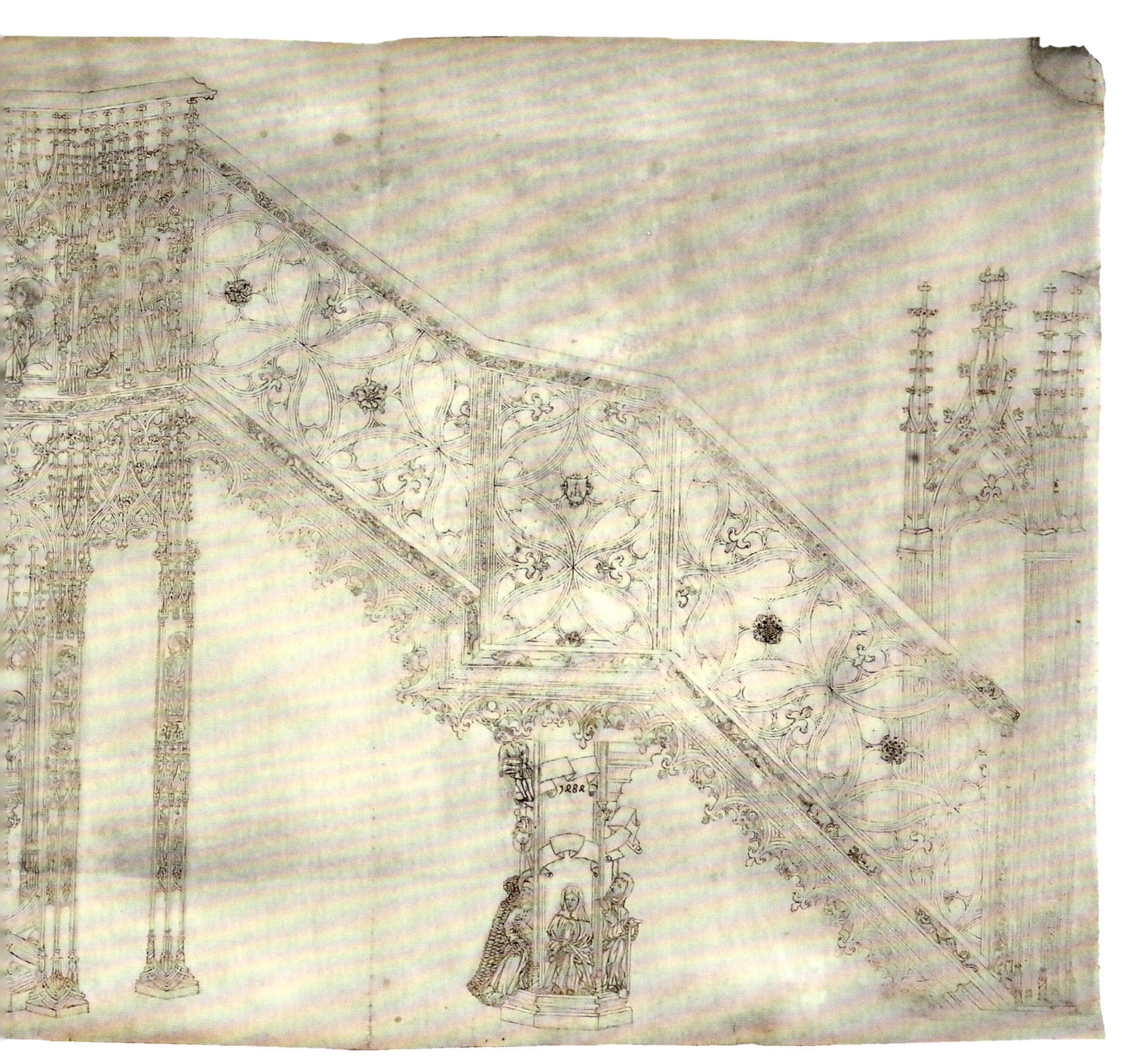

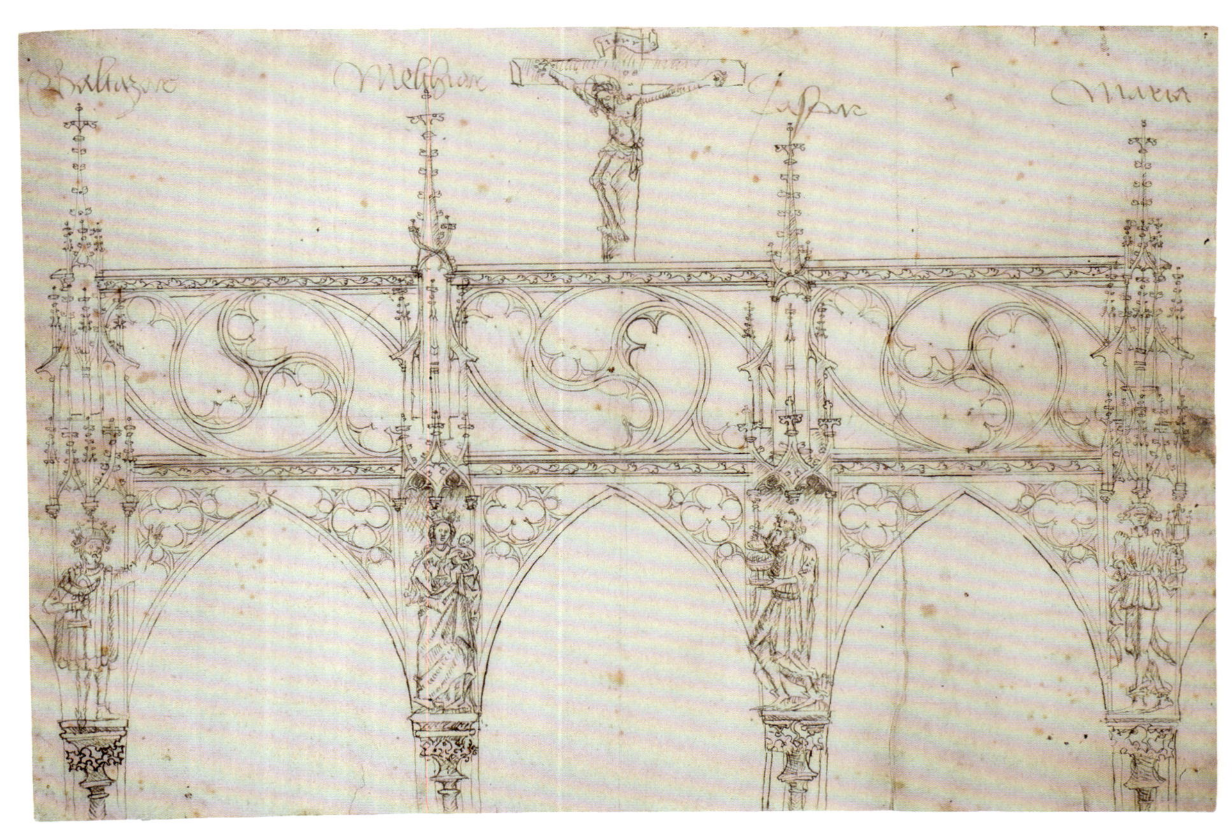

PLATE 27
Attributed to Madern Gerthener or Jost Schilder. Design for a Rood Screen, ca. 1420–50

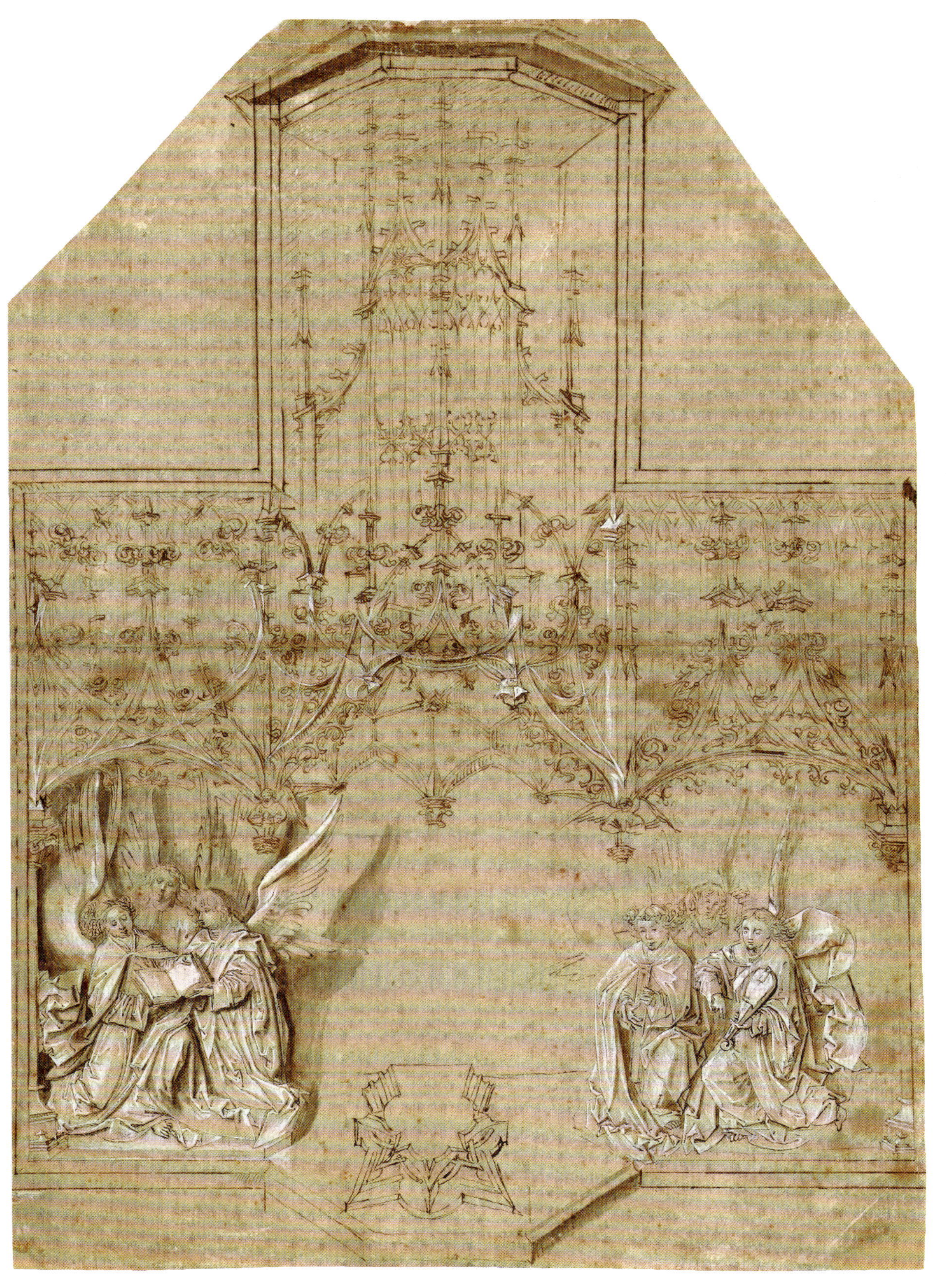

Attributed to Master of the Drapery Studies. Design for an Altar with Angels, ca. 1480–90

119

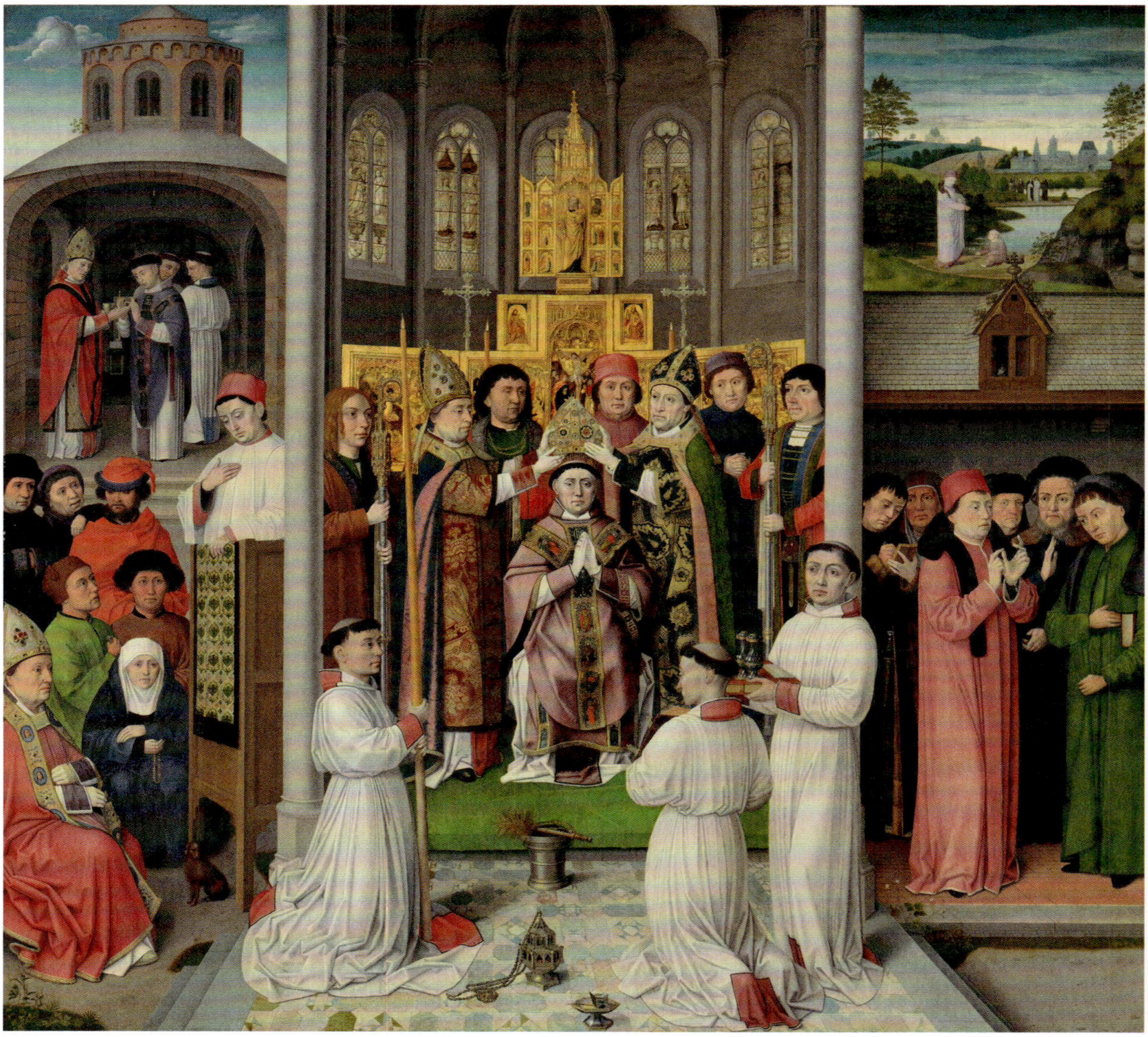

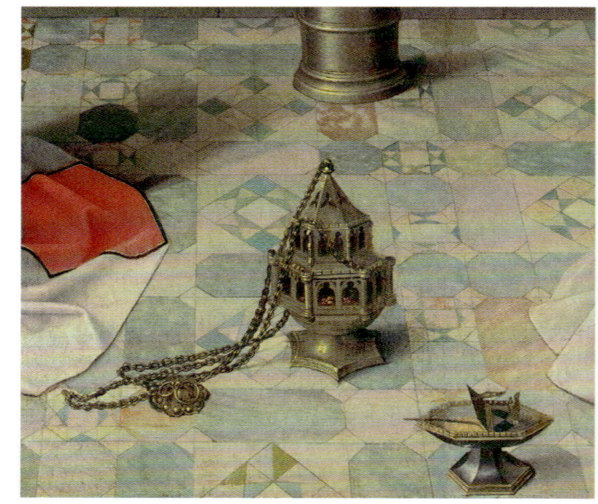

PLATE 29

Master of Saint Augustine. Scenes from the Life of Saint Augustine of Hippo, with a Detail of a Censer, ca. 1490

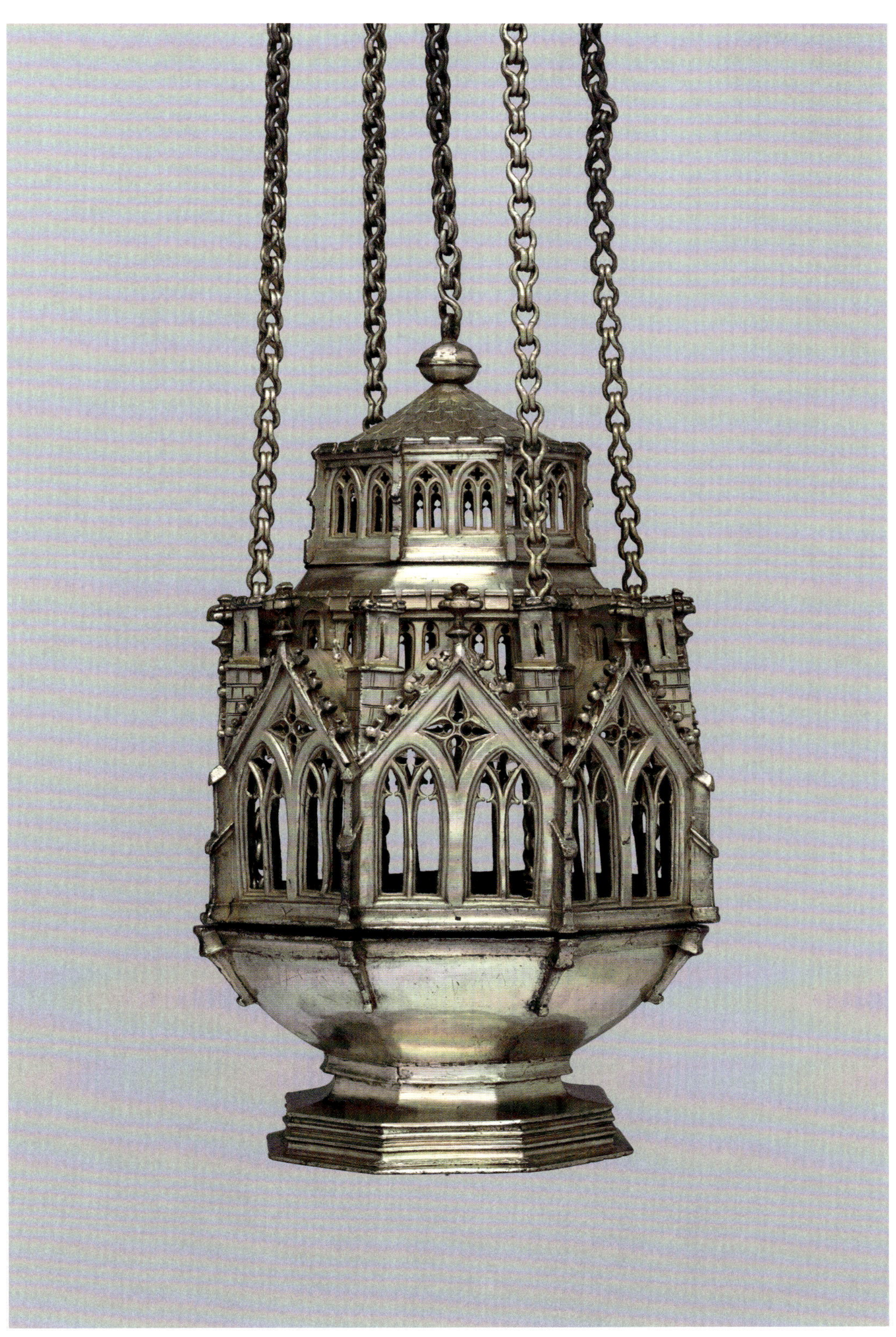

PLATE 30
Unidentified Swiss artist. Censer, before 1477

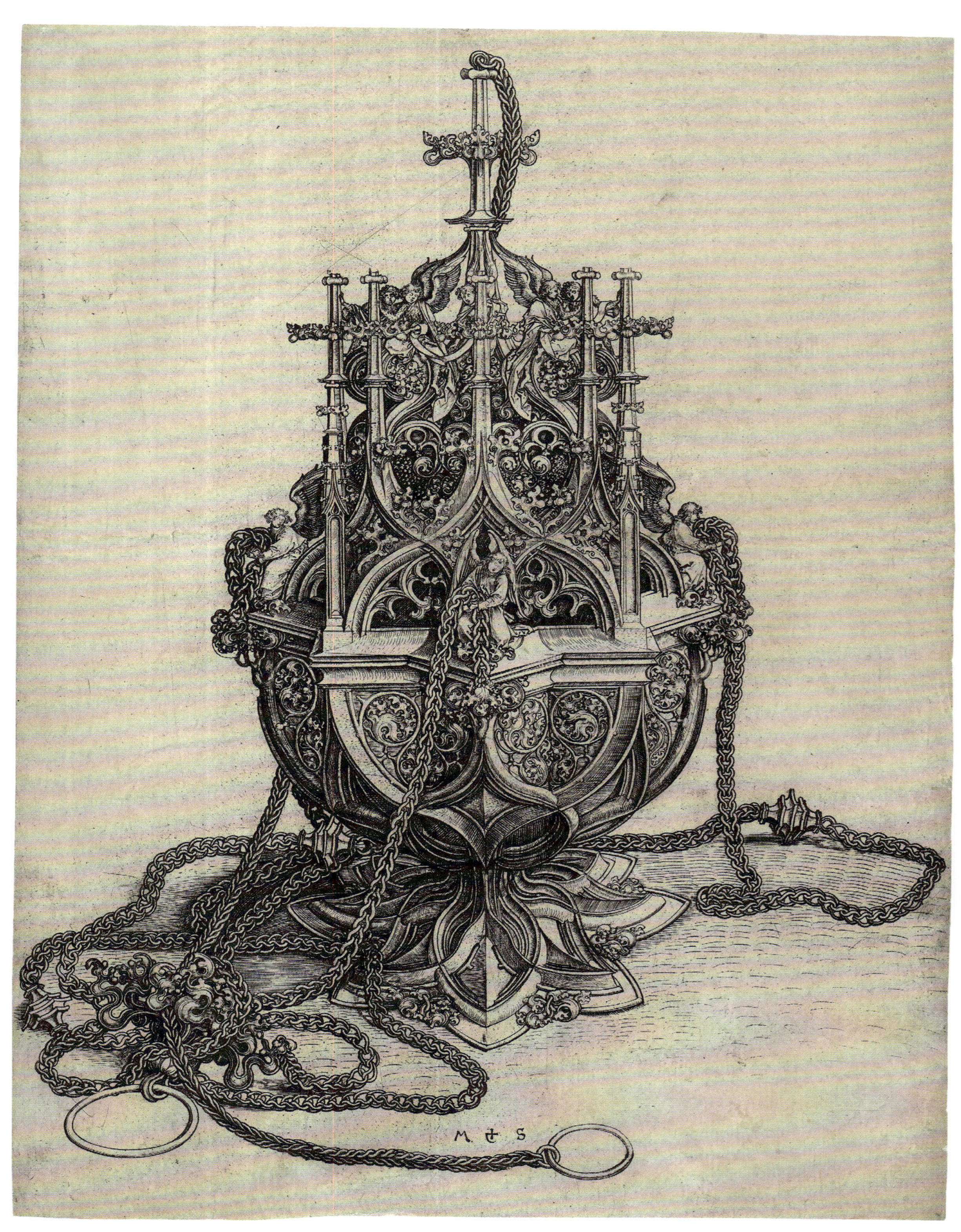

PLATE 31
Martin Schongauer. *The Censer*, 1470–91

122

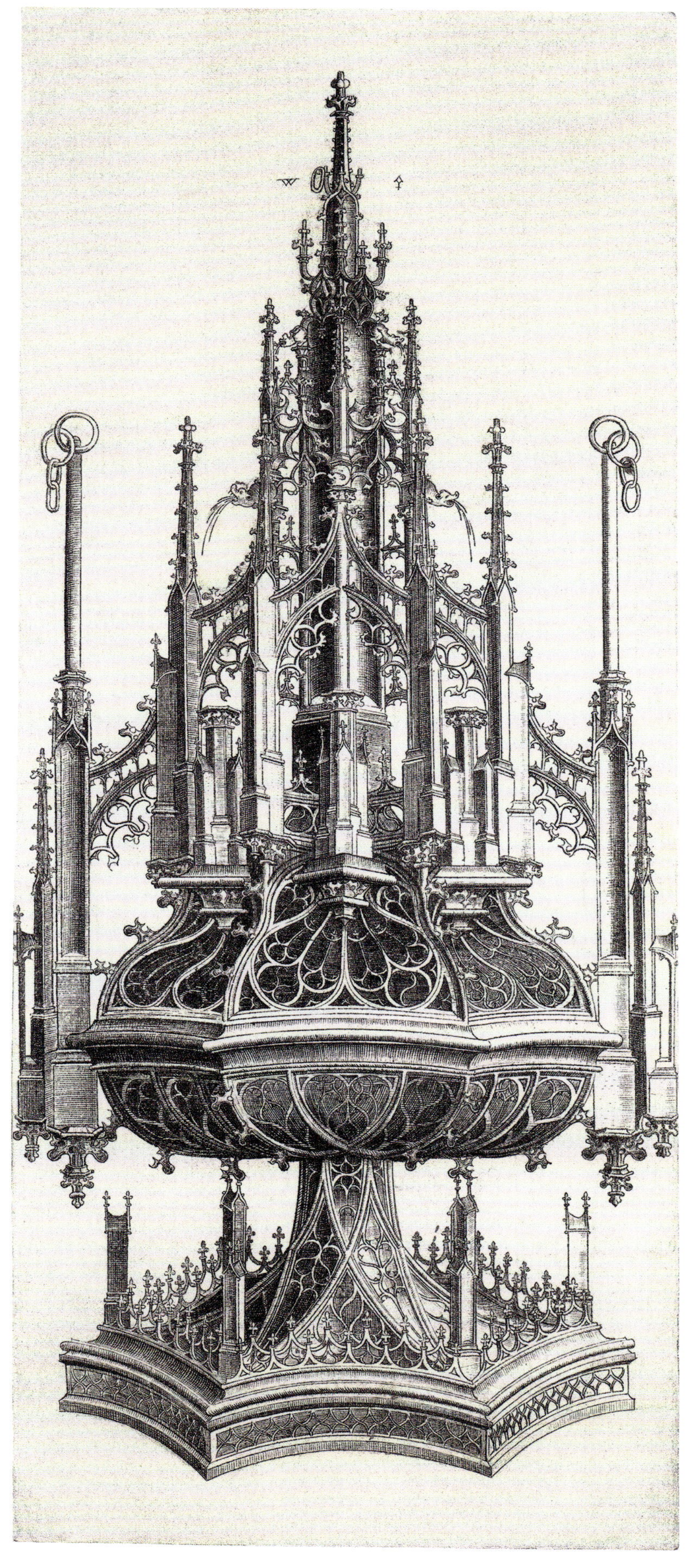

PLATE 32

Master W with the Key. Design for a Censer, ca. 1480–90

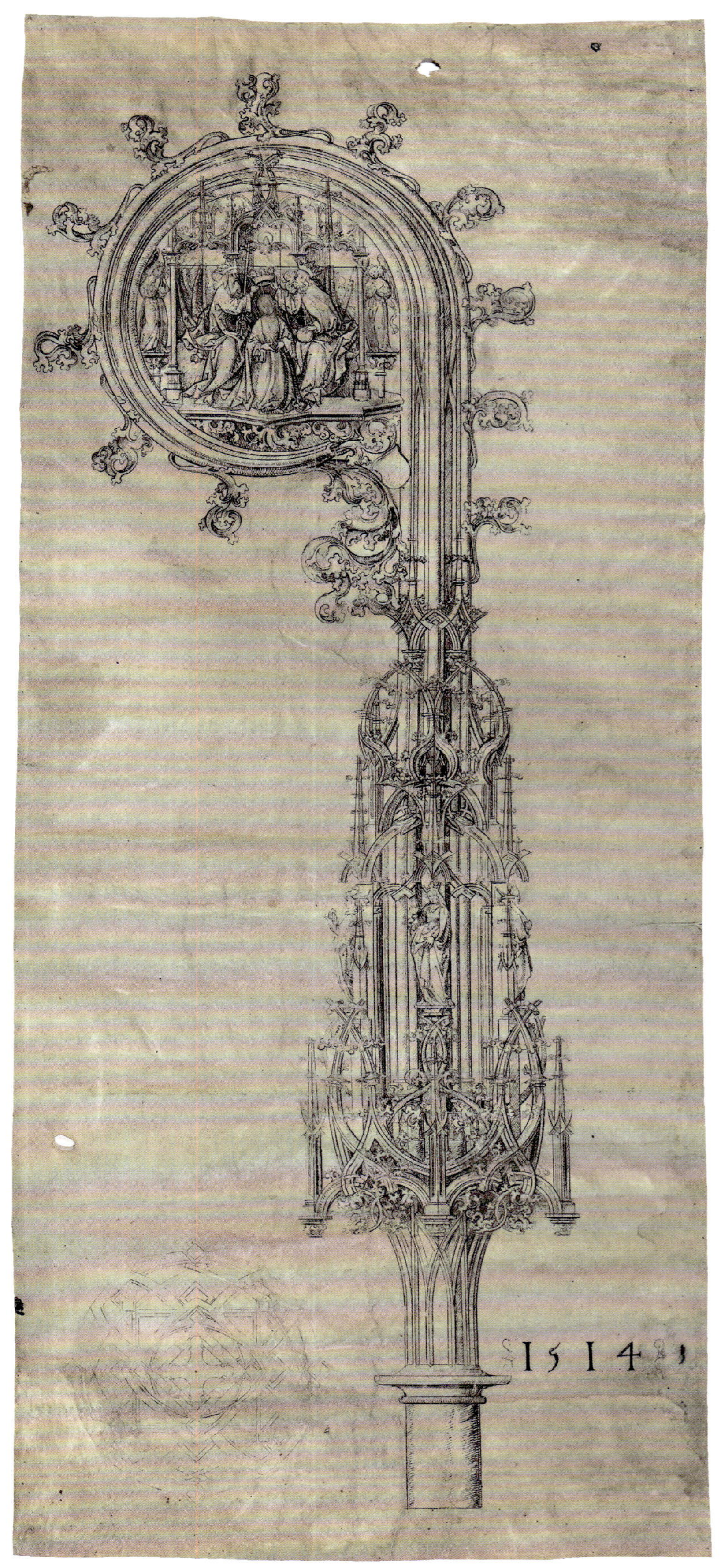

PLATE 33
Hans Holbein the Elder, possibly with Jörg Seld. Design for a Crozier with Plan, 1514

124

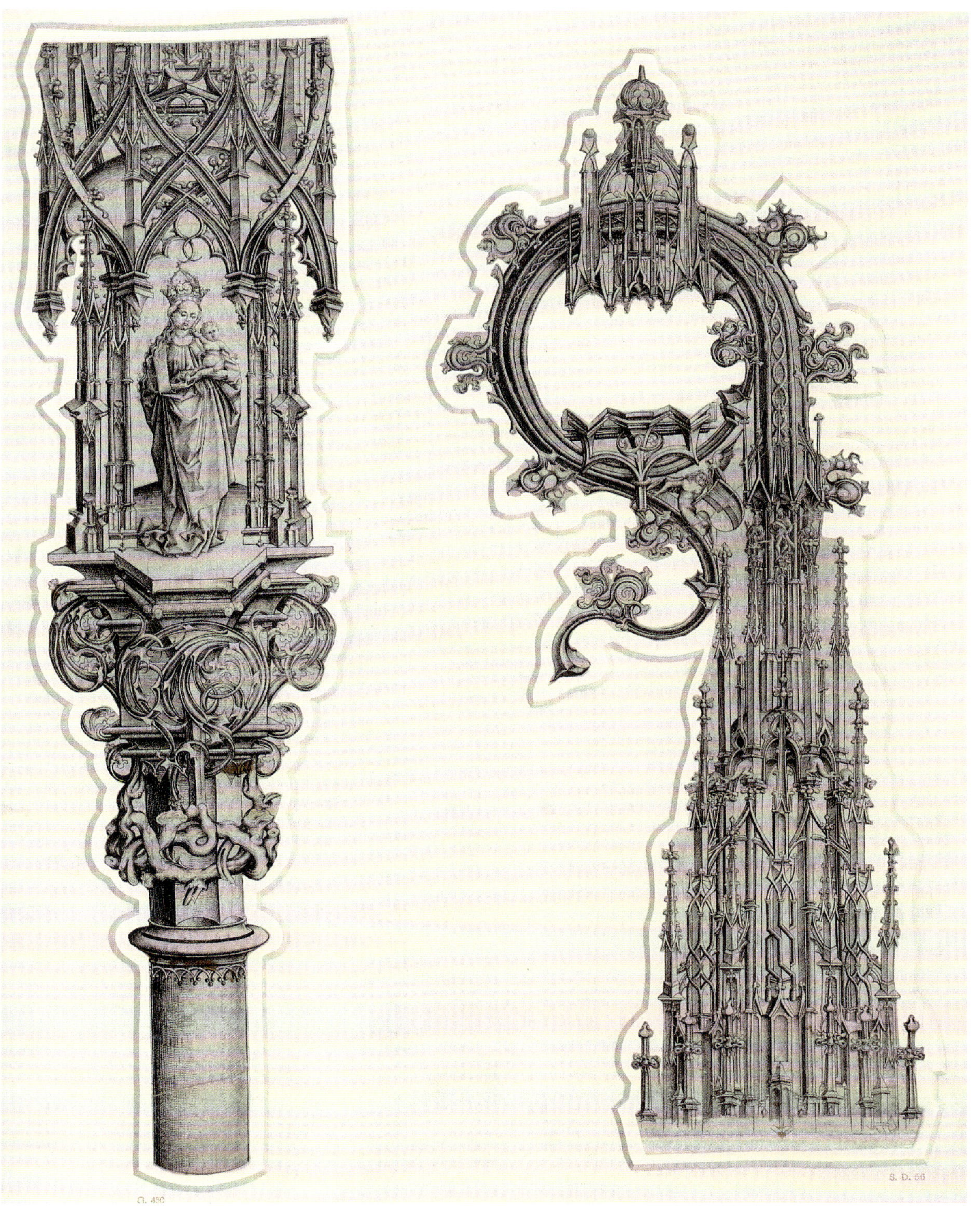

PLATE 34
Israhel von Meckenem. Design for a Crozier (in two parts), with Base (left) and Crook (right),
ca. 1490–1500

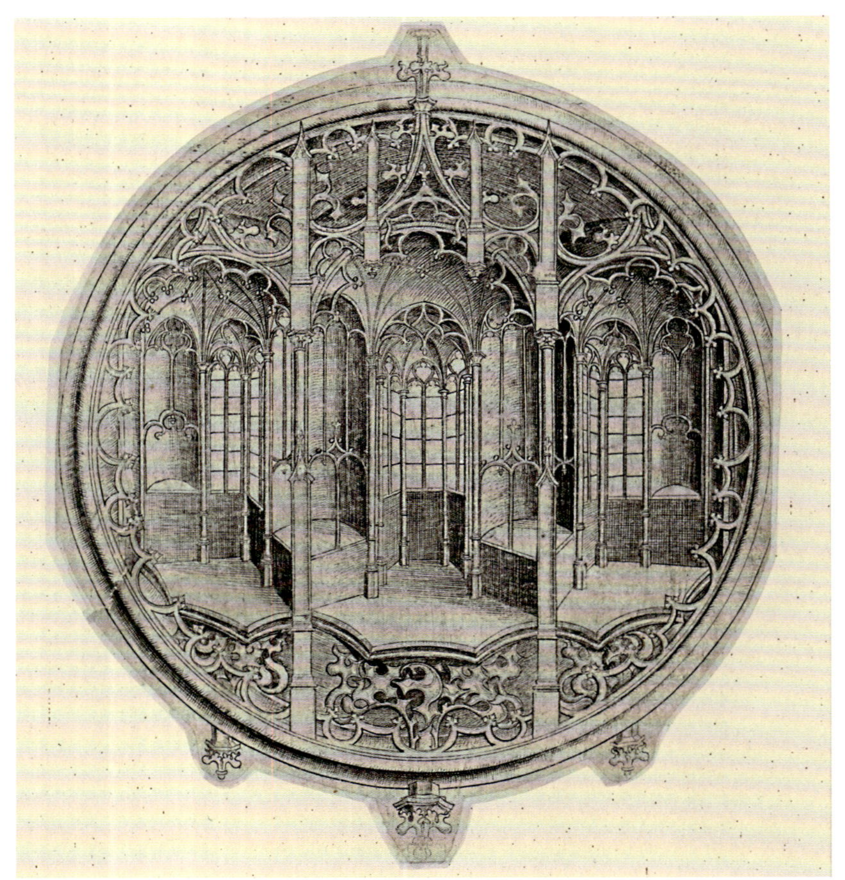

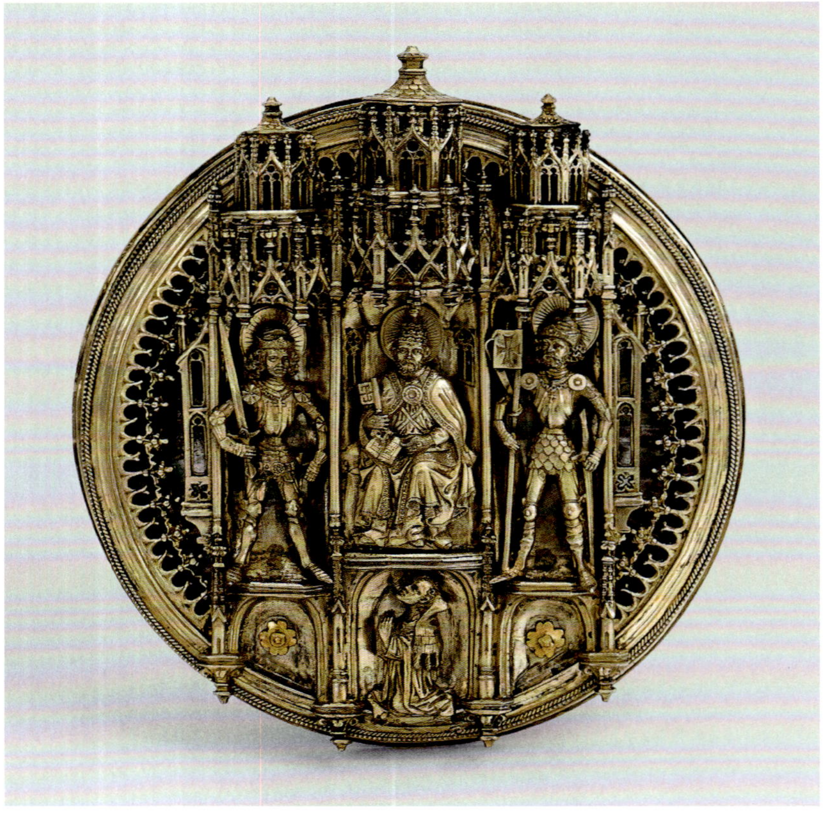

PLATE 35
Master W with the Key. Design for a Morse, ca. 1480–90

PLATE 36
Reinecke vam Dressche. Morse, before 1487

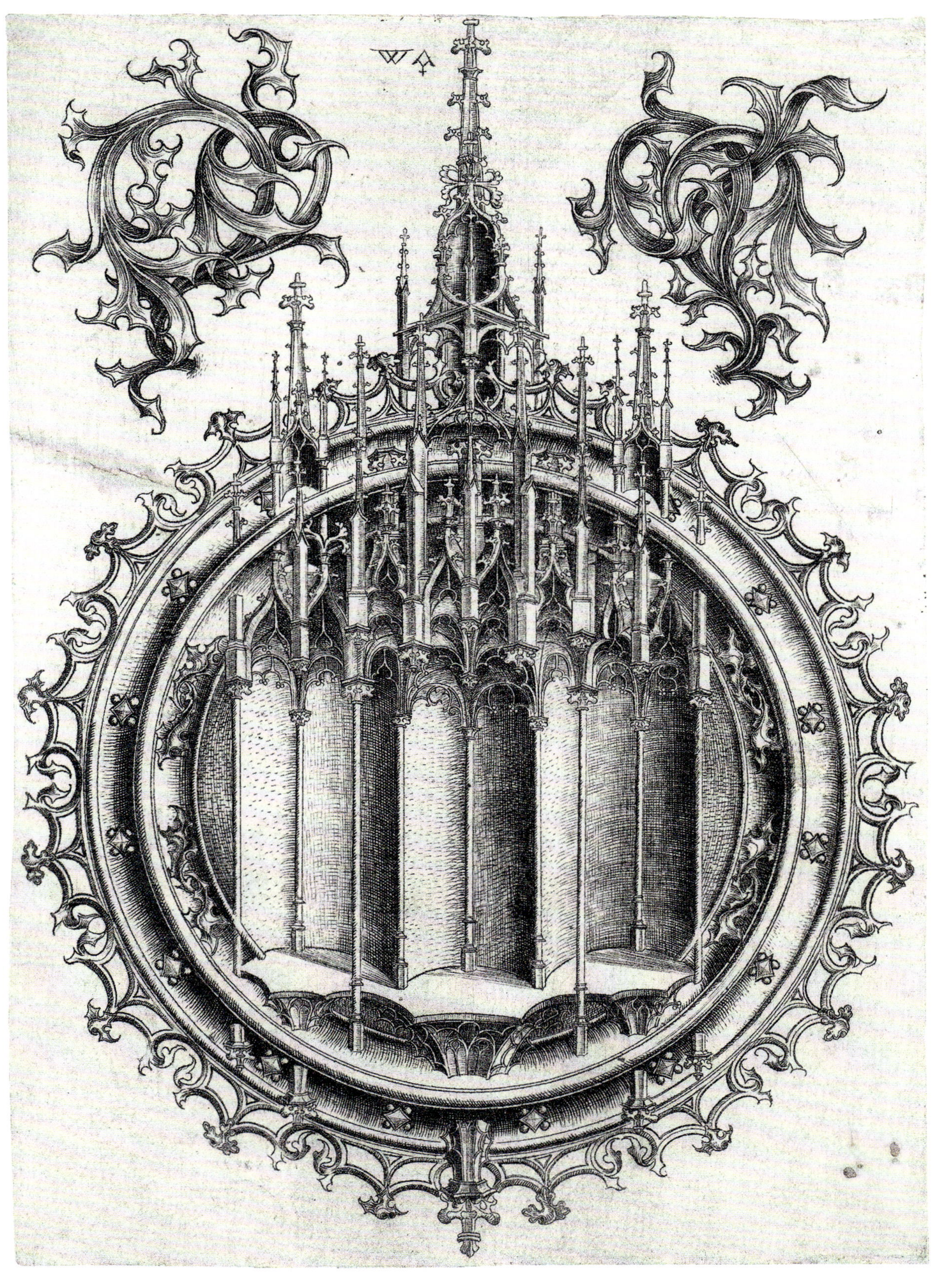

PLATE 37

Master W with the Key. Design for a Morse, ca. 1480–90

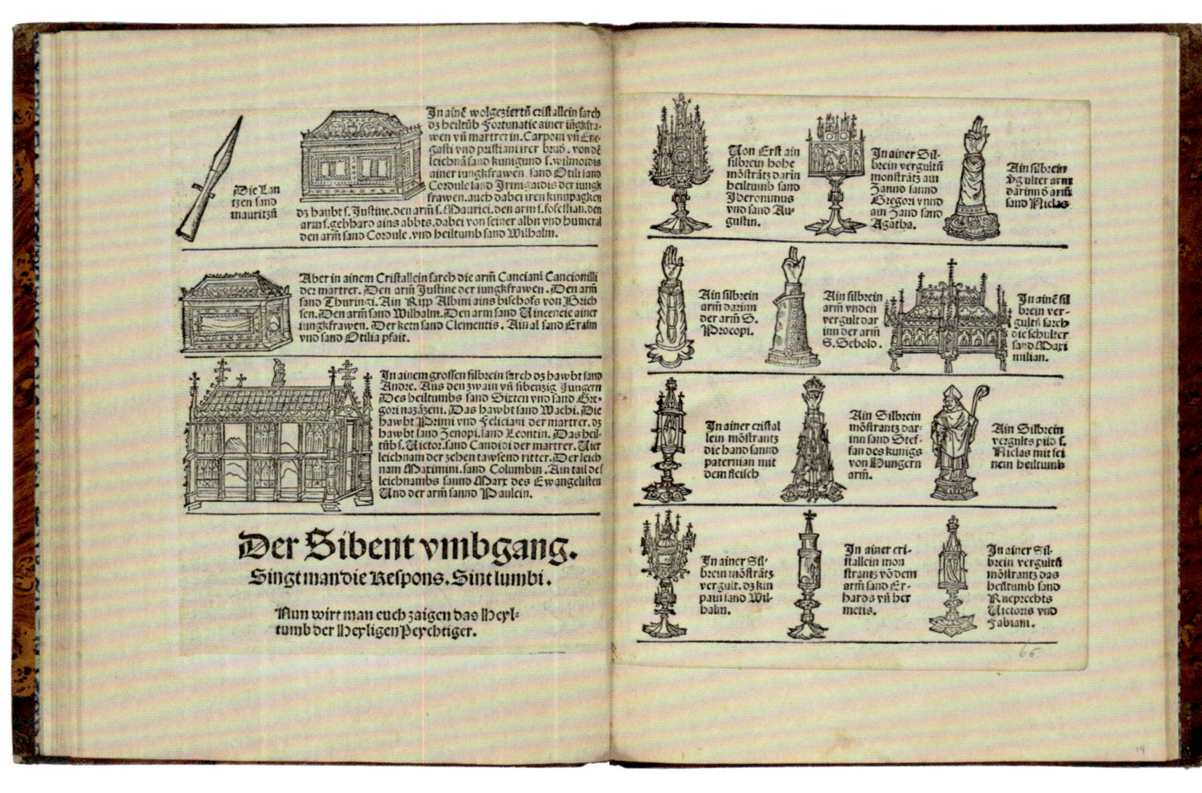

PLATE 38

Relics and Reliquaries, from The Viennese Book of Relics (*Das Wiener Heiligtumsbuch*).
Printed by Johannes Winterburger, Vienna, 1502

PLATE 39

Unidentified Spanish artist. Covered Chalice, late 15th century

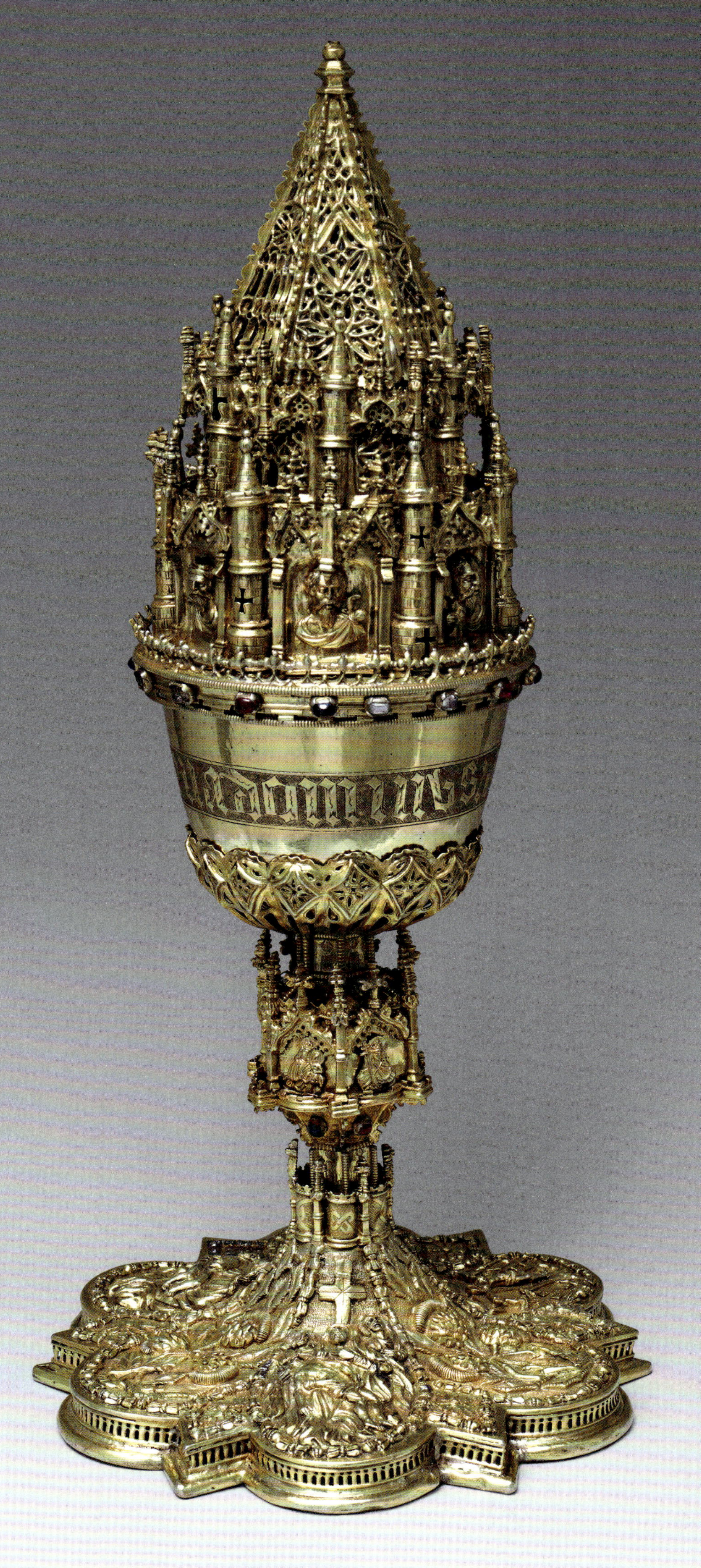

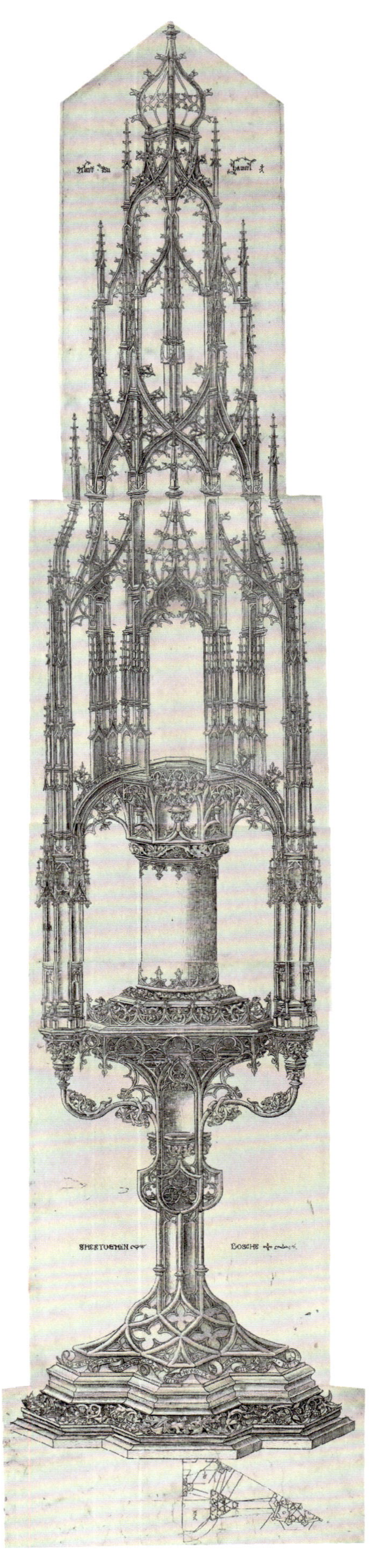

PLATE 40

Alart du Hameel. Design for a Tower Monstrance, ca. 1484

130

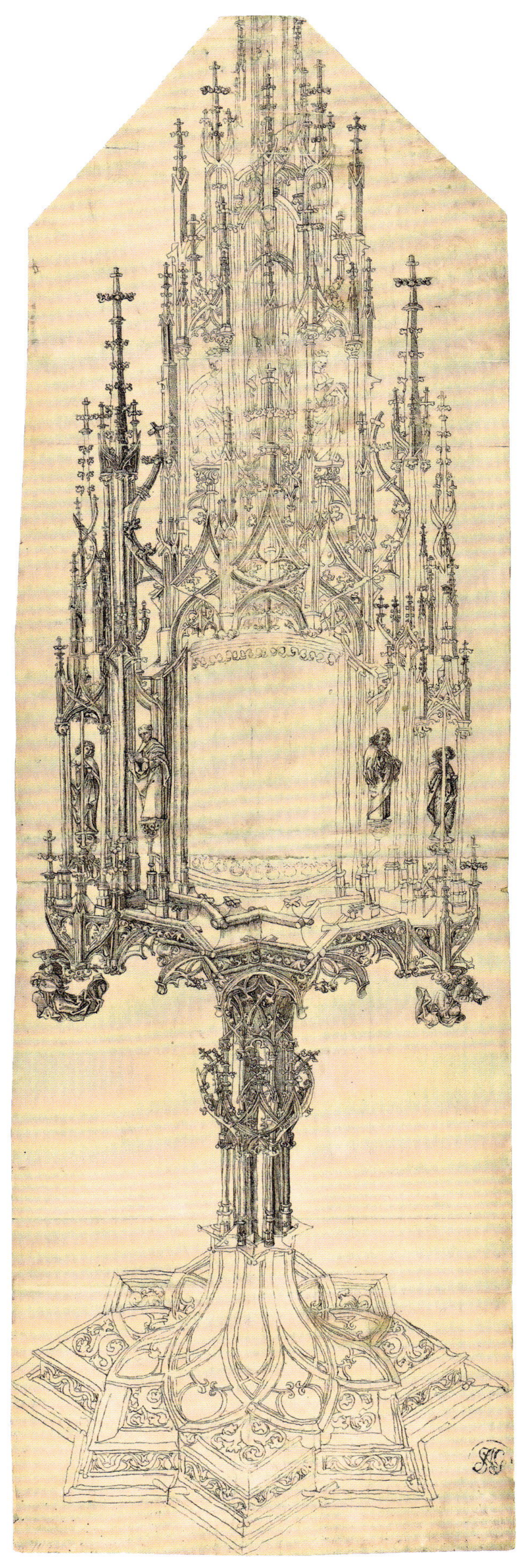

PLATE 41
Jörg Seld. Design for a Tower Monstrance, ca. 1507

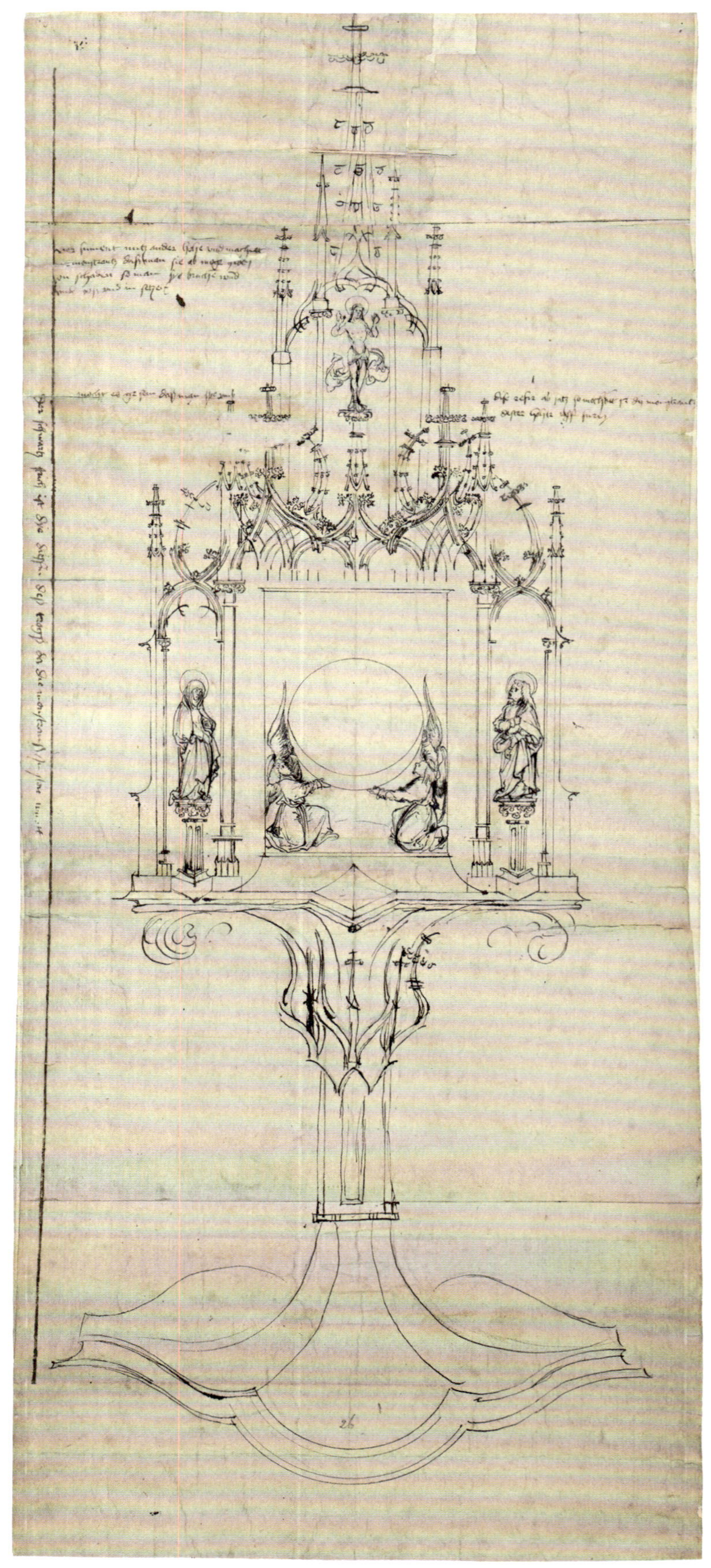

PLATE 42

Circle of Jörg Syrlin the Younger. Design for a Tower Monstrance, ca. 1500–1510

132

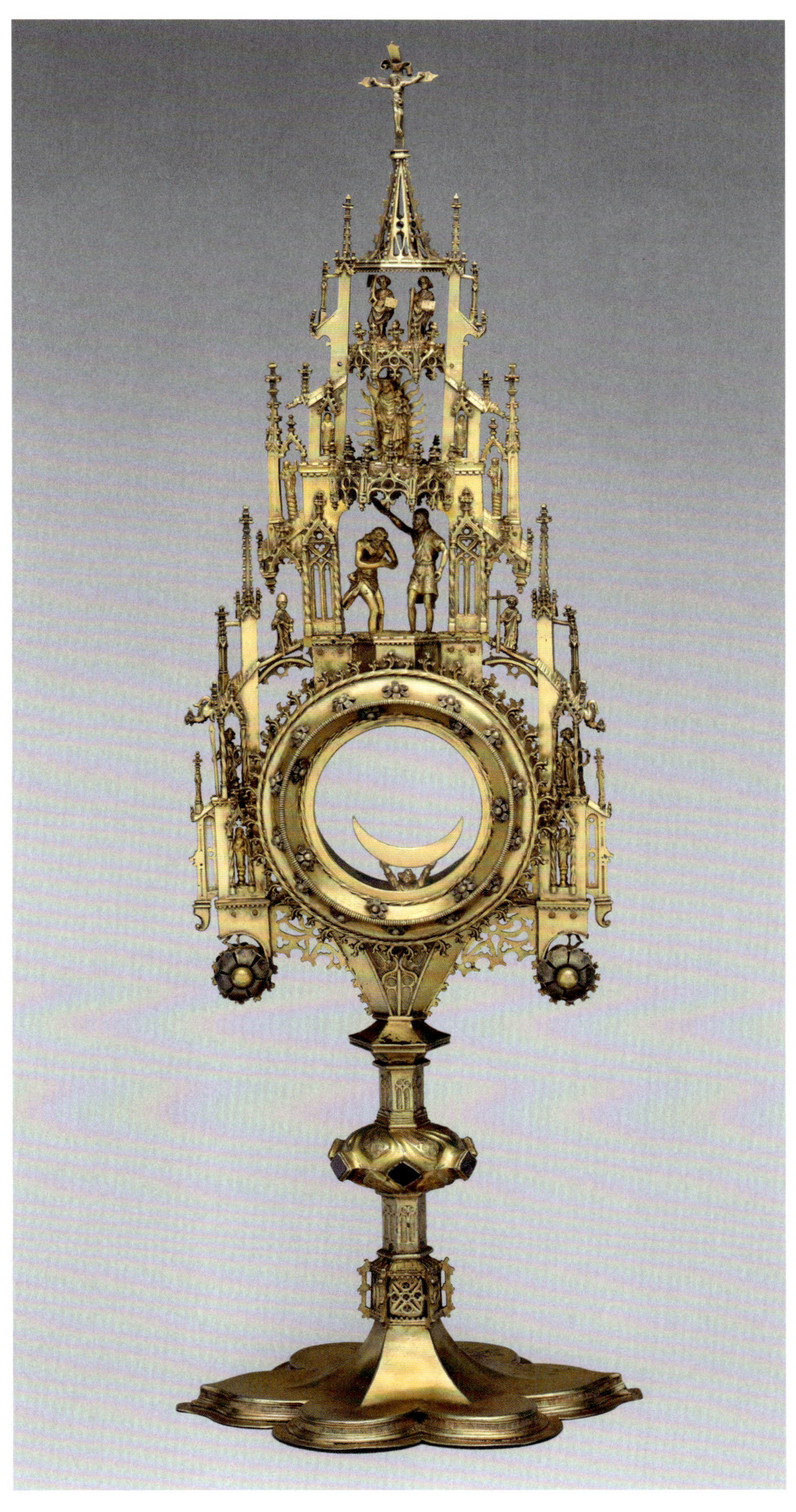

Unidentified German artist. Tower Monstrance, ca. 1450

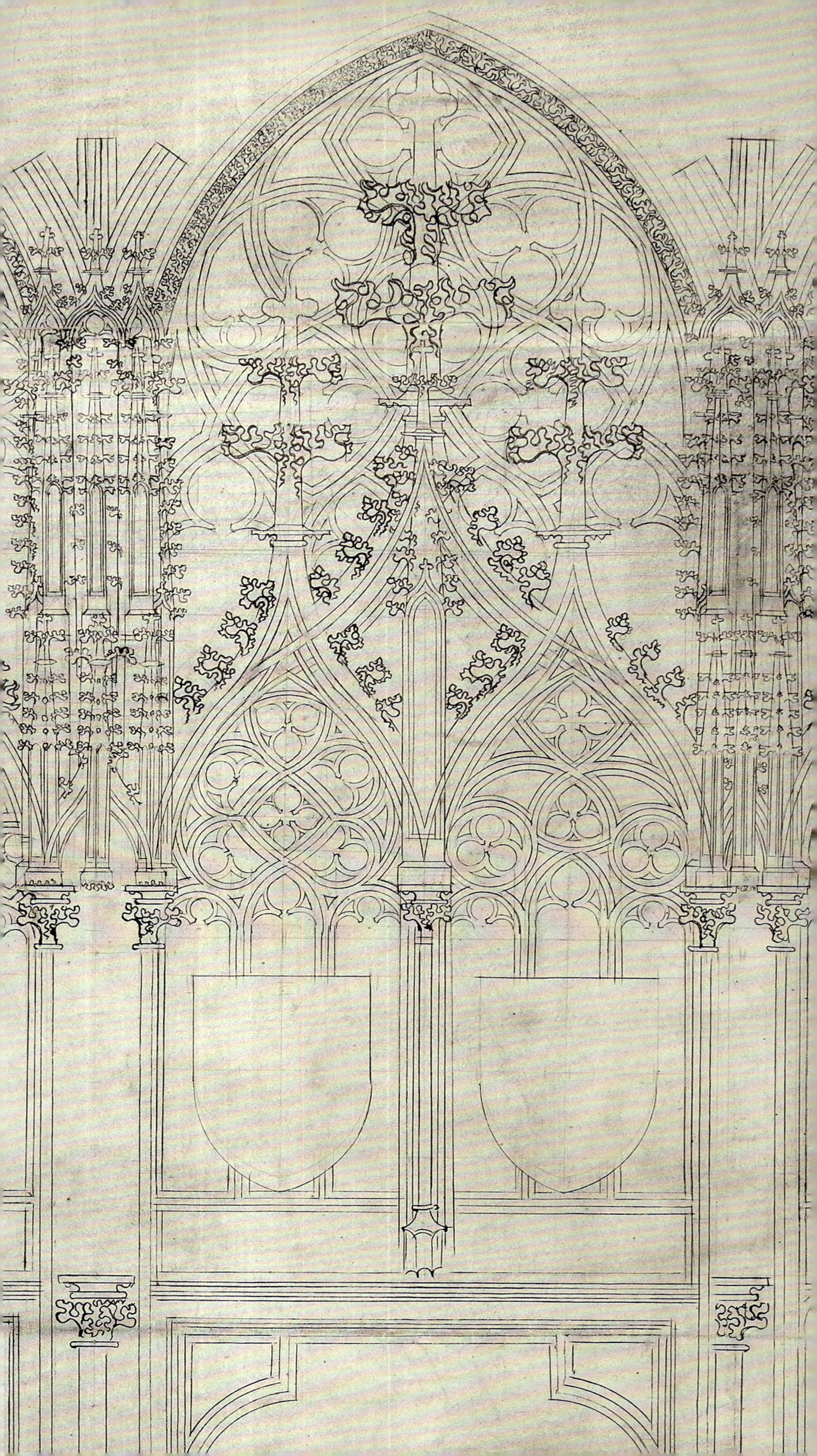

Variation and Transformation

Among the many Gothic architectural drawings from the Viennese Stephansdom (Saint Stephen's Cathedral) is a design for the decoration of the interior of the north tower porch (PL. 48). At first sight, the drawing reads as a relatively straightforward elevation of the wall, showing pilasters and arches filled with tracery. Only closer inspection reveals a subtle but effective program of variations, predominantly in the tracery. The four arches at the top contain two patterns, A and B, which alternate in a simple ABAB scheme. The eight smaller arches below contain three altogether different patterns: C, D, and E. Their layout—CDEC DECC—suggests that multiple options were under consideration in this prospective design, with the left and right sides proposing various rhythms. The final design might have read CDEC ECDC or CC DEDE CC, although other combinations are also possible.

The process of drawing encouraged the development of the many cosmetic details found in Gothic churches and their furnishings.[1] Through systematic exercises of variation and transformation, numerous permutations could be explored, with different ideas juxtaposed on a single sheet or on several sheets laid side by side. The use of a structuring device similar to a poetic rhyme scheme to create patterns of variations, like those described above, resonates with Jacob Burckhardt's concept of "the mathematizing imagination" (*die mathematisirende Phantasie*). The Swiss art historian introduced this term to describe the process of designing Gothic architectural ornament as a mental realm with seemingly endless possibilities governed by an underlying, quasi-scientific logic.[2] Burckhardt's characterization was inspired by an extraordinary group of drawings known as the *Basler Goldschmiederisse* (Basel goldsmith's drawings), now in the Kunstmuseum Basel. These were amassed in the sixteenth century by the Swiss lawyer and professor Basilius Amerbach, who had a particular interest in the process of creation. In 1578, Amerbach acquired the entire workshop inventory of the Basel-based goldsmith family Schweiger. This included a mixture of drawings and prints, both original designs made by the workshop and other works that were collected to serve as inspiration.[3] While commonly referred to as goldsmith's drawings because of their provenance, the collection's scope of subjects is much larger. Among them are designs for altars, bases for goldsmith's vessels, baldachins, geometric pedestals, column bases, monstrances, reliquaries, and various other objects, along with related floor plans and tracery studies.

A strikingly uniform group of pen-and-ink drawings from the study collection, here attributed to the goldsmith Jörg Schweiger the Elder, systematically inventories permutations related to nearly all of the most prominent decorative elements in German Late Gothic architecture (PLS. 53–63, 67, 69–71, 78). As Burckhardt explained, they offer insight into "the laboratory of Gothic invention" and could be used "to architecturize all objects."[4] This characterization highlights both the scalability and transferability of many of the architectural and decorative elements represented in the drawings. A baldachin, for example, could serve in goldsmith's work as the crowning element of a monstrance or reliquary, but one could just as easily sit atop a carved altarpiece or stone sacrament house (PLS. 54–56). Geometric pedestals, similarly, could be shrunk or enlarged, simplified or elaborated for various uses. In Schweiger's drawings, they are incorporated as bases for pillars (PLS. 69, 70), freestanding sculptures (PL. 66), an arm reliquary (PL. 68), and even the cylinder in a monumental monstrance or reliquary (PL. 53). Far from architectural in appearance, this monstrance or reliquary is shaped like a blooming tree with intertwining branches and flowers, and exemplifies the transformation of tracery into the branchwork (*Astwerk*) that became increasingly popular in the final decades of the fifteenth century. While natural in appearance, the growth patterns of the branches nevertheless adhere to the same geometric logic as more traditional forms of tracery (PLS. 60–63).

The line work of the pen-and-ink drawings found in the *Basler Goldschmiederisse* suggests that they are tracings (line-for-line copies) rather than original designs by Jörg Schweiger. This is further confirmed by the discrepancy between the sixteenth-century watermarks in the paper and the stylistic character of the designs, which indicate a fifteenth-century German origin.[5] The *Basler Goldschmiederisse* thus point to an original corpus of drawings (now lost or unknown) that was accessible to the German-born Schweiger during his training or early career as a goldsmith, before he moved to Basel in 1507.[6] Similarities between motifs found in the *Basler Goldschmiederisse* and executed objects, such as wood altarpieces and stone sacrament houses from across Germany, suggest that Schweiger was not the only artist who consulted this corpus. The material likely belonged to a prominent German artist or workshop, and may have been compiled to function as a teaching collection. Ongoing analysis of the subjects found in Schweiger's drawings, now enhanced by computer modeling, may in the future reveal more about the origins of this collection.[7]

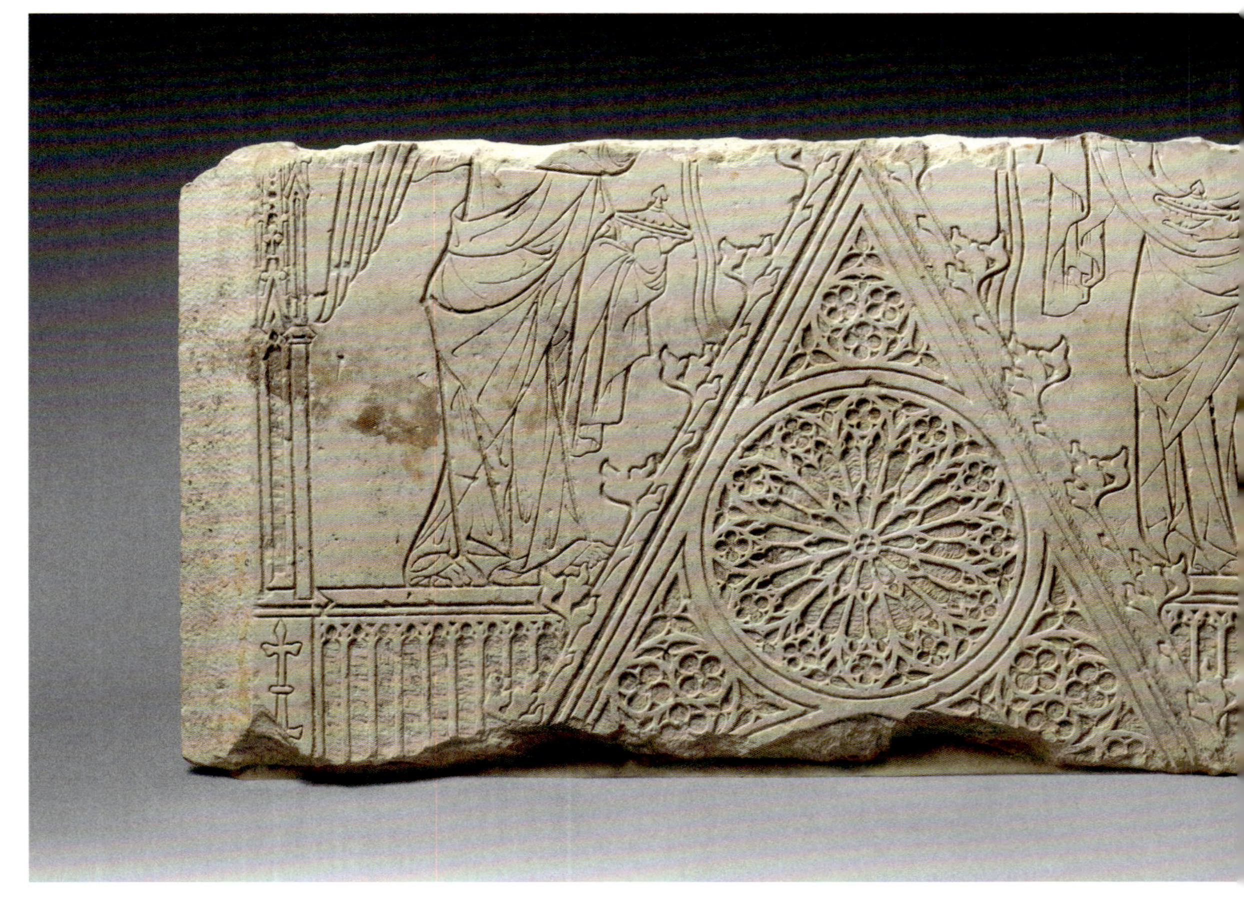

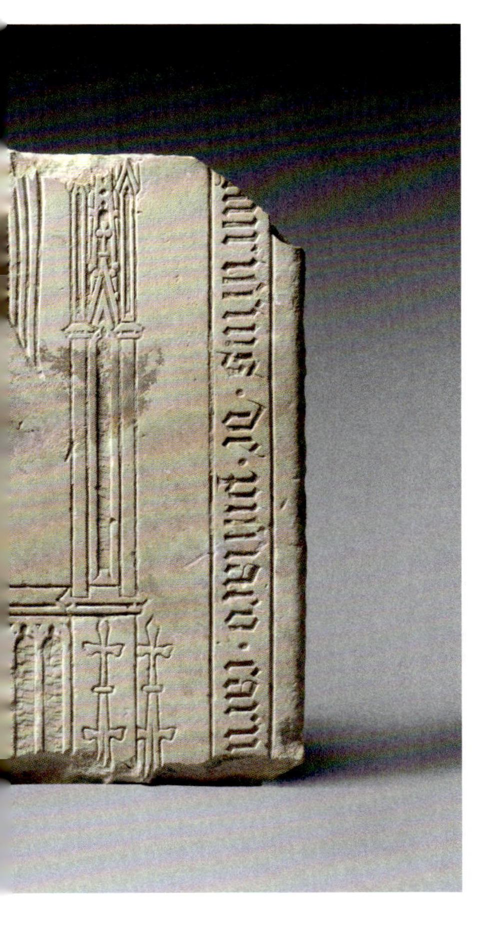

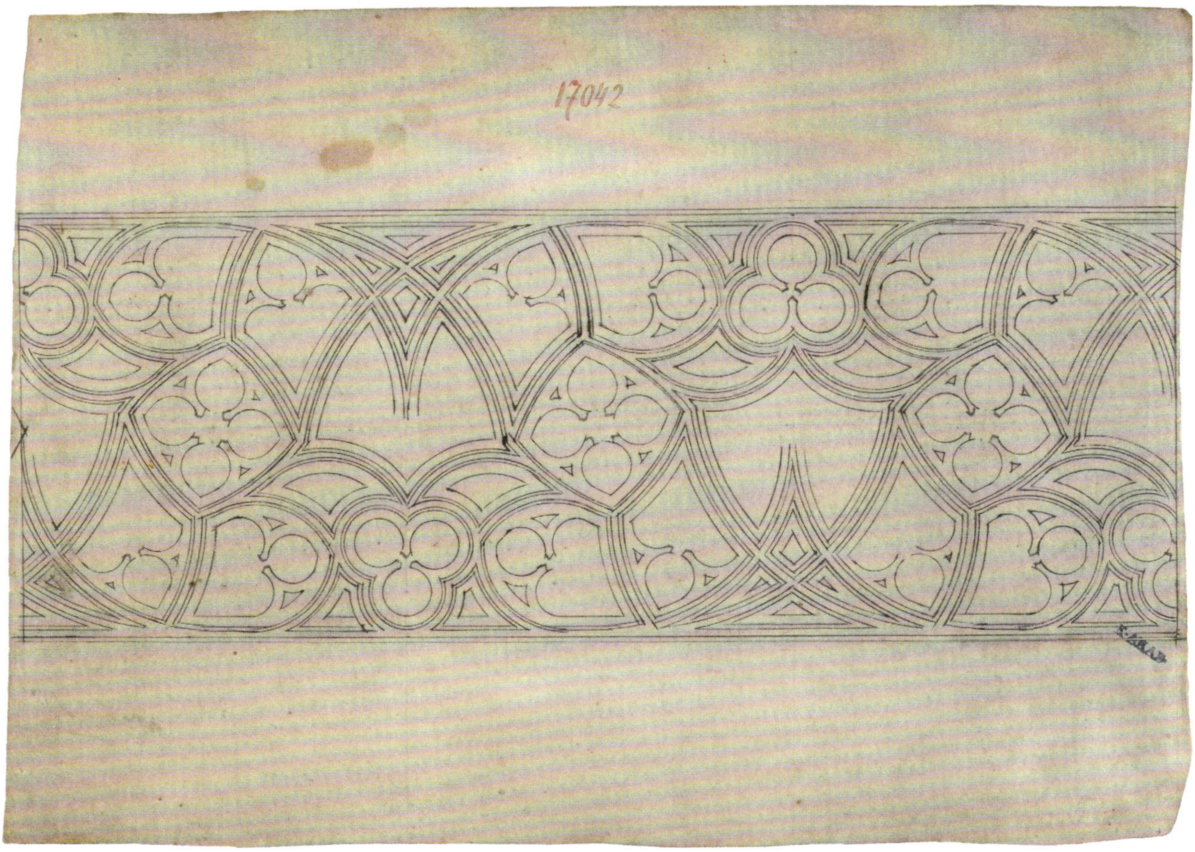

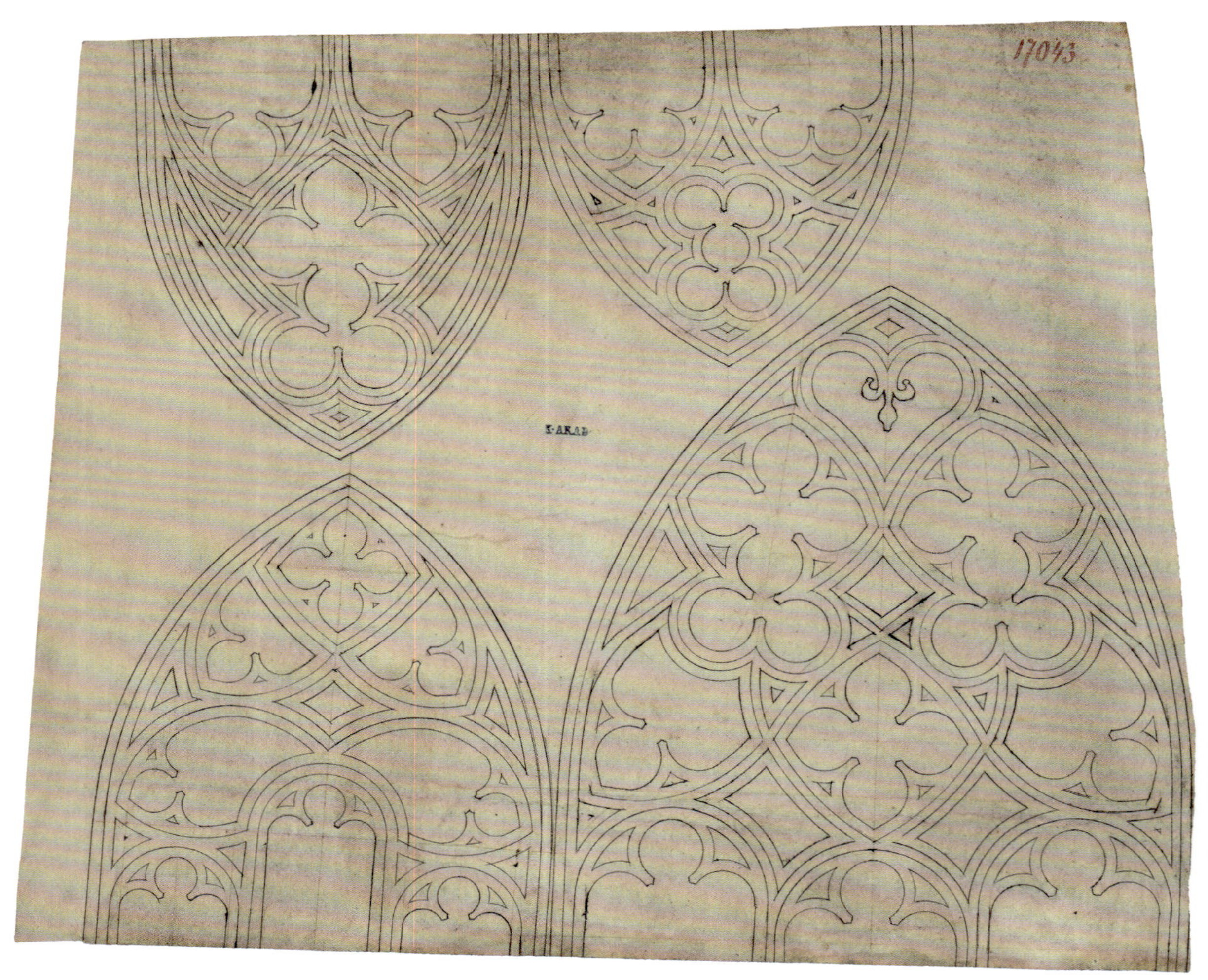

Lorenz Spenning or Workshop. Four Tracery Studies for Arched Windows, ca. 1455–60

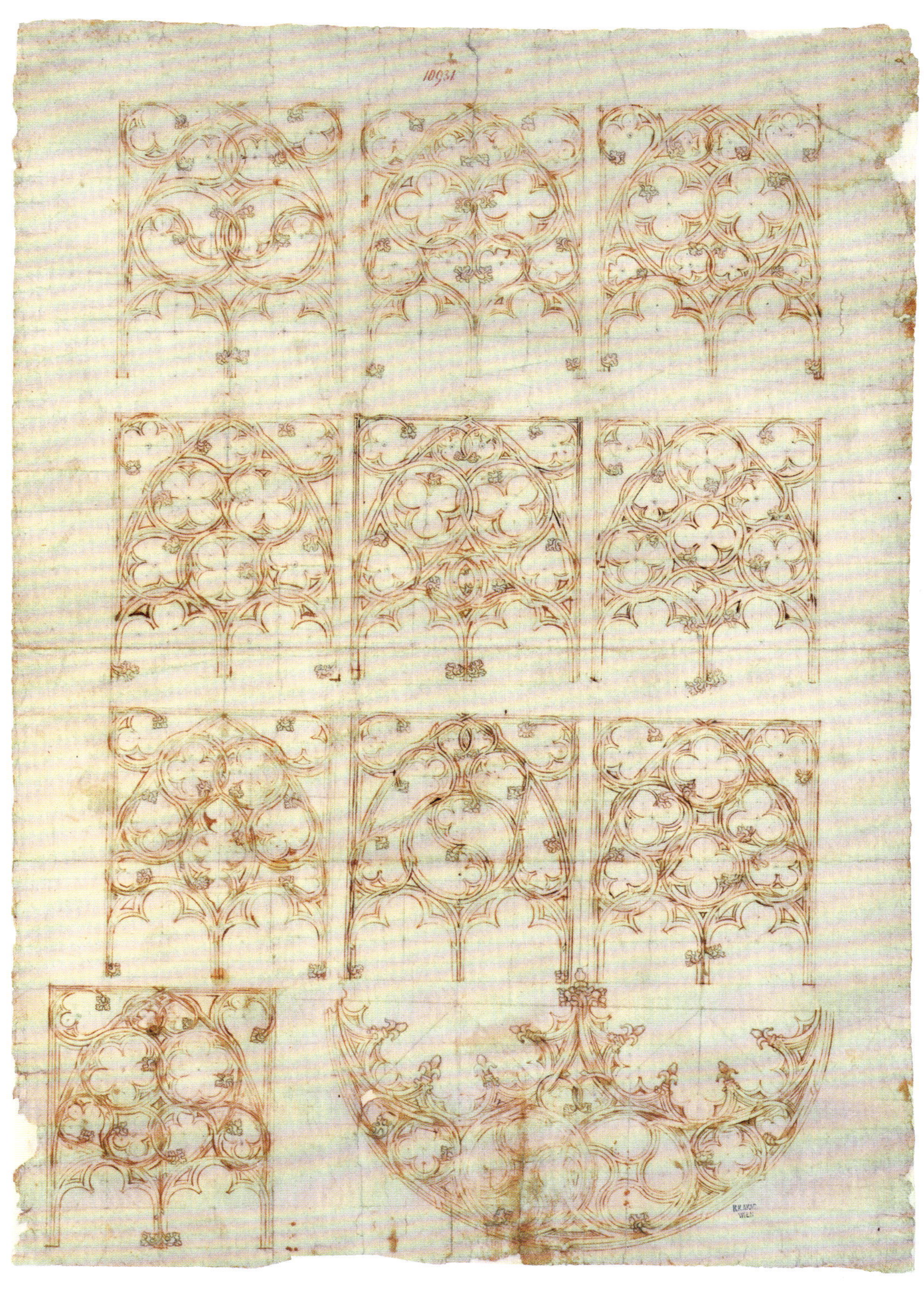

PLATE 47

Attributed to Madern Gerthener. Studies of Tracery Variations, ca. 1410–15

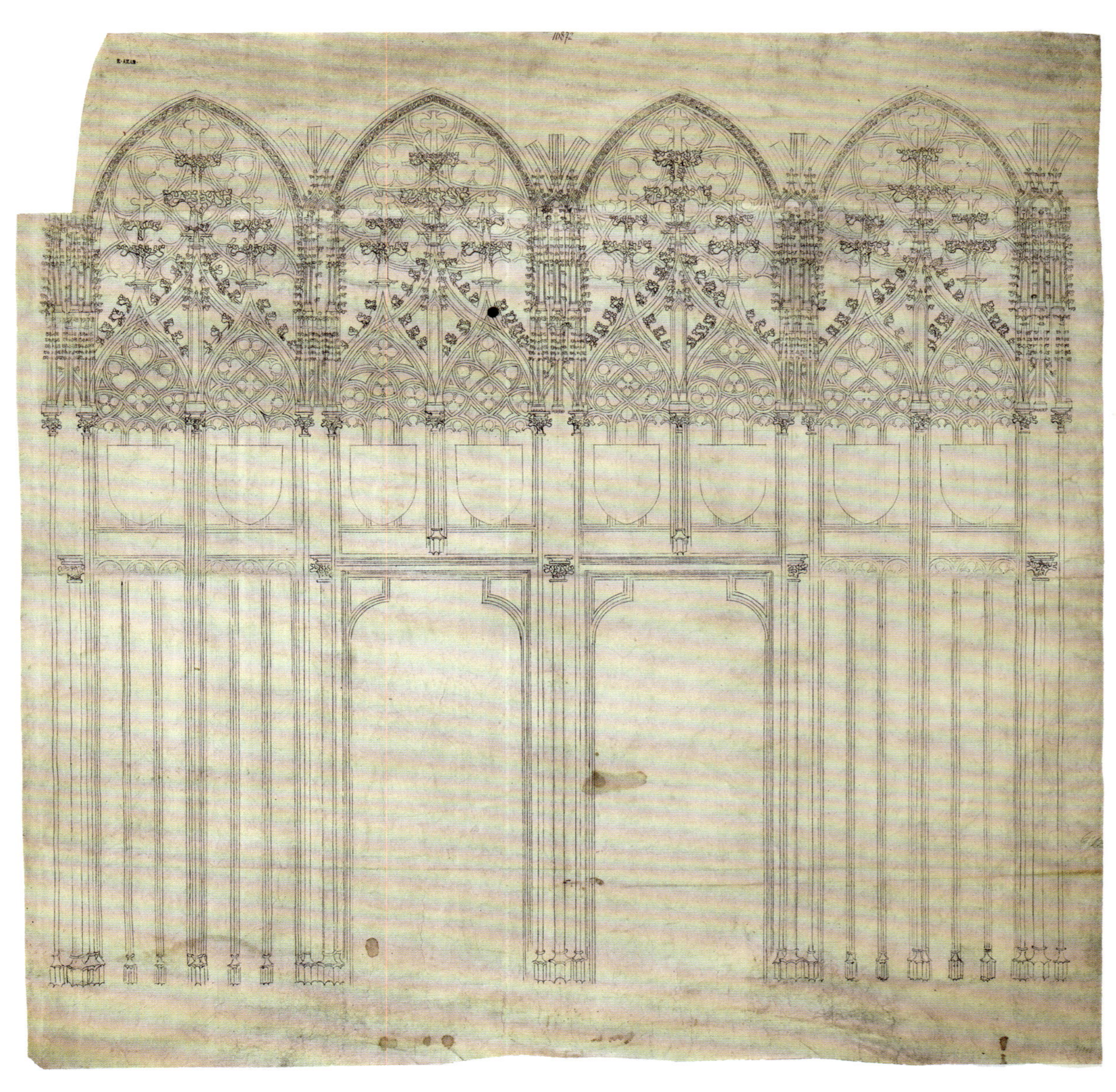

Lorenz Spenning or Workshop. Recto: Elevation of the Inner Walls of the Porch, North Tower, Stephansdom (Saint Stephen's Cathedral), Vienna, before 1467

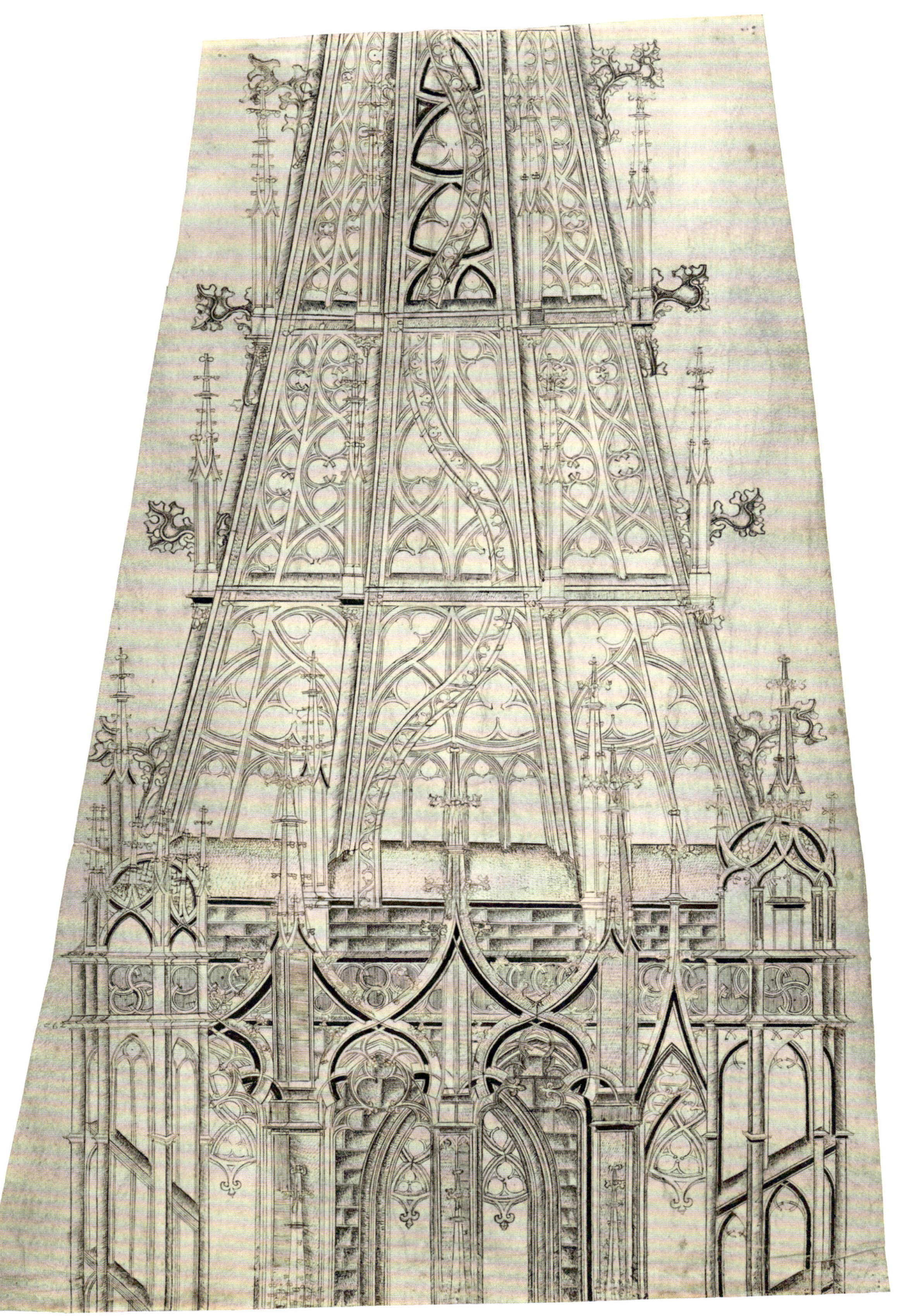

PLATE 49

Bernhard Winkler. Fragment of the Openwork Spire, West Tower, Ulm Minster (Drawing B), ca. 1512–18

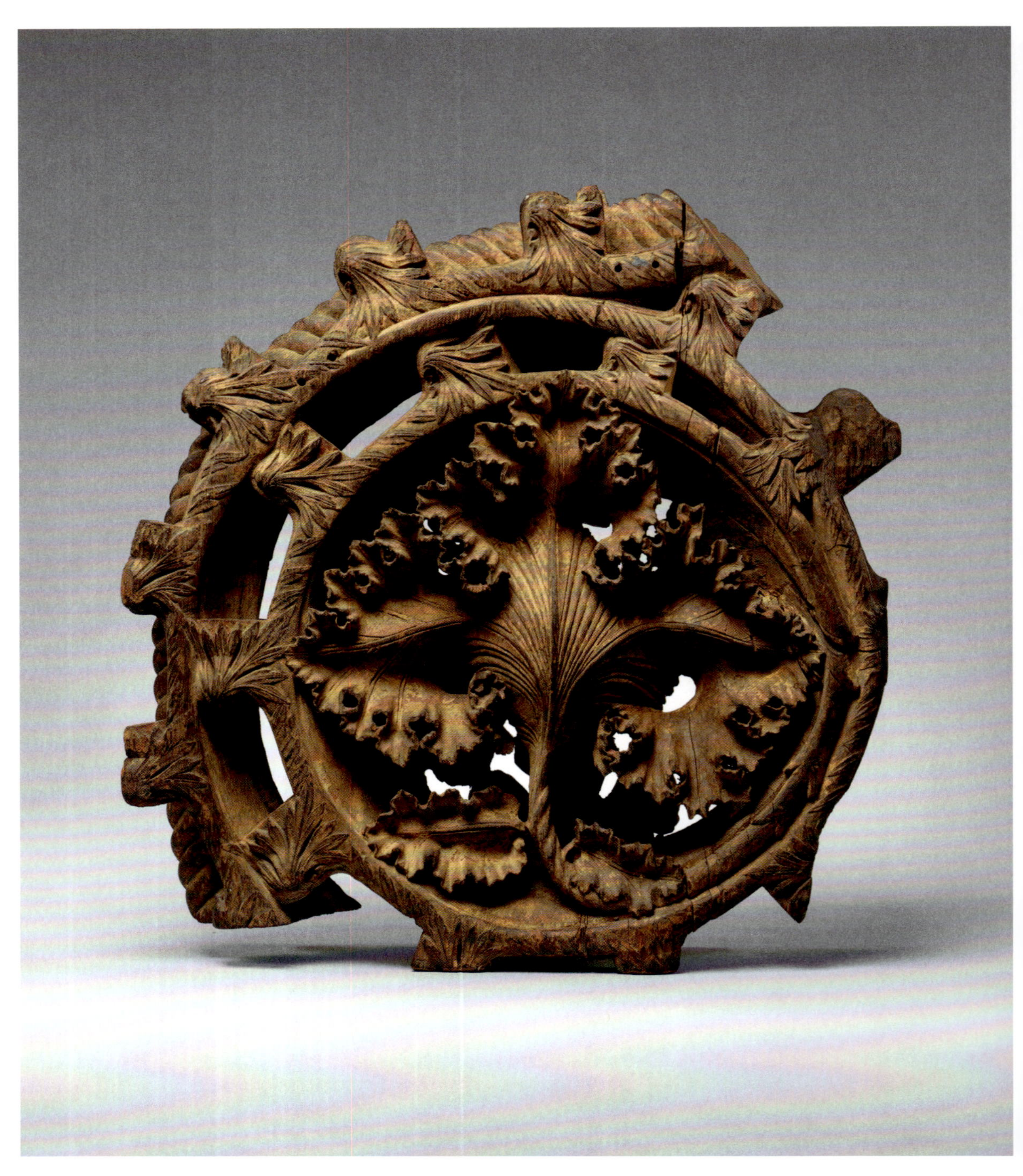

Unidentified British or South Netherlandish artist. Volute with Carved Leafwork, late 15th century

144

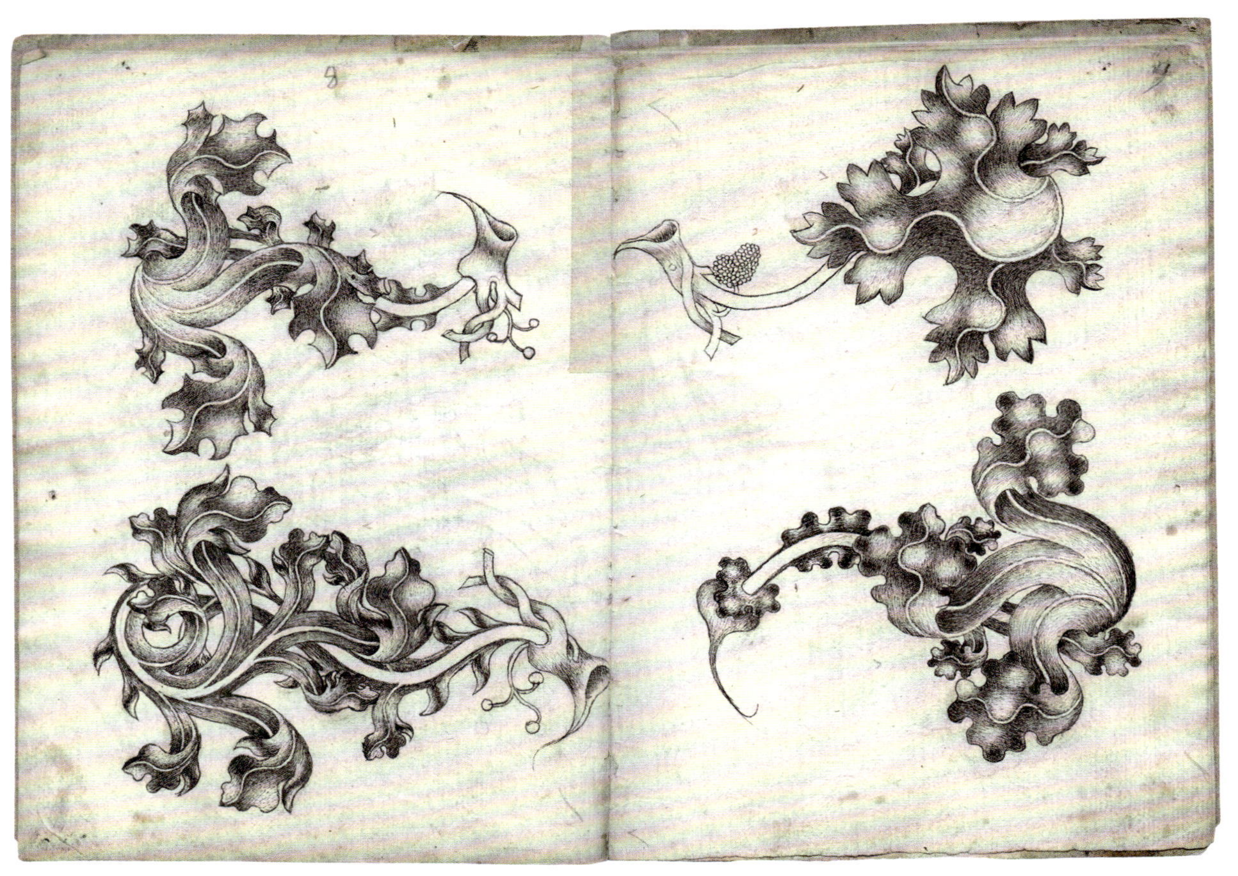

PLATE 51

Hans Böblinger the Elder. Stone Mason's Book of Leaf Designs (*Laubhauermüsterbuch*), 1435

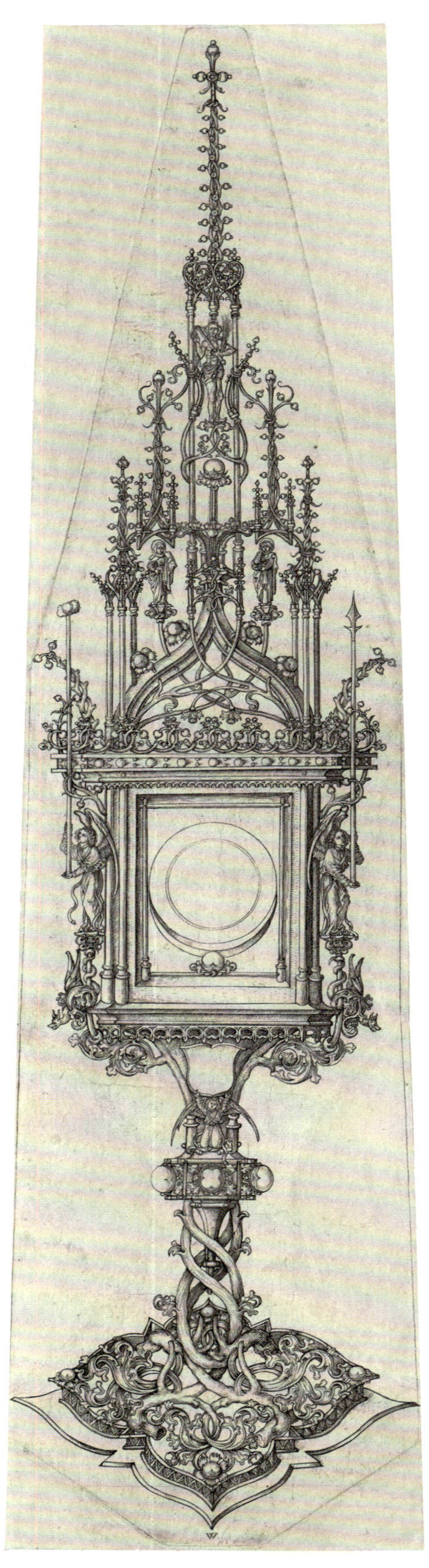

PLATE 52
Wenzel von Olmütz. Design for a Monstrance, ca. 1481–92

146

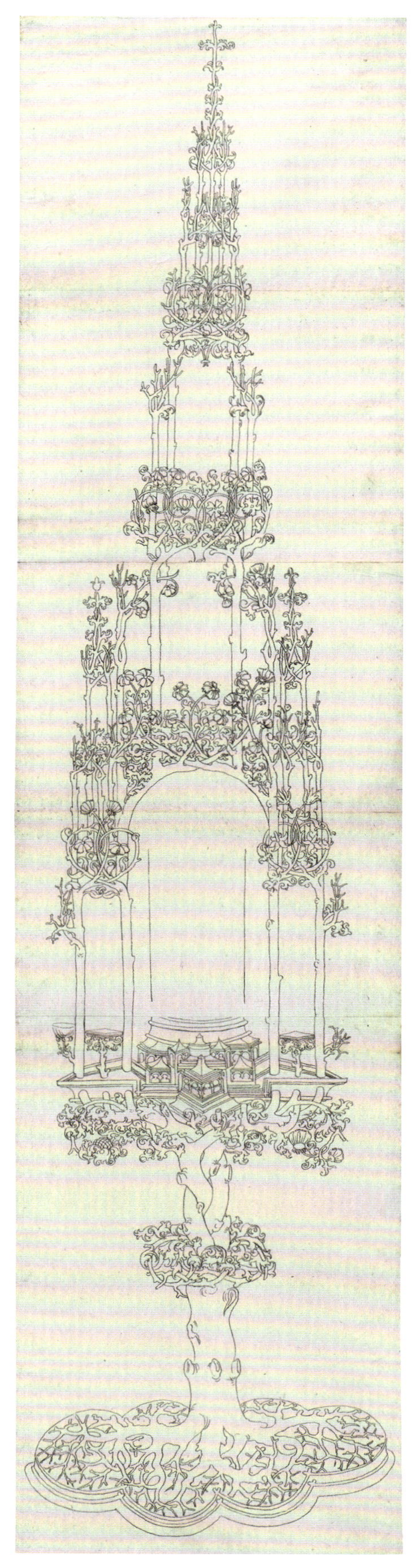

PLATE 53

Attributed to Jörg Schweiger the Elder, after unidentified German artist. Design for a Reliquary with Branchwork (*Astwerk*), from *Basler Goldschmiederisse*, ca. 1500–1510

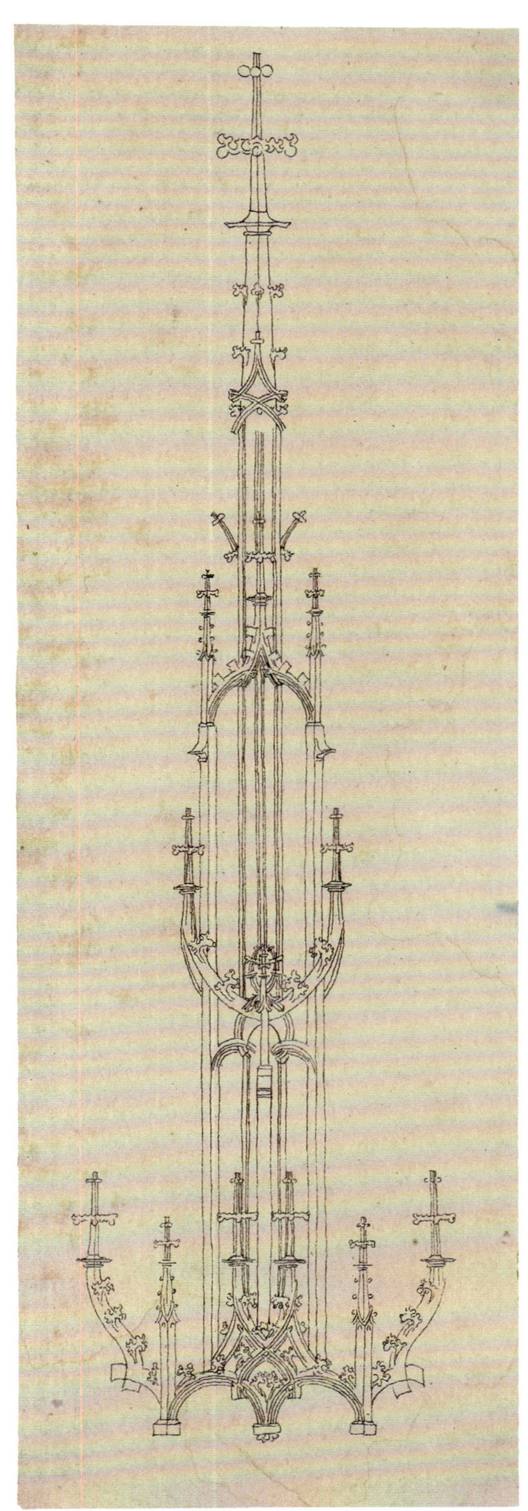

Attributed to Jörg Schweiger the Elder, after unidentified German artist. Elevation of a Baldachin, from *Basler Goldschmiederisse*, ca. 1500–1510

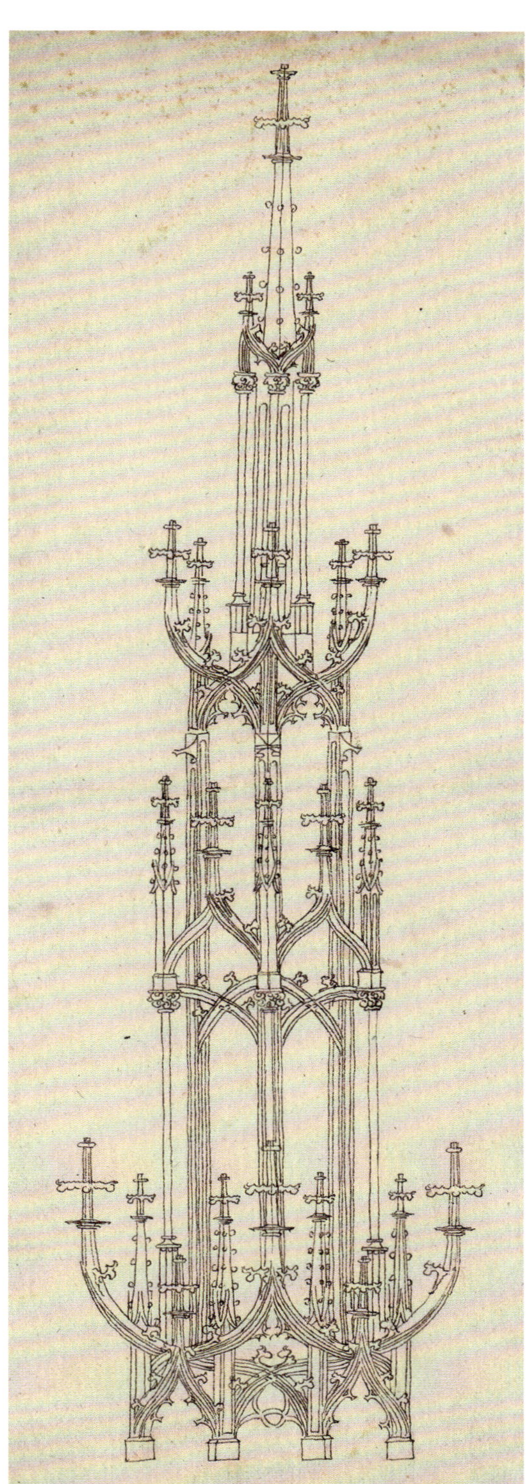

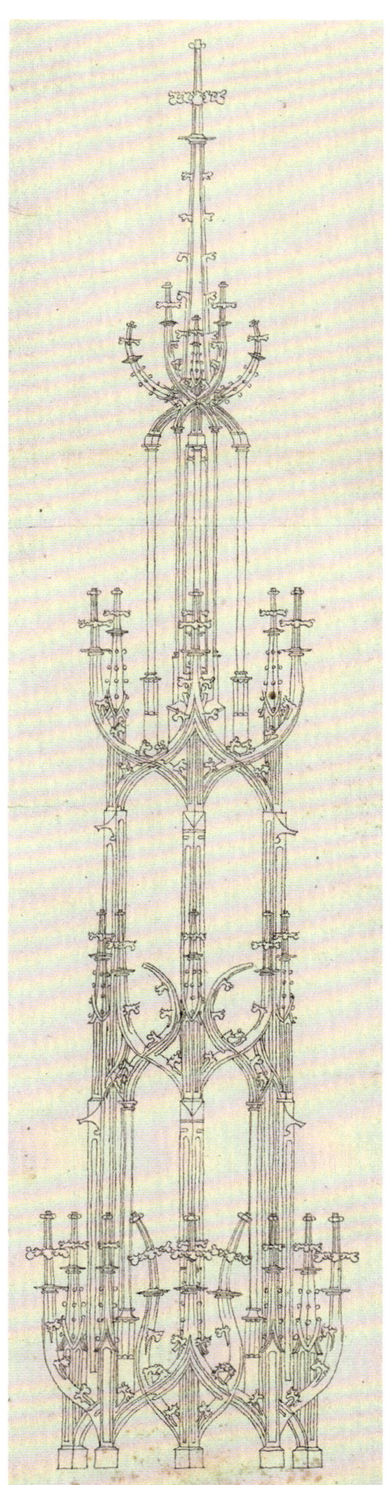

Attributed to Jörg Schweiger the Elder, after unidentified German artist. Elevation of a Baldachin, from *Basler Goldschmiederisse*, ca. 1500–1510

Attributed to Jörg Schweiger the Elder, after unidentified German artist. Elevation of a Baldachin, from *Basler Goldschmiederisse*, ca. 1500–1510

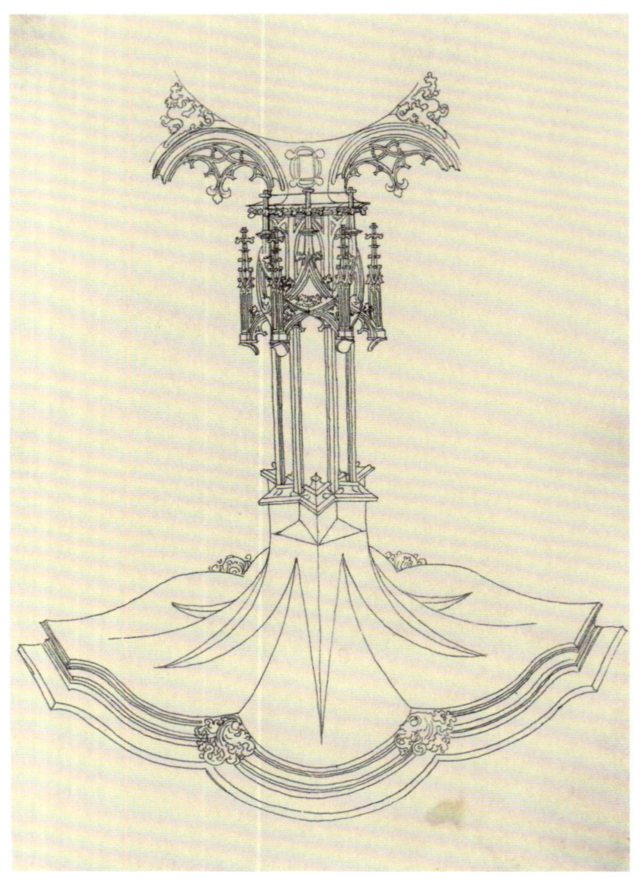

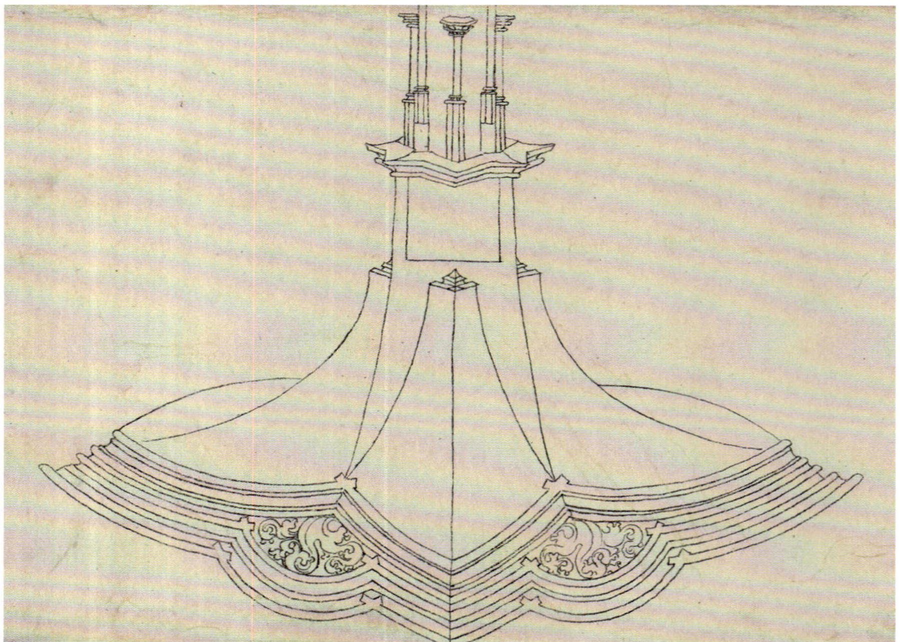

Attributed to Jörg Schweiger the Elder, after unidentified German artist. Stem and Foot of a Monstrance, from *Basler Goldschmiederisse*, ca. 1500–1510

Attributed to Jörg Schweiger the Elder, after unidentified German artist. Foot for a Monstrance or Cup, from *Basler Goldschmiederisse*, ca. 1500–1510

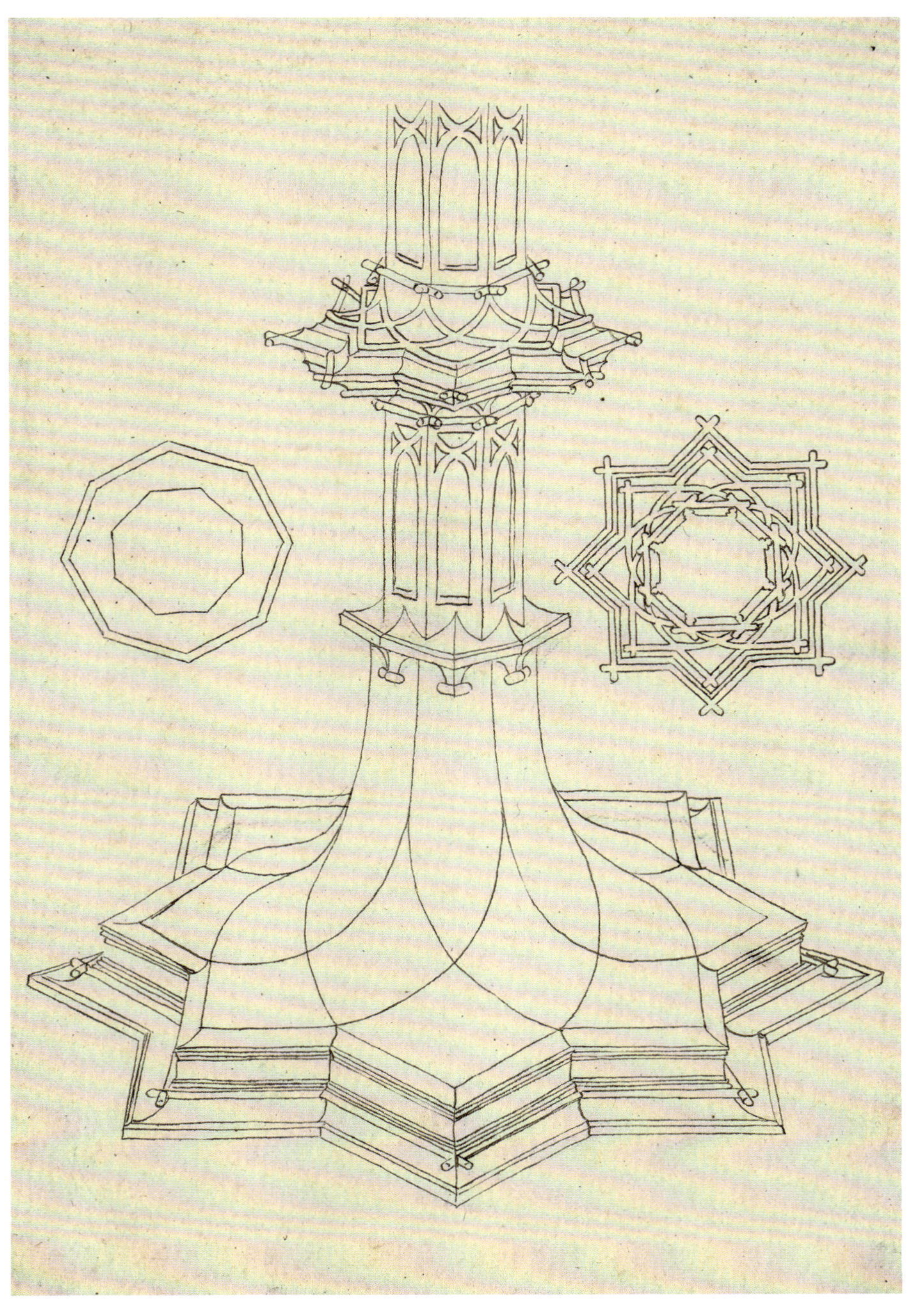

Attributed to Jörg Schweiger the Elder, after unidentified German artist. Stem and Foot of
a Vessel, with Two Related Plans, from *Basler Goldschmiederisse*, ca. 1500–1510

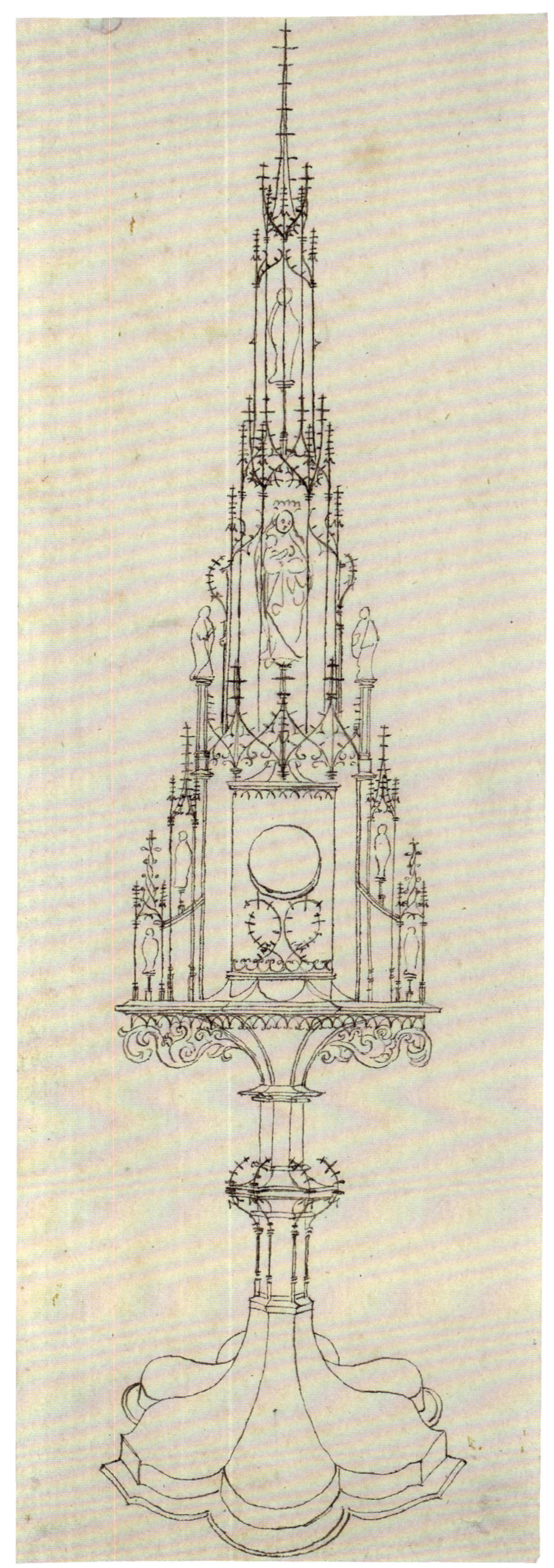

Attributed to Jörg Schweiger the Elder, after unidentified German artist. Elevation of a Tower Monstrance, from *Basler Goldschmiederisse*, ca. 1500–1510

152

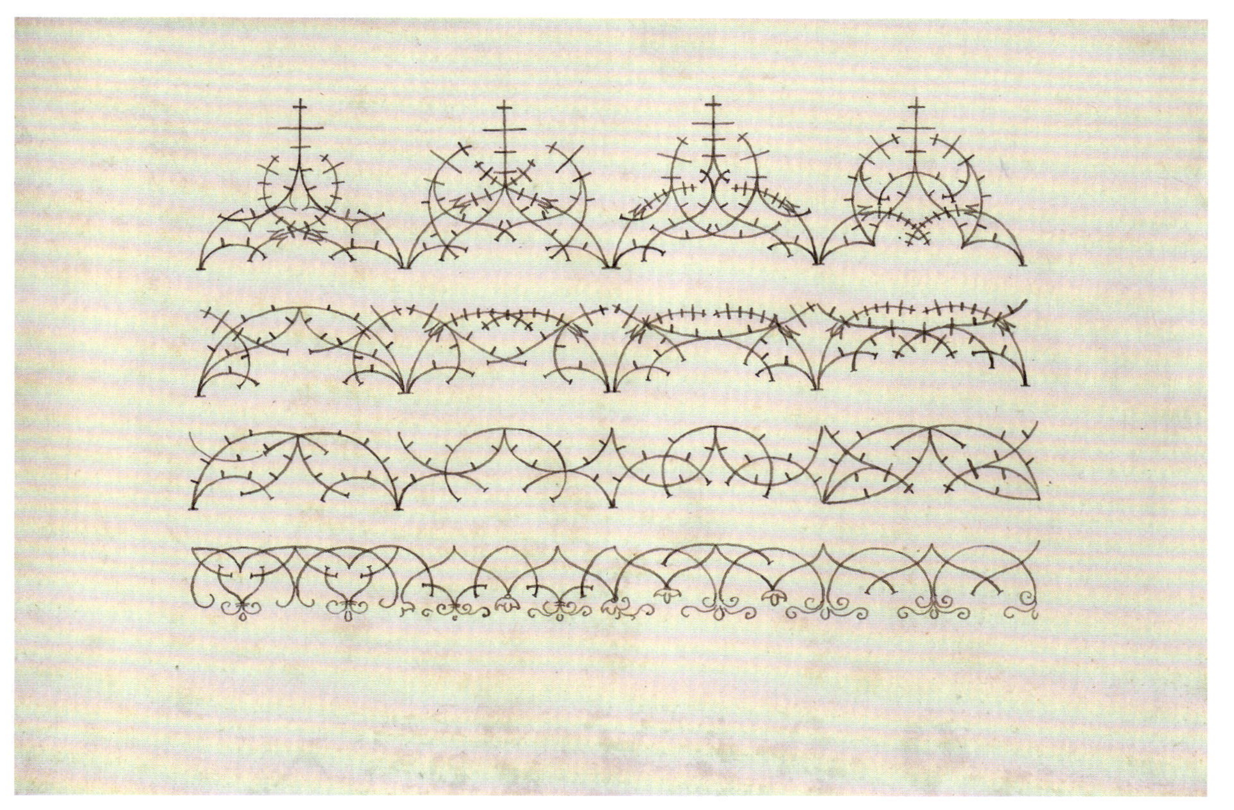

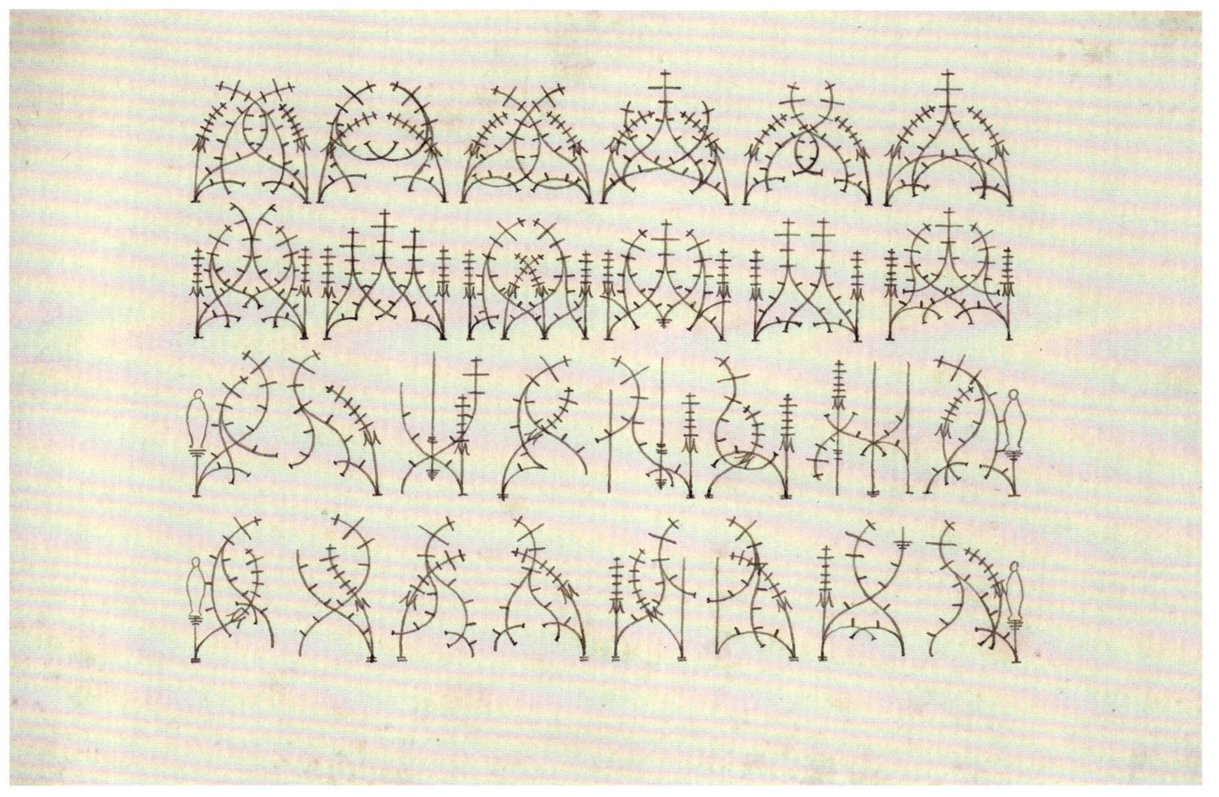

Attributed to Jörg Schweiger the Elder, after unidentified German artist. Schematic
Representation of Tracery Elements and Friezes, from *Basler Goldschmiederisse*, ca. 1500–1510

Attributed to Jörg Schweiger the Elder, after unidentified German artist. Schematic
Representation of Tracery Elements, from *Basler Goldschmiederisse*, ca. 1500–1510

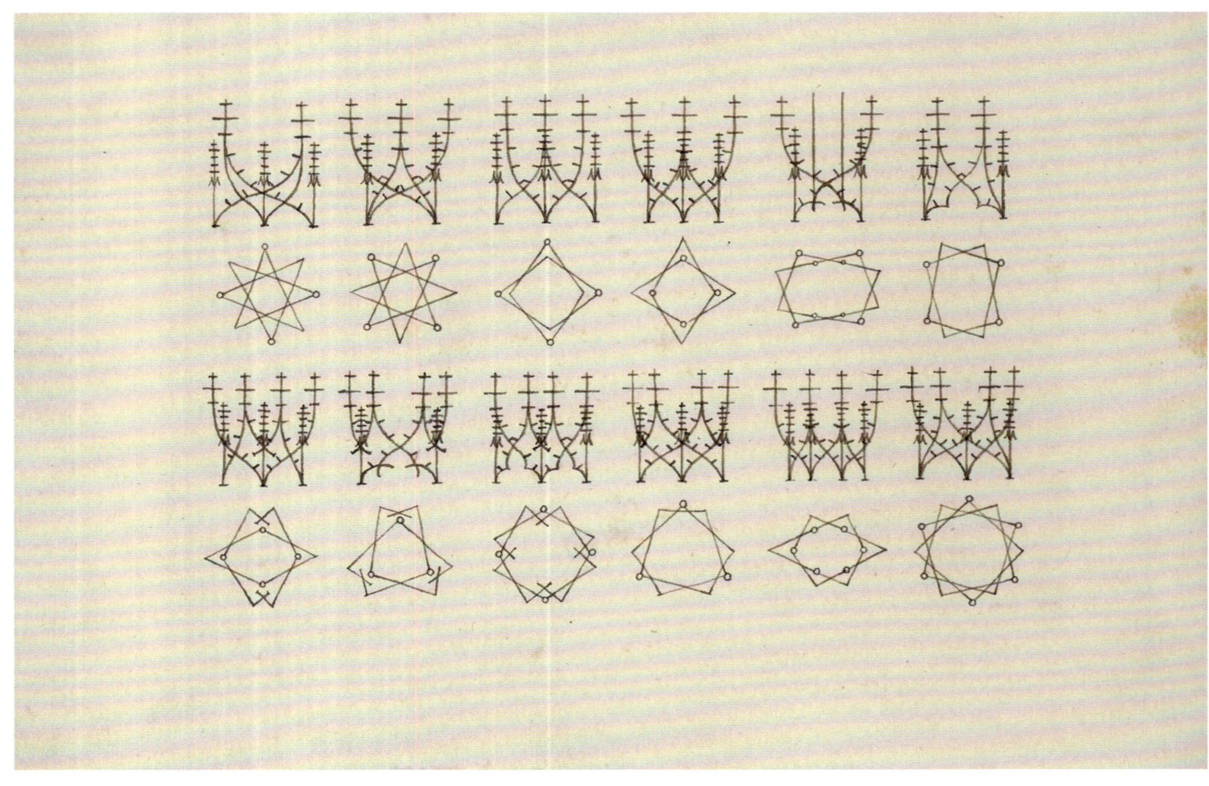

Attributed to Jörg Schweiger the Elder, after unidentified German artist. Schematic Representation of Tracery Elements and Their Plans, from *Basler Goldschmiederisse*, ca. 1500–1510

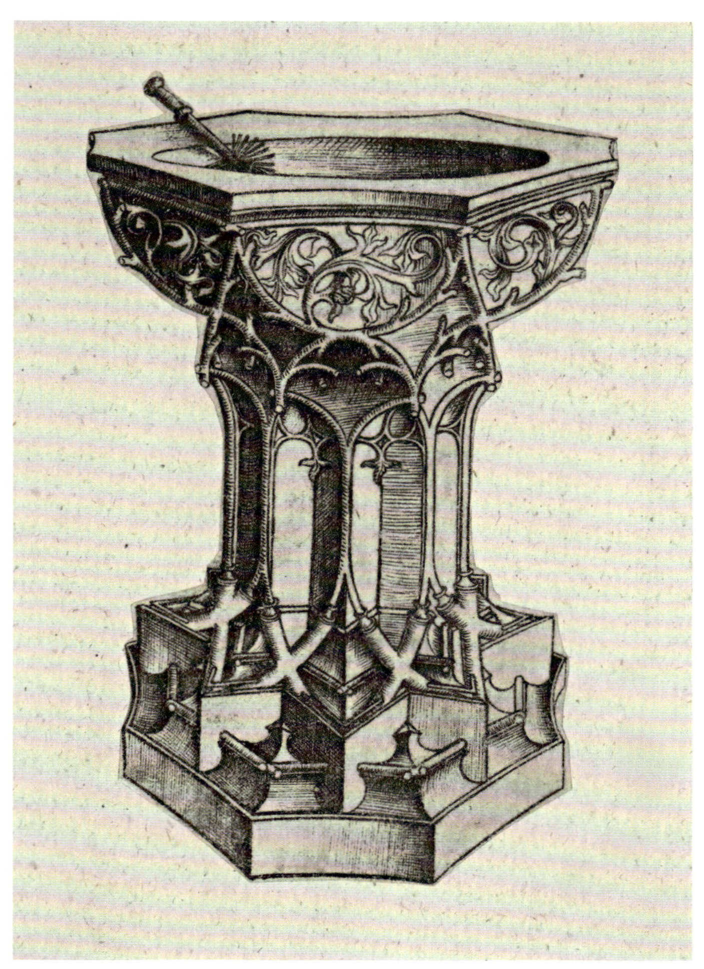

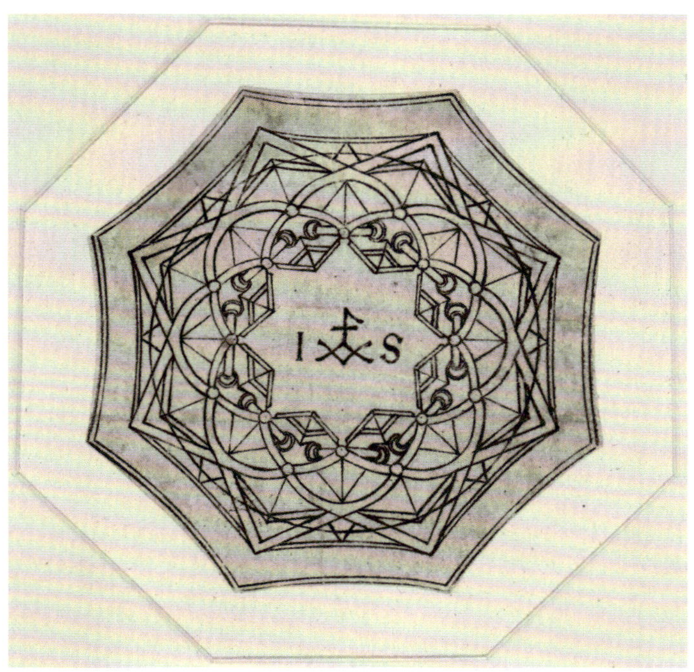

PLATE 64
Jörg Syrlin the Younger, after Matthäus Böblinger. Elevation of a Baptismal Font, ca. 1477–90

PLATE 65
Jörg Syrlin the Younger, after Matthäus Böblinger. Floor Plan of a Baptismal Font, ca. 1477–90

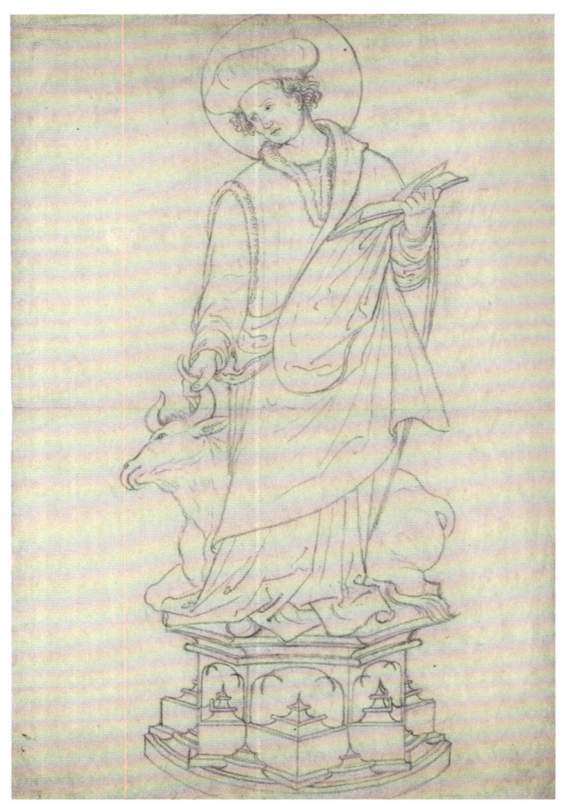

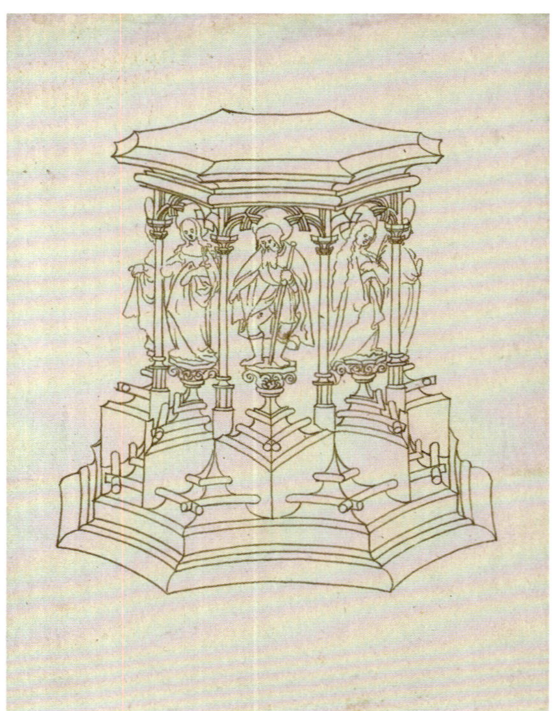

Attributed to Jörg Schweiger the Elder. Reliquary with a Statue of Saint Luke, from *Basler Goldschmiederisse*, ca. 1508–24

Attributed to Jörg Schweiger the Elder, after unidentified German artist. Elevation of a Pedestal with Figures of Saints, from *Basler Goldschmiederisse*, ca. 1500–1510

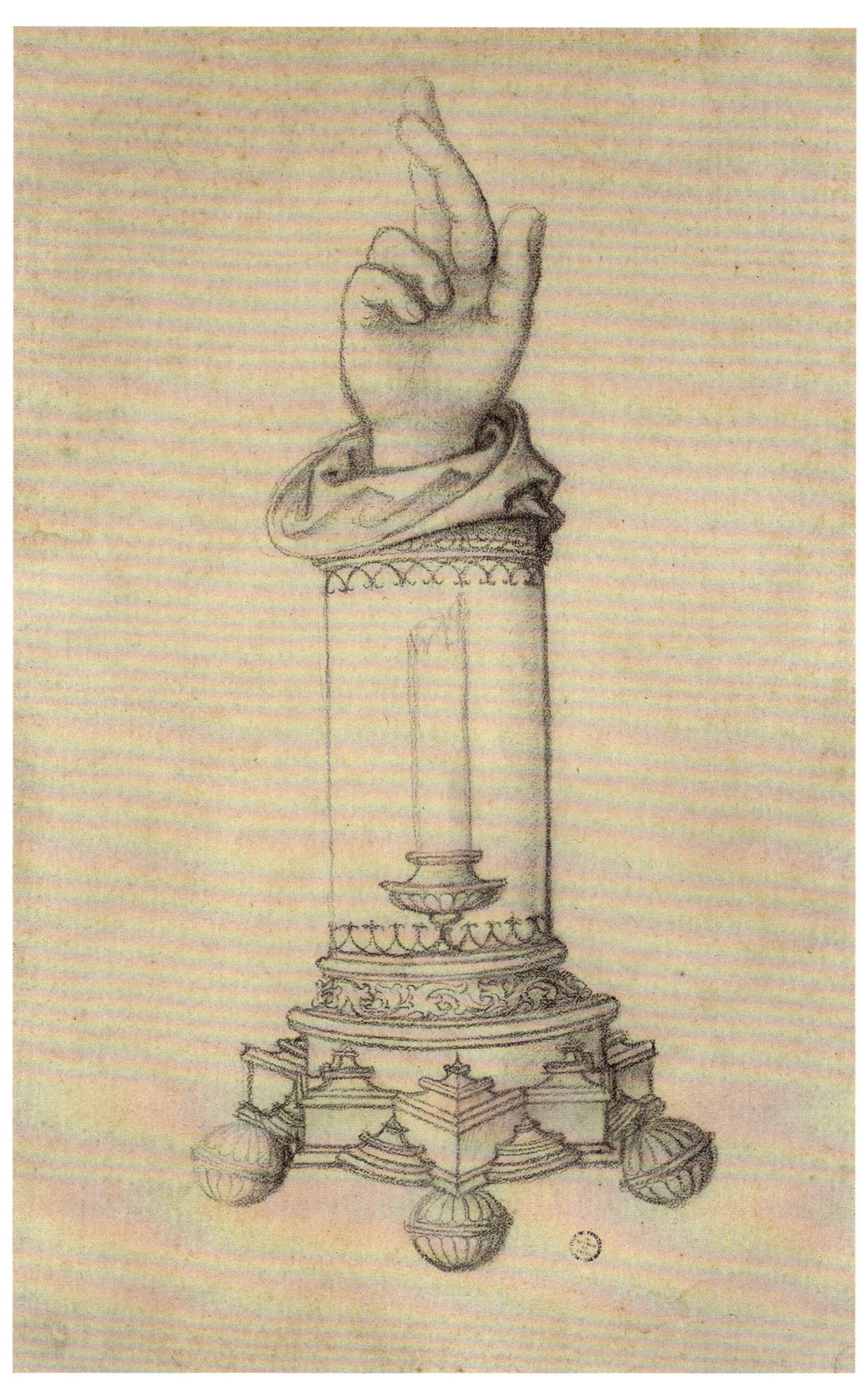

PLATE 68
Attributed to Jörg Schweiger the Elder. Arm Reliquary, from *Basler Goldschmiederisse*, ca. 1508–24

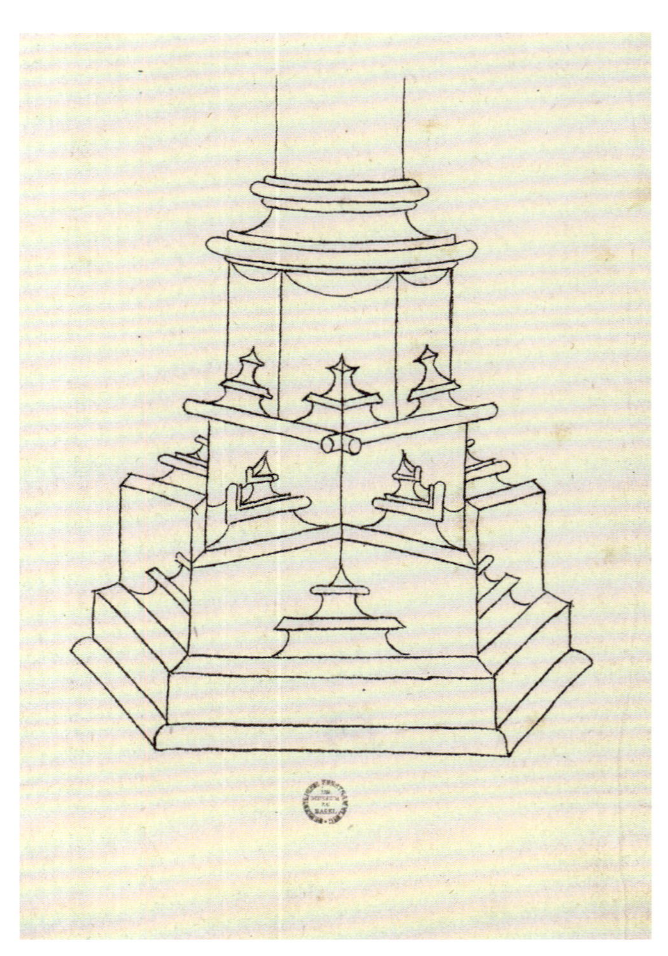

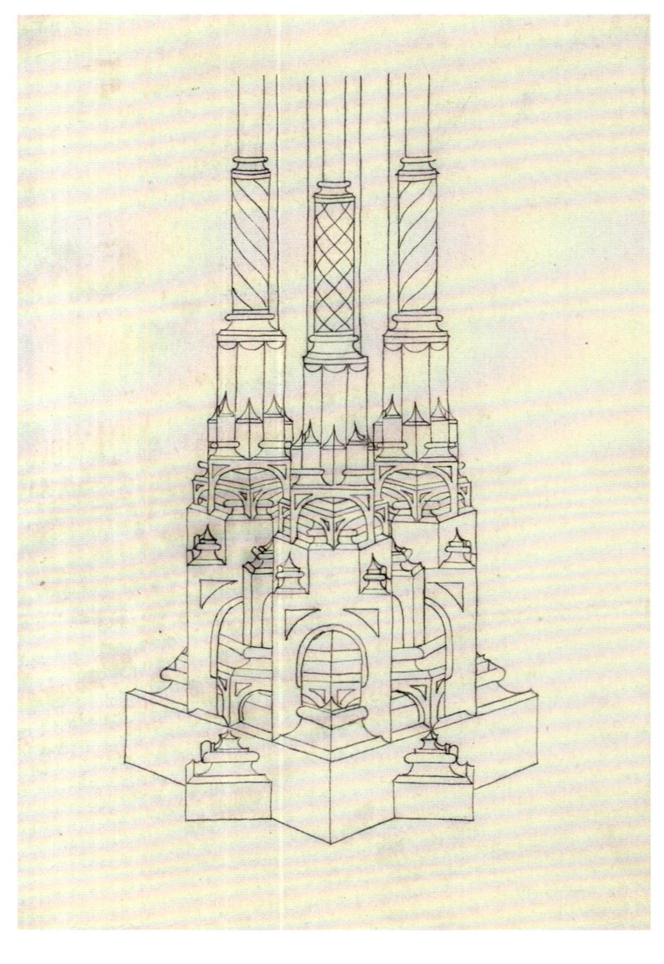

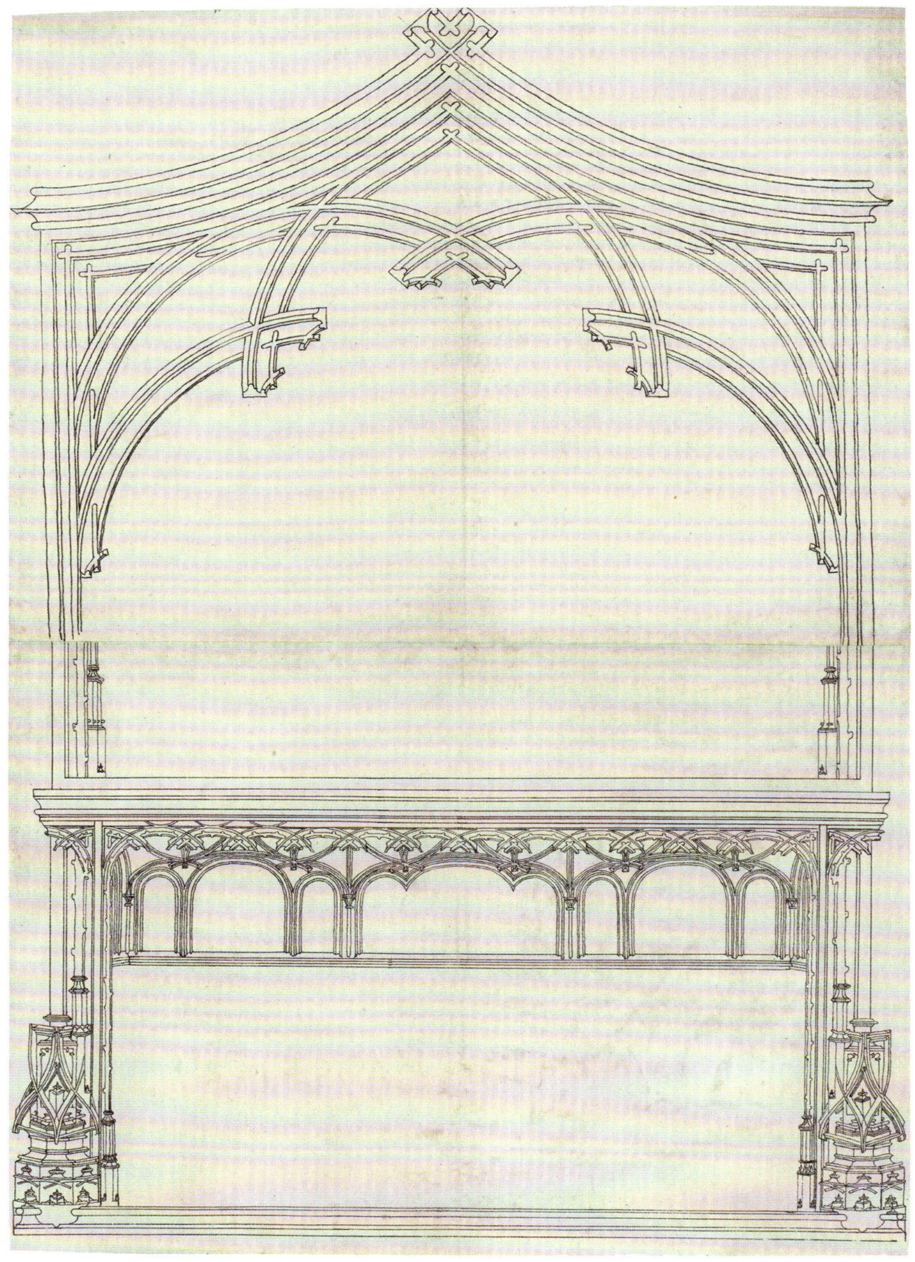

PLATE 69
Attributed to Jörg Schweiger the Elder, after unidentified German artist. Elevation of a Geometric Base for a Pillar, from *Basler Goldschmiederisse*, ca. 1500–1510

PLATE 70
Attributed to Jörg Schweiger the Elder, after unidentified German artist. Elevation of a Geometric Base for a Pillar, from *Basler Goldschmiederisse*, ca. 1500–1510

PLATE 71
Attributed to Jörg Schweiger the Elder, after unidentified German artist. Design for the Architectural Frame of a Wall Monument, ca. 1500–1510

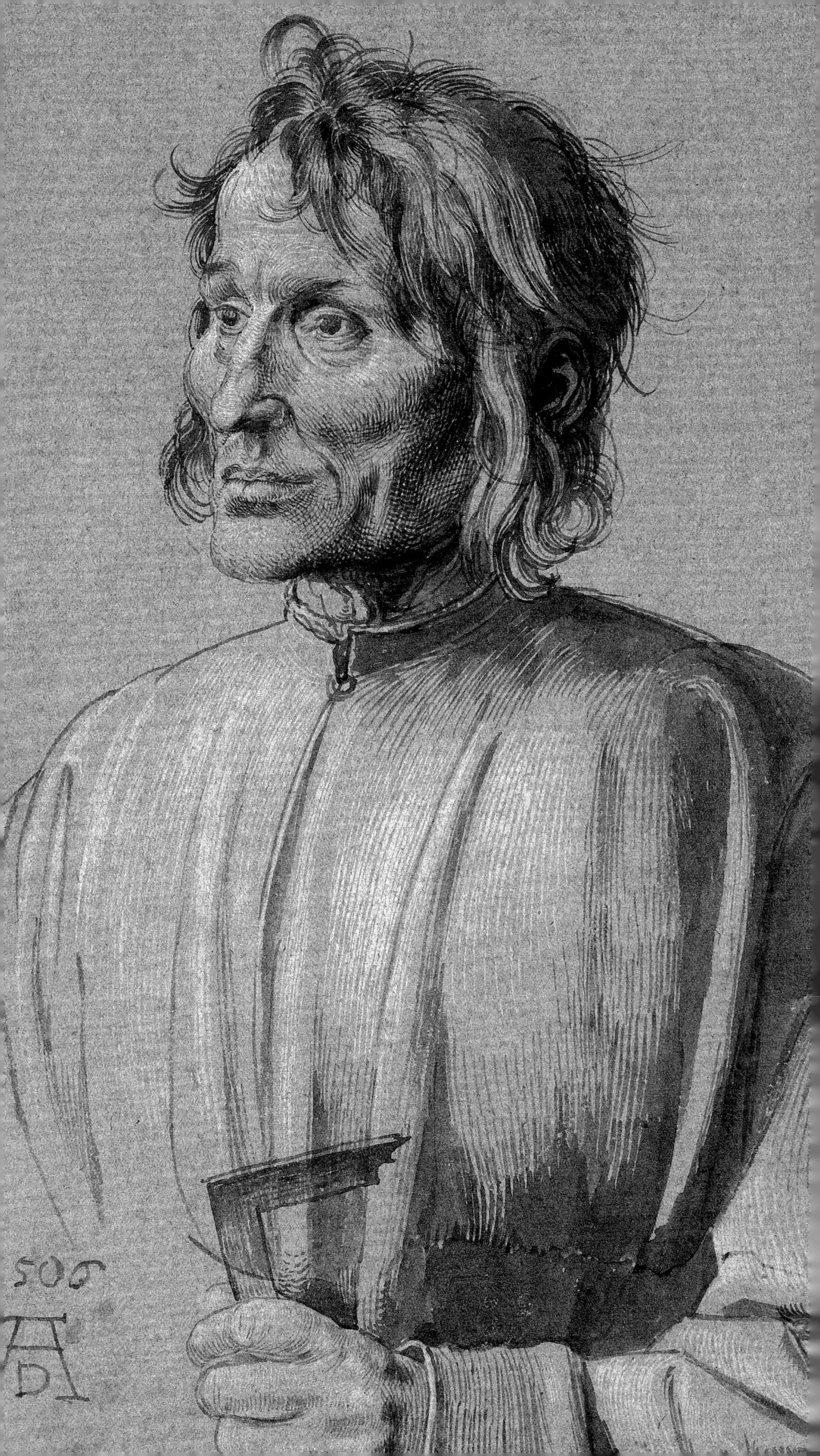

1505

Constructive Geometry

In his portrait study of the architect Hieronymus, a fellow Augsburger active in Venice, Albrecht Dürer shows a man at middle age firmly holding a square, one of the tools of his trade (PL. 83). Alongside the compass (for drawing circles) and straightedge (straight lines), the square (right angles) was one of the principal instruments that facilitated accurate designs and plans. Such implements were indispensable to Gothic architects, whose design practice was deeply grounded in geometry.

Constructive geometry, as the method has come to be known by scholars today, entailed the manipulation of shapes to determine a design's outline and proportions.[1] In addition to circles, most designs were developed with the help of regular convex polygons (the triangle, square, pentagon, hexagon, and octagon), whose relative stability according to the laws of geometry made them the perfect building blocks for architectural pursuits. The triangle in particular stands out for its inherent rigidity, resisting deformation when forces are applied. It is certainly not a coincidence that this shape has come to define Gothic architecture, from the pointed (ogival) arch and window to the tall spires crowning towers and other structures.

The Greek mathematician Euclid was the first to record these geometric principles in writing (*The Elements*; ca. 300 BCE), but the practical application of his theorems seems to have been understood or intuited for much longer, as demonstrated, for example, by the construction of pyramids in ancient Egypt (first recorded during Dynasty III, 27th century BCE) and Maya temples in Mesoamerica (from ca. 1000 BCE). While numerous fragmentary translations of Euclid's text are recorded across Europe beginning about 500 CE, the question of whether and to what extent Gothic architects were aware of geometry's ancient origins remains heavily debated.[2] In his 1486 booklet on how to properly construct pinnacles (PL. 80), for example, the Regensburg master mason Mathes (Matthäus) Roriczer traced his methods back not to the ancients but to the Parler dynasty, which predated him by only a few generations. Evidently this reference to the then renowned family of architects lent Roriczer more authority in 1480s Regensburg than did the name of a comparatively obscure Greek mathematician who had lived nearly two thousand years earlier.

Nevertheless, Gothic architects were able to understand and exploit the practical applications of geometry to create monumental structures in completely novel ways. For example, the graduated stacking of squares in the floor plan for the north tower or *Adlertor* of the Stephansdom (Saint Stephen's Cathedral) in Vienna (PL. 72) might recall the same geometric principles used to design an Egyptian pyramid. Yet the structure, if it had been built, would have resembled the south tower (PL. 12), which looks nothing like a pyramid. Gothic architects did not simply stack stone. Instead, they manipulated the proportions of their building elements, the angles at which they were placed, and their surface finishes to create constructions of unique structural and sculptural appeal.

Technical drawings attest to the intricacy of the working process as well as to architects' dedication to seeing through the practical realization of their artistic ideas. That may seem self-evident, but until the introduction of the modern blueprint, few other surviving architectural drawings from later building traditions include as much information pertaining to the engineering side of construction as do Gothic architectural drawings. This owes in part to the fact that Gothic architects were both designers *and* makers by training. As such, a master mason was responsible not only for the outward appearance of a building, but also for thinking about such aspects as the metal armature needed to reinforce the walls of a tower (see fig. 22, pl. 73 [recto]), the ideal ratio of steps to balustrade segments of pulpit stairs (pl. 84), or the variously shaped elements required to put together the circular rib joints of a complex vaulting structure (pl. 93).

Even after taste shifted from Gothic aesthetics to the classicizing vocabulary of the Renaissance over the course of the sixteenth century, many of the geometric principles that were foundational to Gothic architecture remained in practice. For example, the geometric vaulting systems characteristic of the Gothic tradition retained their relevance well beyond the Gothic period due to their technical sophistication. Their relatively abstract linear appearance also aligned seamlessly with the aesthetics of the new style, thus extending their currency well into the seventeenth century (pl. 95).[3] Other aspects of Gothic expertise persisted as well, predominantly within elements of internal construction, such as the timber framing of houses and roofs.[4] While the eighteenth and nineteenth centuries saw enthusiastic revivals of the Gothic aesthetic, it is in modern-day building practice that Gothic geometry has come into focus once again as a promising answer to challenges of sustainability in construction (see pl. 96).[5]

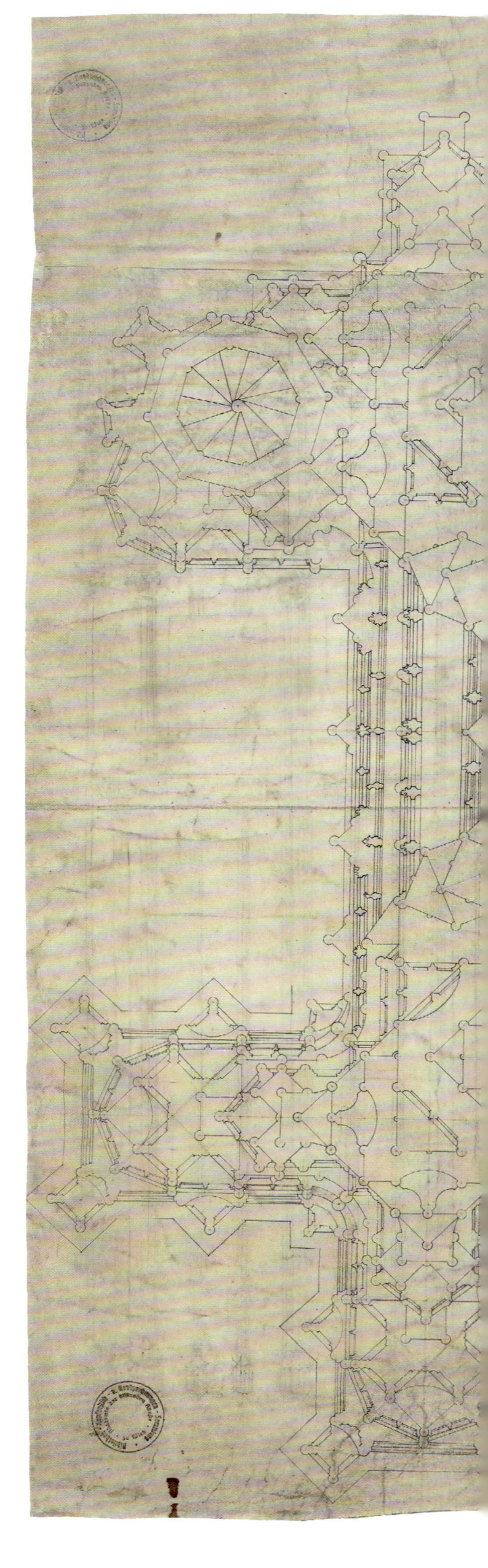

PLATE 72 (FOR RECTO, SEE PL. 48)
Lorenz Spenning or Workshop. Verso: Floor Plan for the North Tower (*Adlertor*), Stephansdom
(Saint Stephen's Cathedral), Vienna, ca. 1470

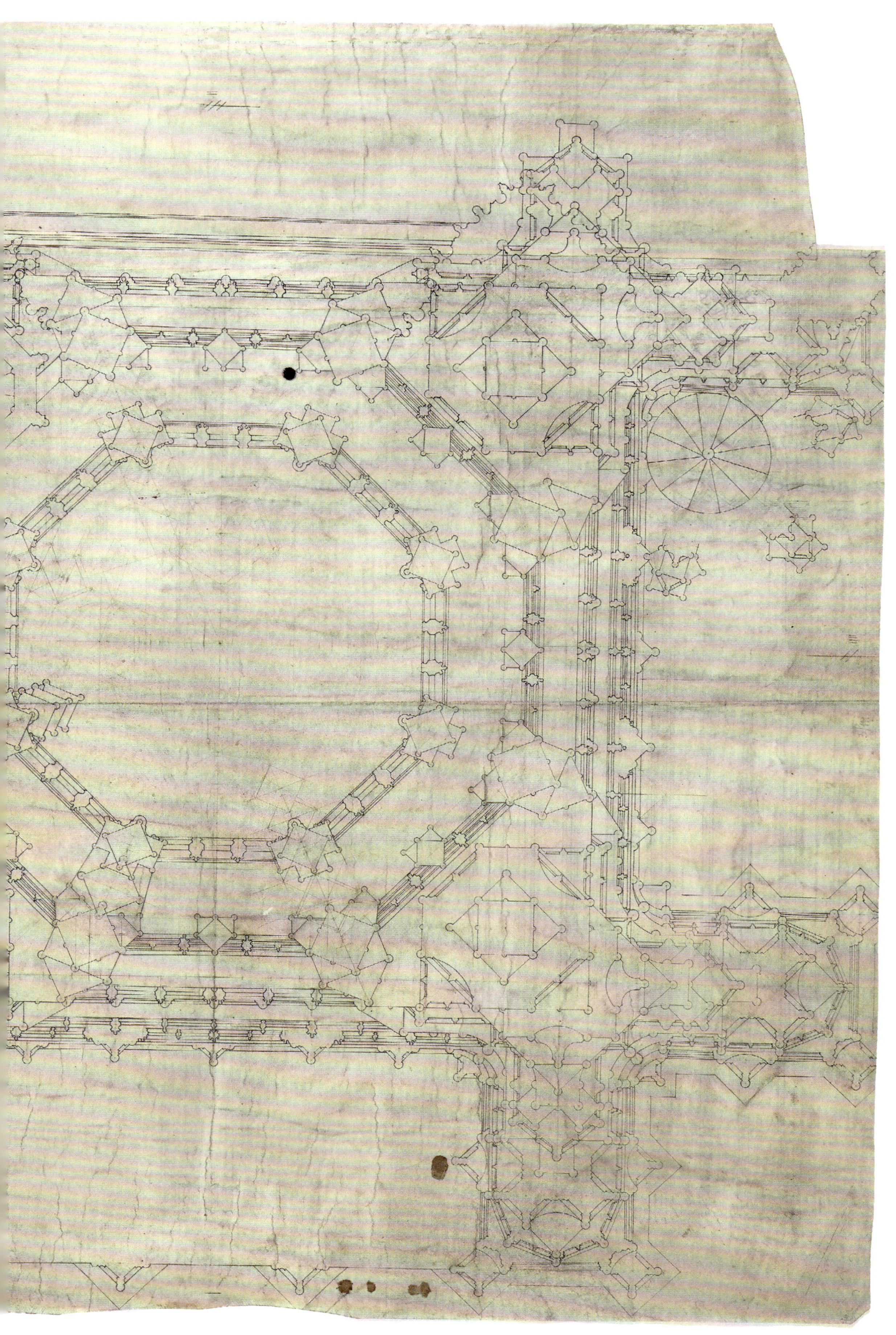

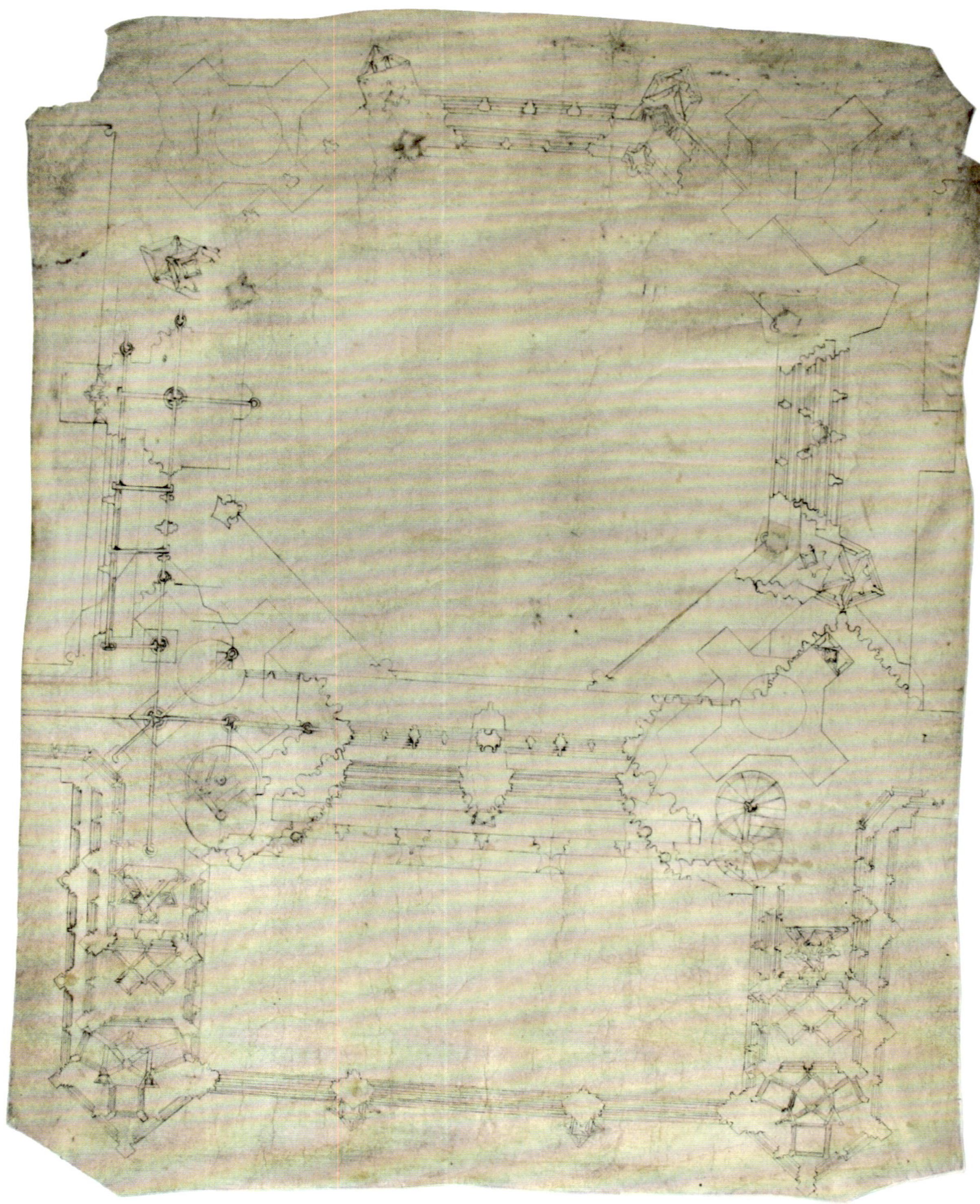

PLATE 73
Attributed to Matthäus Ensinger (recto) and Hans Hammer (verso). Recto (left): Floor Plan of
the Tower and Entrance Portal, Ulm Minster, ca. 1450–60; verso (right): Floor Plan of the
Octagonal Tower, Strasbourg Cathedral, 1480–90 (Drawing IIIC)

166

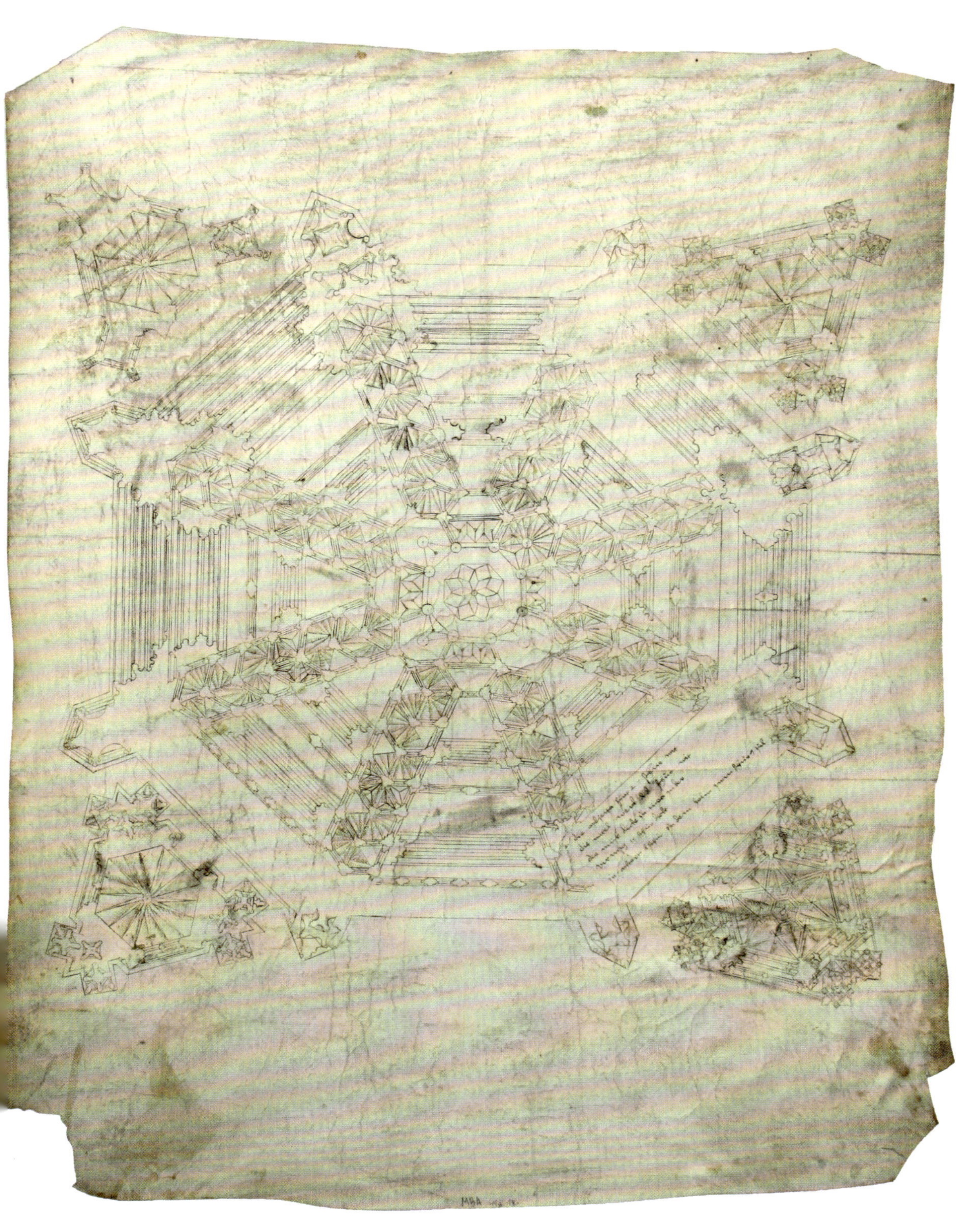

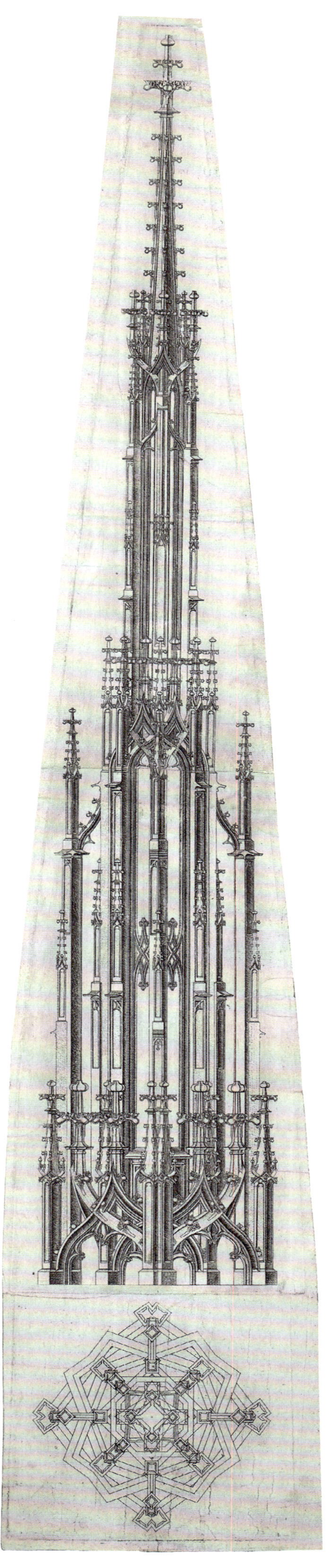
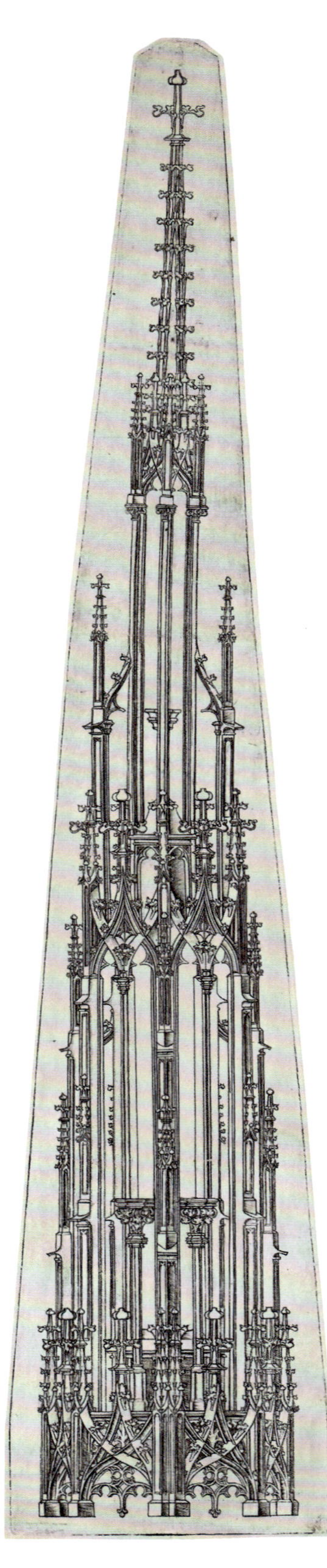
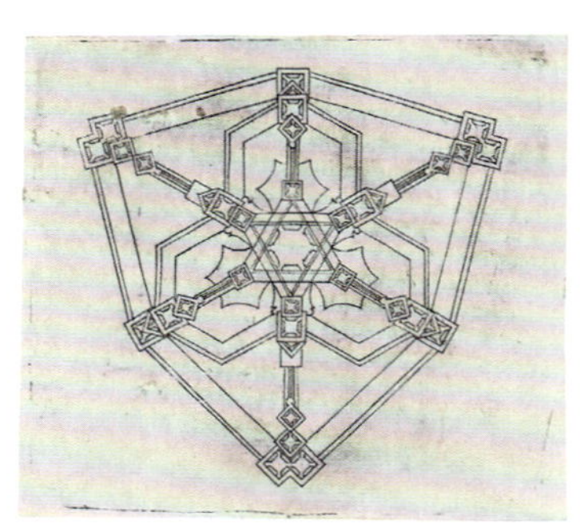

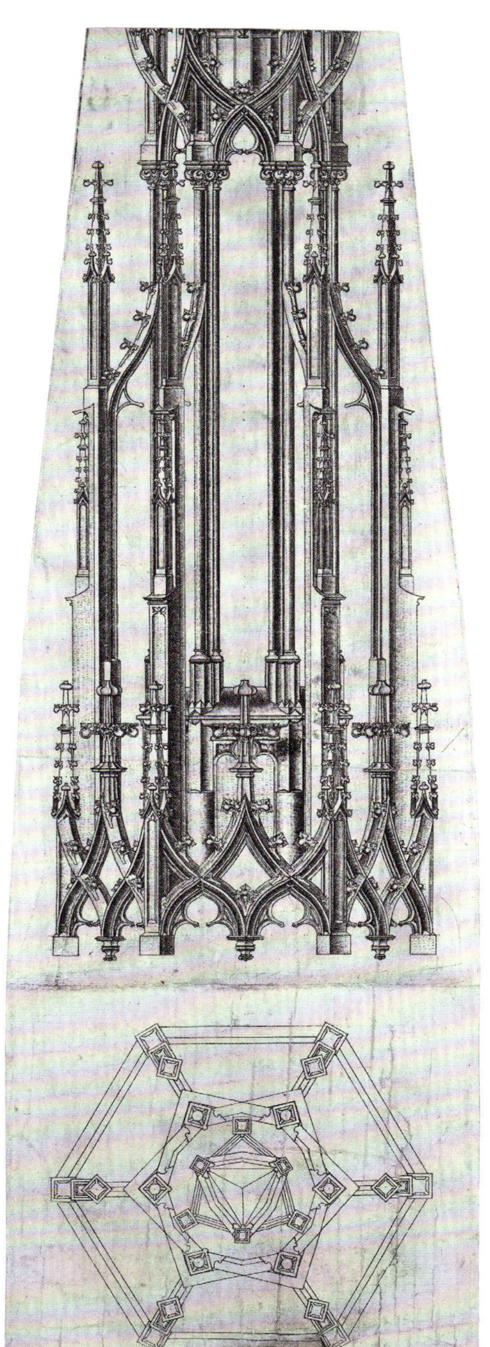

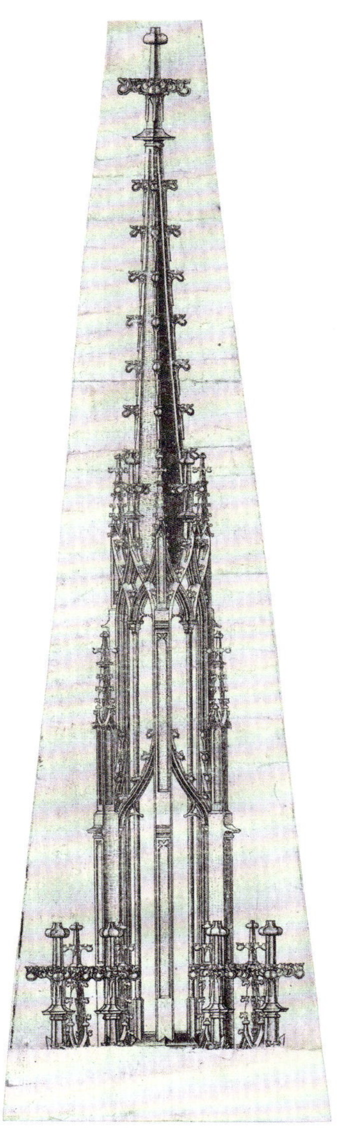

PLATE 74
Wenzel von Olmütz. Design for a Baldachin, with Elevation and Twelve-Sided Plan, ca. 1481–92

PLATE 75
Wenzel von Olmütz. Design for a Baldachin (in two parts), with Elevation (above) and Irregular Hexagonal Plan (below), ca. 1481–92

PLATE 76
Wenzel von Olmütz. Design for a Baldachin (in two parts), with Body and Hexagonal Plan (left) and Spire (right), ca. 1481–92

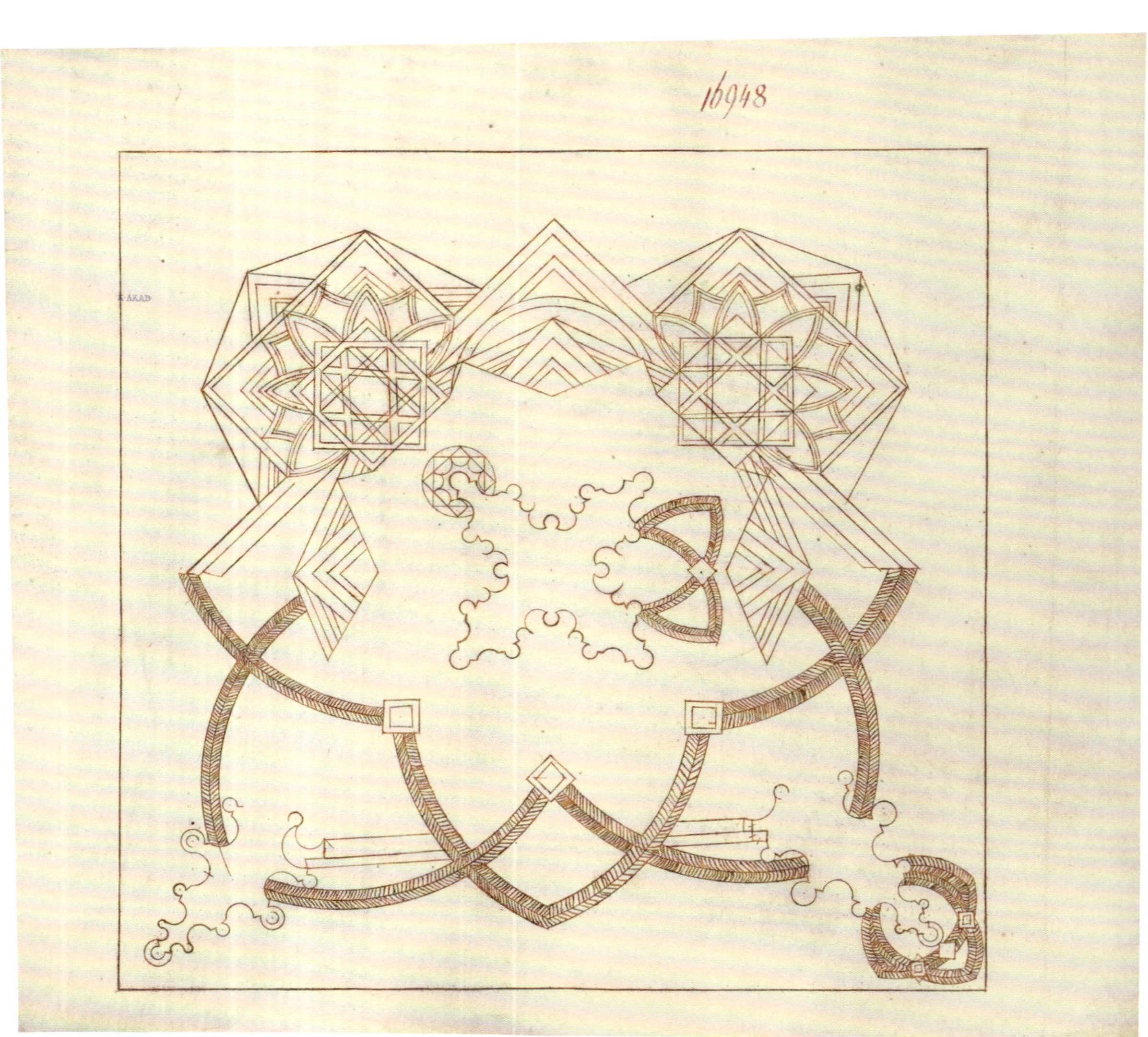

PLATE 77

After Lorenz Lechler. Floor Plan of the Sacrament House in Esslingen, ca. 1500

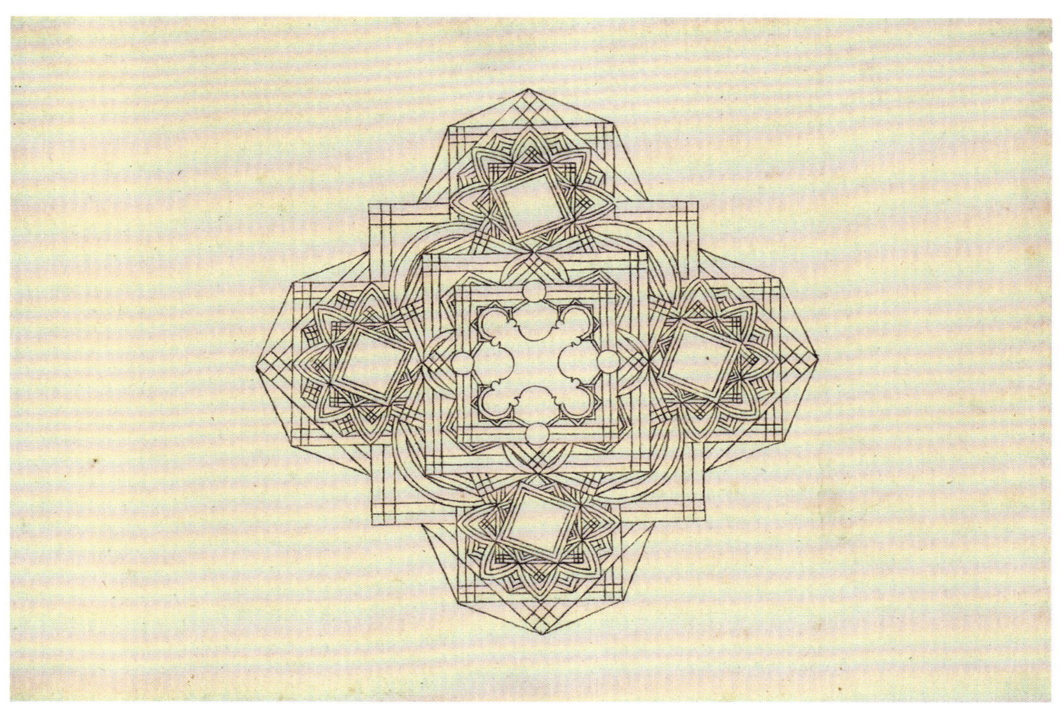

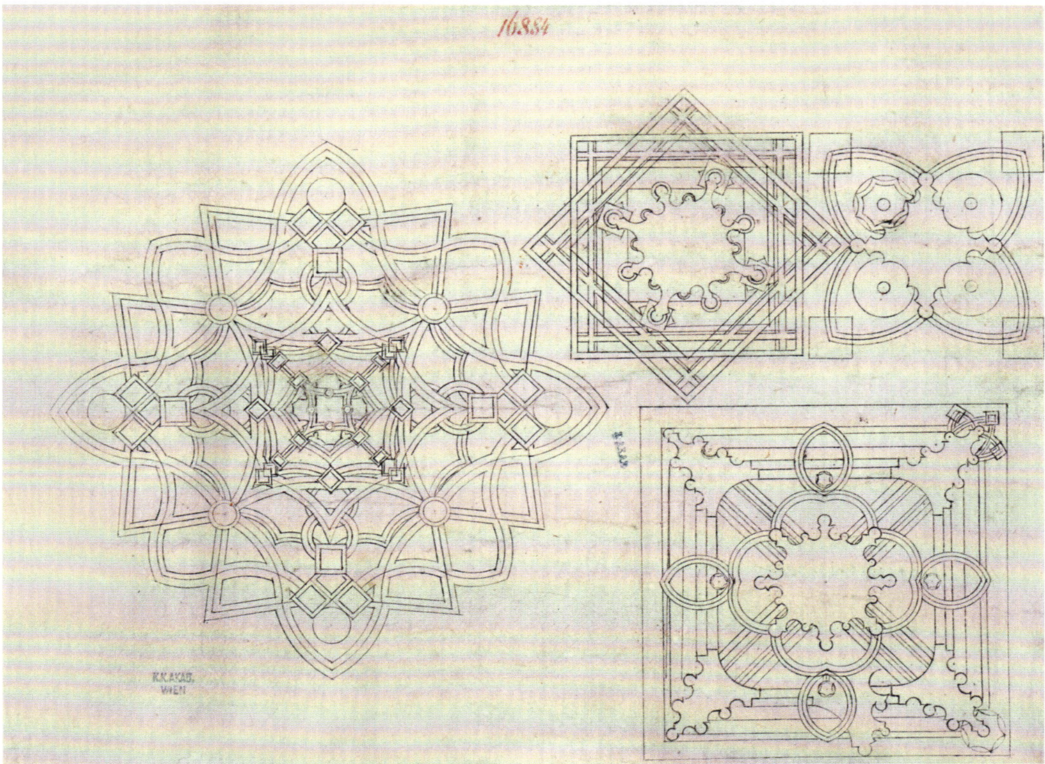

PLATE 78

Attributed to Jörg Schweiger the Elder, after Lorenz Lechler. Ideal Floor Plan of the Sacrament House in Esslingen, ca. 1500–1510

PLATE 79

After Lorenz Lechler. Floor Plans and Sections of the Sacrament House in Esslingen, ca. 1515

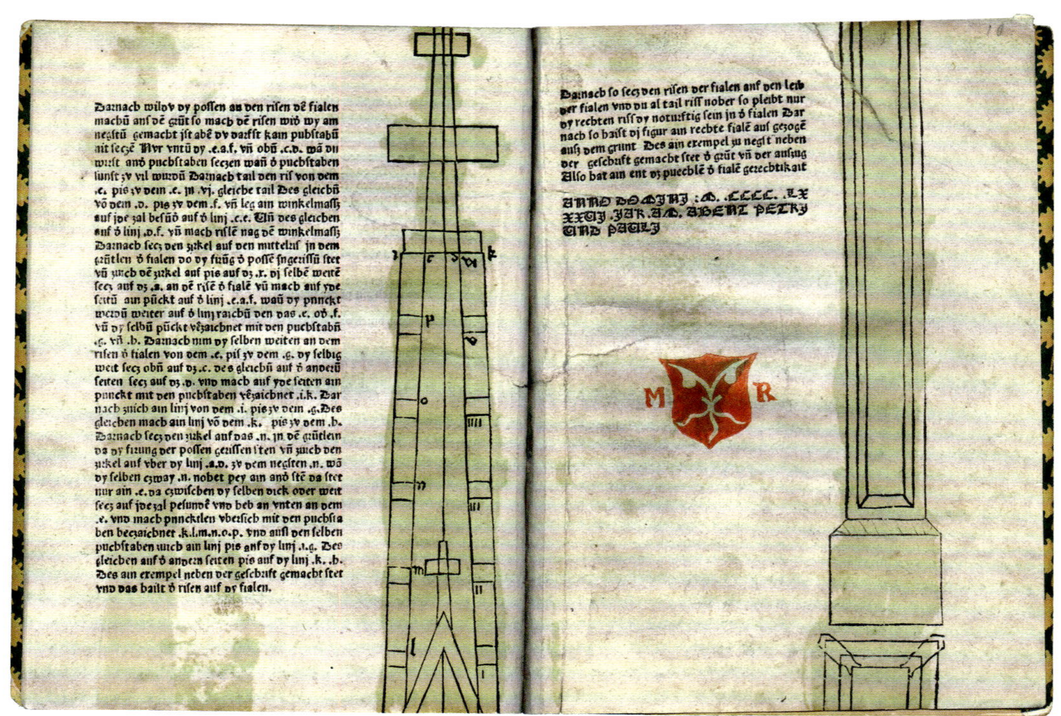

PLATE 80

Mathes (Matthäus) Roriczer. The Booklet on the Proper Construction of Pinnacles (*Das Büchlein von der Fialen Gerechtigkeit*). Printed by Mathes Roriczer, Regensburg, 1486

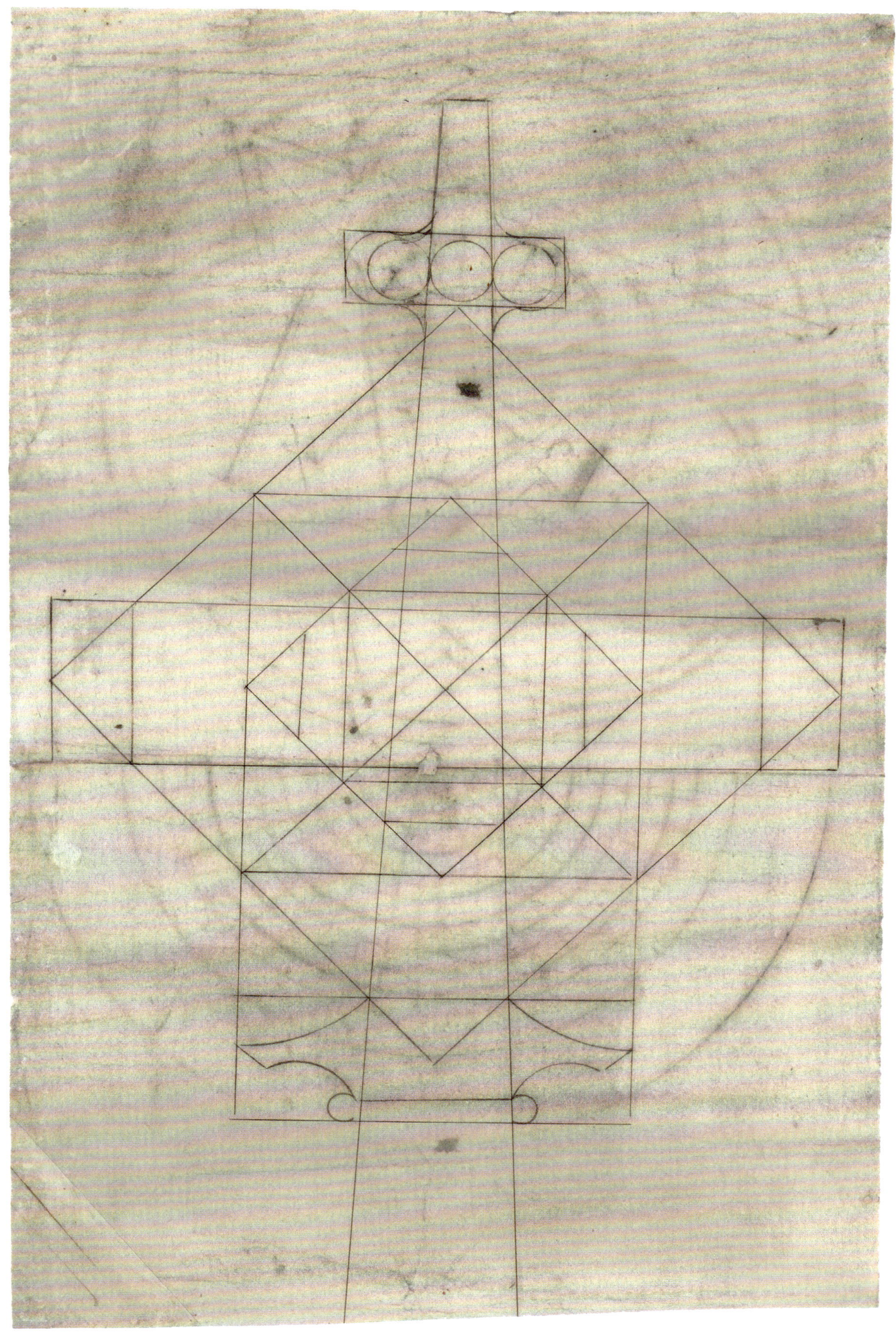

Unidentified Austrian artist. Geometrical Scheme for a Finial, ca. 1515

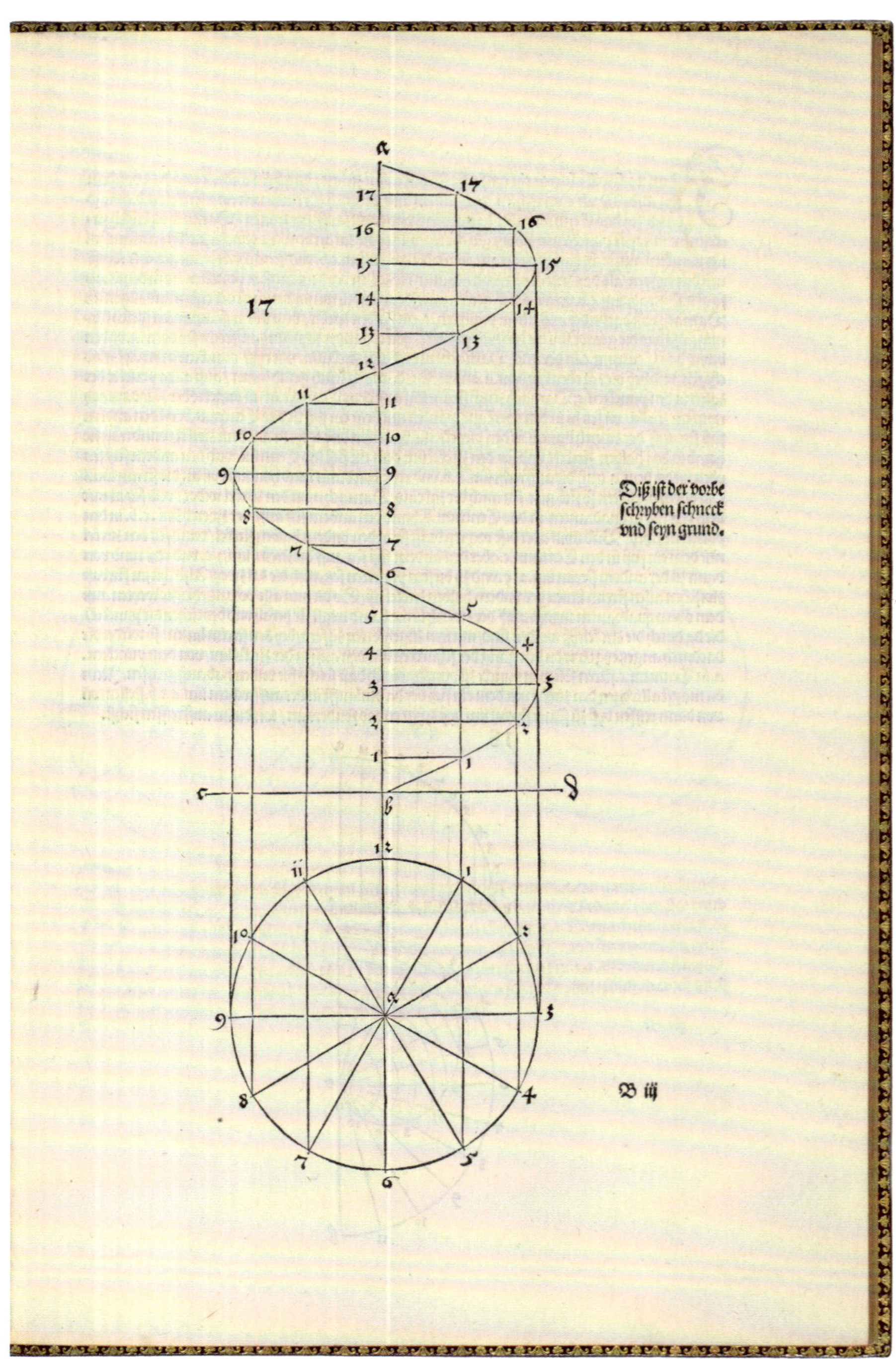

PLATE 82

Albrecht Dürer. Illustration of How to Pull a Spiral Staircase from a Circular Plan, in the Treatise on Measurement (*Underweysung der Messung*). Printed by Hieronymus Andreae, Nuremberg, 1525

174

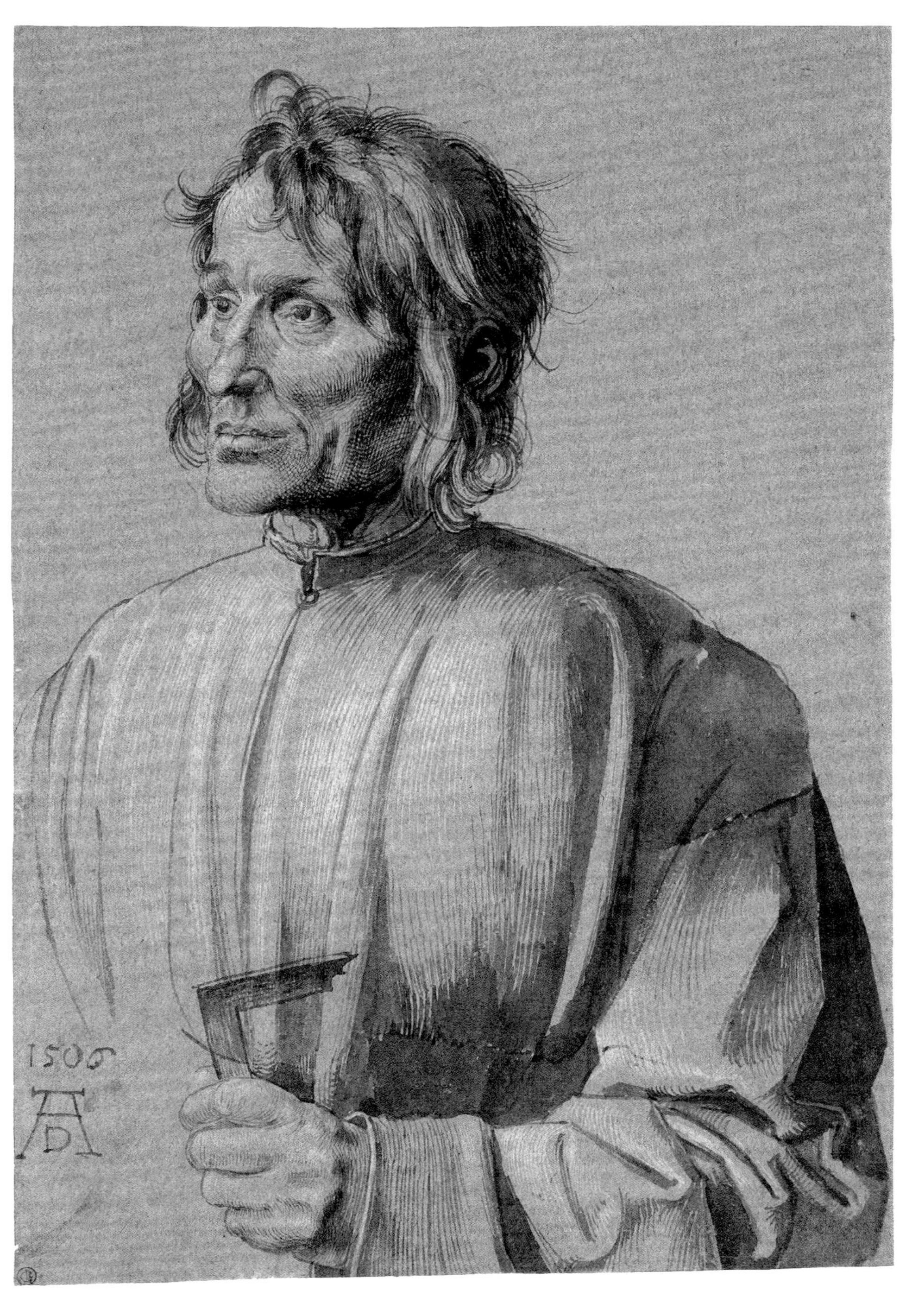

PLATE 83
Albrecht Dürer. Portrait of the Architect Hieronymus of Augsburg, 1506

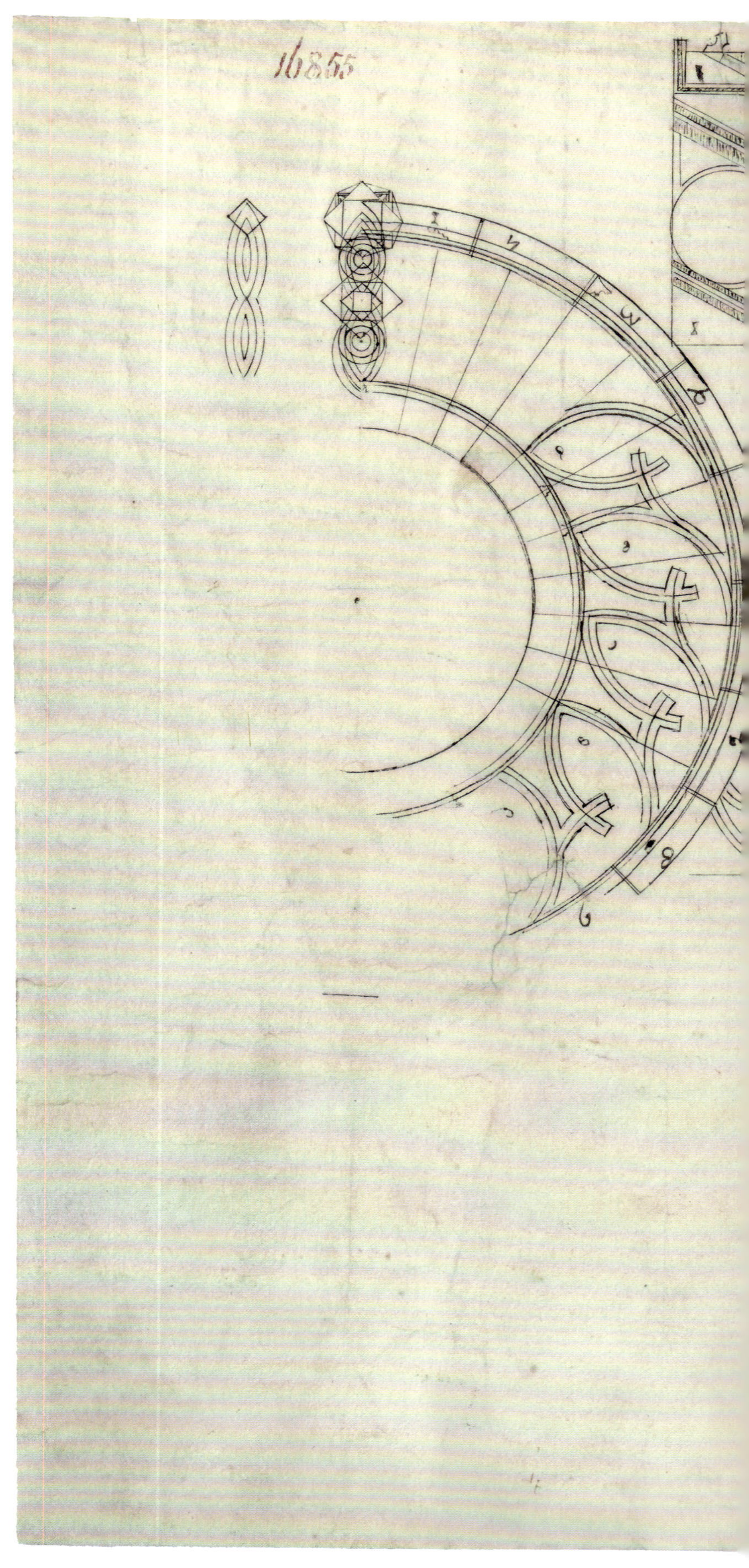

PLATE 84

After Anton Pilgram. Elevation, Section, and Floor Plan for the Stairs to the Pulpit, Stephansdom (Saint Stephen's Cathedral), Vienna, ca. 1515

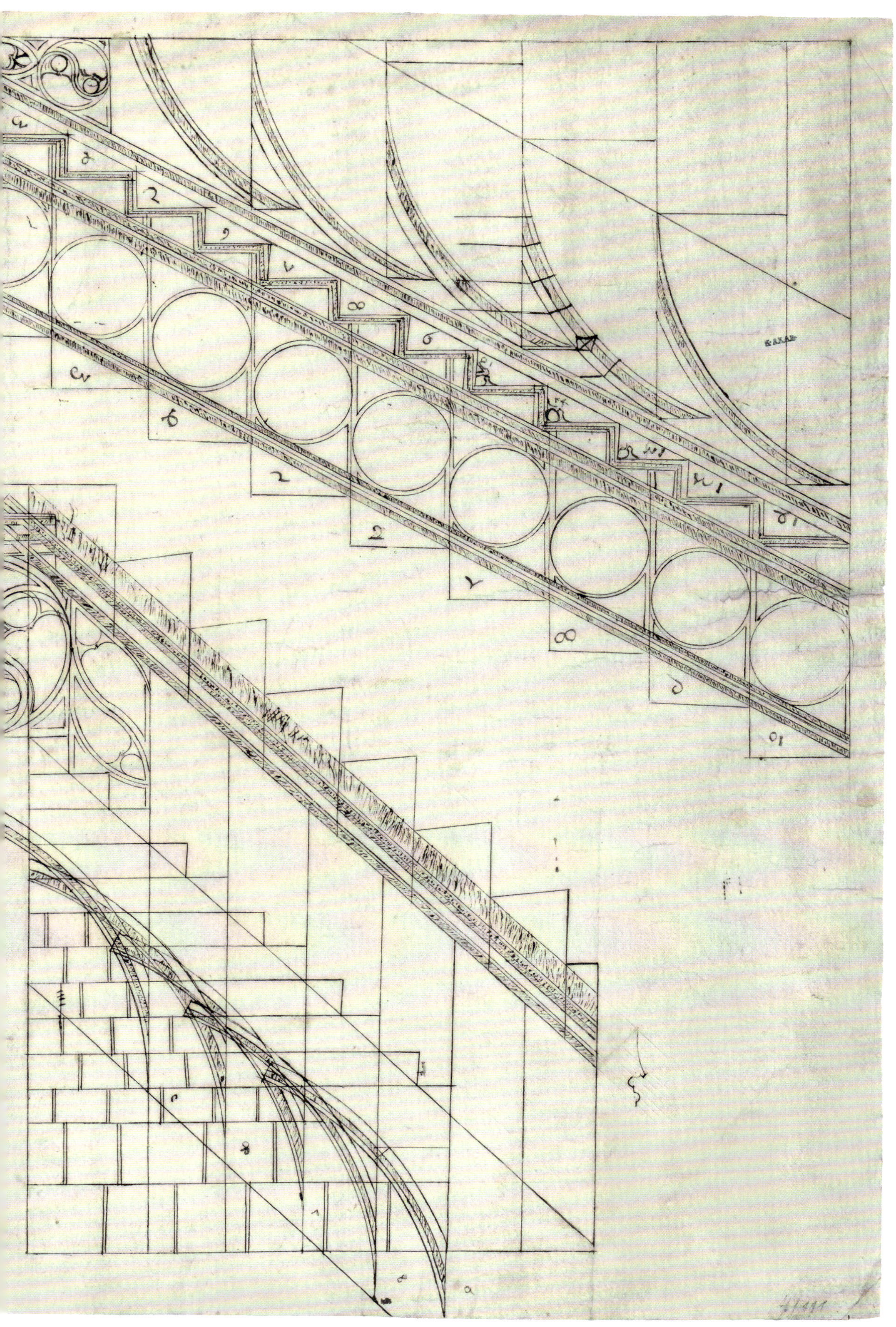

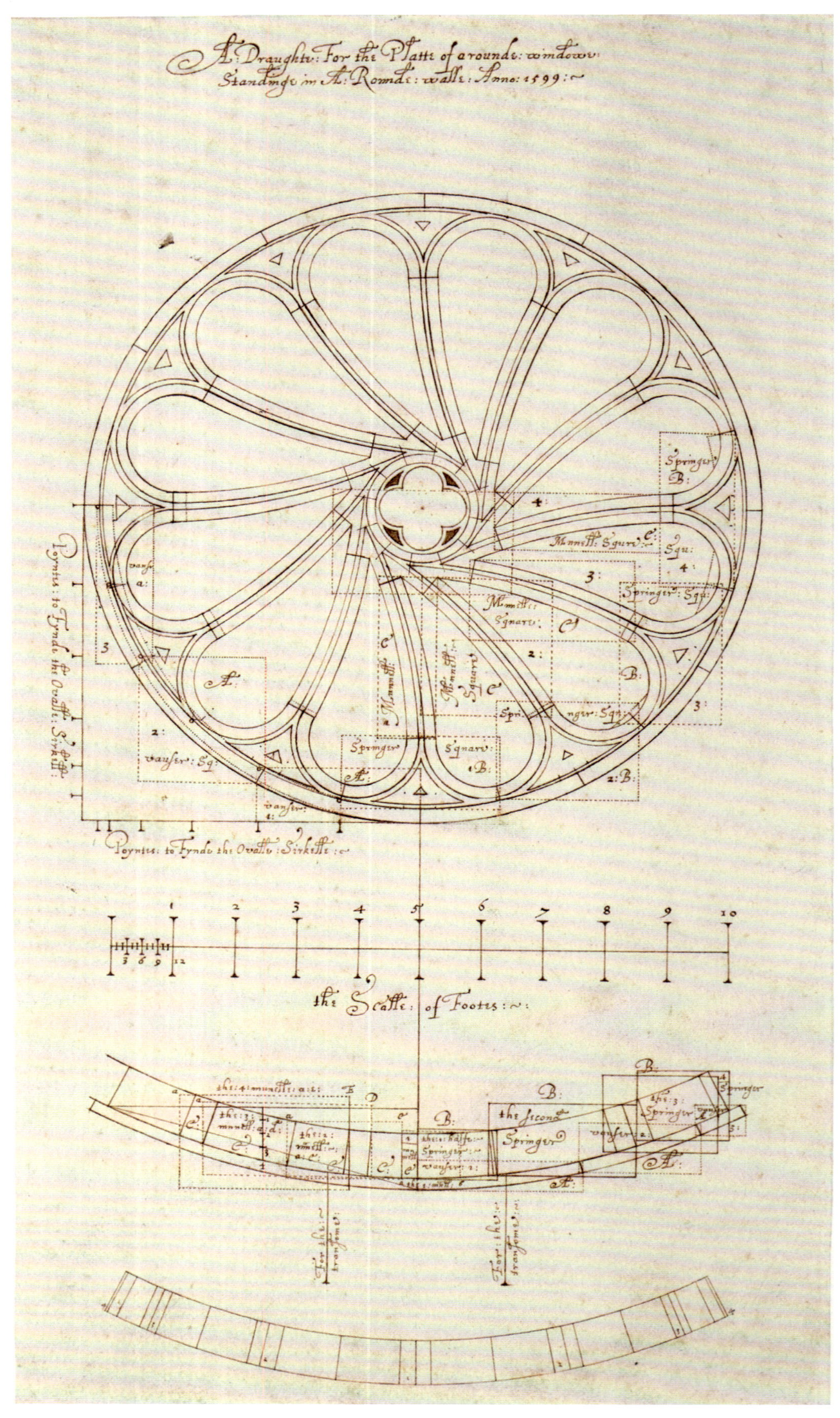

PLATE 85

Robert Smythson. Elevation of a Rose Window, with Measurements, Plans, and a Scale, 1599

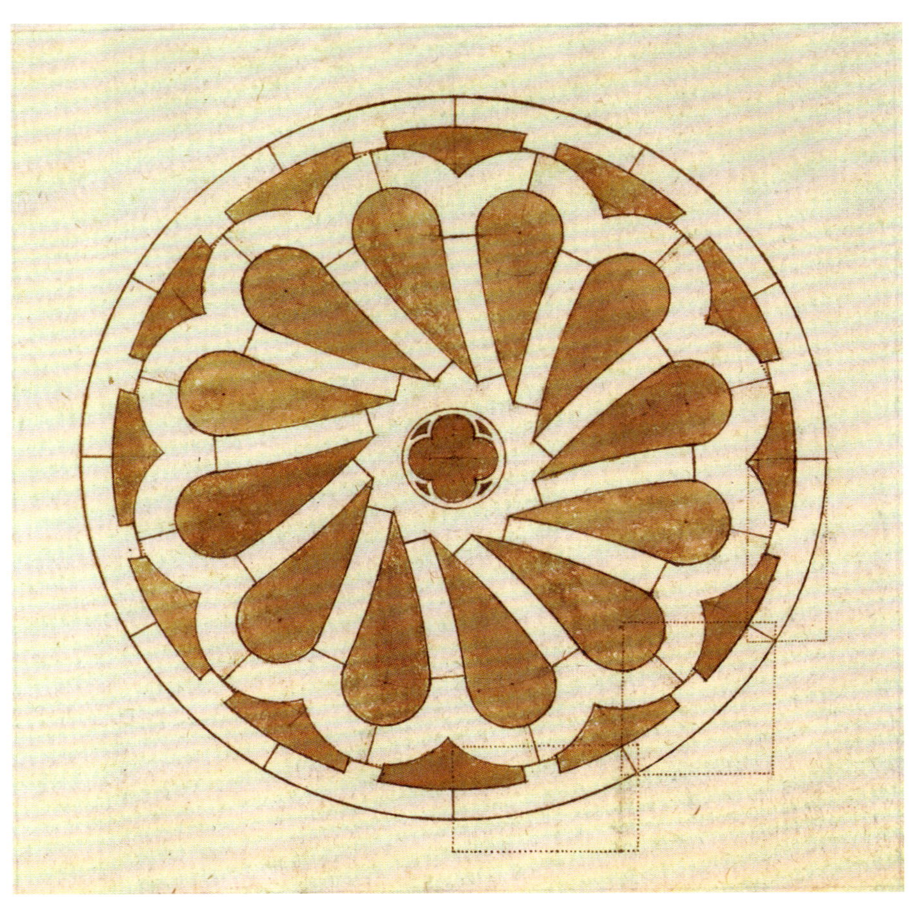

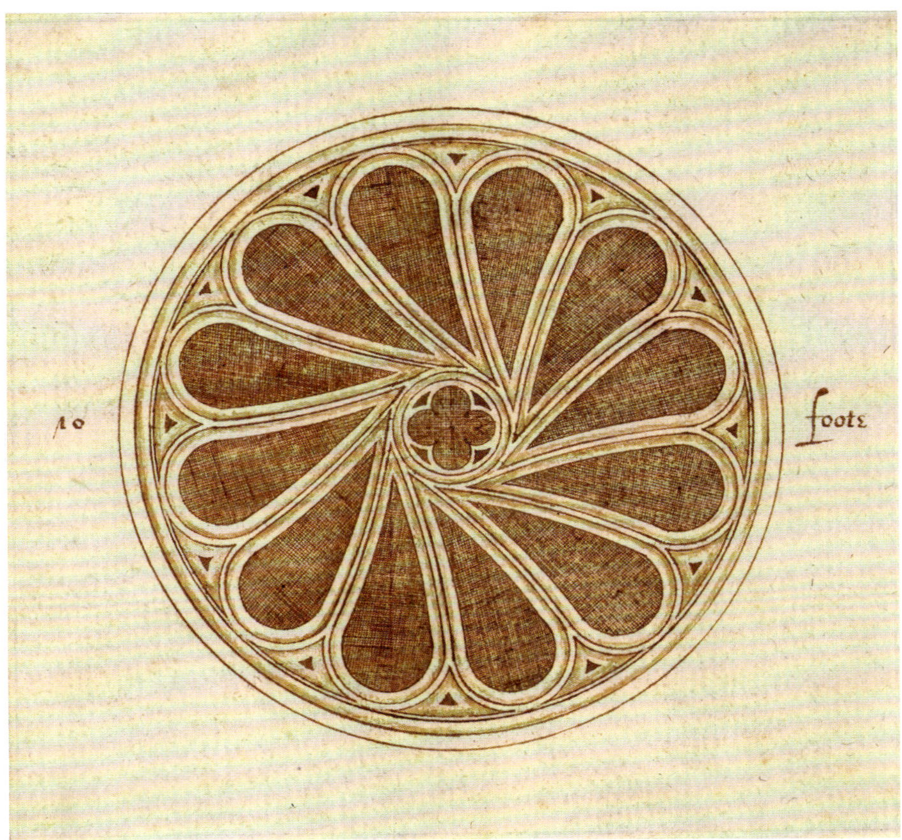

PLATE 86
Robert Smythson. Diagram of a Rose Window Specifying Stone Elements, 1599

PLATE 87
Robert Smythson. Diagram of a Rose Window Specifying the Carved Relief, 1599

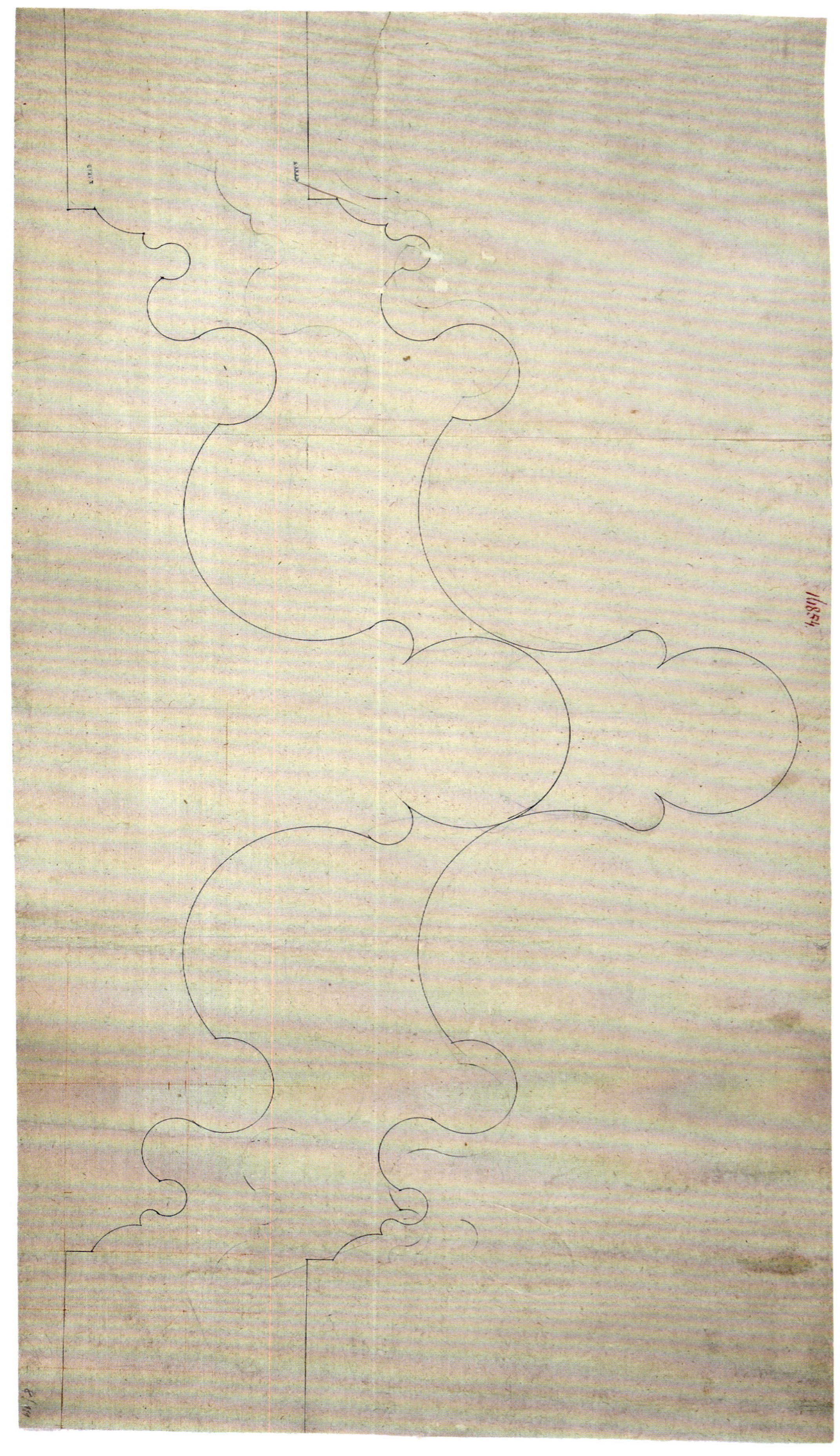

Lorenz Spenning or Workshop. Profile (Template Outline) of the Vaulting Shafts, North Tower, Stephansdom (Saint Stephen's Cathedral), Vienna, ca. 1467–76

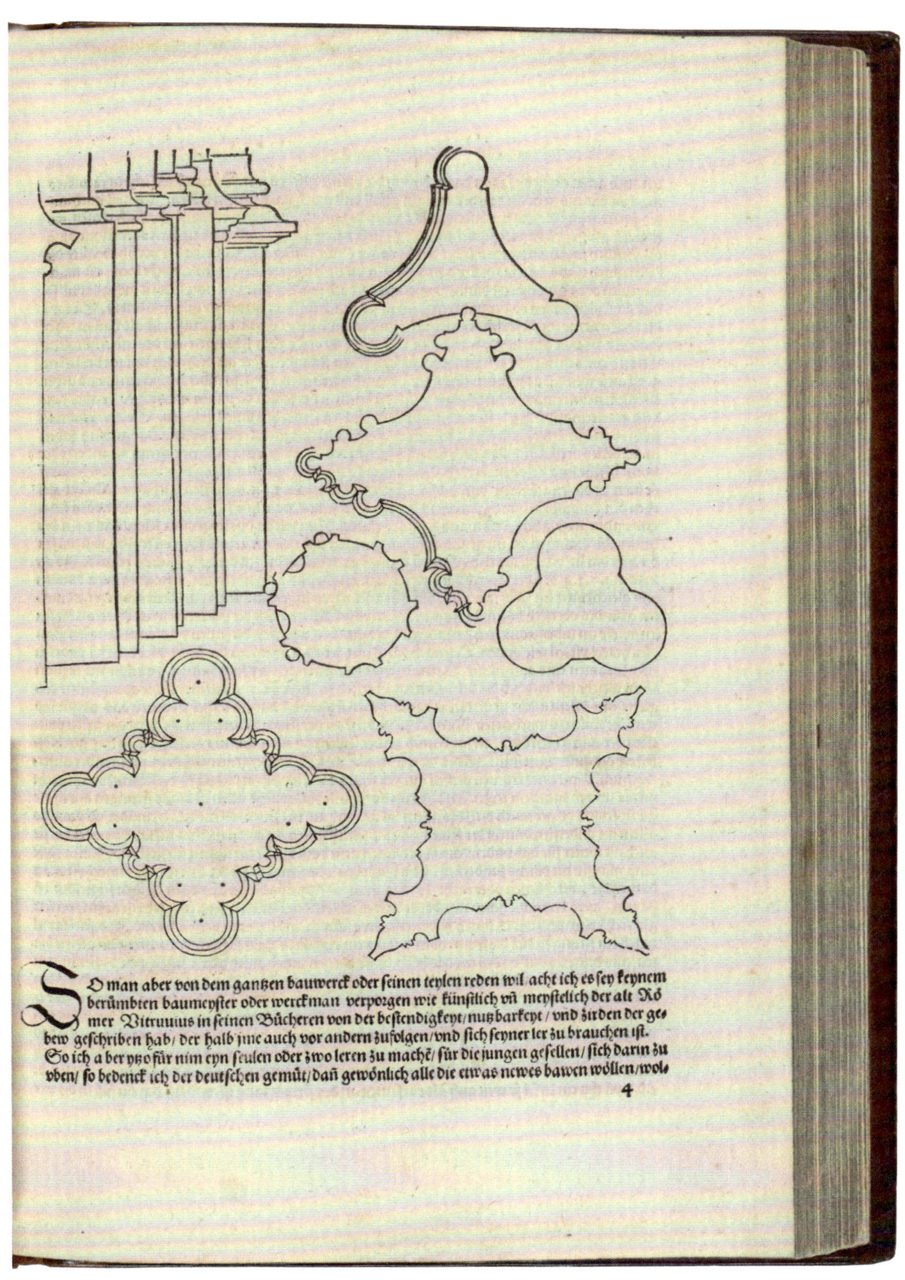

SO man aber von dem gantzen bauwerck oder seinen teylen reden wil/acht ich es sey keynem
berümbten baumeyster oder werckman verporgen wie künstlich vñ meysterlich der alt Rö
mer Vitruuius in seinen Bücheren von der bestendigkeyt/nutzbarkeyt / vnd zirden der ge-
bew geschriben hab/ der halb jme auch vor andern zufolgen/vnd sich seyner ler zu brauchen ist.
So ich a ber ytzo für nim eyn seulen oder zwo leren zu machẽ/ für die jungen gesellen/ sich darin zu
vben/ so bedenck ich der deutschen gemüt/dañ gewönlich alle die etwas newes bawen wöllen/wol-

4

Albrecht Dürer. Illustrations of Pillar Profiles and Silhouettes, in the Treatise on Measurement
(*Underweysung der Messung*). Printed by Hieronymus Andreae, Augsburg, 1525

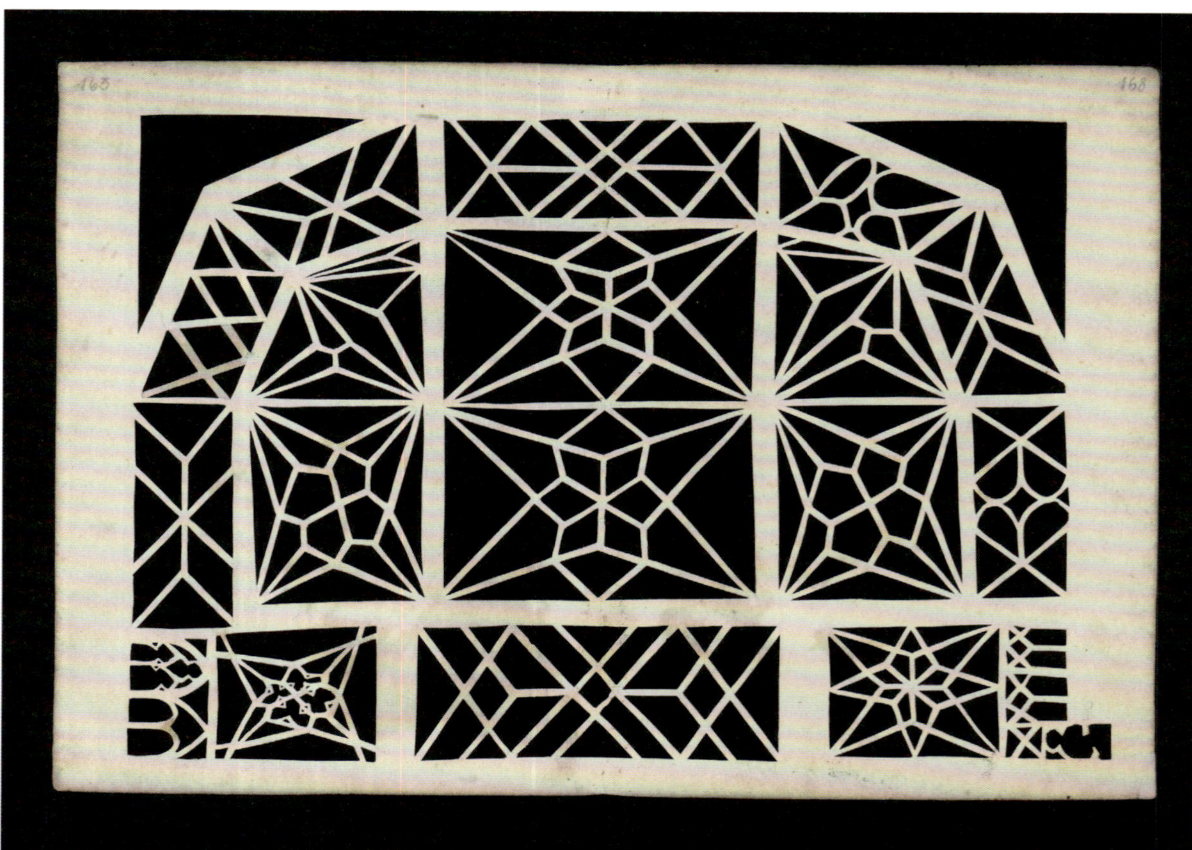

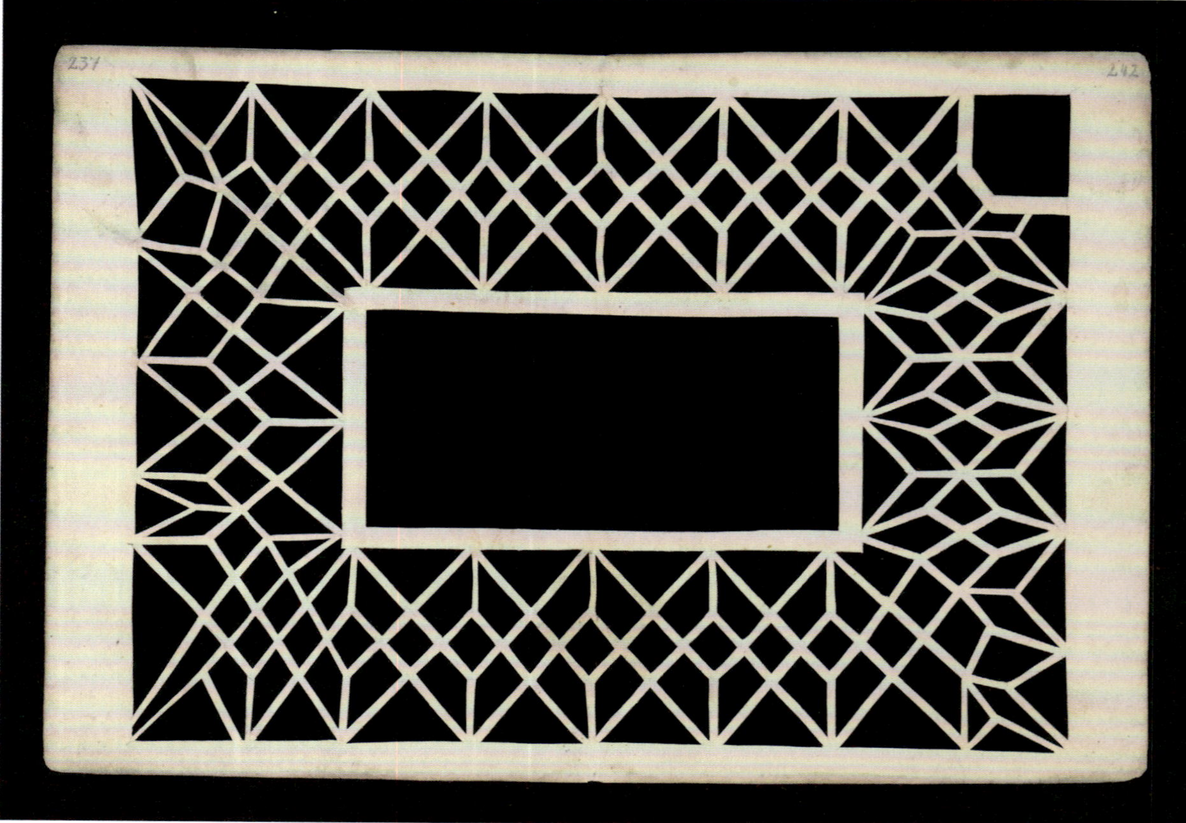

Unidentified German artist (Swabian region). Cut-Paper Vaulting Patterns, from a Lodge Book (*Bauhüttenbuch*), ca. 1470–80; modern ground

Unidentified German artist (Swabian region). Cut-Paper Vaulting Patterns, from a Lodge Book (*Bauhüttenbuch*), ca. 1470–80; modern ground

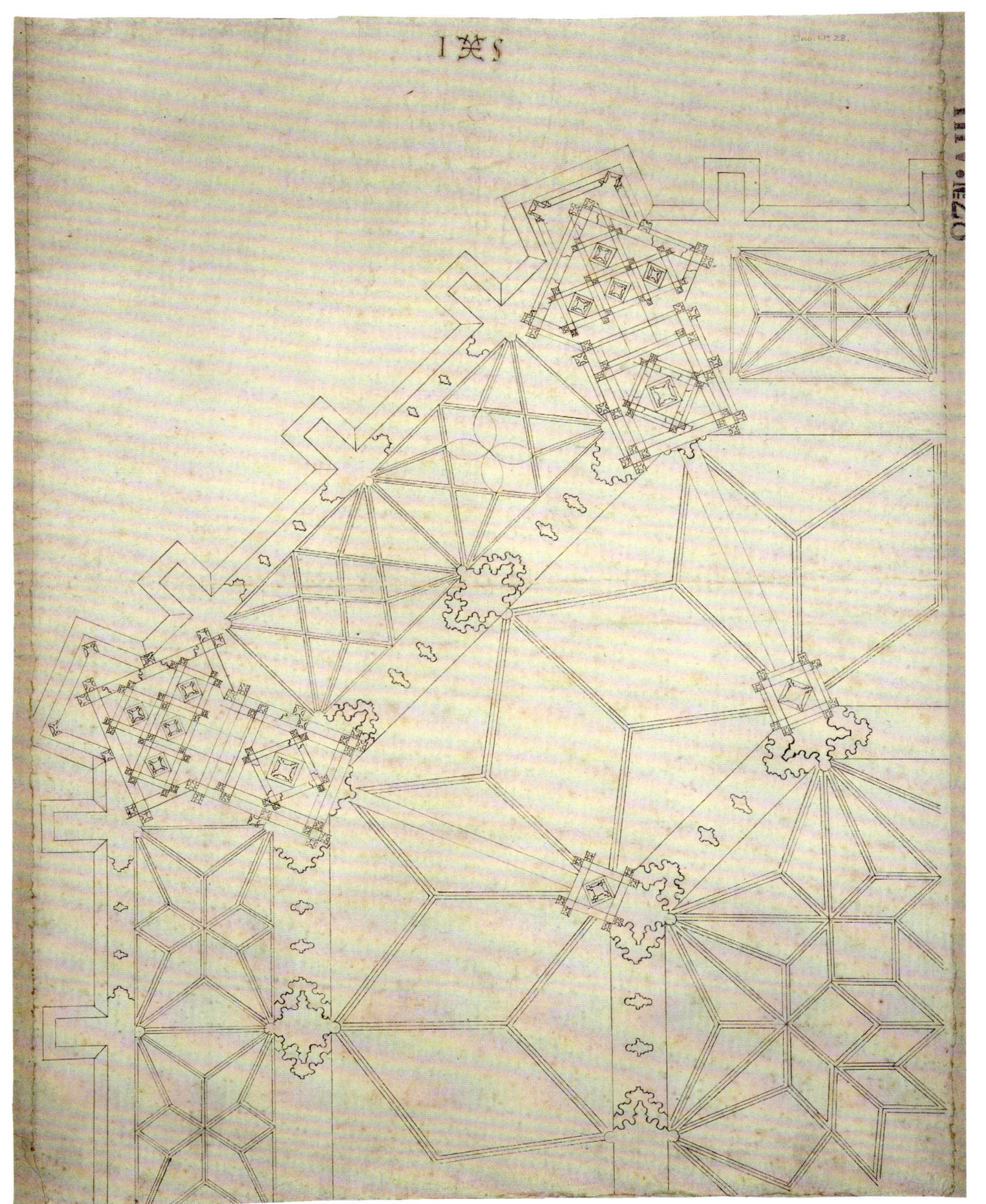

Bernard Nonnenmacher. Vaulting Plan for a Choir and Ambulatory, ca. 1520

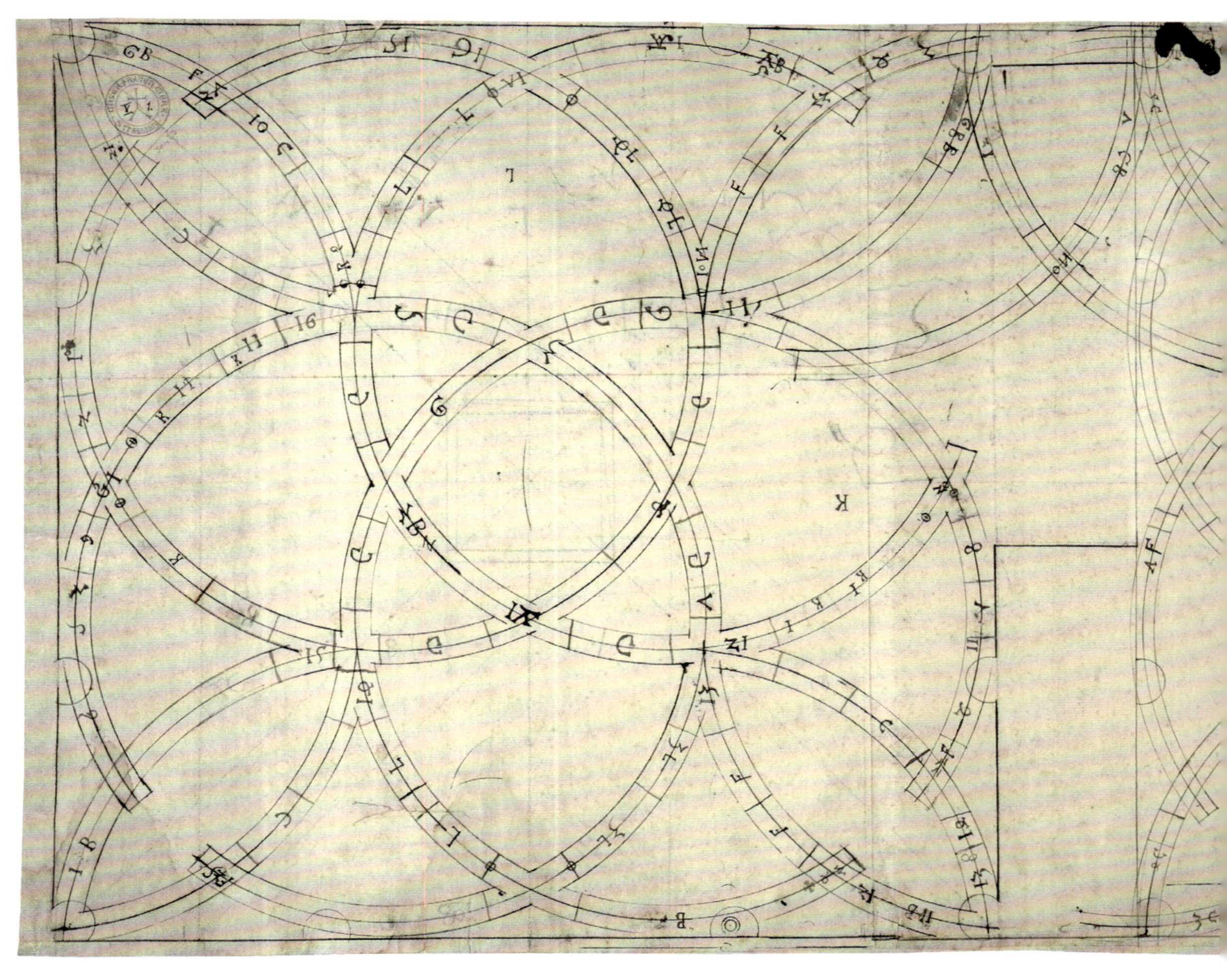

PLATE 93

Bernard Nonnenmacher. Vaulting Plan for the Chapel of Saint Catherine, Strasbourg Cathedral,
with Instructions for the Assemblage of the Vaulting, ca. 1542–46

184

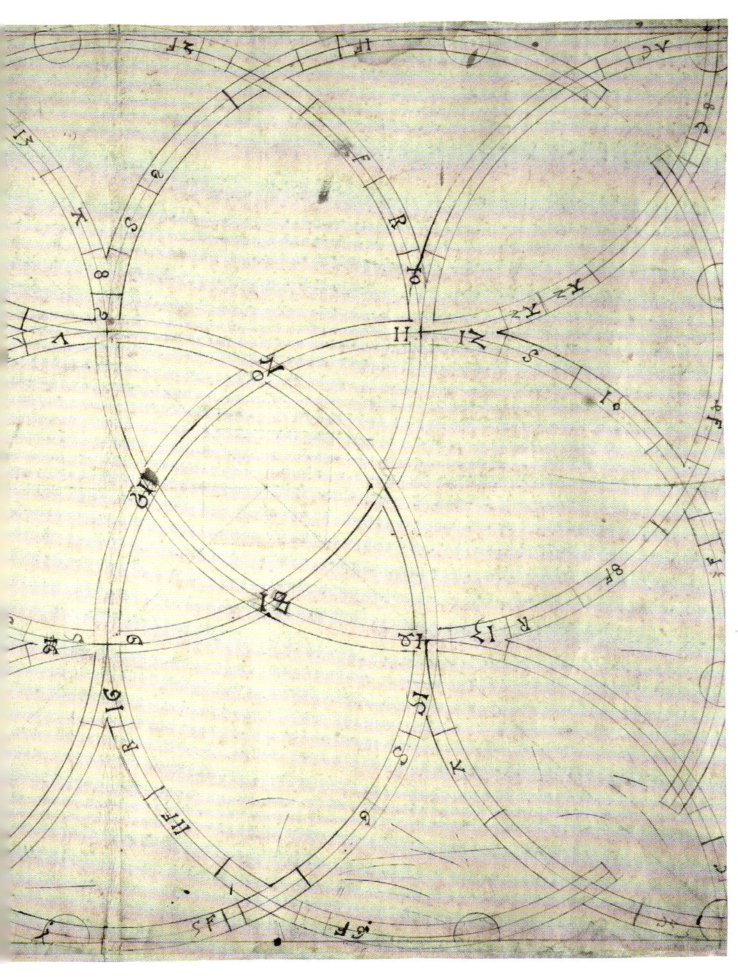

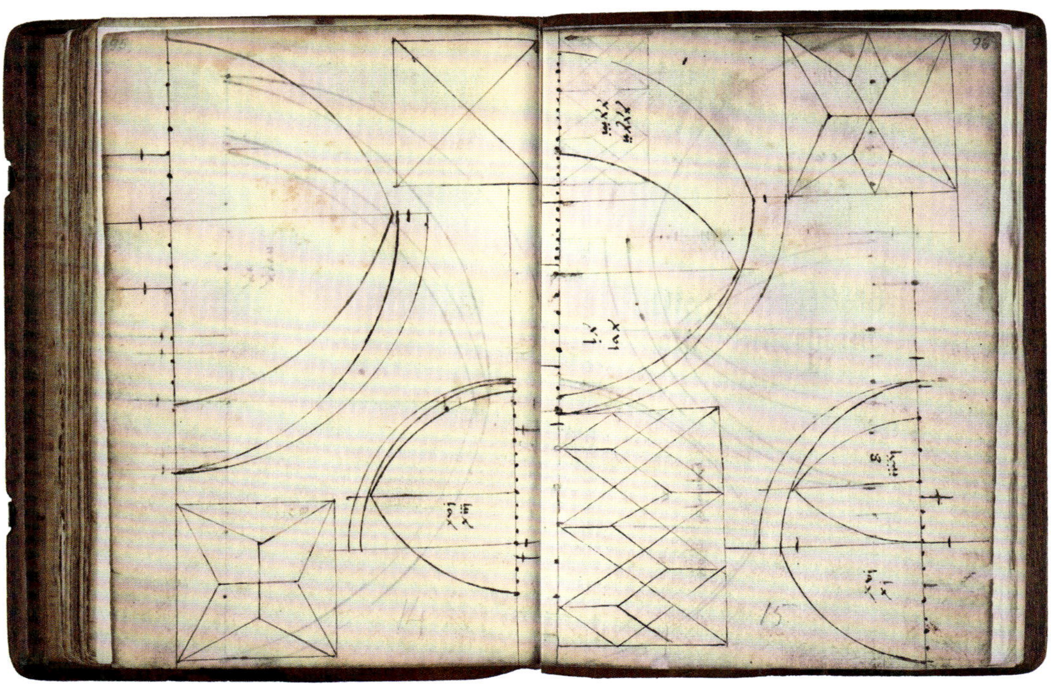

Unidentified German artist (Swabian region). Vaulting Plans and Exercises to Determine Their Height and Angle, in a Lodge Book (*Bauhüttenbuch*), ca. 1470–80

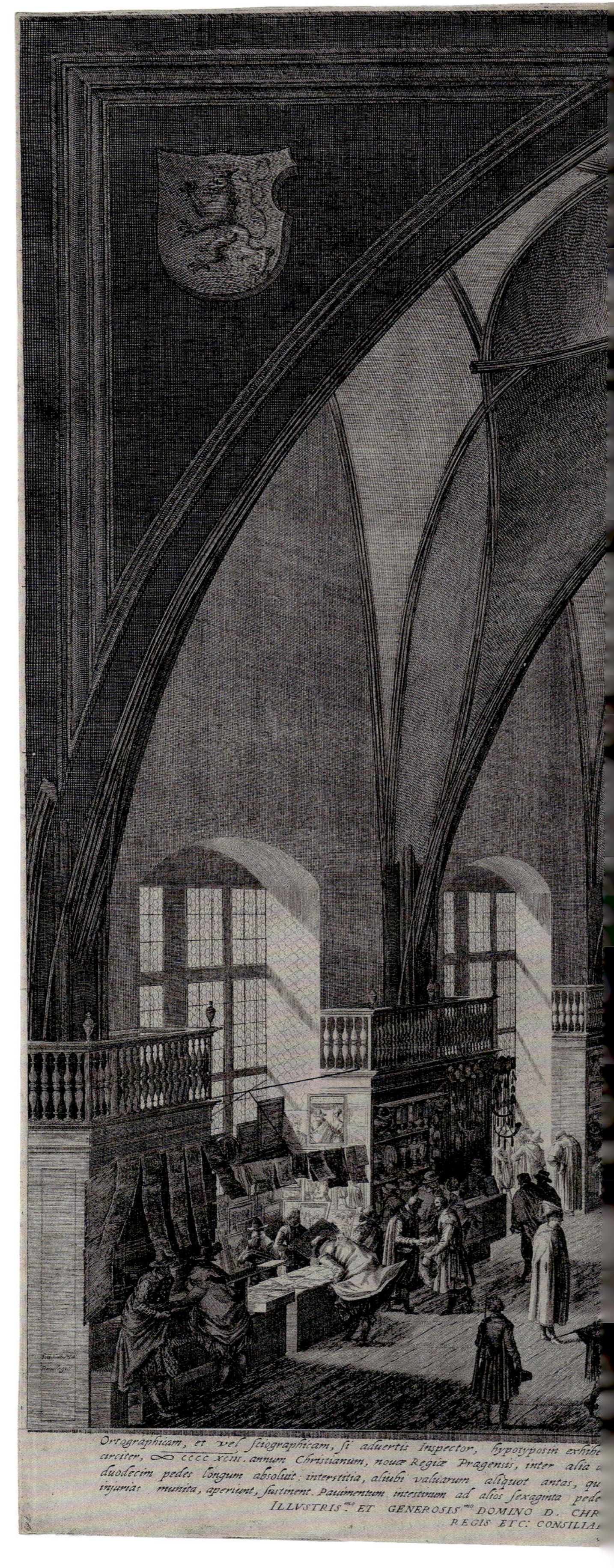

Aegidius Sadeler II. Interior View of Vladislav Hall at Prague Castle during the Annual Fair, 1607

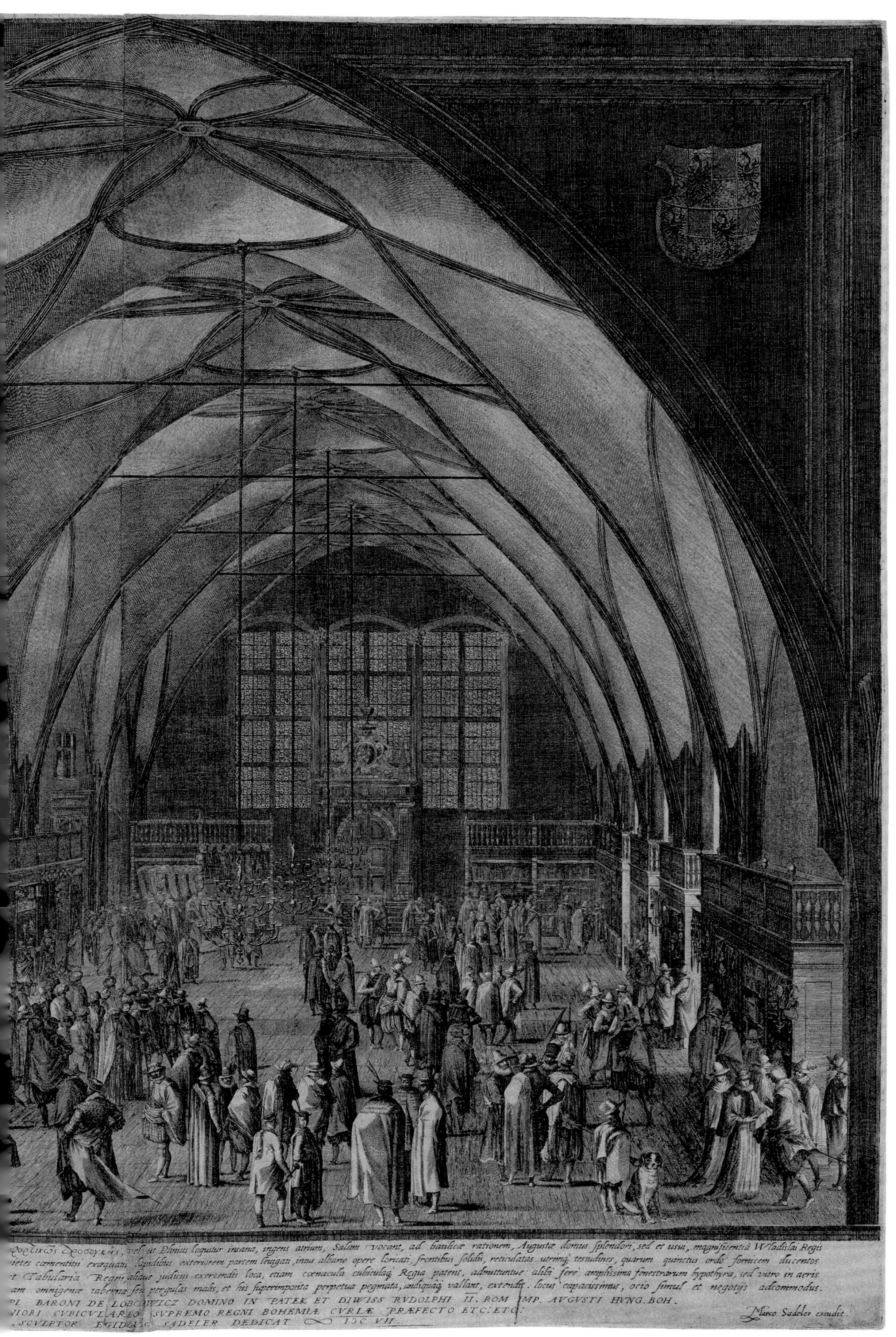
ΠΟΕΤΙΚῶς ΔΟΘΟΟΥΚΗϹ, vel ut Plinius loquitur insana, ingens atrium, Salam vocant, ad basilicæ rationem, Augustæ domus splendori, sed et usui, magnificentiâ Wladislai Regis
...etes cæmentitii exæquati lapidibus exteriorem partem leuigati, intus albario opere loricati, frontibus solidis, reticulatas utrinq testudines, quarum quinctus ordo fornicem ducentos
...t Tabularia Regni, aliaue judicijs exercendis loca, etiam cœnacula cubiculaq Regia patent, admittuntue: alibi ferè amplissima fenestrarum hypothyra, sed vitro in aeris
...am omnigenæ tabernæ seu pergulas malis, et his superimposita perpetua pegmata, undiquaq vallant, extendit. locus capacissimus, ocio simul et negotijs adcommodus.
...PL BARONI DE LOBCOWICZ DOMINO IN PATEK ET DIWISS RVDOLPHI II. ROM IMP. AVGVSTI HVNG. BOH.
...VIORI CVBICVLARIO SVPREMO REGNI BOHEMIÆ CVRLÆ PRÆFECTO ETC: ETC:
...SCVLPTOR EGIDIVS SADELER DEDICAT IↃC VII.
Marco Sadeler excudit.

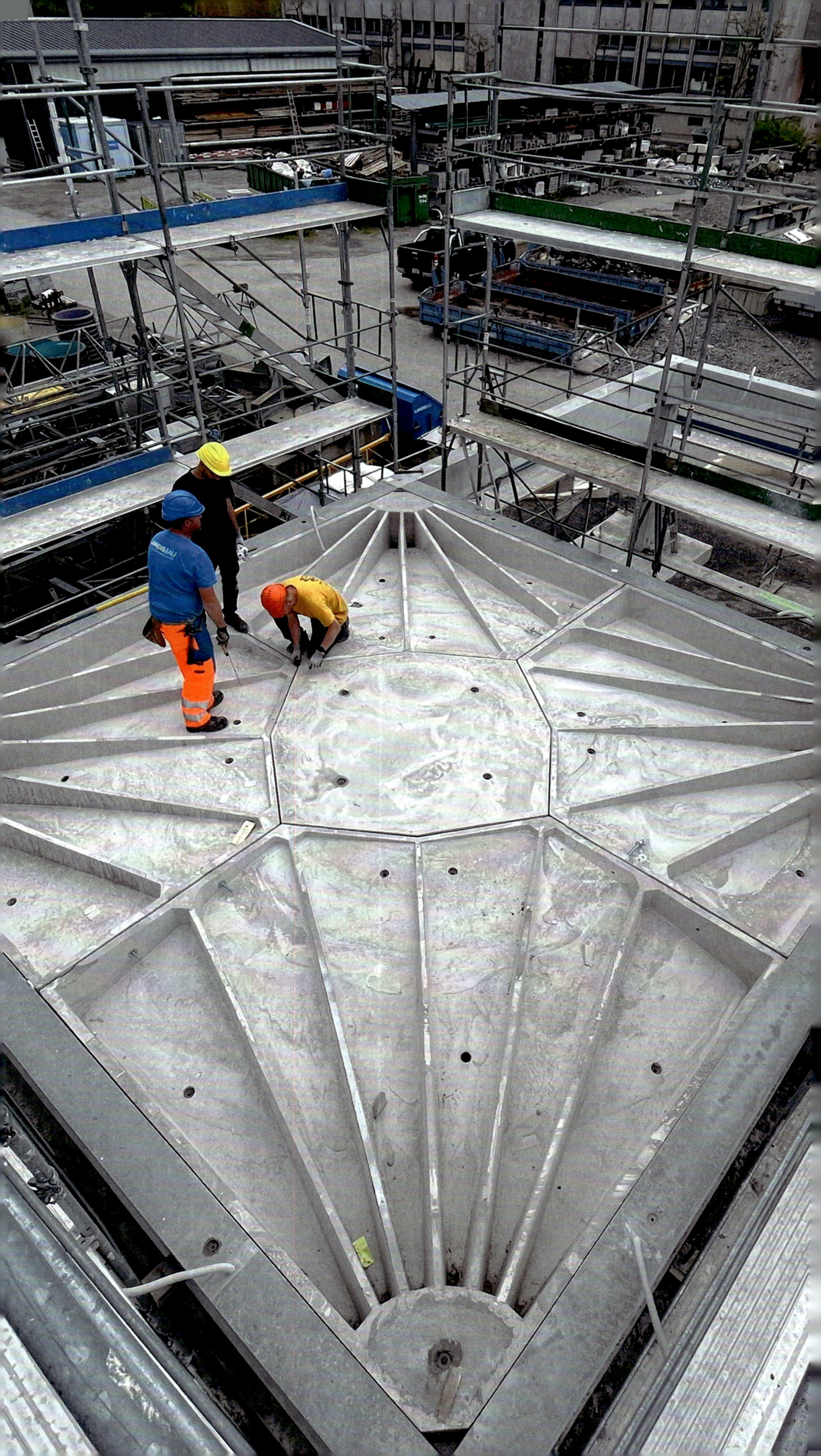

The Promise of Gothic Geometry

The Block Research Group at the Federal Institute of Technology (ETH) Zurich reimagines structural design by integrating historic masonry techniques with computational design and digital fabrication technology. Founded in 2010 and centered on the motto Strength Through Geometry, the research group designs efficient structures by leveraging geometry—in much the same way Gothic architects did—to optimize material use, minimize waste, and enhance structural performance. Its commercial spin-off Vaulted AG translates this pioneering research into practical, market-ready solutions that redefine efficiency and sustainability in construction.

Modern-day environmental challenges demand that structural designers treat ecological responsibility and ethical practice as core objectives of their discipline, along with "the three leading ideals of structural art—efficiency, economy, and elegance," laid out by the engineering scholar David P. Billington.[1] As the global population grows by an estimated two billion people over the next twenty-five years, we will require more than 620 billion square feet of livable space—the equivalent of building New York City every month until 2050. Meeting this demand requires economical and practical, research-driven solutions, as well as forward-thinking practitioners and stakeholders committed to sustainable innovation. Structural designers must therefore embrace solutions that align material efficiency with life-cycle considerations and avoid wasteful or unnecessary projects.

Long before modern engineers articulated the principles of structural engineering, the ideals of efficiency, economy, and elegance were fundamental to the work of Gothic architects. Flying buttresses, slender columns, and filigree ribbed vaulting patterns elegantly expressed the flow of forces; minimized material waste; and created large, open spaces. Although these results were driven by resource scarcity rather than a need for sustainability, circular economy has always been central to masonry structures. It was common to reuse elements from old buildings (spolia) or to employ stone blocks extracted from the construction site. Unreinforced Gothic masonry, such as arches and vaults, and more generally, medieval architects' reliance on structural form rather than over-engineered materials, further contributed to this inherent circularity.

Thanks to advances in technology, we can introduce the principles used by the master builders of the past into today's construction to design beautiful, sustainable structures at scale. One example is the funicular floor, which takes inspiration from Gothic architecture and, in combination with modern materials and smart fabrication, reduces material consumption and carbon emissions by two-thirds (PL. 96). Inspired by the masonry vault, this mono-material concrete floor is designed to follow the natural flow of compressive forces. Loads are efficiently transferred to the floor's supports through arch action, eliminating the need for embedded steel rebars. A slender vault, forming the visible bottom surface of the structure, is shaped to bear the distributed permanent loads—the structure's own weight and those of the floor finishes on top—through compression alone, while a series of ribs on top of the vaulted surface enhances stability and accommodates the additional weight of furniture and occupants, again through simple compression (FIG. 35). Tension ties along the perimeter connect the corners, canceling the outward thrusts generated by the vault. Like a masonry structure, a funicular floor is built from parts. Decoupling compression and tension in the unreinforced, rib-stiffened vault and the ties allows these components to remain separate rather than be fused together, as would be the case in a

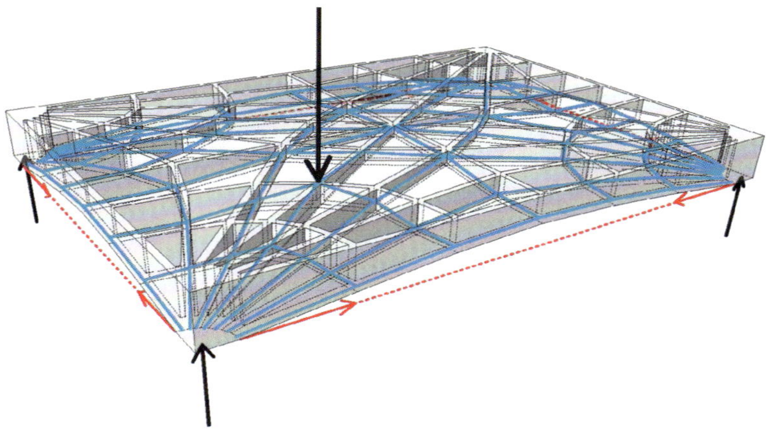

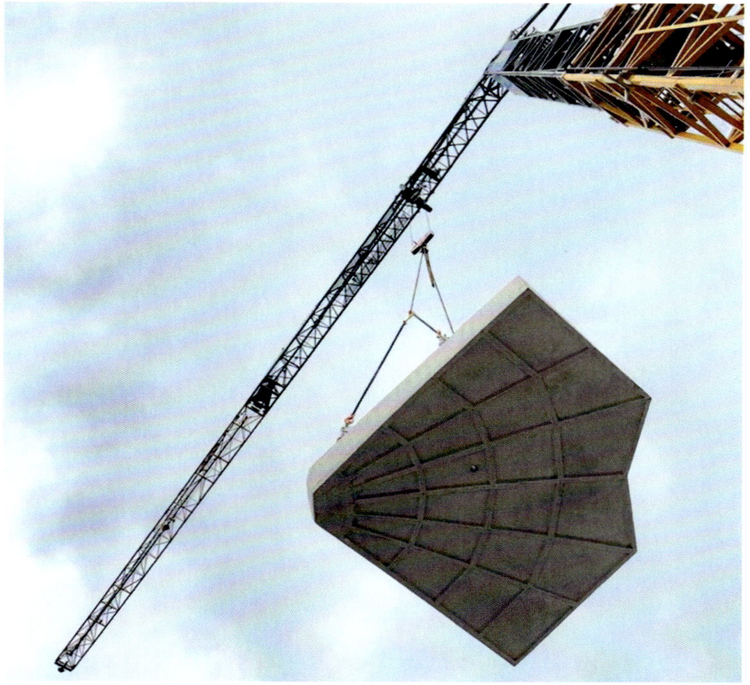

reinforced concrete beam or plate with embedded rebar, and facilitates repurposing and recycling material at the end of a structure's life cycle (FIG. 36). Funicular floors can also be prefabricated in a factory, easily transported, and assembled on-site without the need for complex infrastructure, glue, or mechanical joints.

The funicular floor demonstrates that we can still learn from the structural efficiency that was inherent in Gothic architecture. By integrating such solutions into modern building practice, we can significantly reduce the negative impact of our built environment on the planet.

PB, TVM, FR, ADE

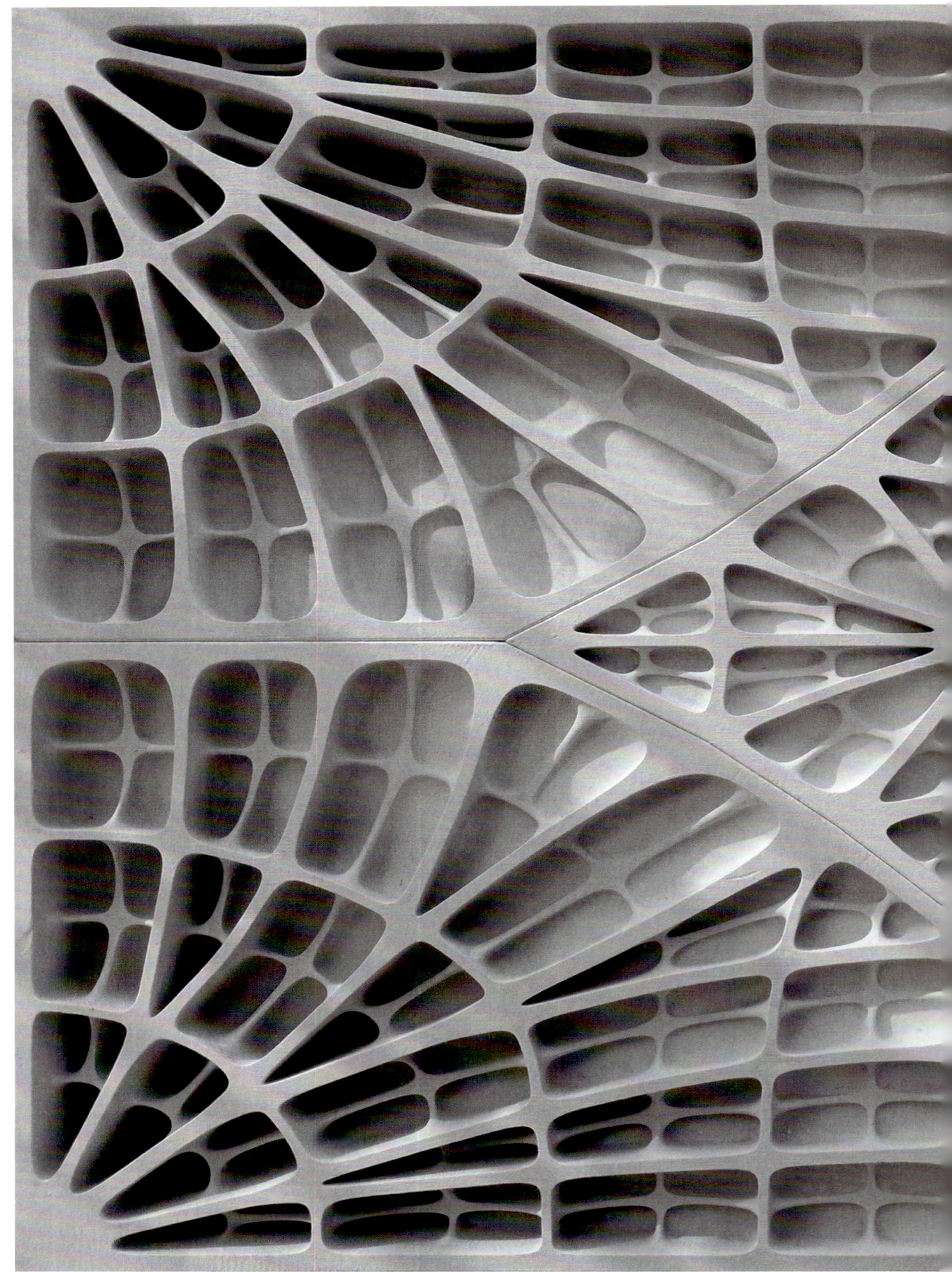

PLATE 96

Block Research Group, Institute of Technology in Architecture (ITA), Federal Institute of Technology (ETH) Zurich / Vaulted AG. Reproduction of the First Prototype of a Discrete Funicular Floor, 2025; original by Matthias Rippmann, 2015

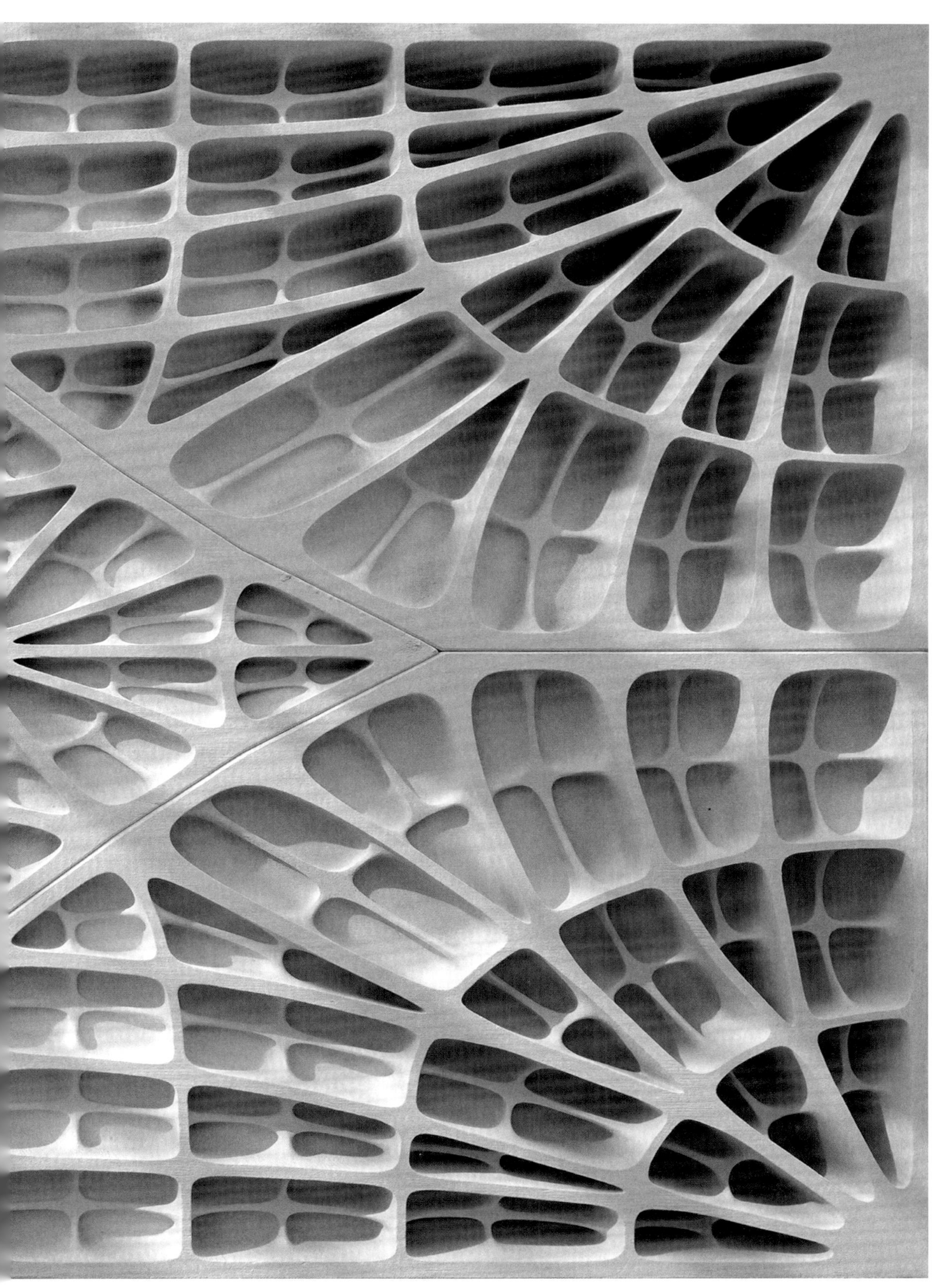

NOTES

ROUGH SKETCHES:
A PREHISTORY OF
ARCHITECTURAL DRAWING
IN THE MIDDLE AGES

1. Jean-Paul Claverie, "Re-Founding Modernity," in *The Fondation Louis Vuitton by Frank Gehry: A Building for the Twenty-First Century*, ed. Anne-Line Roccati (Flammarion, 2014), 6.

2. Claverie, "Re-Founding Modernity," 6.

3. Sonit Bafna, "How Architectural Drawings Work—And What That Implies for the Role of Representation in Architecture," *Journal of Architecture* 13, no. 5 (2008): 535–64.

4. Robert Bork, "Paper Thin? The Evidence for 12th-Century Gothic Design Drawings," *Arts* 12, no. 6 (December 2023): 1–21; and Zachary Stewart, review of *God's Own Language: Architectural Drawing in the Twelfth Century*, by Karl Kinsella, *Journal of the Society of Architectural Historians* 84, no. 4 (December 2025): 577–78. My thanks to Stewart for providing me with an advance copy of his review and his helpful counsel on other aspects of this essay.

5. Robert Branner, "Villard de Honnecourt, Reims, and the Origin of Gothic Architectural Drawing," in *The Engineering of Medieval Cathedrals*, ed. Lynn T. Courtenay (Ashgate, 1997). On the impact and flaws of Branner's argument, see the trenchant remarks in Bork, "Paper Thin?," 5–7.

6. Adomnán, *De locis sanctis*, ed. Denis Meehan, Scriptores Latini Hiberniae 3 (Dublin Institute for Advanced Studies, 1958), 43, lines 33–34.

7. Michael M. Gorman, "Adomnán's *De locis sanctis*: The Diagrams and the Sources," *Revue Bénédictine* 116, no. 1 (2006): 5–41; Thomas O'Loughlin, "Adomnán's Plans in the Context of His Imagining 'the Most Famous City,'" in *Imagining Jerusalem in the Medieval West*, ed. Lucy Donkin and Hanna Vorholt, Proceedings of the British Academy (Oxford University Press, 2012); and Kathryn Blair Moore, "Adomnán's *On the Holy Places*: Pilgrimage Manuscripts and Architectural Translation from Jerusalem to Europe," *Art in Translation* 10, no. 1 (2018): 11–29.

8. P. D. A. Harvey, *Medieval Maps* (British Library, 1991), 12–13.

9. Michael Baxandall, *Painting and Experience in Fifteenth-Century Italy: A Primer in the Social History of Pictorial Style* (Oxford University Press, 1972), 29–32.

10. Emphasis added; Adomnán, *De locis sanctis*, 43, lines 33–34.

11. Arculf indicates that he is Gaulish and that he stayed in Jerusalem for nine months; Adomnán, *De locis sanctis*, 37, lines 4–6.

12. Adomnán, *De locis sanctis*, 47, lines 17–23.

13. Thomas O'Loughlin, "Adomnán and Arculf: The Case of an Expert Witness," *Journal of Medieval Latin* 7 (1997): 127–46.

14. Mary Carruthers described the ninth-century plan of the Monastery of Saint Gall, now in the Stiftsbibliothek, St. Gallen (Cod. Sang. 1092), as a "meditation machine." Mary Carruthers, *The Craft of Thought: Meditation, Rhetoric, and the Making of Images, 400–1200*, Cambridge Studies in Medieval Literature 34 (Cambridge University Press, 1998), 228–31.

15. Carruthers, *Craft of Thought*, 7–24.

16. Walter Cahn, "Architectural Draftsmanship in Twelfth-Century Paris: The Illustrations of Richard of Saint-Victor's Commentary on Ezekiel's Temple Vision," *Gesta* 15, no. 1/2 (1976): 247–54; Walter Cahn, "Architecture and Exegesis: Richard of St.-Victor's Ezekiel Commentary and Its Illustrations," *Art Bulletin* 76, no. 1 (March 1994): 53–68; Leslie Smith, "Jews and Christians Imagining the Temple," in *Crossing Borders: Hebrew Manuscripts as a Meeting-Place of Cultures*, ed. Piet van Boxel and Sabine Arndt (Bodleian Library, 2009); and Karl Kinsella, *God's Own Language: Architectural Drawing in the Twelfth Century* (MIT Press, 2023).

17. Kinsella, *God's Own Language*, 48.

18. Bodleian Libraries, University of Oxford (MS Pococke 295). For a digital facsimile of the *Commentary*, see https://digital.bodleian.ox.ac.uk/objects/b7e0b998-0a85-4a30-851f-58d67be5247d/.

19. Benjamin Williams, "Bringing Maimonides to Oxford: Edward Pococke, the Mishnah and the *Porta Mosis*," in *The Mishnaic Moment: Jewish Law among Jews and Christians in Early Modern Europe*, ed. Piet van Boxel, Kirsten Macfarlane, and Joanna Weinberg (Oxford University Press, 2022), 165–67, esp. n. 35.

20. For two general discussions of the aims of the *Commentary*, see Abraham Joshua Heschel, *Maimonides: A Biography*, trans. Joachim Neugroschel (Farrar, Straus and Giroux, 1982), 33–37; and Joel L. Kraemer, *Maimonides: The Life and World of One of Civilization's Greatest Minds*, 1st paperback ed. (PRH Christian Publishing, 2010), 164–86. For Maimonides's own explanation of his task, see Zvi L. Lampel, trans., *Maimonides' Introduction to*

*the Talmud: A Translation
of the Rambam's Introduction
to His Commentary on the
Mishna* (Judaica Press, 1975).

21. Rachel Wischnitzer,
"Maimonides' Drawing of the
Temple," *Journal of Jewish Art* 1
(1974): 16–27; Esther W.
Goldman, "Maimonides' Illustration of the Temple in Jerusalem
as a Model for Later Copies,"
in *Manuscripts in Transition:
Recycling Manuscripts, Texts and
Images*, ed. Brigitte Dekeyzer
and Jan Van der Stock, Corpus
of Illuminated Manuscripts
15 (Peeters, 2005); and Joshua
Skarf, "Oral Transmission,
Ekphrasis, and Technical Drawings: On the Formation of
Mishnah Middot," *Images* 15,
no. 1 (2022): 18–26. My thanks to
David C. Kraemer for his helpful
comments on this section.

22. *Commentary* (see n. 18), fols.
286r–295r.

23. Translations of Maimonides's
commentary are my own, from
the Hebrew translation (of
the original Judeo-Arabic) available at: https://www.sefaria
.org/Rambam_on_Mishnah
_Middot?tab=contents. "Look
at the figure": I.5; "Although
everything is explained" and
"This requires a lot": II.5.

24. Lampel, *Maimonides'
Introduction*, 182.

25. Carl F. Barnes Jr., *The Portfolio of Villard de Honnecourt
(Paris, Bibliothèque nationale de
France, MS Fr 19093): A New
Critical Edition and Color Facsimile* (Ashgate, 2009). This remains
the single best source for understanding the portfolio, and I
rely on its translations here. For
a digital facsimile of the portfolio, see https://gallica.bnf.fr
/ark:/12148/btv1b10509412z/f1
.item.

26. To say that the literature
on Villard is vast is an under-
statement. For a helpful overview
of the historic debates and

discussions, see Carl F. Barnes Jr.,
*Villard de Honnecourt: The
Artist and His Drawings; A
Critical Bibliography*, A Reference
Publication in Art History
(G. K. Hall & Co., 1982). For
more recent bibliography, see
the various essays in George
Brooks and Maile S. Hutterer,
eds., *The Worlds of Villard
de Honnecourt: The Portfolio,
Medieval Technology, and Gothic
Monuments* (Brill, 2023).
The public exchange between
François Bucher and Peter
Kidson epitomizes the debates
on Villard's professional status.
See François Bucher, *Architector:
The Lodge Books and Sketchbooks
of Medieval Architects*, vol. 1
(Abaris Books, 1979); Peter
Kidson, review of *Architector:
The Lodge Books and Sketchbooks
of Medieval Architects*, by
François Bucher, *Journal of the
Society of Architectural Historians*
40, no. 4 (1981): 329–31; and
François Bucher, "Letter," *Journal
of the Society of Architectural
Historians* 41, no. 2 (1982): 170.

27. Translations from the portfolio of Villard de Honnecourt
follow those in Barnes, *Portfolio*,
53, 70, 98. "I once saw": fol. 6r;
"I have been in many lands":
fol. 9v; "I was once in Hungary":
fol. 15v.

28. Fol. 1v, quoted in Barnes,
Portfolio, 35.

29. See the commentary on indi-
vidual folios in Barnes, *Portfolio*.
Among the many interesting
discussions on Villard's understanding of life drawings are
Stephen Perkinson, "Portraits
and Counterfeits: Villard de
Honnecourt and Thirteenth-
Century Theories of Representation," in *Excavating the Medieval
Image: Manuscripts, Artists,
Audiences: Essays in Honor of
Sandra Hindman*, ed. David S.
Areford and Nina A. Rowe
(Ashgate, 2004); and Jean Givens, "The Testimony of Sight,"
in *Observation and Image-Making
in Gothic Art* (Cambridge Uni-
versity Press, 2005).

30. Though some scholars have
tried to link Pierre de Corbie
to other documented master
masons with similar names, his
identity remains a mystery;
Barnes, *Portfolio*, 95.

31. See, for instance, the figural
drawings on fols. 6r, 8v, 9r,
and 27r.

32. Jean Wirth, *Villard de
Honnecourt: Architecte du XIIIe
siècle*, Titre courant 58 (Droz,
2015).

33. Respectively, George Brooks,
"Villard de Honnecourt:
Gothic Carpenter," in Brooks
and Hutterer, *Worlds*; Carl F.
Barnes Jr., "The Drapery-
Rendering Technique of Villard
de Honnecourt," *Gesta* 20, no. 1
(1981): 199–206; and Carl F.
Barnes Jr., "An Essay on Villard
de Honnecourt and Cambrai
Cathedral," in Brooks and Hut-
terer, *Worlds*.

34. Edward Robbins, "The Social
Uses of Drawing: Drawing
and Architectural Practice," in
Why Architects Draw, 1st paperback ed. (MIT Press, 1997).

VISION MADE VISIBLE: THE
GOTHIC BUILDING TRADITION
AND ARCHITECTURAL
DRAFTSMANSHIP

1. Roland Recht, "Avant-Propos,"
in *Les bâtisseurs des cathédrales
gothiques*, exh. cat., ed. Roland
Recht (Éditions les Musées
de la ville de Strasbourg, 1989),
9. Unless otherwise noted,
all translations are my own.

2. Johann Wolfgang von Goethe,
"On German Architecture
(1773)," in *Goethe's Literary
Essays: A Selection in English*, ed.
J. E. Spingarn (Harcourt, Brace
and Company, 1921), 7–9. See
also Johann Josef Böker, Anne-
Christine Brehm, Julian Han-
schke, and Jean-Sébastien Sauvé,
Architektur der Gotik, vol. 3,
*Rheinlande: Ein Bestandskatalog
der mittelalterlichen Architektur-*

zeichnungen (Müry Salzmann, 2013), 147–48.

3. Böker et al., *Rheinlande*, 145–56.

4. In particular, the fully illustrated three-volume catalogue *Architektur der Gotik*, issued by Johann Josef Böker and a team of architectural historians between 2005 and 2013, offered unprecedented visual and historiographical access. See Johann Josef Böker, *Architektur der Gotik*, vol. 1, *Bestandskatalog der weltgrößten Sammlung an gotischen Baurissen der Akademie der bildenden Künste Wien* (Anton Pustet, 2005); Johann Josef Böker, Anne-Christine Brehm, Julian Hanschke, and Jean-Sébastien Sauvé, *Architektur der Gotik*, vol. 2, *Ulm und Donauraum: Ein Bestandskatalog der mittelalterlichen Archtekturzeichnungen aus Ulm, Schwaben und dem Donaugebiet* (Müry Salzmann, 2011); and Böker et al., *Rheinlande*.

5. François Bucher dedicated several articles to Gothic design methods and objectives in which he juxtaposed drawings, buildings, and objects. He also set out to produce a four-volume study of surviving architects' albums and sketchbooks, but only published one volume during his lifetime. See François Bucher, "Design in Gothic Architecture: A Preliminary Assessment," *Journal of the Society of Architectural Historians* 27, no. 1 (1968): 49–71; François Bucher, "Medieval Architectural Design Methods, 800–1560," *Gesta* 11, no. 2 (1972): 37–51; François Bucher, "Micro-Architecture as the 'Idea' of Gothic Theory and Style," *Gesta* 15, no. 1/2 (1976): 71–89; and François Bucher, *Architector: The Lodge Books and Sketchbooks of Medieval Architects*, vol. 1 (Abaris Books, 1979). Robert Bork systematically analyzes Gothic architectural drawings to learn more about the design methods of medieval architects; a representative study is Robert Bork, *The Geometry of Creation: Architectural Drawing and the Dynamics of Gothic Design* (Ashgate, 2011).

6. Melanie Holcomb, *Pen and Parchment: Drawing in the Middle Ages*, exh. cat. (The Metropolitan Museum of Art, 2009), 3.

7. Hans Sedlmayr, *Die Entstehung der Kathedrale* (Akademische Druck- und Verlagsanstalt, 1976), 613–14.

8. Peter Kurmann, "Gautier de Varinfroy et le problème du style personnel d'un architecte au XIIIe siècle," in Recht, *Bâtisseurs des cathédrales gothiques*, 187.

9. Holcomb, *Pen and Parchment*, 4.

10. Suger refers to the rebuilding of Saint-Denis in three accounts, transcribed and translated from the Latin in Erwin Panofsky, *Abbot Suger on the Abbey Church of St.-Denis and Its Art Treasures*, 2nd ed. (Princeton University Press, 1979). For a criticism of Panofsky's interpretation of the text, see Peter Kidson, "Panofsky, Suger and St Denis," *Journal of the Warburg and Courtauld Institutes* 50 (1987): 1–17.

11. Translations of quotes from Suger are Panofsky's; see Panofsky, *Abbot Suger*, 51.

12. Suger is celebrated as a "great builder" in Jean Gimpel, *Les bâtisseurs des cathédrales* (Éditions du Seuil, 1958), 19, among other sources. On Suger's role as a patron and overseer, see Sumner McKnight Crosby, *The Royal Abbey of Saint-Denis: From Its Beginnings to the Death of Suger, 475–1151* (Yale University Press, 1987), 119–20; Kidson, "Panofsky," 1–2; and Eric Fernie, "Suger's 'Completion' of Saint-Denis," in *Artistic Integration in Gothic Buildings*, ed. Virginia Chieffo Raguin, Kathryn Brush, and Peter Draper (University of Toronto Press, 1995), 85.

13. Alain Erlande-Brandenburg, "Saint-Denis: Le manifeste de l'abbé Suger," in *L'abbé Suger, le manifeste gothique de Saint-Denis et la pensée victorine: Actes du colloque organisé à la Fondation Singer-Polignac (Paris) le mardi 21 novembre 2000*, ed. Dominique Poirel (Brepols, 2001), 21–22.

14. Panofsky, *Abbot Suger*, 101, 103.

15. On Suger's role in the design process, see Kidson, "Panofsky," 1–2, 11–13; and Erlande-Brandenburg, "Saint-Denis," 26.

16. Jules Quicherat, "Notice sur l'album de Villard de Honnecourt, architecte du XIIIe siècle," *Revue archéologique* 6, no. 1 (1849): 65–80.

17. Hans R. Hahnloser, *Villard de Honnecourt: Kritische Gesamtausgabe des Bauhüttenbuches ms. fr 19093 der Pariser Nationalbibliothek* (Schroll, 1935).

18. Carl F. Barnes Jr., "Le 'problème' Villard de Honnecourt," in Recht, *Bâtisseurs des cathédrales gothiques*, 209–23.

19. Carl F. Barnes Jr. and Lon R. Shelby, "The Codicology of the Portfolio of Villard de Honnecourt (Paris, Bibliothèque Nationale, MS FR. 19093)," *Scriptorium* 42, no. 1 (1988): 20–48.

20. Barnes, "'Problème' Villard de Honnecourt," 213.

21. On Villard's process of underdrawing, see Hahnloser, *Villard de Honnecourt*, 184–85; and Robert Bork, "Villard's Laon Tower Drawings and the Visual Transmission of Architectural Ideas," in *New Approaches to Medieval Architecture*, ed. Robert Bork, William W. Clark, and Abby McGehee (Ashgate, 2011), 159.

22. Barnes, "'Problème' Villard de Honnecourt," 215–20.

23. On Villard's possible work in masonry, see James Ackerman, *The Reinvention of Architectural*

Drawing, 1250–1550, Annual Soane Lecture 3 (Sir John Soane's Museum, 1998), 4; as a goldsmith, see Barnes, "'Problème' Villard de Honnecourt," 221; in carpentry, see George Brooks, "Villard de Honnecourt: Gothic Carpenter," in *The Worlds of Villard de Honnecourt: The Portfolio, Medieval Technology, and Gothic Monuments*, ed. George Brooks and Maile S. Hutterer (Brill, 2023), 48–88.

24. Carl F. Barnes Jr., *The Portfolio of Villard de Honnecourt (Paris, Bibliothèque nationale de France, MS Fr 19093): A New Critical Edition and Color Facsimile* (Ashgate, 2009), 229–30; and Carl F. Barnes Jr., "An Essay on Villard de Honnecourt, Cambrai Cathedral, and Saint Elisabeth of Hungary," in Bork et al., *New Approaches*, 77–91.

25. M. F. Hearn, "Villard de Honnecourt's Perception of Gothic Architecture," in *Medieval Architecture and Its Intellectual Context: Studies in Honour of Peter Kidson*, ed. Eric Fernie and Paul Crossley (Hambledon Press, 1990), 127. See also Bork, "Villard's Laon Tower Drawings," 159–67.

26. Robert Bork, "Paper Thin? The Evidence for 12th-Century Gothic Design Drawings," *Arts* 12, no. 6 (December 2023): 4.

27. Bork, "Paper Thin?," 3.

28. Böker et al., *Rheinlande*, 7–13; Anne-Christine Brehm, "Organisation und Netzwerk spätmittelalterlicher Bauhütten: Die Regensburger Ordnung und ihre Initiatoren," *Ulm und Oberschwaben* 58 (2013): 98–101; and Bork, "Paper Thin?," 11.

29. Gimpel, *Bâtisseurs des cathédrales*, 8–10; and Bork, "Paper Thin?," 1.

30. Jacques Le Goff, "Les bâtisseurs des cathédrales," in Recht, *Bâtisseurs des cathédrales gothiques*, 11.

31. Recht, "Avant-Propos," 9; Christoph Luitpold Frommel, "Sulla nascita del disegno architettonico," in *Rinascimento da Brunelleschi a Michelangelo: La rappresentazione dell'architettura*, exh. cat., ed. Henry Millon and Vittorio Magnano Lampugnani (Bompiani, 1994), 101; Robert Branner, "Villard de Honnecourt, Reims, and the Origin of Gothic Architectural Drawing," in *The Engineering of Medieval Cathedrals*, ed. Lynn T. Courtenay (Ashgate, 1997), 63, 66; Erlande-Brandenburg, "Saint-Denis," 7; and Alain Erlande-Brandenburg, *La révolution gothique: 1130–1190* (Picard, 2012), 52, 54, 73.

32. Alessandra Romano and John A. Ochsendorf, "The Mechanics of Gothic Masonry Arches," *International Journal of Architectural Heritage* 4, no. 1 (2010): 59–60.

33. For a wider discussion on the difficulties of communicating Gothic design procedures, see Bork, *Geometry of Creation*, 20–27.

34. Branner, "Gothic Architectural Drawing," 66; and Erlande-Brandenburg, *Révolution gothique*, 73.

35. Wolfgang Schöller, "Le dessin d'architecture à l'époque gothique," in Recht, *Bâtisseurs des cathédrales gothiques*, 227. The thirteenth-century source in fact reads *architectrari*, an error that Schöller corrects.

36. Jean Givens, *Observation and Image-Making in Gothic Art* (Cambridge University Press, 2005), 38, 40; and Holcomb, *Pen and Parchment*, 29–30.

37. On William of Auvergne, see Robert W. Scheller, *Exemplum: Model-Book Drawings and the Practice of Artistic Transmission in the Middle Ages (ca. 900–ca. 1470)*, trans. Michael Hoyle (Amsterdam University Press, 1995), 16; on the resonance

with Villard de Honnecourt, see Roland Bechmann, *Villard de Honnecourt: La pensée technique au XIIIᵉ siècle et sa communication*, rev. ed. (Picard, 1993), 362–63.

38. Givens, *Observation and Image-Making*, 40.

39. Givens, *Observation and Image-Making*, 40–52, 75; and Holcomb, *Pen and Parchment*, 20–22, 89–93, 105–10, 113–19.

40. On the plan of the Monastery of Saint Gall in the Stiftsbibliothek, St. Gallen (Cod. Sang. 1092), see Bork, *Geometry of Creation*, 29–30; and *Der St. Galler Klosterplan: Faksimile, Begleittext, Beischriften und Übersetzung* (Verlag am Klosterhof, 2014). On the Canterbury plan at Cambridge, Trinity College (MS R.17.1, fol. 248v), see Givens, *Observation and Image-Making*, 48, pl. 4; Peter Fergusson, *Canterbury Cathedral Priory in the Age of Becket* (Paul Mellon Centre for Studies in British Art, 2011), 25–36, figs. 4, 5; and Bork, "Paper Thin?," 5.

41. Charles Cotton, ed., *Of the Burning and Repair of the Church of Canterbury in the Year 1174* [. . .], 2nd ed. (Cambridge University Press, 1932); and Givens, *Observation and Image-Making*, 42.

42. Cotton, *Burning and Repair*, 9.

43. Cotton, *Burning and Repair*, 9–11.

44. Cotton, *Burning and Repair*, 10; and Erlande-Brandenburg, *Révolution gothique*, 52–54.

45. Scheller, *Exemplum*, 9–26, touches on closely related issues.

46. John G. Hawthorne and Cyril Stanley Smith, *On Divers Arts: The Treatise of Theophilus* (University of Chicago Press, 1963), 61–62, 70–71.

47. Peter Völkle, *Werkplanung und Steinbearbeitung im Mittelalter: Grundlagen der handwerklichen Arbeitstechniken im mittleren Europa von 1000 bis 1500* (Ebner, 2016), 22–23.

48. James Bugslag, "The Shrine of St. Gertrude of Nivelles and the Process of Gothic Design," *RACAR: Revue d'art canadienne / Canadian Art Review* 20, no. 1/2 (1993): 17; and Scheller, *Exemplum*, 4.

49. Schöller, "Dessin d'architecture," 228; Arnold Pacey, *Medieval Architectural Drawing: English Craftsmen's Methods and Their Later Persistence (c. 1200–1700)* (Tempus, 2007), 35; and Bork, *Geometry of Creation*, 30.

50. Branner, "Gothic Architectural Drawing," 67–68; Böker et al., *Rheinlande*, 9; and Alfonso Jiménez Martín, "Diseño del rosetón del brazo norte del crucero de la catedral de León (ca. 1280)," in *Trazas, muestras y modelos de tradición gótica en la Península Ibérica entre los siglos XIII y XVI*, ed. Javier Ibáñez Fernández (Instituto Juan de Herrera, 2019), 85–87.

51. Michael T. Davis, "On the Drawing Board: Plans of the Clermont Cathedral Terrace," in *Ad Quadratum: The Practical Application of Geometry in Medieval Architecture*, ed. Nancy Wu (Ashgate, 2002), 183–203; and Pacey, *Medieval Architectural Drawing*, 34, 45–58.

52. Schöller, "Dessin d'architecture," 228.

53. Branner, "Gothic Architectural Drawing," 63–80; and Bork, *Geometry of Creation*, 30–31.

54. On the Reims Palimpsest (pl. 4 in this volume), see Robert Branner, "Drawings from a Thirteenth-Century Architect's Shop: The Reims Palimpsest," *Journal of the Society of Architectural Historians* 17, no. 4 (Winter 1958): 9–21; Stephen Murray, "The Gothic Facade Drawings in the 'Reims Palimpsest,'" *Gesta* 17, no. 2 (1978): 51–56; and Bork, "Paper Thin," 1–21.

55. Branner, "Reims Palimpsest," 9, 18; and Murray, "Gothic Facade Drawings," 51–56.

56. Bork, *Geometry of Creation*, 51.

57. Murray, "Gothic Facade Drawings," 51–56; and Branner, "Gothic Architectural Drawing," 74–75.

58. Branner, "Reims Palimpsest," 10–11, 14–15.

59. Robert Branner, "Villard de Honnecourt, Archimedes, and Chartres," *Journal of the Society of Architectural Historians* 19, no. 3 (October 1960): 95–96; Roland Bechmann, "About Some Technical Sketches of Villard de Honnecourt's Manuscript: New Light on Deleted Diagrams; An Unknown Drawing," *British Journal for the History of Science* 21, no. 3 (September 1988): 341–61; and Barnes, *Portfolio*, 49, 51, 62, 82, 86, 130, 140, 146, 177, pls. 1, 2.

60. In a broader context, Bernhard Degenhart has pointed out that the lack of such "autonomous drawings" has led to the erroneous conclusion that there was little artistic creativity during the Middle Ages; Bernhard Degenhart, "Autonome Zeichnungen bei mittelalterlichen Künstlern," *Münchner Jahrbuch der bildenden Kunst*, 3rd ser., vol. 1 (1950): 93.

61. Degenhart, "Autonome Zeichnungen," 114, 135; and Scheller, *Exemplum*, 2.

62. Pacey, *Medieval Architectural Drawing*, 139; Christian Freigang, "Aufrissfragment aus Kloster Eberbach," in *Madern Gerthener und der Pfarrturm von St. Bartholomäus: 600 Jahre Frankfurter Domturm*, exh. cat., ed. Bettina Schmitt and Ulrike Schubert (Schnell & Steiner, 2015), 80–81, no. 8; and Jule Wölk, "Fragment von einem Grundriss des dritten und vierten Turmgeschoss," in *Aufgerissen: Die mittelalterlichen Baurisse des Kölner Domes*, exh. cat., by Leonie Becks and Jule Wölk (Kölner Domschatzkammer, 2022), 25–27.

63. Nancy Wu, "Facade of Strasbourg Cathedral (Plan A1)," in Holcomb, *Pen and Parchment*, 134.

64. Translation from Madeline H. Caviness, "Artistic Integration: A Post-Modern Construct?," in Raguin et al., *Artistic Integration in Gothic Buildings*, 251.

65. A representative overview of medieval illustrations of building sites can be found in Günther Binding, *Baubetrieb im Mittelalter* (Wissenschaftliche Buchgesellschaft, 1993).

66. Wu, "Facade," 133–35; and Böker et al., *Rheinlande*, 162–64, no. 41.

67. Böker et al., *Rheinlande*, 149.

68. Böker et al., *Rheinlande*, 164.

69. Böker et al., *Rheinlande*, 183–87, no. 49.

70. Böker et al., *Rheinlande*, 162.

71. Böker et al., *Rheinlande*, 147, 159.

72. Marc Steinmann, "Funktion und Bedeutung mittelalterlicher Architekturzeichnungen am Beispiel des Kölner Fassadenplanes 'F,'" in *Dispositio: Der Grundriss als Medium in der Architektur des Mittelalters*, ed. Dirk Höhne, Hallesche Beiträge zur Kunstgeschichte 7 (Institut für Kunstgeschichte, Martin-Luther-Universität Halle-Wittenberg, 2005), 62–63; Bork, *Geometry of Creation*, 67–75; and Böker et al., *Rheinlande*, 146.

73. Böker et al., *Rheinlande*, 159.

74. Böker et al., *Rheinlande*, 159–275.

75. Böker et al., *Rheinlande*, 156.

76. Bork, *Geometry of Creation*, 126–65; Böker et al., *Rheinlande*, 87; and Hans W. Hubert, "Vier Risse für den Münsterturm" and "Meister Erwin und Freiburg," in *Baustelle Gotik: Das Freiburger Münster*, exh. cat., ed. Peter Kalchthaler, Guido Linke, and Mirja Straub (Imhof, 2013), 114–17.

77. Böker, *Akademie der bildenden Künste*, 420–21; and Böker et al., *Rheinlande*, 87.

78. Böker et al., *Ulm und Donauraum*, 16, 18.

79. The majority of the drawings amassed by the lodge of the Stephansdom ultimately ended up in the Graphic Collection of the Academy of Fine Arts Vienna through bequest. A smaller body of drawings is now in the Wien Museum. See Böker, *Akademie der bildenden Künste*; and René Schober, "On the Sheaf of Gothic Architectural Drawings in the Graphic Collection," in *Das entwendete Meisterwerk: Bilder als Zeitmaschinen / The Purloined Masterpiece: Images as Time Machines*, exh. cat., ed. Sabine Folie (Walther König, 2023), 214–23.

80. On the Cologne archive, see Marc Steinmann, *Die Westfassade des Kölner Domes: Der mittelalterliche Fassadeplan F* (Kölner Domverlag, 2003), 12–16; Arnold Wolff, "Die Wiederauffindung des Fassadenplanes F und seine Ausstellung im Kölner Dom," *Kölner Domblatt: Jahrbuch des Zentral-Dombau-Vereins* 27 (2007): 275–304; Böker et al., *Rheinlande*, 329; and Leonie Becks, "Riss F – Aufriss der Westfassade des Kölner Domes," in Becks and Wölk, *Aufgerissen*, 24. On the survival of English drawings, see Pacey, *Medieval Architectural Drawing*, 42.

81. Bernhard Degenhart and Annegrit Schmitt, *Corpus des italienischen Zeichnungen, 1300–1450*, pt. 1, *Süd- und Mittelitalien* (Gebr. Mann, 1968), 1:27–30, 215–16.

82. Cécile Dupeux, "Une collection exceptionnelle," in *Dessins: Cathédrale de Strasbourg* (Éditions des Musées de Strasbourg, 2014), n.p.

83. Böker et al., *Rheinlande*, 94–100, 122, 127, 255, nos. 24, 34, 35, 86; and Hubert, "Meister Erwin und Freiburg," 114–15.

84. Böker et al., *Rheinlande*, 94.

85. Böker et al., *Rheinlande*, 94–100, no. 24.

86. Böker et al., *Rheinlande*, 122, 127, nos. 34, 35. For the identification of Breisach Minster, see Anne-Christine Brehm, "Baumeister und Baugeschichte des Breisacher Münsters," *Unser Münster: Neues zur Baugeschichte des Breisacher Münsters* 47 (2012): 6–11.

87. Karl Schuster, "Über Erwin von Steinbachs Beziehungen zum Freiburger Münster," *Freiburger Münsterblätter: Halbjahrsschrift für die Geschichte und Kunst des Freiburger Münsters* 5, no. 7 (1909): 45; and Hubert, "Meister Erwin und Freiburg," 114.

88. Böker et al., *Rheinlande*, 94–100, no. 24.

89. Böker et al., *Rheinlande*, 100.

90. Hubert, "Meister Erwin und Freiburg," 114.

91. Barbara Schock-Werner, "Das Straßburger Münster im 15. Jahrhundert: Stilistische Entwicklung und Hüttenorganisation eines Bürger-Doms" (PhD diss., Christian-Albrechts-Universität zu Kiel, 1981), 214.

92. See Bork, *Geometry of Creation*, 331–36; and Böker et al., *Rheinlande*, 181–82, 187–90, nos. 48, 50.

93. Böker et al., *Rheinlande*, 181–82, no. 48.

94. Böker et al., *Rheinlande*, 187–90, no. 50.

95. Valerio Ascani, "Le dessin d'architecture médiéval en Italie," in Recht, *Bâtisseurs des cathédrales gothiques*, 265–67.

96. Steinmann, *Westfassade des Kölner Domes*; Steinmann, "Funktion und Bedeutung," 59–72; Bork, *Geometry of Creation*, 60–62, 110–23; Böker et al., *Rheinlande*, 348–53, no. 129; and Becks, "Riss F," 20–24.

97. Steinmann, "Funktion und Bedeutung," 59–60; and Böker et al., *Rheinlande*, 335–53.

98. Steinmann, *Westfassade des Kölner Domes*, 54–88; Steinmann, "Funktion und Bedeutung," 61–72; Bork, *Geometry of Creation*, 60, 113, 121; and Böker et al., *Rheinlande*, 348–53, no. 129.

99. Steinmann, *Westfassade des Kölner Domes*, 220–36; Wolff, "Wiederauffindung des Fassadenplanes F," 275–304; and Böker et al., *Rheinlande*, 329.

100. Ernst L. Schlee, "Problemi cronologici della facciata del duomo di Orvieto," in *Il duomo di Orvieto e le grandi cattedrali del Duecento: Atti del Convegno internazionale di studi; Orvieto, 12–14 novembre 1990*, ed. Guido Barlozzetti (Rai Libri, 1995), 110.

101. Böker et al., *Rheinlande*, 302.

102. Böker et al., *Rheinlande*, 285, 288; and Michael Matthäus, "Die Vorgeschichte der Grundsteinlegung des Domturmes aus Sicht der Frankfurter Rates"

and "Vertrag vom 31. Mai 1414 zum Turmbau," in Schmitt and Schubert, *Madern Gerthener*, 57–59, 68–69.

103. Bork, *Geometry of Creation*, 320–30; and Böker et al., *Rheinlande*, 290–98, 302–5, 307–15.

104. Germanisches National-museum, Nuremberg (Hz2667); see Böker et al., *Rheinlande*, 290–98, no. 100.

105. Böker et al., *Rheinlande*, 290–98.

106. Merlijn Hurx, *Architecture as Profession: The Origins of Architectural Practice in the Low Countries in the Fifteenth Century*, Architectura Moderna 13 (Brepols, 2018), 16–19, 280–94.

107. For a transcription of the Regensburg Ordinance, see Binding, *Baubetrieb im Mittelalter*, 110–20. For emphasis on the star architects, see Brehm, "Organisation und Netzwerk," 71–76.

108. Binding, *Baubetrieb im Mittelalter*, 114.

109. Böker et al., *Rheinlande*, 298–302.

110. Böker et al., *Rheinlande*, 302–5, 307–13; and Schmitt and Schubert, *Madern Gerthener*, 72–75.

111. Bork, *Geometry of Creation*, 330; Böker et al., *Rheinlande*, 106, 313–15; and Schmitt and Schubert, *Madern Gerthener*, 76–77.

112. Böker et al., *Rheinlande*, 313.

113. Böker et al., *Rheinlande*, 288.

114. John White, "I disegni per la facciata del duomo di Orvieto," in Barlozzetti, *Duomo di Orvieto*, 78.

115. Böker, *Akademie der bildenden Künste*, 173; and Brehm, "Organisation und Netzwerk," 93.

116. Böker, *Akademie der bildenden Künste*, 170–73; and Peter Morsbach, *Die Erbauer des Doms: Die Geschichte der Regensburger Dommeisterfamilie Roriczer-Engel*, Regensburger Domstiftung 3 (Schnell & Steiner, 2009), 39–44.

117. Kunstsammlungen des Bistums Regensburg, Bischöfliche Zentralarchiv Regensburg (D 1974/0124b).

118. Bork, *Geometry of Creation*, 313–20.

119. Böker, *Akademie der bildenden Künste*, 170.

120. For a family tree of the Parler dynasty, see Binding, *Baubetrieb im Mittelalter*, 243.

121. Bork, *Geometry of Creation*, 208–12.

122. Böker, *Akademie der bildenden Künste*, 74–79.

123. Böker, *Akademie der bildenden Künste*, 74, 77.

124. Bork, *Geometry of Creation*, 205.

125. Böker, *Akademie der bildenden Künste*, 78; and Bork, *Geometry of Creation*, 205, 214–20.

126. Böker et al., *Ulm und Donauraum*, 53–56, 134.

127. Böker et al., *Ulm und Donauraum*, 53–56.

128. Anne-Christine Brehm, *Netzwerk Gotik: Das Ulmer Münster im Zentrum von Architektur- und Bautechniktransfer* (Kohlhammer, 2020), 75.

129. Böker et al., *Ulm und Donauraum*, 53–56.

130. Lon R. Shelby, *Gothic Design Techniques: The Fifteenth-Century Design Booklets of Mathes Roriczer and Hanns Schmuttermayer*, Architectura Medii Aevi 10 (Southern Illinois University Press, 1977), 51–55; and Bork, *Geometry of Creation*, 6.

131. Robert Bork, *Late Gothic Architecture: Its Evolution, Extinction, and Reception* (Brepols, 2018), 4, 119.

132. On Renaissance design, see Christoph Luitpold Frommel and Nicholas Adams, eds., *The Architectural Drawings of Antonio da Sangallo the Younger and His Circle*, vol. 1, *Fortifications, Machines, and Festival Architecture* (Architectural History Foundation, 1994), 10–51.

133. Costanza Beltrami, *Building a Crossing Tower: A Design for Rouen Cathedral of 1516* (Sam Fogg, 2016); and Robert Bork, "Les dessins des tours et flèches gothiques françaises: Analyse de la construction géométrique de trois exemples notables," *Bulletin monumental* 179, no. 2 (2021): 109–24.

134. Beltrami, *Building a Crossing Tower*, 79–93.

135. Translation from Merlijn Hurx, "Collaboration and Competition: Master Masons and Painters in the Production of Architectural Designs in the Low Countries in the 16th century," *Architectural Histories* 11, no. 1 (2023): https://doi.org/10.16995/ah.9179.

136. Bork, "Dessins," 116.

137. Bork, *Late Gothic Architecture*, 164.

138. Mario Carpo, *Architecture in the Age of Printing: Orality, Writing, Typography, and Printed Images in the History of Architectural Theory*, trans. Sarah Benson (MIT Press, 2001), 25, 28.

"ENDOWING MASSIVE WALLS WITH VARIETY": STRUCTURE, ORNAMENT, AND ARTISTIC EXPRESSION IN GOTHIC DESIGN

1. From an addendum to Goethe's 1812 autobiography; see Johann Wolfgang von Goethe, "On German Architecture (1773)," in *Goethe's Literary Essays: A Selection in English*, ed. J. E. Spingarn (Harcourt, Brace and Company, 1921), 14n2.

2. Johann Josef Böker, Anne-Christine Brehm, Julian Hanschke, and Jean-Sébastien Sauvé, *Architektur der Gotik*, vol. 3, *Rheinlande: Ein Bestandskatalog der mittelalterlichen Architekturzeichnungen* (Müry Salzmann, 2013), 227–28, no. 65.

3. Ethan Matt Kavaler, *Renaissance Gothic: Architecture and the Arts in Northern Europe, 1470–1540* (Yale University Press, 2012), 86–88.

4. Goethe, "On German Architecture," 14. See also Robert Bork, *Late Gothic Architecture: Its Evolution, Extinction, and Reception* (Brepols, 2018), 6, 411.

5. For an overview of readings of decadence and decline in Gothic ornament, see the introduction to *Lateness and Modernity in Medieval Architecture*, ed. Alice Isabella Sullivan and Kyle G. Sweeney (Brill, 2023), 5–9.

6. For examples of recent scholarship that recognize the narrative and expressive qualities of Gothic architecture, see Kavaler, *Renaissance Gothic*; Bork, *Late Gothic Architecture*; and Sullivan and Sweeney, *Lateness and Modernity*.

7. Giorgio Vasari, *Le vite de' più eccellenti pittori, scultori e architetti* (2nd ed., 1568; Grandi tascabili economici Newton, 1997), 553–54. See also François Bucher, "Design in Gothic Architecture: A Preliminary Assessment," *Journal of the Society of Architectural Historians* 27, no. 1 (1968): 71; Anne-Marie Sankovitch, "The Myth of the 'Myth of the Medieval': Gothic Architecture in Vasari's *Rinascita* and Panofsky's Renaissance," *Res: Anthropology and Aesthetics* 40 (Autumn 2001): 34; and Robert Bork, *Late Gothic Architecture*, 4.

8. Lon R. Shelby, *Gothic Design Techniques: The Fifteenth-Century Design Booklets of Mathes Roriczer and Hanns Schmuttermayer*, Architectura Medii Aevi 10 (Southern Illinois University Press, 1977), 41; and Robert Bork, "Dynamic Unfolding and the Conventions of Procedure: Geometric Proportioning Strategies in Gothic Architectural Design," *Architectural Histories* 2, no. 1 (2014): 1, 3.

9. Bucher, "Design in Gothic Architecture," 50.

10. Shelby, *Gothic Design Techniques*, 31–38, 81–123; and Wolfgang Strohmayer, *Matthäus Roriczer: Baukunst Lehrbuch* (Guido Pressler, 2009).

11. Peter Kidson, "Roriczer's Iceberg," *Journal of the Warburg and Courtauld Institutes* 71 (2008): 1.

12. Shelby, *Gothic Design Techniques*, 6–7; and Bork, "Dynamic Unfolding."

13. Shelby, *Gothic Design Techniques*, 82–83, references this phrase in the genitive case. See also Bork, "Dynamic Unfolding."

14. Bork, "Dynamic Unfolding," 3.

15. For the *Gothic by Design* exhibition, Zoltán Bereczki (Department of Building Engineering, University of Debrecen, Hungary) and Robert Bork (School of Art, Art History, and Design, University of Iowa) have used Roriczer's method to create a three-dimensional reconstruction of Lorenz Lechler's sacrament house design as proposed in plate 25 of this volume.

16. For a family tree of the Parler dynasty, see Günther Binding, *Baubetrieb im Mittelalter* (Wissenschaftliche Buchgesellschaft, 1993), 243.

17. Bucher, "Design in Gothic Architecture," 52.

18. Bucher, "Design in Gothic Architecture," 52–53.

19. Bork, *Late Gothic Architecture*, 6, 411.

20. Lon R. Shelby, "The Geometrical Knowledge of Mediaeval Master Masons," *Speculum* 47, no. 3 (July 1972): 419.

21. Kidson, "Roriczer's Iceberg," 13.

22. See François Bucher, *Architector: The Lodge Books and Sketchbooks of Medieval Architects*, vol. 1 (Abaris Books, 1979), 375–411; and Peter Völkle, "Hans von Böblingen am Berner Münster," in *Das Berner Münster: Das erste Jahrhundert; Von der Grundsteinlegung bis zur Chorvollendung und Reformation (1421–1517/1528)*, ed. Bernd Nicolai and Jürg Schweizer (Schnell & Steiner, 2019), 288–99.

23. Bucher, *Architector*, 375; Barbara Schock-Werner, "Die Ausbildung der Architekten im Mittelalter," in *Entwerfen: Architektenausbildung in Europa von Vitruv bis Mitte des 20. Jahrhunderts; Geschichte, Theorie, Praxis*, ed. Johannes Ralph (Junius, 2009), 192; Barbara Schock-Werner, "Zur Organisation von Bauhütten im Mittelalter und zum technischen Wandel im Baubetrieb um 1200," in *Aufbruch in die Gotik: Der Magdeburger Dom und die späte Stauferzeit*, exh. cat., ed. Matthias Puhle (Philipp von Zabern, 2009), 1:117; Peter Völkle, *Werkplanung und Steinbearbeitung im Mittelalter: Grundlagen der handwerklichen Arbeitstechniken im mittleren Europa von 1000 bis 1500* (Ebner, 2016), 8; Völkle, "Hans von Böblingen," 288–89; and

Anne-Christine Brehm, *Netzwerk Gotik: Das Ulmer Münster im Zentrum von Architektur- und Bautechniktransfer* (Kohlhammer, 2020), 79–97.

24. Bucher, *Architector*, 376–77.

25. Völkle, "Hans von Böblingen," 288–89.

26. For a transcription of the Regensburg Ordinance, see Binding, *Baubetrieb im Mittelalter*, 110–20; for emphasis on the regulations for journeymen, see Anne-Christine Brehm, "Organisation und Netzwerk spätmittelalterlicher Bauhütten: Die Regensburger Ordnung und ihre Initiatoren," *Ulm und Oberschwaben* 58 (2013): 77–78.

27. Völkle, "Hans von Böblingen," 288–89.

28. Völkle, "Hans von Böblingen," 289, 297.

29. Robert Bork, *The Geometry of Creation: Architectural Drawing and the Dynamics of Gothic Design* (Ashgate, 2011), 208–14, has also called attention to the relationship between the placement of figurative sculpture and gargoyles and the geometrical framework that constitutes a building's elevation.

30. Max Lehrs, *Geschichte und kritischer Katalog des deutschen, niederländischen und französischen Kupferstichs im XV. Jahrhundert*, vol. 7, pt. 5, *Die niederländischen Monogrammisten und der Meister P* von Köln* (Gesellschaft für vervielfältigende Kunst, 1930), 100, no. 78; Bucher, *Architector*, 385, 391; Ronald Glaudemans, *De Sint-Jan te 's-Hertogenbosch: Bouwgeschiedenis en bouwsculptuur 1250–1550* (WBooks, 2017), 131; and Brehm, *Netzwerk Gotik*, 494–95.

31. Böker et al., *Rheinlande*, 42–45, no. 12; and Brehm, *Netzwerk Gotik*, 86–87.

32. Böker et al., *Rheinlande*, 42.

33. The Stephansdom drawings are in the Graphic Collection of the Academy of Fine Arts Vienna (16.893, 16.904, 16.911, 16.949, 16.977, 16.998, 17.004, 17.016, 17.073, 17.037, 17.043 [see pl. 46 in this volume], 17.056, 17.062, 17.071). The album by Antonio Pisano (called Pisanello), known as the Codex Vallardi, is now in the Département des Arts Graphiques, Musée du Louvre, Paris (2528). On Pisanello, see Robert W. Scheller, *Exemplum: Model-Book Drawings and the Practice of Artistic Transmission in the Middle Ages (ca. 900– ca. 1470)*, trans. Michael Hoyle (Amsterdam University Press, 1995), 342–56, no. 33.

34. See Johann Josef Böker, *Architektur der Gotik*, vol. 1, *Bestandskatalog der weltgrößten Sammlung an gotischen Baurissen der Akademie der bildenden Künste Wien* (Anton Pustet, 2005), 57–58; Böker et al., *Rheinlande*, 278–80, no. 97; and Bettina Schmitt and Ulrike Schubert, eds., *Madern Gerthener und der Pfarrturm von St. Bartholomäus: 600 Jahre Frankfurter Domturm*, exh. cat. (Schnell & Steiner, 2015), 82–83, no. 9.

35. Femke Speelberg, "'Noch vil höher, und subtiler Künsten … an tag zu bringen': Renaissance Pattern Books and Ornament Prints as Catalysts of the Design Process," *Zeitschrift für Kunstgeschichte* 87, no. 1 (2024): 48–67.

36. Koninklijke Bibliotheek van België, Brussels (MS II 7617, fol. 68r); see Krista De Jonge, "Early Modern Netherlandish Artists on Proportion in Architecture, or 'de questien der Simmetrien met redene der Geometrien,'" *Architectural Histories* 2, no. 1 (2014): http://doi.org/10.5334/ah.bt, fig. 8.

37. Matthijs Jonker, *The Academization of Art: A Practice Approach to the Early Histories of the Accademia del Disegno and the Accademia di San Luca* (Edizioni Quasar, 2022), 103–22.

38. See the album of Villard de Honnecourt in the Bibliothèque Nationale de France, Paris (MS Fr. 19093, fol. 18).

39. James Bugslag, "The Shrine of St. Gertrude of Nivelles and the Process of Gothic Design," *RACAR: Revue d'art canadienne / Canadian Art Review* 20, no. 1/2 (1993): 17; and Scheller, *Exemplum*, 4.

40. Barbara Schock-Werner, "Ulrich d'Ensingen, maître d'œuvre de la cathédrale de Strasbourg, de l'église paroissiale d'Ulm et de l'église Notre-Dame d'Esslingen," in *Les bâtisseurs des cathédrales gothiques*, exh. cat., ed. Roland Recht (Éditions les Musées de la ville de Strasbourg, 1989), 206–7; and Böker et al., *Rheinlande*, 298.

41. François Bucher, "Micro-Architecture as the 'Idea' of Gothic Theory and Style," *Gesta* 15, no. 1/2 (1976): 72.

42. Bucher, "Micro-Architecture," 71.

43. Emphasis in the original; Gaston Bachelard, *The Poetics of Space*, trans. Maria Jolas (Beacon, 1994), 148. See also Paul Binski, "The Heroic Age of Gothic and the Metaphors of Modernism," *Gesta* 52, no. 1 (2013): 10–11.

44. Paul Binski, "Magnificentia in Parvis: Microarchitecture et esthétique médiévale," in *Microarchitectures médiévales: L'échelle à l'epreuve de la matière*, ed. Jean-Marie Guillouët and Ambre Vilain (Institut national d'histoire de l'art; Éditions Picard, 2018), 14–17.

45. See Nancy Wu, "On 'Microarchitecture': A Gothic Phenomenon," in *Gothic Space: Studies in Celebration of Stephen Murray*, ed. Katherine M. Boivin, Lindsay S. Cook, and Zachary Stewart (Brill, 2026).

46. Anneliese Seeliger-Zeiss, *Lorenz Lechler von Heidelberg und sein Umkreis: Studien zur Geschichte der spätgotischen Zierarchitektur und Skulptur in der Kurpfalz und in Schwaben* (Universitätsverlag Winter, 1967), 5–6; Achim Timmermann, "'Ein mercklich köstlich und wercklich Sacrament gehews': Zur architektonischen Inszenierung des Corpus Christi um die Mitte des 15. Jahrhunderts," in *Kunst und Liturgie: Choranlagen des Spätmittelalters; Ihre Architektur, Ausstattung und Nutzung*, ed. Anna Moraht-Fromm (Jan Thorbecke, 2003), 225–26; and Achim Timmermann, "'Freedom I Do Reveal to You': Scale, Microarchitecture, and the Rise of the Turriform Civic Monument in Fourteenth-Century Northern Europe," *Art History* 38, no. 2 (April 2015): 326.

47. Johann Josef Böker, Anne-Christine Brehm, Julian Hanschke, and Jean-Sébastien Sauvé, *Architektur der Gotik*, vol. 2, *Ulm und Donauraum: Ein Bestandskatalog der mittelalterlichen Architekturzeichnungen aus Ulm, Schwaben und dem Donaugebiet* (Müry Salzmann, 2011), 120–22, no. 46; and Anne-Christine Brehm, "Die steinernen Fragmente von Oktogon und Ölberg: Entdeckungen im südlichen Chorturm und unter dem Ulmer Münsterdach," *Ulm und Oberschwaben* 60 (2017): 104–16.

48. Stefan Roller, "Riss zum Ölberg vor dem Ulmer Münster," in *Michel Erhart & Jörg Syrlin d. Ä.: Spätgotik in Ulm*, ed. Brigitte Reinhardt and Stefan Roller (Konrad Theiss, 2002), 256–57, no. 16.

49. Brehm, "Steinernen Fragmente," 109–13.

50. Böker et al., *Ulm und Donauraum*, 18.

51. On parallels between the Mount of Olives monument spire and Ulm Minster's tower, see

52. Böker et al., *Ulm und Donauraum*, 121.

52. Böker et al., *Ulm und Donauraum*, 18–19.

53. Evangelische Gesamtkirchengemeinde Ulm (Stadtarchiv Ulm, E Münsterbauamt 2); see Böker et al., *Ulm und Donauraum*, 64–69, no. 10.

54. Graphic Collection, Academy of Fine Arts Vienna (16.829); see Böker et al., *Ulm und Donauraum*, 148–49, no. 68.

55. Bucher, "Design in Gothic Architecture," 69–70; Böker et al., *Ulm und Donauraum*, 122; and Brehm, "Steinernen Fragmente," 104–8, 113–15.

56. Kavaler, *Renaissance Gothic*, 167–69; and Böker et al., *Rheinlande*, 153–54.

57. Böker et al., *Rheinlande*, 241–45, no. 75.

58. Böker et al., *Rheinlande*, 154.

59. Peter Anstett, "Ein unbekanntes Baumeisterbildnis von Lorenz Lechler in der Dionysiuskirche zu Esslingen am Neckar," *Nachrichtenblatt der Denkmalpflege in Baden-Württemberg* 7, no. 4 (1964): 97–100.

60. Achim Timmermann, *Real Presence: Sacrament Houses and the Body of Christ, c. 1270–1600* (Brepols, 2009), 129, 132.

61. Seeliger-Zeiss, *Lorenz Lechler von Heidelberg*, 22–23.

62. James S. Ackerman, "'Ars sine scientia nihil est': Gothic Theory of Architecture at the Cathedral of Milan," *Art Bulletin* 31, no. 2 (1949): 90–96; Schock-Werner, "Ulrich d'Ensingen," 205–6; Böker et al., *Ulm und Donauraum*, 15; and Böker et al., *Rheinlande*, 153.

63. Seeliger-Zeiss, *Lorenz Lechler von Heidelberg*, 23; and Anneliese Seeliger-Zeiss, "Studien zum Steinmetzbuch des Lorenz

Lechler von 1516: Ein bisher unbekannt gebliebenes Fragment im Besitz des Badischen Landesbibliothek Karlsruhe," *Architectura* 12 (1982): 132.

64. See Femke Speelberg, "Lorenz Lechler's Tour de Force of Late-Gothic Architectural Draftsmanship," *Master Drawings* 63, no. 3 (Autumn 2025): 293–320.

65. Seeliger-Zeiss, *Lorenz Lechler von Heidelberg*, 17–18, 25.

66. Anstett, "Unbekanntes Baumeisterbildnis," 97–100; Seeliger-Zeiss, *Lorenz Lechler von Heidelberg*, 29; and Timmermann, *Real Presence*, 322.

67. Speelberg, "Lechler's Tour de Force," 309–10, 316.

68. Timmermann, "Zur architektonischen Inszenierung," 210.

69. Brehm, "Steinernen Fragmente," 111–13.

70. The drawing of the sacrament house is now in the Landesmuseum Württemberg, Stuttgart (1956/25), while that of the west tower is in the Stadtarchiv Ulm (F 1 Münsterrisse 14). See also Böker et al., *Ulm und Donauraum*, 58–63, 99–101, nos. 8, 29.

71. Norbert Lieb, *Jörg Seld, Goldschmied und Bürger von Augsburg: Ein Meisterleben im Abend des Mittelalters* (Schnell & Steiner, 1947), 25, 29–30.

72. Bugslag, "Shrine of St. Gertrude," 17; and Scheller, *Exemplum*, 4.

73. Bugslag, "Shrine of St. Gertrude," 16–19; and Johann Michael Fritz, "Martin Schongauer und die Goldschmiede," in *Le beau Martin: Études et mises au point* (Musée d'Unterlinden, 1994), 179.

74. Graphische Sammlung, Fürst Thurn und Taxis Zentralarchiv,

Regensburg (AM 14.1); see Anton Legner, ed., *Die Parler und der schöne Stil 1350–1400: Europäische Kunst unter den Luxemburgern*, exh. cat. (Museen der Stadt Köln, 1978), 1:401–2.

75. Fritz, "Martin Schongauer," 178.

76. Maximilianmuseum, Augsburg (3451). See Franz Bischoff, *Burkhard Engelberg [. . .] und die süddeutsche Architektur um 1500: Anmerkungen zur sozialen Stellung und Arbeitsweise spätgotischer Steinmetzen und Werkmeister* (Wissner, 1999), 268, 270; and Stephan Hoppe, "German Architectural Models in the Renaissance (1500–1620)," in *Les maquettes d'architecture: Fonction et évolution d'un instrument de conception et de réalisation*, ed. Sabine Frommel (Picard, 2015), 133.

77. Lieb, *Jörg Seld*, 30; and Ingrid S. Weber, "Drei Aufrisse spätgotischer Monstranzen im Stadtarchiv Ulm," *Pantheon: Internationale Zeitschrift für Kunst*, n.s., vol. 36 (1978): 20.

78. For an overview, see Larry Silver, *Marketing Maximilian: The Visual Ideology of a Holy Roman Emperor* (Princeton University Press, 2008).

79. Lieb, *Jörg Seld*, 36.

80. Heinrich Röttinger, *Hans Weiditz: Der Petrarkameister* (Strasbourg, 1904), 84, no. 38; Lieb, *Jörg Seld*, 38–41; and Simone Herde, "Seld," in *Neue deutsche Biographie*, vol. 24, *Schwarz–Stader*, 4th ed. (Berlin, 2010), 213. See also Horst Appuhn and Christian von Heusinger, *Riesenholzschnitte und Papiertapeten der Renaissance* (Alfons Uhl, 1976), 45.

81. Vitruvius stated in his *Ten Books on Architecture* that "an architect should be an educated man so as to be remembered by his treatises"; translation from Bucher, "Design in Gothic Architecture," 50.

82. Shelby, *Gothic Design Techniques*, 4–5.

83. Shelby, *Gothic Design Techniques*, 28–31, 38–39, 126–42.

84. Femke Speelberg, "Wenzel von Olmütz in Ulm? Discoveries and New Hypotheses Regarding His Architectural Prints," *Print Quarterly* 41, no. 1 (2024): 3–15.

85. Achim Timmermann, "Vier Kleinarchitekturrisse der Spätgotik," *Das Münster* 55 (2002): 120–21; Timmermann, *Real Presence*, 141–42; and Speelberg, "Wenzel von Olmütz," 6.

86. Lehrs, *Niederländischen Monogrammisten*, 237, 247–49, nos. 3, 10–12.

87. Ch. C. V. Verreyt, "Alart du Hamel of du Hameel, bouwmeester en plaatsnijder," *Oud Holland* 12, no. 1 (1894): 10; Lehrs, *Niederländischen Monogrammisten*, 222, 245–47, no. 9; and Glaudemans, *Sint-Jan te 's-Hertogenbosch*, 321–23.

88. Other architectural elements also correspond to Du Hameel's work in 's-Hertogenbosch, see Glaudemans, *Sint-Jan te 's-Hertogenbosch*, 321–23, 390–401.

89. Ines Braun-Balzer, *Mikro- und Makroarchitektur: Ein Vergliech am Neiderrhein in der Zeit 1394 bis 1521* (PhD diss., Universität Freiburg, 2005), 132.

90. De Jonge, "Early Modern Netherlandish Artists," 9.

MAKING THEIR MARKS

1. Holbein's portrait of Konrad Würffel is in the Kupferstichkabinett der Hamburger Kunsthalle (23907).

2. See Jennifer S. Alexander, "Masons' Marks and the Working Practices of Medieval Stone Masons," in *Who Built Beverley Minster?*, ed. P. S. Barnwell and Arnold Pacey (Spire Books, 2008), 28–29.

3. Peter Völkle, *Werkplanung und Steinbearbeitung im Mittelalter: Grundlagen der handwerklichen Arbeitstechniken im mittleren Europa von 1000 bis 1500* (Ebner, 2016), 33.

4. Franz Bischoff, *Burkhard Engelberg, "Der vilkunstreiche Architector und der Statt Augspurg Wercke Meister"* (Wissner, 1999), 60–64.

5. Bischoff, *Burkhard Engelberg*, 25.

6. Bischoff, *Burkhard Engelberg*, 77–165. See also Franz Bischoff, "Burkhard Engelberg und seine außeraugsburgischen Aufträge: Der Werkmeister als Planlieferant und Bausachverständiger und das Heilig-Kreuz-Münster in Schwäbisch Gmünd," *Zeitschrift des Historischen Vereins für Schwaben* 105 (2013): 25–65.

7. Merlijn Hurx, *Architecture as Profession: The Origins of Architectural Practice in the Low Countries in the Fifteenth Century*, Architectura Moderna 13 (Brepols, 2018), 18.

8. On Steinbach and the Nuremberg Drawing, see the chapter "Vision Made Visible" in this volume, esp. 41, 43.

9. Hurx, *Architecture as Profession*, 18.

10. On Ensingen, see "Vision Made Visible," esp. 50. On Keldermans, see R. Meischke, *De gotische bouwtraditie: Studies over opdrachtgevers en bouwmeesters in de Nederlanden* (Bekking, 1988), 122–26.

11. John Harvey, *English Mediaeval Architects: A Biographical Dictionary down to 1550*, rev. ed.

(Alan Sutton, 1984), 187–89, 194–96.

SCALED ARCHITECTURE

1. James Bugslag, "Architectural Drafting and the 'Gothicization' of the Gothic Cathedral," in *Reading Gothic Architecture*, ed. Matthew Reeve, Studies in the Visual Cultures of the Middle Ages 1 (Brepols, 2008), 57–59.

2. Bugslag, "Architectural Drafting," 62, 64–70.

3. On artists who worked across categories, see the chapter "'Endowing Massive Walls with Variety'" in this volume, esp. 74–75, 78–79.

4. The tallest surviving sacrament house, in Ulm Minster, is just over eighty-five feet tall. See Achim Timmermann, *Real Presence: Sacrament Houses and the Body of Christ, c. 1270–1600* (Brepols, 2009), 80–89.

5. Jacob Burckhardt, "Ueber die Goldschmiederisse der öffentlichen Kunstsammlung zu Basel," *Basler Taschenbuch* 12 (1864): 104.

6. See Paul Binski, "Magnificentia in Parvis: Microarchitecture et esthétique médiévale," in *Microarchitectures médiévales: L'échelle à l'epreuve de la matière*, ed. Jean-Marie Guillouët and Ambre Vilain (Institut national d'histoire de l'art; Éditions Picard, 2018), 14–21; along with the introduction to the same volume, esp. 7–8.

7. On exercise drawings of master-masons-in-training, see the chapter "'Endowing Massive Walls with Variety'" in this volume, esp. 65–66, 69. See also Femke Speelberg, "'Noch vil höher, und subtiler Künsten … an tag zu bringen': Renaissance Pattern Books and Ornament Prints as Catalysts of the Design Process," *Zeitschrift für Kunstgeschichte* 87, no. 1 (2024): 57–63.

8. Johann Michael Fritz, *Goldschmiedekunst der Gotik in Mitteleuropa* (C. H. Beck, 1982), 12.

9. Fritz, *Goldschmiedekunst*, 156.

VARIATION AND TRANSFORMATION

1. Peter Kidson, "Roriczer's Iceberg," *Journal of the Warburg and Courtauld Institutes* 71 (2008): 13.

2. Jacob Burckhardt, "Ueber die Goldschmiederisse der öffentlichen Kunstsammlung zu Basel," *Basler Taschenbuch* 12 (1864): 104, 106–7.

3. Paul Tanner, *Das Amerbach-Kabinett: Die Basler Goldschmiederisse*, exh. cat. (Öffentliche Kunstsammlung Basel, 1991), 7; and Elizabeth Landolt and Felix Ackermann, *Das Amerbach-Kabinett: Die Objekte im Historischen Museum Basel*, exh. cat. (Öffentliche Kunstsammlung Basel, 1991), 11, 102.

4. Burckhardt, "Ueber die Goldschmiederisse," 102–3.

5. For the watermarks, see Tanner, *Basler Goldschmiederisse*.

6. Tanner, *Basler Goldschmiederisse*, 7.

7. Aviv Segall, Jing Ren, Martin Schwarz, and Olga Sorkine-Hornung, "Computational Modeling of Gothic Microarchitecture," in *SIGGRAPH 2025 Conference Papers: Proceedings of the Special Interest Group on Computer Graphics and Interactive Techniques*, ed. Ginger Alford, Hao Zhang, and Adriana Schulz (Association for Computing Machinery, 2025), https://doi.org/10.1145/3721238.3730649.

CONSTRUCTIVE GEOMETRY

1. Lon R. Shelby, "The Geometrical Knowledge of Mediaeval Master Masons," *Speculum* 47, no. 3 (July 1972): 409–20.

2. On Euclid, see Menso Folkerts, *Euclid in Medieval Europe*, Questio de rerum natura 2 (Overdale Books, 1989). On Gothic architects' knowledge of Euclid, see Shelby, "The Geometrical Knowledge," 396–97; and Peter Kidson, "Roriczer's Iceberg," *Journal of the Warburg and Courtauld Institutes* 71 (2008): 4–12.

3. Henri Zerner, *Renaissance Art in France: The Invention of Classicism* (Flammarion, 2003), 11–60; and Ethan Matt Kavaler, *Renaissance Gothic: Architecture and the Arts in Northern Europe, 1470–1540* (Yale University Press, 2012).

4. See, for example, Arnold Pacey, *Medieval Architectural Drawing: English Craftsmen's Methods and Their Later Persistence (c. 1200–1700)* (Tempus, 2007), 117–228.

5. Robert Mark, *Experiments in Gothic Architecture* (MIT Press, 1982), 2–17, 118–25.

THE PROMISE OF GOTHIC GEOMETRY

1. David P. Billington, *The Tower and the Bridge: The New Art of Structural Engineering*, New Princeton Science Library paperback ed. (Princeton University Press, 2022), 5.

(16th century)
The Last Supper
Ca. 1500–1530
Limestone, traces of polychromy
25 × 15½ × 6½ in. (63.5 ×
39.4 × 16.5 cm)
The Metropolitan Museum of
Art, New York, The Friedsam
Collection, Bequest of Michael
Friedsam, 1931 (32.100.143)

Ca. 1480–90
Engraving
8 7/16 × 6 in. (21.5 × 15.3 cm)
Albertina, Vienna
(DG1928/406)

Relics and Reliquaries, from
The Viennese Book of Relics
(*Das Wiener Heiligtumsbuch*)
Printed by Johannes
Winterburger, Vienna, 1502
Letterpress with woodcut
illustrations
9 5/8 × 14 9/16 in. (24.5 × 37 cm)
The Metropolitan Museum of
Art, New York, The Elisha
Whittelsey Collection, The Elisha
Whittelsey Fund, 1951 (51.606)

Unidentified Spanish artist
(active Toledo, 15th century)
Covered Chalice
Late 15th century
Gilded silver, rubies, sapphires,
diamonds, and crystals
17 3/16 × 7 3/4 in. (43.7 × 19.7 cm)
The Metropolitan Museum of
Art, New York, The Cloisters
Collection, 1958 (58.39a, b)

Alart du Hameel (Netherlandish,
ca. 1449–ca. 1507)
Design for a Tower Monstrance
Ca. 1484
Engraving
Crowning element (top sheet):
13 9/16 × 6 3/16 in. (34.4 × 15.7 cm);
corpus (second sheet from top):
13 1/8 × 8 5/16 in. (33.4 × 21.1 cm);
stem and foot (third sheet from
top): 12 1/16 × 8 5/16 in. (30.7 ×
21.1 cm); foot and plan (bottom
sheet): 4 1/2 × 10 1/2 in. (11.5 ×
26.6 cm)
Albertina, Vienna (DG1928/528)

Jörg Seld (German, ca. 1454–1527)
Design for a Tower Monstrance
Ca. 1507
Pen and brown ink on paper
32 3/8 × 10 5/8 in. (82.3 × 27 cm)
Landesmuseum Württemberg,
Stuttgart (WLM 1967-91)

Circle of Jörg Syrlin the Younger
(German, ca. 1455–1522)

Design for a Tower Monstrance
Ca. 1500–1510
Pen and black ink on paper
26 13/16 × 11 9/16 in. (68.1 × 29.3 cm)
Stadtarchiv Ulm (F 1 Münster-
risse 26)

Unidentified German artist
(active Cologne, 15th century)
Tower Monstrance
Ca. 1450
Gilded silver
24 13/16 × 8 3/8 × 6 7/16 in. (63 ×
21.2 × 16.4 cm)
The Metropolitan Museum of
Art, New York, The Friedsam
Collection, Bequest of
Michael Friedsam, 1931
(32.100.226)

VARIATION AND
TRANSFORMATION

Unidentified French artist
(14th century)
Fragment of the Tomb Slab of
Maurice de Poissy
Ca. 1339
Limestone
18 11/16 × 42 1/2 × 3 9/16 in. (47.5 ×
108 × 9 cm)
The Metropolitan Museum of
Art, New York, Purchase,
Larry and Ann Burns Gift, in
honor of Austin B. Chinn,
and The Cloisters Collection,
2024 (2024.489)

Lorenz Spenning (German,
ca. 1400–1477/78) or Workshop
Tracery Study for a Balustrade
Ca. 1460
Pen and black ink, over blind
ruling with stylus, guided by
compass and straightedge, on
parchment
6 × 8 5/16 in. (15.2 × 21.1 cm)
Graphic Collection, Academy of
Fine Arts Vienna (HZ-17042)

Lorenz Spenning (German,
ca. 1400–1477/78) or Workshop
Four Tracery Studies for Arched
Windows
Ca. 1455–60
Pen and black ink, over blind

ruling with stylus, guided by
compass and straightedge, on
parchment
8 5/8 × 10 7/16 in. (21.9 × 26.5 cm)
Graphic Collection, Academy
of Fine Arts Vienna (HZ-17043)

Attributed to Madern Gerthener
(German, ca. 1360–1430)
Studies of Tracery Variations
Ca. 1410–15
Pen and brown ink, over blind
ruling with stylus, guided by
compass and straightedge, on
paper
23 7/16 × 16 7/16 in. (59.5 × 41.7 cm)
Graphic Collection, Academy
of Fine Arts Vienna (HZ-10931)

Lorenz Spenning (German,
ca. 1400–1477/78) or Workshop
Recto: Elevation of the Inner
Walls of the Porch, North Tower,
Stephansdom (Saint Stephen's
Cathedral), Vienna
Before 1467
Pen and black ink, over blind
ruling with stylus, guided by
compass and straightedge, on
parchment
32 5/16 × 32 11/16 in. (82 × 83 cm)
Graphic Collection, Academy of
Fine Arts Vienna (HZ-16872r)

Bernhard Winkler (German,
active 1512–ca. 1550)
Fragment of the Openwork
Spire, West Tower, Ulm
Minster (Drawing B)
Ca. 1512–18
Pen and black ink, over blind
ruling with stylus, guided by
compass and straightedge, on
parchment
29 5/16 × 19 7/8 in. (74.5 × 50.5 cm)
Evangelische Gesamtkirchen-
gemeinde Ulm (Stadtarchiv Ulm,
E Münsterbauamt 4)

Unidentified British or South
Netherlandish artist (15th
century)
Volute with Carved Leafwork
Late 15th century
Oak with traces of polychromy
and gilding

18¾ × 20½ × 4¾ in. (47.6 ×
52.1 × 12.1 cm)
The Metropolitan Museum of
Art, New York, Rogers Fund,
1905 (05.24.15)

seum Basel, Amerbach-Kabinett
1662 (U.XI.11)

Elisha Whittelsey Fund, 1949
(49.97.607a, b)

PLATE 76
Wenzel von Olmütz (Czech,
Moravia, active 1481–97)
Design for a Baldachin (in two
parts), with Body and Hexagonal
Plan (left) and Spire (right)
Ca. 1481–92
Engraving
Elevation (body and spire):
11 13/16 × 1–5 3/16 in. (30 × 2.5–
13.2 cm); plan: 15 1/16 × 5 3/16 in.
(38.3 × 13.2 cm)
The British Museum, London
(E,1.124)

PLATE 77
After Lorenz Lechler (German,
ca. 1460–1516 or after)
Floor Plan of the Sacrament
House in Esslingen
Ca. 1500
Pen and brown ink, over blind
ruling with stylus, guided by
compass and straightedge, on
paper
12 15/16 × 14 3/16 in. (32.8 × 36 cm)
Graphic Collection, Academy
of Fine Arts Vienna
(HZ-16948)

PLATE 78
Attributed to Jörg Schweiger
the Elder (German, ca. 1470/80–
1533/34), after Lorenz Lechler
(German, ca. 1460–1516 or after)
Ideal Floor Plan of the Sacrament House in Esslingen
Ca. 1500–1510
Pen and brown ink, over blind
ruling with stylus, guided by
compass, on paper
8 1/4 × 12 in. (20.9 × 30.5 cm)
Kupferstichkabinett, Kunstmuseum Basel, Amerbach-Kabinett
1662 (U.XI.116)

PLATE 79
After Lorenz Lechler (German,
ca. 1460–1516 or after)
Floor Plans and Sections of
the Sacrament House in
Esslingen
Ca. 1515
Pen and black ink, over blind
ruling with stylus, guided by
compass and straightedge,
on paper
8 5/8 × 11 5/16 in. (21.9 × 28.8 cm)

Graphic Collection, Academy
of Fine Arts Vienna
(HZ-16884)

PLATE 80
Mathes (Matthäus) Roriczer
(German, 1440–1493)
The Booklet on the Proper
Construction of Pinnacles
(*Das Büchlein von der Fialen
Gerechtigkeit*)
Printed by Mathes Roriczer,
Regensburg, 1486
Letterpress with woodcut
illustrations
Closed: 7 9/16 × 5 11/16 in. (19.2 ×
14.5 cm)
Bibliothek, Bayerisches
Nationalmuseum, Munich
(3637)

PLATE 81
Unidentified Austrian artist
(16th century)
Geometrical Scheme for a Finial
Ca. 1515
Pen and brown ink on paper
10 1/2 × 6 5/8 in. (26.7 × 16.9 cm)
Graphic Collection, Academy
of Fine Arts Vienna
(HZ-16868v)

PLATE 82
Albrecht Dürer (German,
1471–1528)
Illustration of How to Pull a
Spiral Staircase from a Circular
Plan, in the Treatise on
Measurement (*Underweysung
der Messung*)
Printed by Hieronymus
Andreae, Nuremberg, 1525
Woodcut
12 3/16 × 16 3/4 in. (31 × 42.6 cm)
The Metropolitan Museum of
Art, New York, Harris Brisbane
Dick Fund, 1941 (41.48.3)

PLATE 83
Albrecht Dürer (German,
1471–1528)
Portrait of the Architect
Hieronymus of Augsburg
1506
Pen and black ink with white
heightening on blue paper
15 3/8 × 10 1/2 in. (39.1 × 26.7 cm)
Kupferstichkabinett,
Staatliche Museen zu Berlin
(KdZ 2274)
NOT IN EXHIBITION

PLATE 84
After Anton Pilgram (Czech,
Moravia, ca. 1460–1515)
Elevation, Section, and Floor
Plan for the Stairs to the Pulpit,
Stephansdom (Saint Stephen's
Cathedral), Vienna
Ca. 1515
Pen and brown ink, over blind
ruling with stylus, guided by
compass and straightedge, on
paper
17 1/4 × 20 5/16 in. (43.8 × 51.6 cm)
Graphic Collection, Academy
of Fine Arts Vienna (HZ-16855)

PLATE 85
Robert Smythson (English,
ca. 1535–1614)
Elevation of a Rose Window,
with Measurements, Plans,
and a Scale
1599
Pen and brown ink, over blind
ruling with stylus, guided by
compass and straightedge, on
paper
13 9/16 × 7 5/16 in. (34.5 × 18.5 cm)
Royal Institute of British Architects, London, RIBA Collections
(SD205/SMY/II/33)

PLATE 86
Robert Smythson (English,
ca. 1535–1614)
Diagram of a Rose Window
Specifying Stone Elements
1599
Pen and brown ink with wash
3 15/16 × 3 15/16 in. (10 × 10 cm)
Royal Institute of British Archi-
tects, London, RIBA Collections
(SE52/SMY/II/34[1])

PLATE 87
Robert Smythson (English,
ca. 1535–1614)
Diagram of a Rose Window
Specifying the Carved Relief
1599
Pen and brown ink with
cross-hatching and wash
3 5/16 × 3 3/4 in. (10 × 9.5 cm)
Royal Institute of British Archi-
tects, London, RIBA Collections
(SE52/SMY/II/34[2])

PLATE 88
Lorenz Spenning (German,
ca. 1400–1477/78) or Workshop
Profile (Template Outline) of

the Vaulting Shafts, North
Tower, Stephansdom (Saint
Stephen's Cathedral), Vienna
Ca. 1467–76
Pen and dark brown ink on
paper
16 5/16 × 29 3/8 in. (41.4 × 74.6 cm)
Graphic Collection, Academy
of Fine Arts Vienna
(HZ-16854r)

Albrecht Dürer (German,
1471–1528)
Illustrations of Pillar Profiles
and Silhouettes, in the Treatise
on Measurement
(*Underweysung der Messung*)
Printed by Hieronymus Andreae,
Augsburg, 1525
Letterpress with woodcut
illustrations
11 × 8 5/16 in. (28 × 21.1 cm)
The Metropolitan Museum
of Art, New York, The George
Khuner Collection, Gift of
Mrs. George Khuner, 1981
(1981.1178.10)

Unidentified German artist
(Swabian region, late
15th century)
Cut-Paper Vaulting Patterns,
from a Lodge Book
(*Bauhüttenbuch*)
Ca. 1470–80; modern ground
Paper on a dark brown ground
8 3/16 × 12 1/16 in. (20.8 × 30.7 cm)
Albertina, Vienna (47111/163,
168)

Unidentified German artist
(Swabian region, late
15th century)
Cut-Paper Vaulting Pattern,
from a Lodge Book
(*Bauhüttenbuch*)
Ca. 1470–80; modern ground
Paper on a dark brown ground
8 1/4 × 12 1/8 in. (21 × 30.8 cm)
Albertina, Vienna (47111/237,
242)

Bernard Nonnenmacher
(German, active 1520–51)
Vaulting Plan for a Choir and
Ambulatory
Ca. 1520

Pen and brown ink, over blind
ruling with stylus, guided by
compass and straightedge, on
paper
22 5/8 × 17 7/8 in. (57.5 × 45.4 cm)
Fondation de l'Oeuvre Notre-
Dame, in custody of Musée
de l'Oeuvre Notre-Dame, Strasbourg (D.22.995.0.29 [OND 28])

Bernard Nonnenmacher
(German, active 1520–51)
Vaulting Plan for the Chapel of
Saint Catherine, Strasbourg
Cathedral, with Instructions for
the Assemblage of the Vaulting
Ca. 1542–46
Pen and brown ink over red
chalk and charcoal underdrawing
19 11/16 × 41 5/16 in. (50 × 105 cm)
Fondation de l'Oeuvre Notre-
Dame, in custody of Musée de
l'Oeuvre Notre-Dame, Stras-
bourg (D.22.995.0.9 [OND 23])

Unidentified German artist
(Swabian region, late
15th century)
Vaulting Plans and Exercises to
Determine Their Height
and Angle, in a Lodge Book
(*Bauhüttenbuch*)
Ca. 1470–80
Pen with black and brown ink
8 3/16 × 11 15/16 in. (20.8 × 30.4 cm)
Albertina, Vienna (Cim. VI,
55 [47111])

Aegidius Sadeler II
(Netherlandish, 1568–1629)
Interior View of Vladislav
Hall at Prague Castle during the
Annual Fair
1607
Engraving
22 1/4 × 24 3/8 in. (56.5 × 61.9 cm)
The Metropolitan Museum
of Art, New York, Harris
Brisbane Dick Fund, 1953
(53.601.10[1])

THE PROMISE OF GOTHIC
GEOMETRY

Block Research Group, ITA,
ETH Zurich / Vaulted AG

Reproduction of the First
Prototype of a Discrete Funicu-
lar Floor, after an Original by
Matthias Rippmann
2025; original 2015
3D-printed sand
78 3/4 × 55 1/8 in. (200 × 140 cm)
Block Research Group, Institute
of Technology in Architecture
(ITA), Federal Institute of
Technology (ETH) Zurich /
Vaulted AG

SELECTED BIBLIOGRAPHY

MEDIEVAL DRAFTSMANSHIP

Evans, M. W. *Medieval Drawings.* Hamlyn, 1969.

Fowler, Caroline. *The Art of Paper: From the Holy Land to the Americas.* Yale University Press, 2019.

Givens, Jean. *Observation and Image-Making in Gothic Art.* Cambridge University Press, 2005.

Holcomb, Melanie. *Pen and Parchment: Drawing in the Middle Ages.* Exh. cat. The Metropolitan Museum of Art, 2009.

Reed, Ronald. *Ancient Skins, Parchments and Leathers.* Seminar, 1972.

Scheller, Robert W. *Exemplum: Model-Book Drawings and the Practice of Artistic Transmission in the Middle Ages (ca. 900–ca. 1470).* Translated by Michael Hoyle. Amsterdam University Press, 1995.

ARCHITECTURAL DRAWINGS

Barnes, Carl F., Jr. *The Portfolio of Villard de Honnecourt (Paris, Bibliothèque nationale de France, MS Fr 19093): A New Critical Edition and Color Facsimile.* Ashgate, 2009.

Böker, Johann Josef. *Architektur der Gotik.* Vol. 1, *Bestandskatalog der weltgrößten Sammlung an gotischen Baurissen der Akademie der bildenden Künste Wien.* Anton Pustet, 2005.

Böker, Johann Josef, Anne-Christine Brehm, Julian Hanschke, and Jean-Sébastien Sauvé. *Architektur der Gotik.* 2 vols. Müry Salzmann, 2011–13.

Bork, Robert. *The Geometry of Creation: Architectural Drawing and the Dynamics of Gothic Design.* Ashgate, 2011.

Bucher, François. "Design in Gothic Architecture: A Preliminary Assessment." *Journal of the Society of Architectural Historians* 27, no. 1 (1968): 49–73.

Bucher, François. "Medieval Architectural Design Methods, 800–1560." *Gesta* 11, no. 2 (1972): 37–51.

Bucher, François. *Architector: The Lodge Books and Sketchbooks of Medieval Architects.* Vol. 1. Abaris Books, 1979.

Neagley, Linda. "A Late Gothic Architectural Drawing at The Cloisters." In *Reading Medieval Images: The Art Historian and the Object,* edited by Elizabeth Sears and Thelma K. Thomas. University of Michigan Press, 2002.

Pacey, Arnold. *Medieval Architectural Drawing: English Craftsmen's Methods and Their Later Persistence (c. 1200–1700).* Tempus, 2007.

Shelby, Lon R. *Gothic Design Techniques: The Fifteenth-Century Design Booklets of Mathes Roriczer and Hanns Schmuttermayer.* Architectura Medii Aevi 10. Southern Illinois University Press, 1977.

Speelberg, Femke. "Lorenz Lechler's Tour de Force of Late-Gothic Architectural Draftsmanship." *Master Drawings* 62, no. 3 (Autumn 2025): 293–320.

Wu, Nancy Y. "Roriczer, Schmuttermayer, and Two Late Gothic Portals at The Cloisters." In *Arts of the Medieval Cathedrals: Studies on Architecture, Stained Glass and Sculpture in Honor of Anne Prache,* edited by Kathleen Nolan and Dany Sandron. Ashgate, 2015.

GOTHIC ARCHITECTURE

Binski, Paul. *Architecture and Affect in the Middle Ages.* University of California Press, 2025.

Bork, Robert. *Late Gothic Architecture: Its Evolution, Extinction, and Reception.* Brepols, 2018.

Clark, William W. *Medieval Cathedrals.* Greenwood, 2006.

Courtenay, Lynn T. *The Engineering of Medieval Cathedrals.* Ashgate, 1997.

Erlande-Brandenburg, Alain. *The Cathedral Builders of the Middle Ages.* Thames & Hudson, 1995.

Frankl, Paul. *Gothic Architecture.* Revised by Paul Crossley. Yale University Press, 2000.

Kavaler, Ethan Matt. *Renaissance Gothic: Architecture and the Arts in Northern Europe, 1470–1540.* Yale University Press, 2012.

Klein, Bruno. *Gothic: Visual Art of the Middle Ages, 1140–1500.* H. F. Ullmann, 2012.

Reeve, Matthew, ed. *Reading Gothic Architecture.* Brepols, 2008.

Wells, Emma J. *Heaven on Earth: The Lives and Legacies of the World's Greatest Cathedrals.* Head of Zeus, 2022.

HISTORICAL FICTION

Falcones, Ildefonso. *Cathedral of the Sea.* Dutton, 2008.

Follett, Ken. *The Pillars of the Earth.* 1st U.S. edition, William Morrow and Company, 1998.

MODERN PRACTICE

Block, Philippe, Tom Van Mele, Matthias Rippmann, and Noelle C. Paulson. *Beyond Bending: Reimagining Compression Shells.* Edition Detail, 2017.

Mark, Robert. *Experiments in Gothic Structure.* MIT Press, 1982.

Mark, Robert. *Light, Wind, and Structure: The Mystery of the Master Builders.* McGraw-Hill, 1990.

ANL/Vienna, Cod. 458, fol. 4: fig. 2; The ALBERTINA Museum, Vienna: fig. 34, pls. 28, 32, 34, 37, 40, 90, 91, 94; Archives départementales de la Marne (ou Arch. dép. Marne, ou AD51): pl. 4; ArtinPrint-Middelburg: p. 107, pl. 21; Bayerisches Nationalmuseum, Bastian Krack: fig. 28, pls. 51, 80; Berner Münster-Stiftung, 3D Fotogrammetrie/Orthofoto: Jan-Ruben Fischer, D-61118 Bad Vilbel: fig. 27; Bibliothèque Nationale de France: figs. 8, 12; © Block Research Group, ETH Zurich: fig. 35; © Bodleian Libraries, University of Oxford: figs. 4–7; bpk Bildagentur / (Kupferstrichkabinett, Staatliche Museen zu Berlin) / (Dietmar Katz) / Art Resource, NY: pls. 35, 52; © Markus Brunetti. Courtesy Yossi Milo, New York: figs. 9, 13, 20, 21, 26; Catholic University of Leuven, Belgium—Public Domain: fig. 31; E-manuscripta, https://www.e-manuscripta.ch/bau/content/zoom/951451 and https://www.e-manuscripta.ch/bau/content/zoom/951452: fig. 30; Evangelische Gesamtkirchengemeinde Ulm (Stadtarchiv Ulm, E Münsterbauamt 1): pl. 14; Evangelische Gesamtkirchengemeinde Ulm (Stadtarchiv Ulm, E Münsterbauamt 4): pl. 49; Evangelische Gesamtkirchengemeinde Ulm (Stadtarchiv Ulm, E Münsterbauamt 3), photo by Cornelia Rauch-Ernst: fig. 22, pl. 73; © Fondation de l'Œuvre Notre-Dame, photo: Simon Woolf: fig. 24; Photo by Dominik Gehl: fig. 25; © Gehry Partners, LLP and Frank O. Gehry: fig. 1; Graphic Collection of the Academy of Fine Arts Vienna: p. 2, pls. 45–47, 77, 79, 81, 84; Graphic Collection of the Academy of Fine Arts Vienna, photo: image industry: p. 134, pls. 8, 48, 72; Graphic Collection of the Academy of Fine Arts Vienna, photo: Pixelstorm: p. 26, pls. 10, 11, 13, 88; Graphic Collection of the FAU Erlangen-Nürnberg, AH 84: fig. 33 (top sheet); Herzog August Bibliothek Wolfenbüttel: Cod. Guelf. 114.1 Extrav: fig. 29; Historisches Museum Frankfurt, Institut für Stadtgeschichte on permanent loan: pls. 16, 17, 27; © Hohe Domkirche Köln, Dombauhütte; Foto: Matz und Schenk: fig. 19; Hz24 © Germanisches Nationalmuseum, Photo: Jens Voskamp: pl. 24; Hz3818 © Germanisches Nationalmuseum, Photo: Georg Janssen: pl. 9; Institute Centrale per la Patologia Degli Archivi e del Libro, Rome: fig. 15; © Kunstmuseum Basel: pls. 53–63, 66–71, 78; Landesmuseum Württemberg, Hendrik Zwietasch: pl. 41; © MAK: pl. 33; Image © The Metropolitan Museum of Art: front cover, pls. 1, 25, 44, 95; Image © The Metropolitan Museum of Art, photo by Katherine Dahab: pl. 20; Image © The Metropolitan Museum of Art, photo by Anna-Marie Kellen: pl. 50; Image © The Metropolitan Museum of Art, photo by Paul Lachenauer: pl. 43; Image © The Metropolitan Museum of Art, photo by Mark Morosse: pls. 31, 38, 75, 82, 89; Image © The Metropolitan Museum of Art, photo by Bruce J. Schwarz: p. 108, pl. 39; Image © The Metropolitan Museum of Art, photo by Juan Trujillo: pls. 23, 29, 30; Musées de la ville de Strasbourg, M. Bertola: back cover, pp. 14, 58, 80, 92–93, figs. 10, 16, 18, pls. 5, 7, 15, 26, 92, 93; Museo Catedralicio-Diocesano de León. Cabildo de la S. I. Catedral de León: fig. 14; Photograph © The Museum of Fine Arts, Houston; Stephen Hanley, Conservation Imaging Specialist, Department of Conservation: fig. 23, pl. 19; B. O'Kane / Alamy: fig. 32; Opera della Metropolitana Aut.N.444/2025: fig. 17; © The President and Fellows of St John's College, Oxford: fig. 3; RIBA Collections: p. 4, pls. 18, 85–87; © Matthias Rippmann / Block Research Group, ETH Zurich: pl. 96; Staatliche Museen zu Berlin, Kupferstichkabinett / Jörg P. Anders: p. 160, pls. 2, 3, 22, 83; Staatliche Museen zu Berlin, Kunstgewerbemuseum / Saturia Linke: pl. 36; Stadtarchiv Ulm, F 1 Münsterrisse 26: pl. 42; Stadtarchiv Ulm, F 1 Münsterrisse 28: fig. 33 (bottom sheet); © 2025 The Trustees of the British Museum: pls. 64, 65, 74, 76; © Vaulted AG / Photo by Philippe Block: fig. 36; © Vaulted AG / Photo by Gabriele Mattei: p. 188; Peter Völkle: fig. 11; Wien Museum Inv.-Nr. 105069/1, CC0 (https://sammlung.wienmuseum.at/en/object/184284/): pl. 6; Wien Museum Inv.-Nr. 105066, CC0 (https://sammlung.wienmuseum.at/en/object/184204/): pl. 12

This catalogue is published in conjunction with *Gothic by Design: The Dawn of Architectural Draftsmanship*, on view at The Metropolitan Museum of Art, New York, from April 16 through July 19, 2026.

The exhibition is made possible by the Placido Arango Fund and the Gail and Parker Gilbert Fund.

Additional support is provided by The Schiff Foundation, Gilbert and Ildiko Butler, and The Michael and Patricia O'Neill Charitable Fund.

This publication is made possible by the Diane W. and James E. Burke Fund.

Additional support is provided by Hubert and Mireille Goldschmidt, and Ann M. Spruill and Daniel H. Cantwell.

Published by
The Metropolitan Museum of Art, New York
Mark Polizzotti, Publisher and Editor in Chief
Peter Antony, Associate Publisher for Production
Michael Sittenfeld, Associate Publisher for Editorial

Edited by Elizabeth Benjamin
Production by Lauren Knighton
Designed by Michael Dyer, Remake
Bibliographic editing by Julia Oswald
Image acquisitions and permissions by Shannon Cannizzaro

Photographs of works in The Met collection are by Imaging Department, The Metropolitan Museum of Art, unless otherwise noted.

Additional photography credits appear on page 219.

Typeset in Jenson
Printed on GardaPat Bianka 135 gsm
Separations by Verona Libri, Verona, Italy
Printed and bound by Verona Libri, Verona, Italy

Front cover: detail of pl. 25. Back cover and p. 14: details of fig. 16. Additional illustrations: p. 2: detail of pl. 84; p. 4: detail of pl. 18; p. 26: detail of pl. 10; p. 58: detail of pl. 15; p. 80: detail of pl. 5; pp. 92–93: detail of pl. 7; p. 107: detail of pl. 21; p. 108: detail of pl. 39; p. 134: detail of pl. 48; p. 160: detail of pl. 83; p. 188: View of an installed funicular floor

The Metropolitan Museum of Art endeavors to respect copyright in a manner consistent with its nonprofit educational mission. If you believe any material has been included in this publication improperly, please contact the Publications and Editorial Department.

Every effort has been made to track object provenances as thoroughly and accurately as possible based on available scholarship, traceable transactions, and the existing archaeological record. Despite best efforts, there is often an absence of provenance information. Provenances of objects in The Met collection are updated as additional research comes to light. Readers are encouraged to visit metmuseum.org and to search by an object's accession number for its most up-to-date information.

Copyright © 2026 by The Metropolitan Museum of Art, New York

First printing

All rights reserved. No part of this publication may be reproduced or transmitted in any form or by any means, electronic or mechanical, including photocopying, recording, or any information storage and retrieval system, without permission in writing from the publishers.

Please note that no part of this publication may be used or reproduced in any manner for the purpose of training artificial intelligence technologies or systems.

The Metropolitan Museum of Art
1000 Fifth Avenue
New York, New York 10028
metmuseum.org

Distributed by
Yale University Press, New Haven and London
yalebooks.com/art
yalebooks.co.uk

Authorized Representative in the EU: Easy Access System Europe, Mustamäe tee 50, 10621 Tallinn, Estonia,
gpsr.requests@easproject.com

Cataloguing-in-Publication Data is available from the Library of Congress.
ISBN 978-1-58839-808-6